THE FIRST SIX BOOKS OF
THE ELEMENTS
OF EUCLID

THE FIRST SIX BOOKS OF

THE ELEMENTS OF EUCLID

IN WHICH COLOURED DIAGRAMS AND SYMBOLS

ARE USED INSTEAD OF LETTERS FOR THE

GREATER EASE OF LEARNERS

BY OLIVER BYRNE

SURVEYOR OF HER MAJESTY'S SETTLEMENTS IN THE FALKLAND ISLANDS
AND AUTHOR OF NUMEROUS MATHEMATICAL WORKS

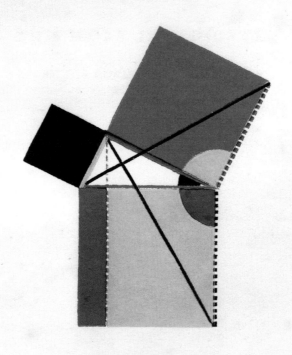

LONDON
WILLIAM PICKERING
1847

Oliver Byrne

THE FIRST SIX BOOKS OF
THE ELEMENTS
OF EUCLID

IN WHICH COLOURED DIAGRAMS AND SYMBOLS
ARE USED INSTEAD OF LETTERS
FOR THE GREATER EASE OF LEARNERS

DIE ERSTEN SECHS BÜCHER
DER ELEMENTE VON EUKLID

*in denen Diagramme und Symbole statt Buchstaben
eingesetzt werden, um das Lernen zu erleichtern*

LES SIX PREMIERS LIVRES
DES ELEMENTS D'EUCLIDE

*dans lesquels des diagrammes en couleur et des symboles sont utilisés
au lieu de lettres pour assurer une plus grande facilité d'apprentissage*

———————————

Essay by / Essay von / Essai par

Werner Oechslin

*The copy used for printing belongs to /
Der Druck erfolgte nach dem Exemplar von / L'impression a été effectuée d'après l'exemplaire de*
John Windle Antiquarian Bookseller

TASCHEN

Euclid.

BOOK I.

PROPOSITION I. PROBLEM.

ON *a given finite straight line* (———) *to describe an equila-teral triangle.*

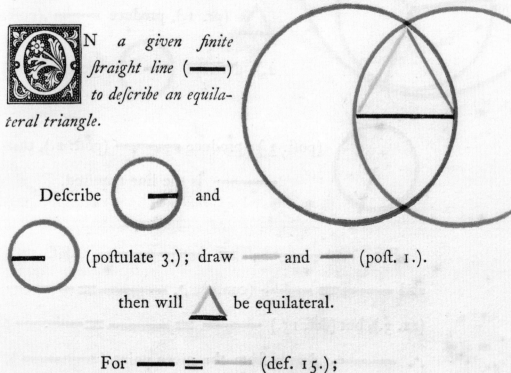

Describe ⬤ and

⬤ (poftulate 3.); draw ——— and ——— (poft. 1.).

then will △ be equilateral.

For ——— = ——— (def. 15.);

and ——— = ——— (def. 15.),

∴ ——— = ——— (axiom. 1.);

and therefore △ is the equilateral triangle required.

Q. E. D.

CONTENTS
INHALTSVERZEICHNIS
SOMMAIRE

ΕΥΚΛΕΙΔΟΥ ΣΤΟΙΧΕΙΩΝ ΠΡΩ=
ΤΟΝ, ΕΚ ΤΩΝ ΘΕΩΝΟΣ ΣΥΝΟΥΣΙΩΝ.

ΣΗΜΕΙΟΝ ἐστὶν, οὗ μέρος οὐθέν. Γραμμὴ δὲ μῆκος ἀπλατές, γραμμῆς δὲ πέρατα σημεῖα. εὐθεῖα γραμμή ἐστιν, ἥτις ἐξ ἴσου τοῖς ἐφ' ἑαυτῆς σημείοις κεῖται. ἐπιφάνεια δέ ἐστιν, ὃ μῆκος καὶ πλάτος μόνον ἔχει. ἐπιφανείας δὲ πέρατα, γραμμαί. ἐπίπεδος ἐπιφάνειά ἐστιν, ἥτις ἐξ ἴσου ταῖς ἐφ' ἑαυτῆς εὐθείαις κεῖται.

σημεῖον. γραμμαί. ἐπι φά νεια.

Ἐπίπεδος δὲ γωνία ἐστὶν, ἡ ἐν ἐπιπέδῳ δύο γραμμῶν ἁπτομένων ἀλλήλων, καὶ μὴ ἐπ' εὐθείας κειμένων, πρὸς ἀλλήλας τῶν γραμμῶν κλίσις. Ὅταν δὲ αἱ περιέχουσαι τὴν γωνίαν γραμμαί, εὐθεῖαι ὦσιν, εὐθύγραμμος καλεῖται ἡ γωνία. Ὅταν δὲ εὐθεῖα ἐπ' εὐθεῖαν σταθεῖσα, τὰς ἐφεξῆς γωνίας ἴσας ἀλλήλαις ποιῇ, ὀρθὴ ἐστὶν ἑκατέρα τῶν ἴσων γωνιῶν. Καὶ ἡ ἐφεστηκυῖα εὐθεῖα κάθετος καλεῖται, ἐφ' ἣν ἐφέστηκεν. Ἀμβλεῖα γωνία ἐστὶν, ἡ μείζων ὀρθῆς, Ὀξεῖα δὲ ἡ ἐλάσσων ὀρθῆς.

ἐπίπεδος γωνία. εὐθύγραμμος. καμπυλόγραμμος. α ὀξεῖα. β ἀμβλεῖα. κάθετος. γ ὀρθή.

Ὅρος ἐστὶν, ὅ τινός ἐστι πέρας. Σχῆμά ἐστι, τὸ ὑπό τινος, ἤ τινων ὅρων περιεχόμενον. Κύκλος ἐστὶ, σχῆμα ἐπίπεδον, ὑπὸ μιᾶς γραμμῆς περιεχόμενον, ἣ καλεῖται περιφέρεια, πρὸς ἣν ἀφ' ἑνὸς σημείου τῶν ἐντὸς τοῦ σχήματος κειμένων, πᾶσαι αἱ προσπίπτουσαι εὐθεῖαι, ἴσαι ἀλλήλαις εἰσί. Κέντρον δὲ τοῦ κύκλου, τὸ σημεῖον καλεῖται. Διάμετρος δὲ τοῦ κύκλου ἐστὶν, εὐθεῖά τις

κύκλος. τρίγωνον. τετράγωνον πέρας τοῦ κύβου. διάμετρος. τμῆμα μεῖζον.

κέντρον.

ἡμικύκλιον. τμῆμα ἔλασσον.

διὰ τοῦ κέντρου ἠγμένη, καὶ περατουμένη ἐφ' ἑκάτερα τὰ μέρη ὑπὸ τῆς τοῦ κύκλου περιφερείας, ἥτις καὶ δίχα τέμνει τὸν κύκλον. Ἡμικύκλιον δέ ἐστι, τὸ περιεχόμενον σχῆμα ὑπό τε τῆς διαμέτρου, καὶ τῆς ἀπολαμβανομένης ὑπ'

α τῆς τε

Euclid's geometry
– (not) a Via Regia?

Euclid is synonymous with geometry, and geometry is tantamount to order and compelling logic in the edifice of our thoughts and speculations. All areas of philosophy, including ethics, had repeatedly striven to achieve the ancient *more geometrico*, which stands for scientific reliability, systematic methodology, and conclusiveness. It is synonymous with syllogisms and inferences, and is a symbol of mathematics – or rather of mathematical thought – as such.

In the early days of printed editions of Euclid, the author's name was usually written as "Euclides Megarensis". The man we now know as Euclid (*c.* 360–280 BC) taught mathematics in Alexandria in the era of Ptolemy I (323–285 BC), but had long been confused with the philosopher Euclid of Megara, who lived more than a century earlier, founded a school, and earned a reputation as a cunning logician. This naturally reinforced the impression, cogently articulated by Girolamo Cardano in his scientific encyclopaedia *De Subtilitate* (1550), that Euclid's Elements were linked with attributes of unshakeably firm theorems and absolute perfection. Only those who adopted the tenets of Euclid were able to distinguish between the truth and fallibility.

This was not possible without restriction and contradiction. Julius Caesar Scaliger granted equal, if not greater, prestige to arithmetic, and it was already quite clear to everyone that geometry and arithmetic are nearly inseparable. This was stated with even greater clarity by Michael Stifel, as well as by Jean Borrel, who followed in his tradition: Euclid's theorems are not Christ's Gospel! On the other hand, it had become commonplace to emphasize the privileged position that Euclid's Elements enjoyed with reference to his skills in didactics.

The learned had always known that Euclid had 'merely' collected and compiled various mathematical treatises written by his long-forgotten predecessors. This is the deeper reason why 'The Euclid' was published from century to century in very different forms and varying degrees of completeness. The allegation of 'obscurity' had caught up with him, too. As with Homer, doubt even arose whether Euclid's name actually referred to a single historical individual.

Euclid's first definitions and theorems, which are arranged in such a beautifully logical sequence, formatively shaped the image we have of him and embodied the solid foundation upon which countless subsequent editions were based and with which Euclid's good reputation was associated. This is readily understandable. Johann Friedrich Lorenz, whose edition of Euclid underwent numerous reprints decade after decade, described Euclid's Alexandrian school as a "school for the world" that endured "throughout a millennium". Robert Simson begins his equally successful text as follows: "I. A point is that which hath no parts, or which hath no magnitude. II. A line is length without breadth. III. The extremities of a line are points. IV. A straight line is that which lies evenly between its extreme points. V. A superficies is that which hath only length and breadth…"

Who could fail to follow this logical progression? And who has never heard of the so-called Pythagorean Theorem, which is introduced as the 47th theorem in Euclid's First Book of Elements? But everything suddenly appears much more difficult and more demanding when one has left the explanations of simple figures behind and is confronted by the doctrine of proportions in the Fifth

Book or, before that, by the challenging theorems about parallels and their behaviour in infinity, which were rediscovered at the beginning of 'non-Euclidean geometry': "If a straight line meets two straight lines, so as to make two interior angles on the same side of it taken together less than two right angles, these straight lines being continually produced, shall at length meet upon that side, which are the angles which are less than two right angles."

As Proclus lamented, geometry simply isn't a royal road: "non est regia ad mathematicam via", as Jean Etienne Montucla repeats in his famous *Histoire des Mathématiques*. At an early date, and taking into account the difficulty and intricacy of mathematics, it had conversely been realized that only a few people would take upon themselves the superhuman task of penetrating the laws of mathematics. This essentially involves more than merely numbers and figures, because Euclid's geometry is inextricably linked with problems of intellectual history in the broadest sense. Francesco Barozzi wrote in 1560 that Euclid had shaped the science of mathematics according to rules of both the utmost order and the highest artistry. Generously interpreted, this means that Euclid's *Elements* is actually a 'work of art', inspiring awe and marvel. Centuries later, Albert Einstein in *Geometry and Experience* (1921) was puzzled and prompted by the "riddle" to wonder why "mathematics, which is a product of human thought and independent of all experience, so excellently fits real objects".

Around the middle of the 19th century, when Euclid's Elements seemed to have finally retired from active service to mathematical science, a trade-school teacher in Winterthur named Carl Adams, with his gaze focused Janus-like both forward and backward, would remark: "The old geometry is distinguished by its austerity of form, the new by its universal way of looking at things." Adams further clarified this in 1845, claiming that Euclid, Archimedes, and Apollonius had "created works of art whose architectonic structure is firm and unalterable" and in which are manifest the "beautiful symmetry" and "elegance of form" that had formerly been "exclusively possessed by the Greeks". This equally well describes the cultural-historical context in which Euclid had come to occupy his precise locus.

The upheaval seems to have occurred in 1847, i.e. the year of publication of Oliver Byrne's *The First Six Books of the Elements of Euclid, in which coloured diagrams and symbols are used instead of letters for the greater ease of learners*, when Byrne again created – albeit unwillingly – a work of art! As early as 1757, in the seventh volume of the *Encyclopédie*, Jean le Rond d'Alembert recognized the limits of a future use of the "Géométrie sublime". On the other hand, he also firmly clung to his opinion that with regard to the application of elementary geometry, no need existed for algebraicizing, because no advantageous simplification would ensue from it. Geometry can thus not be deprived of that didactic benefit that is associated with contemplation by the senses and with a gestalt, which Edmund G. Husserl describes as "finitudes on the horizon of an open infinity" and which Jacques Derrida warns as the danger that arises when a "signe graphique" is connected to "the mundane".

Handling these 'risks' seems to be an easier task for art. Euclid arises anew in Piet Mondrian's work, recognizable 'at a glance' and assigned to aesthetic ideals.

Euclides Megarensis Philosophus clarus habetur
olympiade 90. temporibus Darij Nothi Per=
sarum Regis quinti.

Euklids Geometrie
– (k)ein Königsweg?

Euklid ist gleichbedeutend mit Geometrie und Geometrie mit der Ordnung und Stringenz im Haushalt unseres Denkens und Spekulierens. Das alte, in allen Bereichen des Philosophierens bis hin zur Ethik immer wieder bemühte *more geometrico* steht für wissenschaftliche Verlässlichkeit, systematisches Vorgehen und Schlüssigkeit. Ja, es ist gleichbedeutend mit dem Syllogismus, der Schlussfolgerung, und steht auch symbolhaft für Mathematik – oder eben mathematisches Denken – an und für sich.

In der Frühzeit der gedruckten Euklideditionen erschien Euklid meist als „Euclides Megarensis" zitiert. Man hatte Euklid (ca. 360–280 v. Chr.), der in Alexandria in der Zeit Ptolemäus I. (323–285 v. Chr.) Mathematik lehrte, lange Zeit mit dem gut 100 Jahre früher tätigen Philosophen und Schulbegründer Euklid von Megara verwechselt. Dieser galt als gewiefter Logiker, und so verstärkte sich der Eindruck, den Girolamo Cardano auf den Punkt brachte, als er in seiner Wissensenzyklopädie *De Subtilitate* (1550) Euklids Elemente mit den Attributen unerschütterlicher Festigkeit der Thesen und absoluter Perfektion verband. Nur wer Euklid folge, könne wahr und falsch unterscheiden.

Ohne Einschränkung und Widerspruch ging das nicht. Für Julius Caesar Scaliger war die Arithmetik genauso, wenn nicht noch höher, einzuschätzen. Und dass sich die Geometrie kaum von der Arithmetik ablösen ließe, war ohnehin jedermann klar. Michael Stifel und in seiner Nachfolge Jean Borrel sagten es deshalb umso deutlicher. Das Evangelium Christi seien Euklids Sätze nicht! Man hatte sich andererseits schon früh darauf verlegt, den Vorrang der Elemente Euklids in didaktischer Hinsicht hervorzuheben.

Es war auch bekannt, dass Euklid ja ‚nur' verschiedene mathematische Schriften vergessener Vorgänger gesammelt und zusammengefügt hatte. Das ist der tiefere Grund, weshalb ‚der Euklid' über die Zeit in ganz verschiedener Form und Vollständigkeit publiziert worden ist. Der Vorwurf der ‚Dunkelheit' hat ihn ohnehin eingeholt. Und es kam sogar – analog zu Homer – der Zweifel hoch, ob sich mit seinem Namen überhaupt eine Person verbinde.

Die ersten Definitionen und Sätze Euklids, die sich so schön logisch aneinanderreihen, haben wesentlich das Bild geprägt, das man sich von ihm machte. Es bildete jene solide Grundlage, deren Folge die unzähligen Ausgaben waren und mit der sich der gute Ruf Euklids verband. Man kann das mühelos nachvollziehen. Johann Friedrich Lorenz, dessen Euklid jahrzehntelang immer wieder aufgelegt wurde und der Euklids Alexandrinische Schule als eine „ein Jahrtausend hindurch" wirksame „Schule für die Welt" bezeichnet, beginnt mit: „1. Ein Punkt ist, was keine Theile hat. 2. Eine Linie aber eine Länge ohne Breite. 3. Das Aeusserste einer Linie sind Punkte. 4. Eine gerade Linie ist, welche zwischen den in ihr befindlichen Punkten auf einerley Art liegt. 5. Eine Fläche ist, was nur Länge und Breite hat ...".

Wer würde dem nicht folgen können, und wer kennt nicht den sogenannten Pythagorassatz, der als 47. Satz des ersten Buches der Elemente Euklids vorgestellt wird. Aber wenn man die Erläuterung der einfachen Figuren erst einmal verlassen hat, um im fünften Buch auf die Proportionslehre oder schon zuvor auf die anspruchsvollen, am Anfang der ‚nicht-euklidischen Geometrie' wieder neu entdeckten Sätze zu den Parallelen und ihrem Verhalten im Unendlichen zu stoßen, sieht alles plötzlich sehr

Ill. 3
Diogenes Laertius, *Delle Vite de' Filosofi …
accresciute, & migliorate … da Gio. Felice
Astolfi …*, Venice 1611, p. 14
– This idealized portrait of Euclid by Gioseffo
Salviati, which depicts the philosopher lying
down and contemplating geometric figures, is
also used in the same book as a portrait of
Parmenides.
– Das von Gioseffo Salviati ausgeführte Ideal-
bild des liegenden und über geometrischen Figuren sinnierenden Philosophen Euklid ist in
demselben Buch auch Parmenides zugeordnet.
– Réalisé par Gioseffo Salviati, le portrait idéal
du philosophe Euclide couché, méditant sur
des figures géométriques est aussi relié dans le
même livre à Parménide.

3

viel schwieriger und anspruchsvoller aus: „Wenn eine Gerade zwei
Geraden trifft und mit ihnen auf derselben Seite innere Winkel
bildet, deren Summe kleiner ist als zwei rechte, so treffen sich die
beiden Geraden, wenn man sie auf dieser Seite verlängert."

Es ist eben doch so, wie schon Proklus moniert, ein Königsweg
ist die Geometrie nicht, „non est regia ad mathematicam via", wie
Jean Etienne Montucla in seiner berühmten *Histoire des Mathématiques* wiederholt. Früh hat man umgekehrt, die Schwierigkeit
und den hohen Anspruch der Mathematik im Auge, festgestellt, es
seien eben nur wenige, die diese übermenschliche Aufgabe, in die
mathematischen Gesetze einzudringen, auf sich nehmen würden.
Es geht schließlich um mehr als bloß um Zahlen und Figuren; es
sind im umfassendsten Sinne geistesgeschichtliche Probleme, die
sich mit Euklids Geometrie verbinden. Francesco Barozzi schrieb
1560, Euklid hätte die mathematische Wissenschaft in gleicher
Weise nach den Regeln höchster Ordnung und höchster Kunst
gebildet. Großzügig interpretiert heißt das, Euklids Elemente
sind eben auch ,Kunstwerk', das Staunen hervorruft – bis zu
Albert Einstein, der sich in *Geometrie und Erfahrung* (1921) über
das „Rätsel" wundert, „dass die Mathematik, die doch ein von aller
Erfahrung unabhängiges Produkt des menschlichen Denkens ist,
auf die Gegenstände der Wirklichkeit so vortrefflich passt."

Um die Mitte des 19. Jahrhunderts, als die Elemente Euklids
ihren Dienst an der mathematischen Wissenschaft endgültig quittiert zu haben scheinen, bemerkt dann beispielsweise der Win-
terthurer Gewerbschullehrer Carl Adams im Blick nach vorn
und zurück: „Die alte Geometrie zeichnet sich durch Strenge der
Form, die neue durch Allgemeinheit der Betrachtungsweise aus."

1845 verdeutlicht dies derselbe Autor, indem er festhält, Euklid,
Archimedes und Apollonius hätten „Kunstwerke geschaffen, deren
architektonisches Gefüge fest und unverrückbar" sei. „Schöne
Symmetrie" und „Eleganz der Form", ehedem „ausschliessliches
Eigenthum der Griechen" würden sich hier manifestieren. Das
beschreibt gleichsam den kulturgeschichtlichen Rahmen, in dem
Euklid seinen präzisen Ort eingenommen hat.

1847, im Jahr des Erscheinens von Oliver Byrnes *The First Six
Books of the Elements of Euclid, in which coloured diagrams and symbols
are used instead of letters for the greater ease of learners* scheint jener
Umbruch vollzogen, und Byrne schafft erneut – wider Willen –
ein Kunstwerk! Schon Jean le Rond d'Alembert hat 1757 im siebten
Band der *Encyclopédie* die Grenzen einer künftigen Anwendung
der „Géométrie sublime" erkannt. Er hielt andererseits daran fest,
dass es bezogen auf die Anwendung der elementaren Geometrie
keinerlei Bedarf an Algebraisierung gäbe, weil daraus keinerlei
Vorteil an Vereinfachung entstünde. So ist der Geometrie jener
didaktische Vorzug nicht zu nehmen, der sich mit sinnenhafter
Anschauung und einer Gestalt verbindet, was Edmund G. Husserl mit „Endlichkeiten im Horizont einer offenen Unendlichkeit"
umschreibt und was bei Jacques Derrida erneut an die Gefahren
eines an die „Weltlichkeit" gebundenen „signe graphique" gemah-
nen lässt.

Der Umgang mit diesen ,Risiken' scheint der Kunst leichter
von der Hand zu gehen. Euklid ersteht neu bei Piet Mondrian, ,auf
einen Blick' erkennbar und den ästhetischen Idealen zugewiesen.

La géométrie d'Euclide – une voie royale ?

Le nom d'Euclide rime avec géométrie et on associe à celle-ci l'ordre et la rigueur de la pensée et des spéculations. L'ancien *more geometrico* auquel on a sans cesse recours dans tous les domaines de la philosophie jusqu'à l'éthique, représente la fiabilité scientifique, le travail méthodique et concluant. Oui, il est l'équivalent de syllogisme, de conclusion et symbolise aussi les mathématiques – ou la pensée mathématique – à proprement parler.

A l'époque des premières éditions imprimées d'Euclide, celui-ci est cité le plus souvent sous le nom d'« Euclides Megarensis ». C'est qu'on a longtemps confondu Euclide (vers 360–280 av. notre ère) qui vivait à Alexandrie sous le règne de Ptolémée Ier (323–285 av. notre ère) et enseignait les mathématiques avec le philosophe Euclide de Mégare, actif un bon siècle plus tôt et qui a fondé l'Ecole mégarique. Ce dernier étant considéré comme un logicien adroit, cette impression se renforça, impression que Jérôme Cardan précise lorsqu'il associe dans son encyclopédie *De Subtilitate* (1550), les Eléments d'Euclide à la solidité inébranlable des thèses et à la perfection absolue. Seul celui qui suivait Euclide était capable de distinguer le vrai du faux.

Cela n'allait pas sans restrictions et objections. Julius Caesar Scaliger estimait que l'arithmétique était de valeur égale, si ce n'est supérieure. De toute façon, tout le monde était conscient qu'il n'était guère possible de dissocier la géométrie de l'arithmétique. C'est pourquoi Michael Stifel et à sa suite Jean Borrel le dirent encore plus clairement : les propositions d'Euclide ne sont pas parole d'évangile ! D'autre part, on s'était déjà accoutumé de bonne heure à mettre en avant la primauté des Eléments d'Euclide au point de vue didactique.

Il était aussi notoire que « le seul mérite » d'Euclide était d'avoir collectionné et rassemblé divers écrits de mathématiciens oubliés qui l'avaient précédé. C'est la raison plus profonde pour laquelle « l'Euclide » a été publié au cours du temps sous des formes différentes et de manière plus ou moins complète. Le reproche d'être « obscur » l'a de toute façon rattrapé. Et à l'instar d'Homère, on a même douté de son existence historique.

Les premières définitions et propositions d'Euclide qui s'enchaînent de manière si logique ont essentiellement marqué l'image que l'on se faisait de lui. Elle formait cette base solide dont ont découlé les innombrables éditions et à laquelle est associée la bonne réputation d'Euclide. Cela est facile à comprendre. Johann Friedrich Lorenz, auteur d'une des éditions les plus souvent éditées et rééditées appelait l'Ecole alexandrine d'Euclide une « école du monde » dont l'impact s'est fait sentir pendant « un millier d'années ». Et Didier Henrion, lui aussi, auteur d'un « Euclide » longtemps utilisé, commence ainsi : « 1. Le poinct, est ce qui n'a aucune partie. 2. La ligne, est une longueur sans largeur. 3. Les extremitez de la ligne, sont poincts. 4. La ligne droicte, est celle qui est également comprise & estendue entre ses poincts. 5. Superficie, est ce qui a longueur & largeur tant seulement… »

Voici la logique parfaite d'Euclide. Jusqu'ici tout le monde est capable de suivre et tout le monde se rappelle le théorème dit de Pythagore présenté comme la 47e proposition du Livre I des Eléments d'Euclide. Mais lorsqu'on a quitté l'explication des figures simples pour tomber dans le Livre V sur la théorie des proportions ou déjà avant, sur les propositions sophistiquées de parallèles, redécouvertes au début de la « géométrie non-euclidienne », et

III. 4
Nicola Tartaglia, *Euclide Megarense Philosopho:
Solo Introduttore delle Scientie Mathematice:
diligentemente reassettato, et alla integrità ridotto ...*, Venice 1543

4

leur comportement dans l'infini, tout semble soudain beaucoup
plus ardu : « Si une ligne droicte tombant sur deux autres lignes
droictes, faict les angles interieurs d'un mesme costé plus petits
que deux droicts, icelles deux lignes estans continuées à l'infiny,
se rencontreront du costé où les angles sont plus petits que deux
droicts. »

Il faut bien reconnaître, ainsi que nous le rappelle Proclus, que
la géométrie n'est pas une voie royale, « non est regia ad mathematicam via » – Jean Etienne Montucla le répète d'ailleurs dans sa
célèbre *Histoire des Mathématiques*. Ayant en tête la difficulté et
l'aspect exigeant des mathématiques, on a autrefois, inversement,
constaté qu'étaient rares ceux qui assumeraient la tâche surhu-
maine de pénétrer dans les lois mathématiques. En fin de compte,
il s'agit de bien davantage que de nombres et de figures ; globalement ce sont des problèmes philosophiques qui s'attachent à la
géométrie d'Euclide. En 1560, Francesco Barozzi écrit qu'Euclide
aurait formé la science mathématique pareillement selon les règles
de l'ordre et de l'art les plus hauts. Interprété librement cela signi-
fie que les Eléments d'Euclide sont aussi une « œuvre d'art » qui
suscite l'étonnement. On pense à Albert Einstein qui se demande
dans *La Géométrie et l'Expérience* (*Geometrie und Erfahrung*, 1921)
« comment se fait-il que les mathématiques qui sont pourtant un
produit de la réflexion indépendant de l'expérience, se conforment
si excellemment à la réalité ? ».

Vers le milieu du XIXᵉ siècle, lorsque les Eléments d'Euclide
semblent ne plus servir la science mathématique, Carl Adams, enseignant dans l'école professionnelle de Winterthur, fait un état
des lieux et remarque par exemple : « L'ancienne géométrie est ca-
ractérisée par la rigueur de la forme, la nouvelle par la généralité
du mode d'observation. » En 1845, le même auteur se montre plus
explicite lorsqu'il consigne qu'Euclide, Archimède et Apollonius
auraient « créé des œuvres d'art dont la structure architectonique »
serait « résistante et immuable ». Une « belle symétrie » et « l'élé-
gance de la forme », autrefois « propriété exclusive des Grecs » se
manifesteraient ici. Cela décrit quasiment le cadre historico-culturel dans lequel Euclide a trouvé sa place.

En 1847, l'année où paraît *The First Six Books of The Elements
of Euclid, in which coloured diagrams and symbols are used instead of
letters for the greater ease of learners*, cette mutation semble accom-
plie et Oliver Byrne crée à nouveau – à son corps défendant – une
œuvre d'art ! En 1757, dans le septième volume de l'*Encyclopédie*,
Jean le Rond d'Alembert reconnaît déjà les limites d'une future
utilisation de la « Géométrie sublime ». Il soutenait d'un autre côté
qu'en ce qui concerne l'utilisation de la géométrie élémentaire il n'y
aurait aucun besoin d'algébrisation, parce qu'il n'en naîtrait aucun
avantage sur le plan de la simplification. Ainsi on ne peut ôter à
la géométrie cet avantage didactique qui s'associe à l'intuition
sensible et à une forme, ce qu'Edmund G. Husserl décrit comme
« des finitudes à l'horizon d'un infini ouvert » et qui chez Jacques
Derrida fait penser à nouveau aux dangers d'un « signe graphique »
lié à la « mondanéité ».

Il semble que l'art gère plus facilement ces risques. Euclide voit
à nouveau le jour chez Piet Mondrian, reconnaissable « au premier
coup d'œil » et affecté au domaine esthétique et ses idéaux.

BOOK III.

DEFINITIONS.

I.

EQUAL circles are those whose diameters are equal.

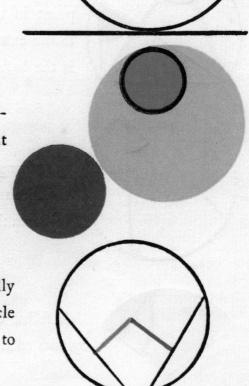

II.

A right line is said to touch a circle when it meets the circle, and being produced does not cut it.

III.

Circles are said to touch one another which meet but do not cut one another.

IV.

Right lines are said to be equally distant from the centre of a circle when the perpendiculars drawn to them from the centre are equal.

"To facilitate their acquirement"

Oliver Byrne's *The First Six Books of the Elements of Euclid*
– didactic, colourful, and eccentric

What could impel a Surveyor of Her Majesty's Settlements in the Falkland Islands to conceive and to publish the most attractive edition of Euclid that the world had ever seen? This edition comes down to us today in colours reminiscent of Mondrian, modern and *avant la lettre*. No one who holds it in his hands can resist the fascination of its illustrations. The pictures are all the more captivating because they simply suggest, concretely demonstrate *ad oculus*, and thus assist in the comprehension of mathematical laws that initially seem most difficult and abstract.

The crucial issue of "the visual depiction of forms of thought"

"Mathematicians who would prefer not to enter the labyrinthine maze of philosophy are politely requested to cease reading the foreword here."
– Frege, *Grundgesetze der Arithmetik*, 1893[1]

Later generations have not dealt gently with Oliver Byrne. This harshness primarily involves the science of mathematics and its relationship to its own history, in which the name "Oliver Byrne" is seldom or never mentioned. One can search in vain for the spectacular Euclid edition in Max Steck's *Bibliographia Euclideana*, although Steck is kindly disposed to the "mathematical gestalt" and took appreciative notice of the "demonstrative self-evidence" ("Schaufähigkeit") of Proclus's commentary about Euclid. From here he moved onward via Nikolaus Cusanus to Johannes Kepler and the "renewal of Pythagorean motifs", then continued to Gottfried Wilhelm Leibniz, where he explored a synthesis in which the *mundus intelligibilis* and the *mundus sensibilis*, i. e. the abstract and that which can be experienced with the senses, would be viewed together and reshaped into a unified whole.[2]

Oliver Byrne, for his part, never intended to venture so far either from an historical or from a fundamental point of view. His intentions remained didactically directed toward the immediate understanding and use of mathematics. Nonetheless, his *Euclid* could have led, and indeed must lead, to those fundamental considerations. Steck was convinced that mathematics, "unlike pure logic", could not be derived from mere concepts and that, instead, the following assertion holds true: "The participation of contemplation in its realizations is inarguable because *mathemata* are not possible from concepts, but only from their construction."[3] Steck oriented himself according to Andreas Speiser and his *Die Mathematische Denkweise* (1932), and with regard to the scientific formation of concepts *(Grenzen der naturwissenschaftlichen Begriffsbildung)* also to Heinrich Rickert, who in his day had noted that mathematics did not have recourse to previously existing material and that mathematics itself must create its material. This, Rickert says, is why questions about heuristic definitions of the straight line (the "absolutely simple") are obsolete, just as the attempt "to define blue or red" can only be regarded as an "indication".[4] Definitions are sufficient unto themselves. In his first chapter, which is devoted to "limits", Andreas Speiser called attention in 1932 to the "basis of lawfulness" ("Rechtsgrund"), which is to be found, in all conceivable other interests and exuberances, "for mathematics in the mathematical insight".[5]

Speiser dedicated his *Die Mathematische Denkweise* to Raoul La Roche, who had commissioned the architect Le Corbusier. For him, simply because of the verdicts of their scope of applicability, i. e. their "basis of lawfulness", there could be no doubt about the proximity of mathematical and artistic worlds. The sciences would be "determined by the basis of their lawfulness, and here mathematical and artistic insights belong to the intellectual arena, whereas experiment and tradition belong to the external world".[6] This naturally lends support to the view that mathematical forms and figures should be philosophically regarded and evaluated as spontaneous human inventions, rather than merely being viewed and appraised as the result of scientific requirements. But a more comprehensive "system of our knowledge (i. e. the system of total experience)"[7] demands such a "scientific context of achievement", in which the "visible intelligibility of the empirical world" and all of psychology insist upon their rights.[8] In his discussion of *Die Grenzen der naturwissenschaftlichen Begriffsbildung*, Heinrich Rickert analyses the opposition between the "logical perfection" (of a concept) and empirical contemplation, but then immediately afterwards blurs this distinction when considering the actual efficacy of corporeal worlds. Nothing can circumvent these difficulties.[9] This opposition is further exacerbated by cultural views when, for example, the attempt is made to apply mathematical statements to aesthetic effects. In his Würzburger Dissertation (1908), Ernst Bloch cites methodical "deviations" as an essential characteristic of Rickert's philosophy and illustrates this by calling attention to the changes and diverging interests that arose around 1850.[10]

In their specific accentuation and exacerbation, these questions thus occupy their own historical space. What began in 1847 with the "formal logic"[11] of Oliver Byrne's critic Augustus De Morgan matures into a crisis with Edmund G. Husserl, who situates this predicament under the concept of "mathematization" and associates it with science's loss of vital significance.[12] Rickert states in 1910–11 that the "objectifying weltanschauung" is incapable of grasping the meaning of life.[13] Husserl, who was concerned at this time with the ideals of a "strict science", grants that the foundations and independence of the strict natural sciences and liberal arts, "as well as new purely mathematical disciplines", would be achieved as the "only ripe fruit" of efforts conducted "through the medium of critical reflection".[14] For philosophy, which had been left out in the cold, so to speak, and building upon the critique of the unavoidable "indirect methods" that had been voiced by the "most impressive sciences of the modern era, i. e. mathematics and physics", he hoped for a science "which would be free from all indirect symbolizing and mathematizing methods, free from the apparatus of conclusions and proofs, yet which would gain many rigorous insights that would be decisive for all subsequent philosophy".[15] This ought to be of service to a "phenomenological cognition of the essential" in "the correct sense of philosophical intuition".[16]

Viewpoints and interests had long since diverged. Gottlob Frege published his *Begriffsschrift, eine der arithmetischen nachgebildete Formelsprache des reinen Denkens* in 1879, and Oliver Byrne's *Euclid* justifiably deserves a place, in the broadest sense, in the prehistory of Frege's book. Afterwards, in 1882, Frege noted that "a visually comprehensible presentation of the forms of thought" would have "a significance that transcends mathematics".[17] He urged philosophers to "grant importance to the topic".[18] It is not surprising that, in his dispute with Husserl, the psychology of all perception was paramount for both thinkers. With regard to Frege, one should also interpret this as meaning that he wasn't so unphilosophical after all. Just the opposite: his initial and fundamental explications in the first volume of the *Grundgesetze der Arithmetik* (1893) are followed by the footnote: "Mathematicians who would prefer not to enter the labyrinthine maze of philosophy are politely requested to cease reading the foreword here."[19] He then proceeds to explore the question of what can and should be thought and represented. Of course, Frege argues against an abusive "psychological falsification of logic".[20] On the other hand, he calls for limiting "arbitrary fabrication" ("Erdichtungswillkür").[21] Arithmetic, for him, is undoubtedly a branch of logic.[22] "I regard it as a sure sign of error when logic has need of metaphysics and psychology, two sciences that are themselves in need of logical underpinnings. Where, then, is the genuine primal foundation upon which all else rests? Or is it as it is for Münchhausen, who pulled himself out of the swamp by the hair of his own head?"[23]

Time and again, the questions that arise revolve around what mathematics can and should do, what is permissible and impermissible for it, and what leads astray into the "imagined".[24] In criticism of Benno Erdmann, Frege asserts that anyone who puts the latter into the foreground is an incorrigible idealist.[25] At the beginning of his *An Essay on the Foundations of Geometry* (1897), Bertrand A. W. Russell remarks: "Geometry throughout the 17th and 18th centuries remained in the war against empiricism, an impregnable fortress of the idealists."[26] Thus the warring hosts stand in full array upon the battlefield. Russell, who follows his scolding of idealism with a presentation of the trajectory of geometry's path since it moved away from Euclid, questions the axiom of parallels and continues, via Nikolai Ivanovich Lobachevsky and János Bolyai, onward to untrammelled shores.[27]

Precisely this, the incunabula of non-Euclidian geometry, preceded Oliver Byrne's efforts. Later, by 1854, at least a narrow circle of scholars was familiar with Bernhard Riemann's "Ueber die Hypothesen, welche der Geometrie zu Grunde liegen". Riemann's speculations begin with the fact that geometry presup-

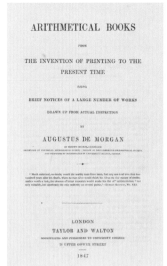

Page/Seite/Page 14

Ill. 5
Oliver Byrne, *The First Six Books of the Elements of Euclid*, London 1847
– Book III. Definitions.
– Buch III. Definitionen.
– Livre III. Définitions.

Ill. 6
Augustus De Morgan, *An Essay on Probabilities, and on their Application to Life Contingencies and Insurance Offices*, London 1838

Ill. 7
Augustus De Morgan, *Arithmetical Books ... being brief notices of a large number of works drawn up from actual inspection*, London 1847

6   7

poses the notion of space and that the reasons underlying the axioms are entirely obscure. He therefore recommends that this darkness, which neither mathematicians nor philosophers "from Euclid to Legendre" have ever elucidated, ought gradually to be subjected to work, making use of experiences and facts, with an eye toward "the reality underlying space".[28] This points toward physics. For the ceremony commemorating the founding of the Friedrich-Wilhelms-Universität in Berlin in 1878, Hermann von Helmholtz delivered his famous speech entitled *Die Thatsachen in der Wahrnehmung* (The Facts in Perception), in which he explained the old and the new contradiction.[29] He contrasts the "older notion of contemplation" ("Anschauung"), which relates to that which "immediately comes into consciousness with the sense impression", with his own scientific notion: "To prove that something can be experienced, I demand only that the resulting sense impressions be unambiguously given for each mode of observation; if necessary, by using scientific knowledge of their laws, from which, for someone who knows these laws, it would become evident that the thing under consideration, or the contemplating relationship, is indeed present."[30]

Helmholtz consciously opts not to include the "lightness, speed and sudden self-evidence" which are inherent in the "earlier notion of contemplation", namely, to immediate sense impression.[31] The uncoupling has occurred. Helmholtz situates his criticism precisely where Immanuel Kant asserted that the Euclidean laws are necessarily correct and that deviations from them are inconceivable, so that he could then clarify and describe the form of contemplation in a wholly traditional manner: "Our eye sees all it sees as an ag-gregate of coloured planes in the field of view; this is its manner of viewing."[32] But mathematics and Helmholtz explicitly sought nothing more than this. Husserl, on the other hand – and also with an eye toward the advantages that indwell the sense of sight e.g. "sudden self-evidence", or "blitzähnliche Evidenz"), which were now to be done without – accused Frege of straying "into infertile hyper-subtleties",[33] whereas Husserl, for his part, calls attention to "elementary psychic data". "No one can define" notions such as "quality, intensity, place, time and the like".[34] Husserl goes on to link this with "elementary relations" such as "equality, similarity, increase, whole and part, multiplicity and unity".[35] Phenomenology concerns itself with abstract, pure ideas! Husserl, as is well known, intends to establish phenomenology as a "fundamental science of philosophy" and to connect phenomenology to the "natural knowledge and experience" that he calls "the world".[36]

The claims of geometry were indeed extensive in bygone years. Those "elementary relations" in particular belonged – and still belong! – to the domain of geometry. With didactic intentions, one can still try to understand them in this sense and can strive to orient them in this (idealist) direction. Anyone who did so around the year 1850 was participating in a tradition that was admittedly significant in cultural history, but that is no longer part of the scientific community, which is moving toward the "new, purely mathematical disciplines", whose importance, incidentally, Husserl had fully recognized. But this cannot expunge the crisis as though it had never happened. "What is truth in our contemplation and thought? In what sense do our notions correspond to reality? Philosophy and natural science confront this problem

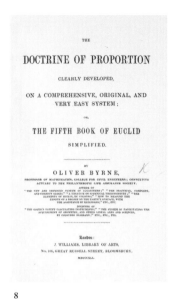

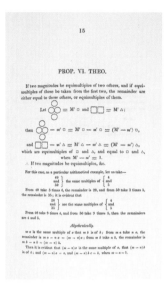

8

9

Ill. 8
Oliver Byrne, *The Doctrine of Proportion*,
London 1841

Ill. 9
Oliver Byrne, *The Doctrine of Proportion*,
London 1841, p. 15

from two diametrically opposite sides; it is their mutual task."[37]
This formulation, which Helmholtz penned in 1879, describes the
double and separate access to the problem. Considering the im-
possibility of overlooking the fact that the interests and efforts of
the two disciplines are drifting apart, the appended phrase about
"their mutual task" sounds as though it were glossing over the
problem. For Euclidean geometry and its mediating tradition, at
least in the relevant science, it stands as a valediction.[38]

The anachronistic and eccentric mathematician Oliver Byrne and his detractor Augustus De Morgan

"Oliver Byrne's Euclid *in symbols and colored diagrams
was not taken seriously, but was regarded a curiosity."*
– Cajori, *A History of Mathematical Notations*, 1928[39]

With only moderate exaggeration, one can describe the precari-
ous situation in 1847 as follows. Byrne's "coloured diagrams" and
his blind faith in arbitrary forms of representation position him,
from a mathematical perspective, in the era prior to 1850, while
simultaneously transporting him, from an artistic viewpoint, dec-
ades ahead, into modern times. His gaze focuses primarily on the
ancient intention of the *adaequatio rei ac intellectus*, i.e. the corre-
spondence sought between knowledge and its object, as well as the
corresponding form of perception ("Anschauungsform"), which is

closely related to the senses, through his didactic figures and symbols, which is the unmistakeable, immediate, and explicit goal of
his *Euclid*. It is not coincidental that Byrne's *Euclid* is mentioned
in the grand presentation that Florian Cajori devoted in 1928 to
the symbols and figures used in mathematics.[40] But Cajori mentions Byrne only in passing: "Oliver Byrne's *Euclid* in symbols and
colored diagrams was not taken seriously, but was regarded a curiosity."[41] Byrne's *Euclid* was perceived as an oddity – and accordingly dismissed! But none other than Cajori himself also says that
the use of colours in the presentation of geometrical problems was
mentioned by Heron of Alexandria, who claimed that such usage
follows a Pythagorean tradition.[42] Cajori also cites Martianus
Capella, who correlated plane and colour with one another and
who is amenable to all aspects of figure formation. Tradition sides
with Oliver Byrne!

Cajori believes that the more profound reason for the disin-
terest in Byrne's *Euclid* lies in the opinion that the slightly older
Augustus De Morgan had expressed, and that he reinforced with
his full authority, at the time, i. e. in 1849, which was two years after
the publication of the work: "Those who introduced algebraical
symbols into elementary geometry, destroyed the peculiar character of the latter to every student who has any mechanical associations connected with those symbols; that is, to every student who
has previously used them in ordinary algebra. Geometrical reasons,
and arithmetical process, have each its own office; to mix the two
in elementary instruction, is injurious to the proper acquisition of
both."[43] That's quite a severe verdict, especially when we consider
that the interrelationship between arithmetic and geometry was

frequently the explicit subject of research and served as a useful field of observation at this time, not least by Augustus De Morgan himself. Was De Morgan's harsh criticism deliberately aimed at Byrne's *Euclid*? If so, it would primarily target Euclid's Fifth Book, which is devoted to magnitudes and to the relationships between numbers.[44]

A "curiosity", to repeat the word that Cajori chose to describe the (dearth of) appreciation for Byrne's *Euclid*, seems instead to smack of the deliberate avoidance of a more precise description of the quality of the signs and symbols that Byrne had chosen. Does Cajori mean their anachronism or their indeterminacy in a wider spectrum of pictorial description, as it were, between iconoclasm and idolatry? Isn't Augustus De Morgan's criticism of the mixing of geometric and arithmetic languages more likely a pretext to conceal his fundamental personal dislike for Byrne? We do not know. It is known, however, that De Morgan reviewed *The creed of St. Athanasius*, which Oliver Byrne published in 1839 under the pseudonymous anagram E. B. Revilo and which he included in his *A Budget of Paradoxes*, into which he put everything he could unearth that he deemed guilty of mathematical, Pythagorean, or cabalistic abstruseness. His verdict reads as follows: "This author really believed himself, and was in earnest. He is not the only person who has written nonsense by confounding the mathematical infinite (of quantity) with what speculators now more correctly express by the unlimited, the unconditional, or the absolute."[45] In the much later treatment by David Eugene Smith, we again find, with direct allusion to Byrne's *Euclid*, that Byrne is classed among the "minor mathematical writers".[46] No one seems to have anything good to say about Byrne! In its most recent printing (1974), Augustus De Morgan's anthology of marginal mathematical viewpoints and theories appeared under the title *The Encyclopedia of Excentrics* [*sic*], and thus Oliver Byrne indeed found his way into the fringe of mathematical curiosities and eccentricities![47]

Byrne is an eccentric, of course, as is Augustus De Morgan, about whom it is rumoured that ever since he lost an eye during his first year of life in India, he spent the rest of his life with nothing else but abstract numbers in his mind. Of course, such anecdotes cannot explain the crisis surrounding the issue of pictorial presentation in 19th-century mathematics. The fact remains that Augustus De Morgan and Oliver Byrne are linked by many of the issues that concerned the British world at the time. De Morgan, for his part, is especially interested in the problems of didactics and teaching. He shares the view that his teacher and friend William Whewell expressed in 1836 in the title of his book: *Thoughts on the study of mathematics, as part of a liberal education.*[48] Mathematics serves education and is a discipline that simultaneously trains both the moral and the rational capacity. Furthermore, the pedagogical orientation shapes mathematics and imbues it with societal status. This is meant to be understood quite concretely.

His *Essay on Probabilities* (1838), which bears the subtitle *On their Application to Life Contingencies and Insurance Offices* (ill. 6), should be taken literally and understood as a contribution toward dispelling "public ignorance of the principles of insurance".[49] De Morgan was a prominent member of the Society for the Diffusion of Useful Knowledge, which was established in 1826, and he wrote more than 700 articles for its organ, the *Penny Cyclopedia*.[50] In 1841 he published in it a short text entitled *Proportion*, in which he discusses Euclid's Fifth Book.[51] This prompts him to occupy himself all the more with the notions of number, arithmetic, algebra, logic, and probability (ill. 7). The same year that Byrne's *Euclid* appeared, De Morgan published his *Formal Logic*, which was followed by a series of related research papers.[52] De Morgan, and with him the mathematics leading toward symbolic logic, seem to have wanted to exclude precisely that which Byrne and his *Euclid* elevate to a didactic principle: namely, clarification by means of figures and symbols. Of course, illustrative elucidation had been practised long before Byrne either in kindred manner, differently, or at least rudimentarily, so Oliver Byrne was by no means as isolated as he may seem. Colour, too, soon became more frequently used in the context of scientific illustrations.[53] Only for mathematics did it seem necessary to keep things apart that belong neatly separated.[54] What most contributed toward Byrne's reputation as an outsider was probably the fact that the development of geometry, within the discipline of mathematics, had long since evolved away from Euclid and turned its attention toward new problems, for example, the questions of formal logic. The topic of symbols is comparatively obsolete. Nonetheless, De Morgan seems to use every available opportunity to cast his vote against them and to serve logic all the more: "Every science that has thriven has thriven upon its own symbols: logic, the only science which is admitted to have made no improvements in century after century, is the only one which has grown no symbols."[55]

The degree to which empiricism in general – and also in mathematics – would ultimately assert itself 'a priori' against the actual or the alleged is an entirely different issue. In his autobiography, John Stuart Mill speaks out against "the German, or a priori view of human knowledge, and of the knowing faculties" and argues in favour of both his *System of Logic* and his exchange with Whewell: "But the 'System of Logic' supplies what was much wanted, a textbook of the opposite doctrine – that which derives all knowledge from experience, and all moral and intellectual qualities principally from the direction given to the associations."[56] No place remains here for the age-old *more geometrico*, nor is any room left for German idealism![57] Induction was the order of the day! Whewell's *The Philosophy of the Inductive Sciences, founded upon their history* (1840) not only lastingly influenced his students De Morgan and Mill, but also exerted a fundamental and determining effect on the new course of scientific development and its moral underpinnings.

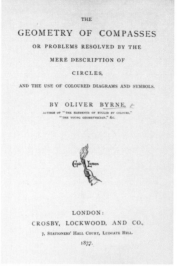

Ill. 10
Oliver Byrne, *The Geometry of Compasses*,
London 1877, frontispiece

Ill. 11
Oliver Byrne, *The Geometry of Compasses*,
London 1877

10   11

When Chiswick Press published Byrne's *Euclid* in 1847, the second edition of Whewell's *Philosophy of the Inductive Sciences* was nearly simultaneously published. Afterwards, in typical British fashion, it was augmented by a *Novum Organum Renovatum*.[58] And that added the decisive accent!

Byrne held the outmoded view that the elements of Euclid were "by common consent, the basis of mathematical science all over the civilized globe". He thus took a firm stance on the historical side of mathematics.[59] Considering the most recent developments, it would seem old-fashioned to position oneself in favour of the search for truth and, in the process, to borrow and apply Euclid's (old) symbols and figures in order to present mathematical laws in a comprehensible way: namely, to leave them in the realm of the visible. Byrne, on the other hand, wrote in the introduction to his *Euclid* (1847): "All language consists of representative signs, and those signs are the best which effect their purposes with the greatest precision and dispatch."[60] The progress of formal logic had convinced most logicians that this view was obsolete. Cajori, incidentally, notes that all individual approaches toward ideographic presentation would be overruled by a consensus that pointed in the opposite direction.[61]

With Augustus De Morgan's seemingly rigid rejection of the mixing of geometrical and arithmetical languages or other symbols, it is clear that here, too, the tradition had long since been abandoned which Proclus, as well as Martianus Capella, had expounded in all its extremely effective richness. The assertion that "geometry teaches how to discover and prove laws which express the attributes of figures" had elsewhere been connected for many

years with the necessary effort, "without which one cannot have profit and satisfaction in science or life".[62] In 1852 Professor Arthur Arneth, who taught in Heidelberg, held the achievements of geometry in particularly high esteem: "Geometry, among all the branches of mathematics, offers us the most instructive picture. We see how human beings, from the beginning of pure thought, have sought to cling to the singular, wanting only – and being solely able – to know this with certainty."[63] Byrne, for his part, expressly refers to the authority of all those philosophers in the Platonic tradition who stood for this history. Now, however, that which was thought to be valid was what Max Bense had described as the "detachment of mathematics from philosophy" and what he had declared with the strenuous articulation of the "discipline's own precise language".[64] In Bense's interpretation, this would rectify the tendency of "mathematical problems and solutions to run ahead of their actual mathematical overcoming".[65] This, however, seems more reminiscent of the footrace between Hercules and the tortoise!

The progress of the era pushed Oliver Byrne out of the recent history of mathematics and caused the undignified dunce hat of 'a curiosity' to be placed upon his head. One is referred to different horizons, to art, for example, where languages and figures and their manifold meanings continue to be employed. The less uplifting consequence that results from the anachronism of Byrne's *Euclid* involves the fact that Byrne seems more likely to pique our interest merely for typographical and aesthetic reasons.[66] The typographer and designer Ruari McLean, whose work took its cue from Jan Tschichold, became aware of Byrne's *Euclid* in this way. His appraisal, which he expresses in *Victorian Book Design and Colour Printing* (1963), emphasizes just that. He describes Byrne's book as "a decided complication of Euclid" and recalls the triumphal presentation at the Great Exhibition in London in 1851 of Charles Whittingham's book, which was published by William Pickering in an edition of 1,000 copies. This is connected to the anecdote claiming that that lavish book drove its publisher into bankruptcy and forced him to abandon the famous Chiswick Press, which had been founded by his eponymous uncle.[67]

Byrne's method and argumentation – and the goal reached with the 'colourful' *Euclid* of 1847

"This Work has a greater aim than mere illustration; we do not introduce colours for the purpose of entertainment, or to amuse by certain combinations of tint and form, but to assist the mind in its researches after truth, to increase the facilities of instruction, and to diffuse permanent knowledge. If we wanted authorities to prove the importance and usefulness of geometry, we might quote every philosopher since the days of Plato. Among the Greeks, in ancient, as in the school of Pestalozzi and others in recent times, geometry was adopted as the best gymnastic of the mind."
– Byrne, *Euclid*, 1847[68]

One simply has no other choice but to come to terms with the fact that, together with Byrne, we have arrived in the era of "outmoded Euclid".[69] Byrne and his geometric views are, of course, not mentioned in the relevant literature on logic, from Augustus De Morgan to Willard Van Orman Quine's *Philosophy of Logic* (1970). But the age-old urge to make our notions visible under the conditions of plausibility, and the advantages, cited by von Helmholtz, of "lightness, speed, sudden self-evidence", are still on the table. Artists should devote their efforts to it! Oliver Byrne and his *Euclid* entirely put their trust in the old, outmoded view that holds that geometry not only mediates, but also fundamentally assists us in the quest for truth, because it is an exercise that strengthens the mind. One must follow Oliver Byrne and Euclid where mathematics had not yet pursued the history of the discipline and its specialized fields after 1850, where it continues to be devoted, or rather, is for the first time truly devoted, to the great cultural and historical tradition, to which Max Steck would later add the admittedly rather broadly based maxim: "All great mathematicians were simultaneously also philosophers."[70] Steck appends to this "universal view" other and no less generalized statements: "All great mathematicians had an intimate relationship to art, and most of them were also practising artists" and "All great mathema-

ticians felt at home in intellectual and art history, especially in that of their own people, until the middle of the 19th century."[71]

Although euphoric judgements of this sort don't make it any easier to assign Byrne's *Euclid* to the place it deserves in the long history of Euclid's *Elements* and the nearly equally lengthy history of the tome's editions, the key questions have been raised and now the task is to consider the wider cultural context. This is inevitable for Byrne because precisely this consideration sheds light on his work's profounder meaning and greater usefulness. Part of this also obliges us to realize that the interconnections between geometry, figure, and form merit respect as an effective and powerful cultural tradition. Essential to this is the realization that contemplation ("Anschauung") is anchored in sensory perception. This lends support to the didactic aspect of Byrne's *Euclid*, even if this is at first introduced in rather self-effacing and apologetic terms: "Illustration, if it does not shorten the time of study, will at least make it more agreable [*sic*]."[72] One must follow the thread of Byrne's reasoning.

The didactic introductory notes, which he inserts into his books at regular intervals, are sufficiently remarkable on their own. Byrne repeatedly emphasizes the distinction between his work and the pure science of mathematics: "Much indeed has been written by learned and experienced Mathematicians, but their works seem rather addressed to the proficient, than to the uninitiated student in the science. Their long formulae, complicated rules, and demonstrations, &c., perplex rather than instruct the beginner, who perhaps, terrified at the mass of difficulties before him, gives up in disgust the study of a subject, which, treated in a simple manner, he had easily acquired."[73] Byrne recalls his firsthand experience with the frightening effects of mathematics, both during his student years and in his role as a teacher, and he wants to improve this situation: "I have therefore written in the same manner in which I should have explained it by oral communication with my pupils."[74] He intends his prose to be practical and readily understandable for classroom use or home study. In 1835 this is the intention with which Byrne introduces his spherical trigonometry, the subtitle of which expressly alludes to a "few simple rules" and conversely promises to avoid major difficulties.

Analogous statements and recommendations are a recurrent theme in Oliver Byrne's numerous and obviously didactically conceived publications. The first sentence of the introduction to his *Handbook for the artisan, mechanic, and engineer* (1853) promises its readers that even those who are as yet unacquainted with the material will soon be capable of understanding even the most difficult problems.[75] Byrne also doesn't shy away from comparison with his metier's leading lights – indeed, he positively invites it. In the foreword to his *The Young Dual Arithmetician* (1866), which is lauded as "new art, designed for elementary instruction and the use of schools", he says of the tables of logarithms: "They are equal in power to Babbage's and Collet's combined, and take up less than one eighth part of their space."[76] Oliver Byrne's work on logarithms earned him, also in Germany, admiring notice at an early date, especially and significantly wherever the "application of logarithms in everyday life" was sought. Praise of this sort could be read in the subtitle of a publication by the Eisenach school director Adolf Lorey: the prologue of *Das Neueste und Interessanteste aus der Logarithmotechnik* (1852) begins with a reference to Byrne and M. Philippe Koralek, and emphasizes the "technical skill, especially in the instantaneous calculation of logarithms".[77] The introduction begins with a comparison: "The logarithms are as powerful and effective for calculations as steam is for machinery."[78]

One can see from these testimonies that Byrne was above all interested in teaching the subject in the most straightforward and effective way. The urge to achieve quick comprehension was paramount. This same intention also guided him in his works on geometry. Byrne first emphasized this in his *The Doctrine of Proportion clearly developed, on a comprehensive, original, and very easy system; or, The Fifth Book of Euclid simplified*, which was published in 1841 while he was serving as a professor of mathematics at the College of Civil Engineers at Putney and which he dedicated to the directors, organs, and students of that institution (ills. 8, 9).[79] The title proclaims that this is an "easy system", in which the Fifth Book of Euclid is "simplified". That same year other publications of Byrne were publicized, as was the case of *The First Six Books of the Elements of Euclid*. In many respects, what follows in the *Doctrine of Proportion* is a prelude to the corresponding parts of his *Euclid* of 1847, where some of the symbols introduced in 1841 reappear in altered form. Conversely, in 1847, he refers to the preceding publication and especially to the algebraic and arithmetic elucidations that are explained at length in the earlier book but skimmed over in the more recent work.[80]

The starting point of Oliver Byrne's opus is clear. He regards the relevant research as being fraught with lacunae and errors, which he traces, by way of Adrien-Marie Legendre, to Isaac Newton. He contrasts this, on the other hand, with the cliché about Euclid's absolutely consistent, error-free logic.[81] Byrne is unshakeably convinced that "Euclid's Fifth Book is a master-piece of human reasoning".[82] He accordingly devotes his undivided attention to the tasks of explaining, elucidating, and presenting, for which purposes he relies on symbols, about which he says – in contradiction to De Morgan and Cajori's later view: "The introduction of symbols into works of geometry is every day becoming more general."[83] These symbols and their usefulness are so self-evident that he deems no further justifications necessary. In 1841, however, he feels obliged to mention, with regard to arithmetical and algebraic modes of presentation, that the subject itself ought solely to decide "whether the structure be raised upon numbers,

symbols, or lines, &c.".[84] The doctrine of proportions repeatedly made use of all these means in various ways.

Explanations that follow place geometric symbols beside the familiar algebraic formulae and thus compare the "visible symbols with the abstractions for which they stand". Byrne's interest ultimately lies in the usage "in ordinary language", a means whose success he had discovered during his earlier career as a surveyor.[85] The crux of the matter is clearly to discern and understandably to convey the differences among symbols; the method must accordingly be "logical, strict, and convincing ... without being attended with that tediousness and circuitous detail which frequently accompany other methods".[86] It was already clear to Byrne that different colours would be helpful in clarifying differentiation.[87] In his foreword (dated 19 November 1840) to the *Doctrine of Proportion*, he unmistakeably states that this had been his intention, but that he was obliged to abandon his polychrome printing plans by then because of the expenses involved.[88]

It is obvious that Byrne, long before his Euclid of 1847, had acquired specific experience with his method and had accordingly earned both praise and criticism. For example, in the fifth definition of the Fifth Book, where Euclid discusses the multiplicities of magnitudes and their proportional identities, this involved replacing the phrase "any equimultiples", which Robert Simson had used in the edition of Euclid that was most widespread at the time, with the phrase "every equimultiples."[89] Even here, Byrne's didactic intention is evident. He didn't want to follow this with arbitrary – and arbitrarily many – tests of this sort, but sought instead to set a standard. No one would contradict him that definitions, as well as the individual parts and concepts therein, should stand on their own without further explanation. This goes hand in hand with his didactic objective: teaching must be the highest aim for everyone who writes about elementary things.[90] But here Byrne also abstains from a more profound analysis and interpretation of the Euclidean definition, which had always been recognized as being an especially difficult one. Augustus De Morgan, of all people, devoted his attention to this question and to the significance of ratio and proportionality, and published his thoughts about them in the *Penny Cyclopedia* in 1841.[91] Unlike Byrne, De Morgan, against his usual abstract predilections, had conducted tests to check the usability and plausibility of the Euclidean formula, and for this project he had made use, of all things, of a colonnade of pillars to aid the imagination and visualization.[92]

Recognition of Euclid's fundamental significance was obviously a high priority for Oliver Byrne in 1841. His *Doctrine of Proportion* was intended to prove that Euclid's Fifth Book is the only legitimate doctrine of geometrical proportion. He also planned to show here "that proportions should be treated algebraically and arithmetically as well as geometrically, as it equally belongs to all".[93] The symbols that he used to illustrate the Fifth Book of Eu-

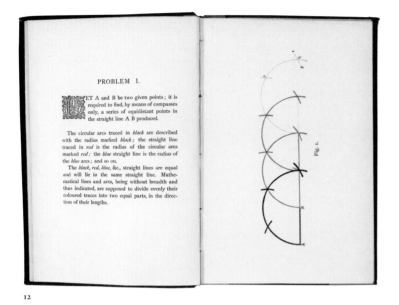

Ill. 12
Oliver Byrne, *The Geometry of Compasses*, London 1877
– *Problem I*, with illustration and text.
– *Problem I*, mit Abbildung und Text.
– *Problème I*, avec illustration et texte.

clid and that reappear in colour and slightly altered in 1847, tread a middle path and are most similar to later symbolic writings and forerunners of logicians' "Begriffsschriften". They clearly differ from the geometrical or geometricizing symbols with which Byrne illustrated Euclid's other books.

Byrne is unquestionably cognizant of the difficulties that might arise from this method: "Care must be taken to show that colour has nothing to do with the lines, angles, or magnitudes, except merely to name them."[94] But considering these didactic measures, which relied specifically on this visual aid, how should one understand this caveat? It's important to note that Byrne symbolically, i. e. indirectly, depicted points and lines through the overlapping of coloured planes. To truly discover point, line, and plane, one must abstract from the coloured planes that are visible in the illustration.[95] This precedes a rather long-winded rendering of the old explanation: "A mathematical line, which is length without breadth, cannot possess colour yet the junction of two colours on the same plane gives a good idea of what is meant by a mathematical line; recollect we are speaking familiarly, such a junction is to be understood and not the colour, when we say the black line, the red line or lines &c."[96] The thing itself is depicted through the touching and overlapping of coloured planes. In his *Underweysung der messung* (1525), Albrecht Dürer found an easier and more straightforward way to solve the problem caused by the lack of means of depicting an abstract line – he simply drew a thick and therefore visible line: "Because through this means, the interior understanding must be shown in the exterior work."[97] Byrne was aware of the risks that such indicative methods entail. His colours and coloured

diagrams would perhaps initially seem to be "a clumsy method"; but then he promised to offer a "means more refined and extensive than any that has been hitherto proposed".[98] This is undoubtedly true. But the "coloured diagrams", it seems, take on an independent life of their own. One cannot rid oneself of the suspicion that Byrne would like to add, to the Euclidean system, a second and graphic system, the usefulness of which he never tires of proving. "The experience of all who have formed systems to impress facts on the understanding, agree in proving that coloured representations, as pictures, cuts, diagrams, &c. are more easily fixed in the mind than mere sentences unmarked by any peculiarity."[99]

"More easily fixed in the mind." Isn't that precisely what Byrne had been striving for all along? The project that he first announced in 1841 ultimately succeeded in 1847 with the publication of a multicoloured *Euclid*, designed so that its contents are most readily comprehensible because the visual design takes into account all of Byrne's experiences with sense perception. Soon thereafter, polychrome printing went on to conquer the world of scientific publication. To cite only two examples: when Edward L. Youmans's *Chemical Atlas* was published in New York in 1856, its title alluded indirectly to Byrne's publications and emphasized that it contains "a series of beautifully colored [sic] diagrams" and that it has been expressly "designed for the use of students" (ills. 18–20, 32, 39). Ezekiel Webster Dimond followed suit in Worcester in 1867 with his publication of *The Chemistry of Combustion* "in language as simple and definite as possible" and naturally relying on colours to take the place of chemical symbols: red for oxygen, yellow for hydrogen, blue for nitrogen, and black for carbon (ills. 21–23, 33).[100]

12

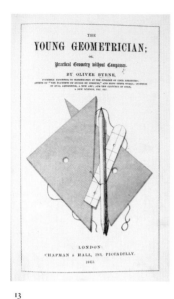

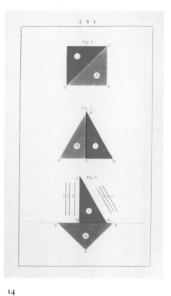

13   14

Ill. 13
Oliver Byrne, *The Young Geometrician*,
London 1865

Ill. 14
Oliver Byrne, *The Young Geometrician*,
London 1865, p. 3

Youmans wrote in his introduction: "It is especially in natural science, where definite and exact ideas of properties and relations are to be communicated to the mind, that the employment of visible diagrams is most useful."[101] Many years ahead of his time, he was aware that illustrations are particularly useful wherever the object under consideration cannot be seen.[102] Youmans cites geometry as his first example of such a situation. The corresponding method is to "diagramize geometrical conceptions", i. e. to translate geometrical notions into visible diagrams.[103]

Byrne had already joined this discussion in 1841 and had demonstrated the paramount importance of colour in the illustration of scientific subjects. He reached his goal in 1847, when, through poetic allusions, he demonstrated the intensity with which he concerned himself *avant la lettre* with this psychophysical question. He quoted Horace and Aesop to show the superiority of the sense of sight. Gustav Theodor Fechner shared this view in 1860 when he declared in the foreword to his *Elemente der Psychophysik:* "Ancient with regard to the task at hand", the novelty lies in the "mathematical connection of experienced facts".[104] What could be more reasonable than to use these facts for the presentation of scientific subjects? This undoubtedly forms the basis of Byrne's approach. In both the act and the fact, interest shifts from the scientific subject to its presentation and its didactic communication. It impels him to emphasize this in the introduction to his *Euclid* and to accentuate it visually and concretely. Byrne recommends dyed chalks for schools and coloured pencils for private use by those who wish to intensify their study of his *Euclid*.[105]

The didactic impetus and its necessary measures

*"Among the Greeks, in ancient, as in the school of
Pestalozzi and others in recent times, geometry was
adopted as the best gymnastic of the mind."*
– Byrne, *Euclid*, 1847[106]

Byrne mentions Johann Heinrich Pestalozzi right at the start of his *Euclid.* He's interested here in "the best gymnastic of the mind",[107] i. e. exercising the cognitive capacity. The didactic principle orients itself according to classroom instruction, "oral demonstrations", and the optimal interplay of visual and audible impressions. Comprehension ultimately occurs when "reason, and fact, and proof" all conjoin and leave a lasting impression. It is of lesser importance whether the indication from the text to the diagram runs through colour and form as a sign or whether it runs through the corresponding parts of the diagram itself; what matters most is the "simplicity" and that it facilitates "concentration".[108] Precisely this is what Pestalozzi sought to achieve with his *Elementarlehre* and *Anschauungslehre der Zahlenverhältnisse*, namely: a method or "exercise of the art", in order to bring the learning of mathematics into harmony with the development of the "power of thought" (ills. 24, 25). This is exactly what Byrne strives to accomplish by means of symbol, figure, and colour, to the advantage of learning in and of itself.[109] "For the greater ease of learning" is the ultimate aim, and Euclid is a means toward that goal. This is part of a long tradition in which mathematics was primarily assigned the role of a mediator. Mathematics is not a science per se, wrote Giovanni Pico della Mirandola in the first of his theses about mathematics; mathematics does not lead directly to happiness; rather, it ranks among the helping sciences that pave the way to other sciences.[110] It all depends on the *medietas*, i. e. the status as a means and mediator.

When one approaches the subject in this way, the uncertainties associated with Euclid and the *obscuritas* ascribed to him become less important. In his discussion of Euclid's postulate of parallels, Giovanni Alfonso Borelli says that the reason why everyone says this is so difficult to grasp is because they lack the requisite foundations, namely: understanding infinity.[111] But this doesn't make him abandon hope. He, too, claims that new insights can be acquired through the (classical) progress of the intellect from the known to the unknown,[112] and he published his *Euclides restitutus* accordingly.

One comes to terms with this situation and searches for aids. In 1684, i. e. long before Oliver Byrne, St. George Ashe wrote an article about Euclid for the *Philosophical Transactions* of the Royal Society of London, entitling it "A new and easy way of demonstrating some propositions of Euclid".[113] In it, he orients himself on the "pre-eminence of Mathematical knowledge", subsequently and all the more clearly insisting upon the importance and reliability of the mathematical method. The foreground is occupied by the few axioms and postulates that ought to be kept separate from all trifling and lack of precision.[114] In a letter that he wrote in 1686, we learn that Ashe had consulted John Pell's *An Introduction to Algebra* for assistance with his own efforts to present Euclid's Second and Fifth Books.[115] To what degree these efforts are connected with *The Elements or Principles of Geometrie*, which was anonymously published in London in 1684, must remain an unanswered question (ills. 26–28).[116] The fact is that this textbook of geometry, which is clearly a successor of Borelli's work, is followed by an introduction with definitions, axioms, and an explanation of the subsequently used signs, some of which are similar to those that Oliver Byrne used in 1847. The intentions are similar. The fastest and most efficient route toward an adequate understanding is sought, which benefits everyone who wants to arrive, with the greatest possible speed, at the practical questions of this examination.[117] Such people will find the introductory definitions useful, although they must bear in mind that points, lines, and angles are immaterial things, and their inherent immateriality justifies the use of symbols. But the author is not yet satisfied with this explanation; he therefore appends another, in which he even more clearly emphasizes the value of demonstration: "Demonstration is the highest degree of Proof that any matter admits of."[118] He stresses the fundamental use of geometry and the indirect use of Euclid's methods, both of which train the mind and protect it against error and misapprehension.[119] The didactic usefulness is immediately noted.[120] That's why it is also necessary to create the clarifying preconditions, to which also ultimately belong, alongside the definitions, the tables with the "Explication of the Notes", in which there is a list of the graphic symbols representing functions or meanings such as "equal to" or "like" or "continued proportion", as well as the figures of triangle or circle.[121]

The didactic objectives, along with a corresponding method of presentation, seem to have long since taken possession of Euclid. Indeed, they would appear to have been inherent in Euclid through and through. Oliver Byrne's evocative words in the introduction to his *Euclid* resound in our ears: the colours aren't intended for purposes of entertainment, but to "assist the mind in its researches after truth" and to clear the path toward long-lasting knowledge.[122] One could also say that the more Euclid's infamous *obscuritas* continues to exert its after-effects, the more important are the methods of presentation, demonstration, and a didactic approach.[123] The more clearly the application occupies the foreground, the greater is the need for appropriate models. "A teacher of mathematics should elucidate all equations by means of models or, when he doesn't have them at his disposal, he should try to augment his lecture with clear and complete diagrams."[124] This ranks among the absolutely indispensable preconditions, Peter Heinrich Christoph Brodhagen writes in 1792 in his *Anleitung zum gemeinnützigen Unterricht*, which is expressly intended for artisans, artists, and mechanics.

With Pestalozzi, to whom Byrne refers, these interests are strengthened, the methods undergo greater refinement, and especially the question of the senses that come into play is raised more frequently. The adaptation to the senses ceases to be merely an accompaniment and soon becomes paramount. The illustration separates itself out and comprises a new logic in itself or, to speak of it in modern terms, it becomes a pictorial discourse. This process can be observed in Byrne's writing. The intentions of his *Euclid* are in harmony with the efforts of his era. For example, Johann Georg Heinrich Feder declared in 1793 that "in cognition, much depends upon the quality of the signs" and this statement, of course, builds upon Johann Heinrich Lambert's *Neues Organon* (1764),[125] which was also well known in Great Britain, and ultimately prompted Byrne to state that all languages consist of representative signs.[126] The senses are granted even greater importance, as Byrne affirms by repeatedly expressing his preference for oral teaching. For Heinrich Stephani, the contrast between the "heard language" and the "seen language" forms the starting point for his research, which he published in Erlangen in 1814 under the title *Ausführliche Beschreibung meiner einfachen Lese-Methode*.[127] In Stephani's view, the letters of the alphabet are essentially "only for the eye, which they serve as arbitrarily chosen signs of the various spoken sounds", but he nevertheless wanted them to be understood as "the real notes

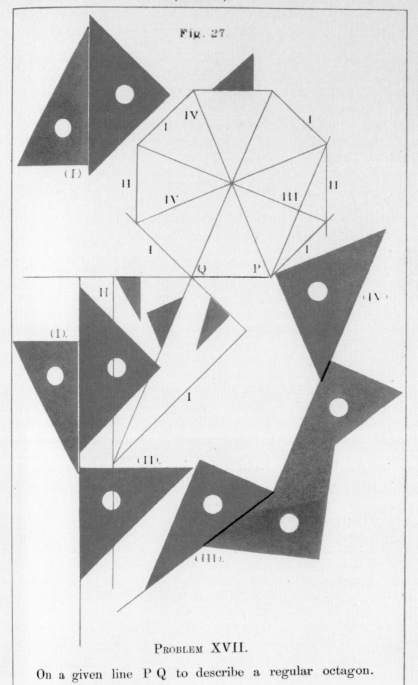

Fig. 27.

PROBLEM XVII.

On a given line P Q to describe a regular octagon.
Fig. 27.

Ill. 15
Oliver Byrne, *The Young Geometrician*, London 1865,
p. 26
– *Problem XVII. On a given line PQ to describe a regular octagon.*
– *Problem XVII. Auf einer gegebenen Linie PQ ein regelmäßiges Achteck beschreiben.*
– *Problème XVII. Tracer un octogone régulier sur une ligne donnée PQ.*

of our speaking instrument".[128] To speed up this process, he calls upon the memory, which can take note of things and, as it were, mechanically recall them more quickly and not only letter by alphabetical letter, but from the letter to the syllable and from the syllable to the entire word, which ought to be recognizable "at a glance".[129] Stephani builds upon Pestalozzi, but also abides by ancient mnemonic techniques that enable us to deduce the letter from the word, e.g. to move from "tulip" to "p" and from "fir" to "r". It soon becomes apparent that the entire project isn't quite as simple as the book's title promises. One still finds oneself in the state of experimentation.

Nevertheless, one cannot doubt the earnestness of the didactic promises. The principle of "at a glance", which Alfred North Whitehead (1927) describes with regard to an optimization of "sense-perception" as "presentational immediacy", is neither easily achieved nor can its effects be readily guaranteed.[130] Incidentally, scepticism with regard to unconventional visual aids was part of the order of the day. Johann Wolfgang von Goethe, in the foreword to his *Farbenlehre* (1812), questions the fashion of adding illustrative plates to works of natural history:

"Highly unsatisfactory surrogates here are the plates that are customarily included in such publications. An autonomous physical phenomenon that is effective on all fronts cannot be captured in lines, nor can it be indicated by averages. No one has the idea of elucidating chemical experiments with the aid of figures; but such illustrations are commonplace for the closely related physical experiments because such visual aids can accomplish the one and the other equally well. But these figures very often represent mere concepts; they are symbolic aids, hieroglyphic modes of communication, which gradually insinuate themselves into the place of the phenomenon and the place of nature, and which obstruct genuine understanding rather than encourage it."[131]

Goethe, too, was aware of the danger that ensues when such symbols become autonomous, and he could not imagine that they could be truly useful, for example, in the field of chemistry. Nonetheless, in the next sentence, he concedes that such plates and symbols do indeed have a certain degree of usefulness: "We also cannot entirely dispense with illustrative plates; but we have tried to arrange them so that one can readily take them in hand for didactic and polemical use, and regard them as a part of the necessary apparatus."[132] Goethe, too, excuses himself by citing didactic expedience.

Finally, Kant also expresses his views on this matter when he seeks an answer to the question "What is the meaning of: to orient oneself in thought?" Kant says, "We can elevate our ideas as high as we wish, and we can abstract from the senses as far as we wish, but visual conceptions still cling to them, and their real purpose is to make them, which are otherwise not derived from experience, capable of experiential use ('Erfahrungsgebrauch')."[133] Kant thus comes to speak of contemplation ("Anschauung") and finds, as a minimal condition, "a certain guiding medium"[134] for what he and Moses Mendelssohn would like to assign to the "evidence of demonstration" or to orientation. Kant, too, is interested in the question of how we assign our concepts to experiential use.

From signs and symbols to mathematical philosophy

"Such for all common purposes are the audible signs called words, which are still considered as audible, whether addressed immediately to the ear, or through the medium of letters to the eye. Geometrical diagrams are not signs, but the materials of geometrical science, the object of which is to show the relative quantities or their parts by a process of reasoning called Demonstration."
– Byrne, *Euclid*, 1847[135]

"The concept of reflection is thus also the concept of reproduction."
– Wagner, *Mathematische Philosophie*, 1851 (a)[136]

"Experiential use", "symbolic aids", or generally simply "guiding medium"! One wants to know how these affect the imagination and contemplation ("Anschauung"), and one seeks in this demonstration the benefits of precision and the shortest route. These are the linguistic problems of great interest during this era. The train of thought that Oliver Byrne began when he declared that language is a system of signs, leads to the conviction that, in his case, the use of coloured symbols, signs, and diagrams could increase the precision and speed of the cognitive process.[137]

The theme is in the air and working on language is de rigueur. Among the Germans, Karl Philipp Moritz devoted himself to what he would describe in a speech to the Royal Academy of Sciences in Berlin as "the educability ('Bildsamkeit') of the German language".[138] He decries, for example, the "lack of German neologisms ('Kunstwörter') in the theory of proportions".[139] Friedrich Adolf Trendelenburg, who championed the idea of a *lingua rationalis*, writes: "When the life we live together sprouts new twigs, it naturally also sprouts new words."[140] The researcher extracts "the lasting character for his result of language".[141] Because "even the most abstract thinking exists with and in language" and because of the urge to "return to a simple concept through a simple description", the comprehension and the concept should be brought together in this "ascending line" from the "self-motivation of inner contemplation".[142]

Oliver Byrne discovered the advantages of geometric, figurative – and colour-assisted – language, and was able to demonstrably quantify the time saved through quicker perception.[143] There is no shortage of attempts to compare and to merge the various languages, each with its own advantages. Johann Jakob Wagner writes in his *Philosophie der Erziehungskunst* (1803) about the "ease of translating mathematics into philosophy".[144] Logic had always

seemed insufficient to him and he "had always searched in mathematics for the architecture of the world and of knowledge".[145] In mathematics, he saw "the form of objectifying the intellectual, i. e. language". Finally, the "dualism" of arithmetic and geometry prompted him to assume the existence, on a higher plane, of something that both have in common, namely: "contemplation" ("Anschauung").[146] In his *Organon*, which was first published in 1830 and appeared in a second edition in 1851, Wagner presents the entire spectrum of different languages and linguistic forms.[147] He distinguishes numerical and linear writing, which includes lines, figures, "trigonometry, i. e. interrelationships", "bodies, i. e. gestalts", and the compounding of lines and figures.[148] He calls geometry, which provides the "basics of a theory of gestalts", a "relational writing", and an "abstraction from pictorial writing".[149] He believes that the schema of word–number–figure–image underlies the "construction of language", and from this he draws analogies to poetry–music–painting–sculpture or man–beast–plant–mineral.[150] He refers to the "parallel series" of idea–concept–perception–imagination or symbol–example–sign–picture.[151] Furthermore, his *Mathematische Philosophie* places all this in an historical perspective, according to which "speculative knowledge" is presented in a Pythagorean manner as number and figure, which, under the dominance of the word, became translated into a "mechanical" thing "called mathematics".[152] The image, he laments, has declined to the status of "an arbitrary game", and "our art produces only appearances".[153] The interrelationship among word–number–figure thus remains the focus of interest with regard to the scientific question. This particularly occupies Wagner's attention in his attempt to translate mathematics into philosophy. He wants to revive mathematics from its status as a "dead mechanism" and to rehabilitate it as "the natural language of ideas or the language of the mind" and as "the sole universal science or philosophy".[154]

It behoves us to follow the characteristic line of this presentation – language! – according to this mathematical-philosophical understanding. The first example, which Wagner symbolically chooses in his *Philosophie der Erziehungskunst* in 1803, is Pythagoras's geomtrical figure that also appeared on the title page of Oliver Byrne's *Euclid* in 1847: "Every line is the expression of motion, the path of a moving body, determined in space from the viewpoint of external observation, but constructible only by the inner power of reasoning, and mobile in time."[155] Now the figure is constructed: "Let there be given a line as a path; and let another line approach this one along the same path but in the opposite direction; in this instance, both lines ... will meet, and if their forces are equal, they shall reduce to a point of zero motion."[156] A discussion of this sort requires a certain effort, so Wagner adds visual and physical examples (e. g. the comparison of a line with a "lever" or with a "pendulum"), which he hopes will facilitate the process, so that "our pupil can become acquainted with the reciprocal reflections between mind and nature".[157] The "explanation by means of things" ("Sacherklärung") has long since become an "explanation by means of words" ("Worterklärung"), "according to which concepts are first formed", as Ephraim Salomon Unger stated in 1833 in his introduction to the body of Euclid's teachings.[158] Didactic intentions have caught up with explanations, which also serve as their basis.

In this way, Wilhelm von Türk, a follower of Pestalozzi, created a more comprehensive "doctrine of forms", which he styled, in accordance with the prevailing fashion and with clear didactic intentions, as a Socratic dialogue between teacher and pupils.[159]

"Teacher: (drawing a point, a straight line, and a curved line on the blackboard and pointing to 1) What is the name of this sign here?
Children: A point.
Teacher: (pointing to 2 and 3) And these two signs here?
Children: Lines."

One after another, these exercises were conducted with all five senses and were designed to include form, colour, and direction. The ultimate goal was to find and form a "language for inner contemplation".[160] Everything came together again in the recommendations that Oliver Byrne later combined with his "oral demonstrations", which simultaneously prioritized both the eye and the ear.[161] As Wilhelm von Türk explicitly stated in the title of his handbook, sense perceptions were the point of departure and thus also the central theme of the discussion. After all, also in times of enlightenment, and if one follows the *Allgemeine Theorie des Denkens und Empfindens* with which Johann August Eberhard won the prize of the Royal Academy of Sciences in 1776, the "discoveries in the theory of perception" would be especially recognized as progress within the "new speculative philosophy".[162] Eberhard emphasized this in a special first point, citing "the discoveries made about the nature of several derived characteristics ... of bodies, namely: the colours".[163] In harmony with so many other efforts, the mission was "to pull knowledge of the world down from the celestial firmament of the schools and bring it into human society".[164]

———

Byrne's *Euclid* – a work of art after all!

"La logique veut que l'art soit l'expression plastique de tout notre être."
– MONDRIAN, *Néo-Plasticisme*, 1920[165]

Following Pestalozzi and his *Anschauungslehre der Zahlenverhältnisse*, everything – including the most abstract things – was moving back into the physical, three-dimensional, or "plastic" world. Oli-

ver Byrne's opinion of Euclidean geometry as "the best gymnastic of the mind" indicates this motion involuntarily and with exaggerated clarity. This, too, corresponds to an old insight. Isaac Newton wrote on 8 May 1686 in the introduction to his *Philosophiae Naturalis Principia Mathematica* that the descriptions of straight and curved lines, on which geometry rests, belong to mechanics.[166] Furthermore, geometry postulates; explanations must be sought elsewhere.[167] On the other hand, geometry needs augmentations of all sorts in order to become accessible and understandable. Newton calls for this with his remark that geometry is only one part of a much more comprehensive *mechanica universalis*. One can arrive empirically at such a "physical geometry", just as one can arrive at laws through observation.[168] It would not be out of place here to recall Albert Einstein and his famous lecture "Geometry and Experience", in which he regards "practical geometry" as a natural science and as the oldest branch of physics.[169] This was preceded by his statement that it is "nonetheless certain that mathematics in general and geometry in particular owe their existence to the need to learn something about the existence of real things".[170] This doesn't detract one iota from the high value of the axioms, which he hails as "those independent creations of the human mind", although he adds, with regard to developments in the handling of symbols: "Terms in axiomatic geometry such as 'point', 'line' and so forth should be understood only as conceptual schemata, and these are devoid of content."[171] This is not a satisfactory situation, and a connection to reality is expressly needed. The explosiveness lies in the connection, to which each of these thinkers – every one with a different emphasis – has devoted his attention.

Mathematicians and artists meet here. Clear contours separating the two metiers disappear from time to time through their reciprocal interest and usage of means. After all, why should one ascribe less creativity to a mathematician than to an artist and vice versa? Mystical darkness is not less alien to Euclid than to modern inventors of images, especially when one considers the beginnings of the great tradition of creating figures and symbols. In 1901 Max Simon answered the question raised by Hubert Müller in his publication *Besitzt die heutige Schulgeometrie noch die Vorzüge des Euclid-Originals?* (Does Geometry, as Taught in Today's Schools, Still Possess the Advantages of Euclid's Original Geometry?): "Geometry as taught in German schools never possessed those advantages."[172] Much is wishful thinking and an idealized notion of a mathematically rigorous way of thinking. The call for an exact science, which penetrates deep into the liberal arts,[173] and the need for a "sharp-edged tool"[174] repeatedly led people to forget the actual physical difficulties. This view, which credits all precision to geometry and blames all deviations from precision on mechanics, i. e. praxis, is neatly summarized in Newton's words: "The error lies not in the thing itself, but in the user" ("Attamen errores non sunt artis, sed artificum").[175]

If one now looks to art, on the other hand, one cannot talk about a "gestalt crisis" of the sort that Max Steck espoused in 1942 with regard to mathematics.[176] Rather, it seems that Leibniz's motto that he had chosen – *Mathesis est scientia imaginabilium*, i. e. mathematics is a science of the imagination – acquires a much wider scope of meaning than had perhaps been suspected. Mathematical aspects at this time had long since entered, as they never had in the past, not only the realm of the imagination, but also the visible realm of the actually physical and mechanical, and their introduction came about not as a result of genuine need, but with enthusiastic intentions. Beginning with Mondrian, afterwards discussed by Amedée Ozenfant and Le Corbusier and later transferred to architecture, the notion of the sculptural ("plastique"), which is similar in some respects to the idea of gestalt, describes that which powerfully forces itself out of the intellectual insight into an outwardly visible form. This involves fundamentals and not merely formal analogy or the quest for forms on the basis of geometry or stylization. Neither does the mere allusion to cleansing and simplicity suffice "because the abstract remains the plastic functional expression of the universal: it is the most profound interiorization of the exterior and the purest exteriorization of the interior".[177] In 1920 Piet Mondrian expressed this uncompromising rejection of all merely superficial geometrisms – which would only be ignored anyway. Only when they are most profoundly understood and comprehended can the abstract, the mathematical, and the geometric be drawn into reality and – by necessity – be brought into an artistic form. It's clear that connections are most likely to result where this necessary relationship to perception, in the sense of physical geometry, is viewed as a problem and where, for the purpose of demonstration, it is expressly sought, as it was by Oliver Byrne. Only now – *a posteriori* – can one become genuinely conscious of the remarkable status and uniqueness of Byrne's *Euclid*.

The statement that Byrne's wrote in 1847 in the introduction to his *Euclid*, where he makes it quite clear that he is interested not in pleasant entertainments but in the search for truth and knowledge, neatly accords with analogous assertions such as those voiced by Mondrian,[178] for whom the issue was the quest for a universal plastic medium. Leading the reader into his manifesto *Le Néo-Plasticisme* (ill. 42), Mondrian advocates that an artist achieves three-dimensional expression by way of the consciously known. Accordingly, the appearance of art is the overall plastic expression of the unconscious and the conscious mind; art reveals the relationship between the two and it undergoes changes, but art per se remains immutable.[179] At the same time, the aspects of didactically conveying and making visible, which Byrne included in his *Euclid* of 1847, are clarified, and the corresponding objectives explained in a new view of art. For Mondrian, too, the highest priority is not the (apparent) form that arises as a result of this process. Conversely, form as a general and fixed appearance in a picture ought to be avoided and, in its place, the focus should be in the process that leads to precision and abstraction as universal plastic means.[180] To make this clearer, Mondrian expressly criticizes the (merely exterior) process of cleansing and simplification, which could also occasionally be seen in the architecture of his day. Only a select few individuals would achieve the plastic effect of the abstract.[181]

The modern age proclaims itself from atop the new and the old pedestal of the controversial body-mind conflict, and a new quest for the *raison* gets underway. In the first issue of *L'Esprit Nouveau*, Paul Dermée wrote that, as far as intelligence is concerned, everything occurs in consciousness and in a brightly lit room.[182] Light! In spite of this, he saw the necessary counterweight and the desirable balance between intelligence and the fashionable new buzzword *lyrisme*. Léonce Rosenberg contributed two formulations to the discussion, quoting the first from Georges Braque and modifying the other himself: "J'aime la règle qui corrige l'émotion" (I love the rule that rectifies emotion), followed by Rosenberg's humanized version: "J'aime le sentiment qui humanise la Règle" (I love the sentiment that humanizes the Rule).[183] Ethics and morals in particular had sought to discover the deeper meaning of mathematics in Oliver Byrne's Great Britain, but now psychology was paying its courtesy call, striving to bring pure thought into the world. Restraint was needed. To the erstwhile order of the day, i. e. to "rebuter l'intelligence" (away with intelligence), Paul Dermée added his own recommendation: "pas de logique apparent" (no ostentatious logic).[184] The inclination toward lawfulness should not be permitted to express itself too obviously. Amedée Ozenfant and Charles-Edouard Jeanneret (later known as Le Corbusier) – who, on the next page of the first issue of *L'Esprit Nouveau*, would seek to derive reliability, constants, and universality for their artistic work from the mechanical origin of sculptural ("plastique") sensitivity – soon realized that this could no longer serve as the basis and starting point.[185]

Communication, clarification, and mindfulness of the essentials were again necessary. The first sentence in Oliver Byrne's *Euclid*, here admittedly divorced from its context, declares: "The arts and sciences have become so extensive, that to facilitate their acquirement is of as much importance as to extend their boundaries."[186] In his *La pensée mathématique pure*, which is based on the lectures he delivered at the Collège de France in 1914–15 and 1918–19, Edouard Le Roy undertakes to characterize his notion of pure mathematics as imaginative and to link the sensory perspective with the intellectual point of view.[187] This relates particularly to geometry, for which reason he talks about the specific "intuition géométrique". Geometry repeatedly forces itself into reality and the perceptible world.[188] Le Roy thus takes into account the interaction and the fact of a physical geometry. Geometry seems to him to be a sort of mathematics that has become discernible

Ill. 16
Oliver Byrne, *The First Six Books of the Elements of Euclid*, London 1847, p. 158
– An illustrated and multicoloured text to elucidate Euclid's Fifth Book.
– Figürliche und farbige „Begriffsschrift" zur Erläuterung des fünften Buchs Euklids.
– « Idéographie » figurée et coloriée expliquant le Livre V des Eléments d'Euclide.

Ill. 17
Johann Andreas Christian Michelsen, *Euclides Elemente, für den gegenwärtigen Zustand der Mathematik bearbeitet, erweitert und fortgesetzt*, Berlin 1791, p. 193
– Presentation of the identical Euclidean theorem about the "equimultiples".
– Darstellung des identischen euklidischen Lehrsatzes zu den „Gleichvielfachen".
– Représentation du théorème euclidien identique se rapportant aux « équimultiples ».

16   17

to the senses; it is of this world.[189] He finds pure mathematics in analysis and thus, either consciously or unconsciously, he follows in Leibniz's footsteps.[190]

Geometry and Euclid are thus more strongly exposed to compromise with the sensibly perceptible. This has long since become part of their history and culture. De Stijl and Mondrian were accordingly closer to the subject than were mere daubers and picture-makers. As Léonce Rosenberg succinctly put it: painting is the means, not the goal.[191] Even if a painter's intention is colour and paint, Oliver Byrne's reasoning seems comparable to the ideas expressed by Ozenfant and Le Corbusier. The programmatic text about *Purisme* unequivocally asserts: "Quand on parle peinture, on parle forcément couleur" (when one talks about painting, one necessarily talks about colour). This text commences at the point where logic, at the beginning of the train of thought, is derived from human constants and installed to guard against the sometimes implausible roaming of intuition.[192] Taken by themselves, colours would be risky and downright dangerous.[193] They ought to serve the task at hand and they should be used constructively.[194] A few pages later in *Purisme* one reads that "a painting is the linkage of purified, associated, and 'architecturalized' elements".[195] The parallels to Byrne are impossible to overlook.[196] Even the greater speed with which human vision recognizes colours is mentioned, a fact that Byrne had explicitly emphasized. Colour, with regard to its priority in human perception, is akin to shock: because of its immediate visual perception, the awareness of colour precedes the recognition of form, which is at least partly a creation of the brain.[197]

If one considers how much importance Byrne placed on the didactic aspect of his *Euclid*, one finds even clearer parallels in the writing of Gyorgy Kepes, who published his *Language of Vision* in 1944 in the tradition of De Stijl and under the direct influence of Gestalt psychology (ill. 34, 35, 37, 41).[198] The viewpoint of language and communication has come home to roost. In the footsteps of Mondrian, Kepes talks about plastic organization, clarifying his description as "the shaping of sensory impressions into unified, organic wholes".[199] The process of form-giving takes precedence, but "visual representation" and the created picture naturally also feature prominently. It's nonetheless astonishing to see how much importance Kepes grants to the overlapping of coloured planes. This no longer serves to depict fundamental geometric shapes, as it had for Byrne, but is now put at the service of the "colour balance" and the visual phenomena in general.[200]

Kepes's historical retrospective acknowledges Helmholtz, fleetingly mentions Leonardo da Vinci and Goethe, and recalls Arthur Schopenhauer. In the first sentence of his early study *Ueber das Sehn und die Farben* (1816), Schopenhauer describes the larger context and the inherent problems: "All contemplation is intellectual in nature, because without reason, we would never again arrive at contemplation, perception, and the apprehension of objects, but would remain with mere sensations, which, as a feeling of pain or a sense of wellbeing, could possibly have meaning in relation to volition, but would otherwise be only an alternation of meaningless conditions and would not be anything that bears a similarity to knowledge."[201] Schopenhauer neither wanted to, nor could he, grant Goethe's *Zur Farbenlehre* the status of a theory. On

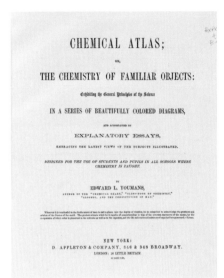

18

the other hand, his thoughts would provide psychophysics with decisive arguments.

In Great Britain during the time of Oliver Byrne and Augustus De Morgan, every attempt and every need to venture beyond the narrow limits of mathematics seemed to lead toward ethics and morals. In the modern era psychology devotes attention to the borderline areas and to the many difficulties associated with the body-mind problem. Psychophysics directly affected the arts at precisely the moment when the latter began to recall invariable laws, firm rules, and naturally also geometry in a particular way.[202] It's understandable that Gestalt psychology takes a special interest in questions concerning a focusing of the senses ("Prägnanzmomenten"), or the ways in which people are affected by colours. All of this had already played an important part in Oliver Byrne's *Euclid*.

Wilhelm Wundt dedicates his introduction to *Beiträge zur Theorie der Sinneswahrnehmung* (1862) to questions of method: "The attempt to erect psychological facts atop a metaphysical foundation is inherently allied with psychology's mathematical way of handling things. This is an almost unavoidable consequence of the fact that metaphysical psychology includes the deductive method."[203] In a downright imperative way, this indicates the degree to which geometry and its sensualization ("Versinnlichung") can be and are subjected to questioning. Wundt continues: "When a science derives a large number of facts from its own axioms through a series of more or less tangled conclusions, without the simple methods of formal logic being sufficient to arrive at this derivation, then that science is forced to require assistance from

the language of mathematical signs."[204] Kant postulated that nature, sometimes, would have to be forced to answer to the questions of reason.[205] It needs the support of the human capacity for knowledge. Wundt accordingly states: "This [language of signs] is only an effective aid for thought, merely a multiple application of logical laws that determine, through certain signs, the results of thought at each step along a series of conclusions."[206]

Wundt added at this juncture a footnote containing his appraisal of the developmental status of mathematics in this regard: "Mathematicians might well object that this definition goes too far, because mathematics to date has indeed not yet discovered such a generalized application. But it seems to me to be impossible to deny that all of the more recent efforts in mathematics strive toward this generalization of calculus, which makes it merely an expanded logic."[207]

The paths of development frequently pursued separate routes from this point onward. The extent to which Byrne's "Mondrianic" Euclid matches this development, or one of these developments, is a question that may remain unanswered. In any event, those mathematicians showed little or no interest in Byrne. Not even the Euclideans took much notice of him. On the other hand, each of the various sciences has always been preoccupied with itself, and has all too eagerly wielded its "incisive principles and methods" against the less potent philosophy in its own circle, whatever "philosophy" was thought to mean.[208] Fechner's psychophysics, too, a new branch of science that is grafted onto an ancient bough and that begins with such wide-ranging questioning, ought, according to an initial definition proposed in 1860, "to briefly [offer] an exact

PLATE II.

METALS AND THEIR COMPOUNDS WITH OXYGEN.

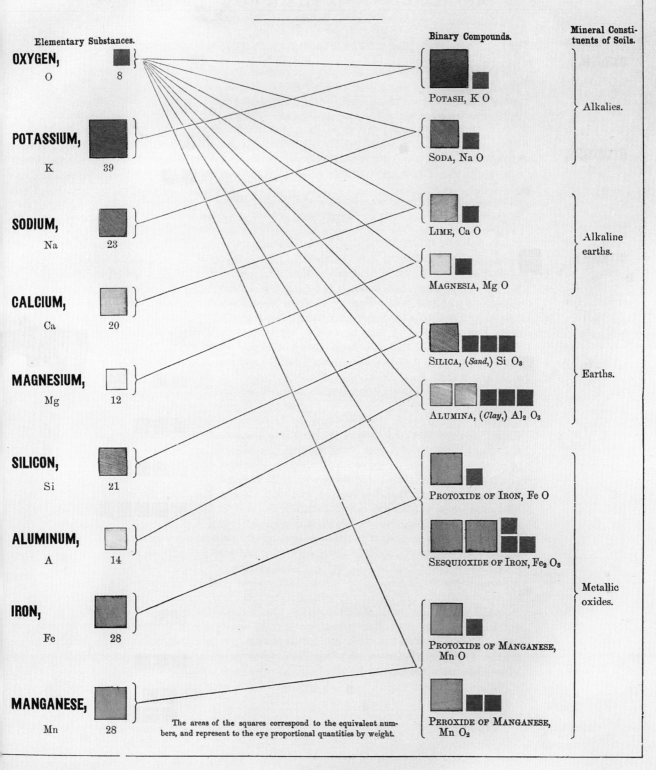

Elementary Substances.

Binary Compounds.

Mineral Constituents of Soils.

OXYGEN, O 8

POTASSIUM, K 39

SODIUM, Na 23

CALCIUM, Ca 20

MAGNESIUM, Mg 12

SILICON, Si 21

ALUMINUM, A 14

IRON, Fe 28

MANGANESE, Mn 28

POTASH, K O

SODA, Na O

LIME, Ca O

MAGNESIA, Mg O

SILICA, (Sand,) Si O₃

ALUMINA, (Clay,) Al₂ O₃

PROTOXIDE OF IRON, Fe O

SESQUIOXIDE OF IRON, Fe₂ O₃

PROTOXIDE OF MANGANESE, Mn O

PEROXIDE OF MANGANESE, Mn O₂

Alkalies.

Alkaline earths.

Earths.

Metallic oxides.

The areas of the squares correspond to the equivalent numbers, and represent to the eye proportional quantities by weight.

doctrine of the relationships between body and soul".[209] Indeed, it ought to become precise and scientific!

Oliver Byrne's *Euclid* remains unique, but the book's sheer solitariness makes it all the more interesting and heuristic to search for potential connections to Pestalozzi, to the mathematical philosophy of a thinker such as Wagner, to the viewpoint of language, or the perspective of geometry. Byrne's *Euclid* is more closely akin to the 'facts' espoused by a scientist such as Helmholtz than one would suspect at first glance. "Geometry always involves ideal figures, whose physical depictions are really nothing but approaches to the needs of the concept; whether or not a body is solid, its surfaces are even, and its edges are straight will be decided only by means of the same statements whose actual correctness would need to be shown by empirical testing."[210] These are approaches to the universal truths that attracted the mathematician Byrne just as strongly as they appealed to the artist Piet Mondrian. Perhaps geometry really isn't the unshakeable, conclusively described edifice that, for lack of other secure foundations, is typically credited to Euclid; perhaps it is actually more Pythagorean, a conception of the world in forms and figures, admittedly less conclusive from this viewpoint, yet capable of being experienced at a single glance. Oliver Byrne imbued this notion with colour and thus anticipated a language that would become known, in the modern period, by the phrase *Neue Gestaltung*, which is also the title of Theo van Doesburg's well-known book.

Theodor W. Adorno prefaced his *Negative Dialektik* with Walter Benjamin's pronouncement: "... one must cross the icy wasteland of abstraction to succinctly arrive at concrete philosophizing".[211] This terrain is abstract, but it is by no means a frozen wilderness that one would like to put behind oneself as quickly as possible! In any case, everything for Byrne and Mondrian revolves around this abstraction and how it forces itself into the visible world. One doesn't want to give it up, but to make it visible! "L'abstrait reste l'expression plastique en fonction de l'universel: c'est l'intériorisation la plus approfondie de l'extérieur et l'extériorisation la plus pure de l'intérieur."[212] In this sentence, which was published in *Le Néo-Plasticisme* in 1920, Mondrian alluded to "De Nieuwe Beelding in de Schilderkunst", i.e. to the third part of remarks that he had published in *De Stijl*, where he had devoted himself in particular to the relationship between the abstract and the mathematical.[213] The corresponding equivalence can be traced as far back as Aristotle. In fact and in truth, Mondrian still stands here most clearly in that tradition, which was especially conveyed to him by Mathieu Schoenmaekers.[214] It is a tradition in which interest is kept alive in universal concepts. Geometry has always served as its starting point and Euclid has always been its key witness. And it is even more comprehensively expressed in Oliver Byrne's words: "If we wanted authorities to prove the importance and usefulness of geometry, we might quote every philosopher since the days of Plato."[215]

Notes

1 Frege 1893, p. xiv, note 1.

2 Cf. Steck 1981, p. 179 seq. Cf. also and esp. Steck 1943, p. 131 seqq., esp. passim and p. 133 ("Schaufähigkeit").

3 Translated from a quotation in Knittermeyer 1939, p. 59 seq.: in Steck 1943, note 24, p. 148.

4 Cf. Steck 1981, p. 180.

5 Cf. Speiser 1932, p. 14.

6 Ibid. He thus embraces a tradition that extends back to Schelling (1797, preface, p. iii seqq.), who argued against the "bisherige [...] Vermischung ganz heterogener Principien" in philosophy and divided these into "rein" (pure) and "angewandt" (applied) principles: "Die reine theoretische Philosophie beschäftigt sich bloß mit der Untersuchung über die Realität unsers Wissens überhaupt."

7 Cf. Schelling 1797, p. iv.

8 Cf. Rickert 1913, pp. 189 and 188.

9 Rickert 1913, p. 191, adds here: "... so lange eine mechanische Theorie fehlt", but shortly before that he says that the path of their perfection "eine naturwissenschaftliche, d. h. eine mechanische Erklärung eines physischen Vorganges geradezu mit einer Veranschaulichung identifiziert werden müsse".

10 Cf. Bloch 1909.

11 Cf. below.

12 Cf. Husserl 1936, p. 77 seqq. Decisive for our context (cf. also below) is the analysis of the meaning of geometry before and after Galileo (p. 103 seqq.), which existed "ohne dass er, und wohlbegreiflich, das Bedürfnis empfand, in die Art, wie die idealisierende Leistung ursprünglich erwuchs (nämlich wie sie erwuchs aus dem Untergrunde der vorgeometrischen sinnlichen Welt und ihrer praktischen Künste), einzugehen und sich in Fragen zu vertiefen nach dem Ursprung der apodiktischen mathematischen Evidenz".

13 Cf. Rickert 1910–11, p. 1 seqq., esp. p. 7.

14 Cf. Husserl 1910–11, p. 289 seqq., esp. p. 289.

15 Id., p. 341.

16 Ibid.

17 Cf. Frege 1882, p. 48 seqq., esp. p. 56; id., in Frege 1964, p. 106 seqq., esp. p. 114.

18 Ibid.

19 Cf. Frege 1893, foreword, p. xiv.

20 Id., p. xxv.

21 Id., p. 3.

22 Id., p. 1 seqq., with allusion to the earlier publication *Grundlagen der Arithmetik*, Breslau 1884.

23 Id., p. xix. On the other hand, he naturally defends himself (p. xii) against assumptions such as *metaphysica sunt, non leguntur* and *mathematica sunt, non leguntur*.

24 Id., pp. xvii seqq. and xx.

25 Id., p. xxi.

26 Cf. Russell 1897, p. 1.

27 Id., p. 10 seqq.

28 Cf. Riemann 1892, p. 272 seqq., esp. pp. 272 and 286. The critique of geometry, which begins with the notion of space, is more readily understandable when one recalls Wolff's notion of mathematics; the first definition of the initial grounds of geometry is: "Die Geometrie ist eine Wissenschaft des Raumes, den die cörperlichen Dinge nach ihrer Länge, Breite und Dicke einnehmen" (quoted from a later edition: Wolff 1755, p. 65). But at the same time, one also finds the usual definition of "Geometrie, das ist, die Wissenschaft der Massen, oder der Grössen, in so fern sie als an einander hangend können gemessen werden [...]", that is the 'Messkunst' (cf. Fabricius 1752, p. 454).

29 This was preceded, in a direct allusion to Riemann, by the article "Über die Tatsachen, die der Geometrie zugrunde liegen" (in *Nachrichten von der Königlichen Gesellschaft der Wissenschaften und der Georg-Augusts-Universität aus dem Jahre 1868*, no. 9, p. 193 seqq.; reprinted in Helmholtz 1968, p. 32 seqq.).

30 Cf. Helmholtz 1879, p. 25.

31 Ibid.

32 Id., p. 23.

33 Cf. Husserl 1891, p. 131: "Das Ziel, das sich Frege setzt, ist also ein chimärisches zu nennen."

34 Id., p. 130.

35 Ibid.

36 Cf. esp. Husserl 1913, introduction, pp. 1 and 7 seqq.

37 Cf. Helmholtz 1879, p. 7.

38 In his introduction to Frege (1973, p. viii), Lothar Kreiser emphasizes how anachronistic Frege's conceptual text was.

39 Cajori 1928, p. 429.

40 Cf. id.

41 Ibid.

42 Id., note 4, with a reference to Heiberg 1912, p. 20.

43 Cited here after Cajori 1928, p. 429 seq. (after De Morgan 1849, p. 92 seq.).

44 Cf. also below.

45 Cf. De Morgan 1872, p. 199.

46 Cf. De Morgan 1915, p. 329, note 1. Likewise see p. 344 for a critique of Oliver Byrne's *Theory of Parallels* (1840).

47 All too often, that marginal fringe is the larger frame within which mathematical history is made! Cf. Casselman 2000, p. 1257 seqq. (on Byrne, cf. p. 1260).

48 Cf. Phillips 2005, p. 105 seqq.

49 Cf. De Morgan 1838, foreword, p. xvi.

50 Cf. Grattan-Guinness 1992, p. 1 seqq.; Phillips 2005, p. 105 seqq.).

51 De Morgan's definitions of *ratio* and proportion were still regarded by Thomas L. Heath as the best (cf. Heath 1956, p. 116 seqq.) Eutocius and the notion of *pelikotes* or *pelikos* had, however, been discussed in detail long before De Morgan, by Meibomius 1655, p. 11.

52 This same year also saw the publication that confirmed the arithmetical foundations of De Morgan's mathematical research and interests. Cf. De Morgan 1847.

53 Cf. below.

54 A methodical intention was, of course, the primary underlying reason for such statements. Understandably, there was a strong interest at the time in the overlaps in geometry and arithmetic. Inspired by one of Gauss's observations, in 1846 Hermann Scheffler published his *Über das Verhältniß zur Arithmetik zur Geometrie, insbesondere über die geometrische Bedeutung der imaginären Zahlen*, in the introduction to which he emphasized the different assignations given to "pictorial" presentation and to the "undivided act of the cognitive capacity". De Morgan would naturally appear in the wrong light if one were to associate him solely with this statement, quoted by Cajori.

55 From the archives of the Cambridge Philosophical Society, vol. 10, 1864, p. 173 seqq.: cited here after Church 1936, p. 121 seqq., esp. p. 128.

56 Cf. Mill 1873, p. 225.

57 To complete this picture, one must recall Mill's mixed reactions to Auguste Comte (cf. id., p. 209 seqq.).

58 Cf. Whewell 1840 and 1847; Whewell 1849; Whewell 1858.

59 Cf. Byrne 1847, introduction, p. vii.

60 Ibid.

61 Cf. Cajori 1928, p. 431: "Individual workers who in elementary fields proposed to express practically everything in ideographic form have been overruled." Cajori interprets it as a trend toward "conservatism" with regard to the use of symbols and seems to explain it as a result of peer pressure: "by large groups or by representatives of large groups". And he concludes these thoughts in a Sibylline fashion: "The problem requires a consensus of opinion, the wisdom of many minds. That wisdom discloses itself in the history of science. The judgement of the past calls for moderation."

62 Cf. Hesse 1865, preface.

63 Cf. Arneth 1852, p. 288.

64 Cf. Bense 1946, p. 53.

65 Ibid.

66 Even what is probably the only more recent treatment of Byrne's *Euclid* fails to go into any greater depth: cf. Tufte 1990, p. 84 seqq.

67 Cf. Casselman 2000.

68 Byrne 1847, introduction, p. vii.

69 The phrase appears in Krbek 1954, p. 205 seqq., together with the subtitle and motto: "Form is the visible sister of number".

70 Cf. Steck 1946, p. 17.

71 Ibid.

72 Cf. Byrne 1847, introduction, p. vii.

73 Cf. Byrne 1835, 2002, foreword.

74 Ibid.

75 Cf. Byrne 1853, foreword, p. vii: "Although this work is written to guide the experienced and accomplished artisan, yet the descriptions and directions are of so practical a nature, that any mechanic or amateur, previously unacquainted with the subjects treated of, may, by following its pages as a text-book, succeed in his earliest attempts to accomplish even the most difficult processes inscribed."

76 Cf. Byrne 1866, foreword, p. vi.

77 Cf. Lorey 1852, p. iii.

78 Id., introduction, p. 1.

79 Cf. Byrne 1841.

80 Cf. Byrne 1847, p. 210.

81 Cf. Byrne 1841, p. viii: "... while there is not one mistake, oversight, or logical objection in the whole of Euclid's Fifth Book".

82 Ibid.

83 Id., p. xv.

84 Id., p. xiv.

85 Cf. note 74 above.

86 Cf. Byrne 1841, p. xvi.

87 Ibid.

88 Ibid.

89 Cf. the later translation, in which "the same equimultiples" are used for clarification. Heath 1956, p. 120.

90 Cf. Byrne 1841, p. xviii: "To teach should be the highest aim of a writer on elementary subjects, and not to adopt (which is too often the case) that stiff and formal manner so prejudicial to and inconsistent with the ideas of a learner; every thing likely to embarrass should be explained, and that authorial kind of scientific dignity should be set aside when the object is to instruct others."

91 Cf. above.

92 Cf. Heath 1956, p. 122 seq.

93 Byrne 1841, p. xviii.

94 Byrne 1847, p. xiii.

95 For the corresponding proofs, see id., pp. xiii and xiv.

96 Id., p. xiii.

97 Cf. Dürer 1525, fol. A ij recto: "Dann durch solche weyß muß der innerliche verstand im eussern werck angetzeigt werden".

98 Cf. Byrne 1847, p. xiii.

99 Id., p. xii.

100 The commentary in the foreword reads: "Technical terms always present a formidable obstacle to practical men in the investigation of any scientific subject." Cf. Dimond 1867, p. vi.

101 Cf. Youmans 1856, introduction, p. 9.

102 Ibid.: "Whenever the object to be contemplated cannot itself be seen, and consists of such fixed elements or qualities as are capable of being represented or delineated to the eye, pictorial illustrations become indispensable."

103 Ibid.

104 Cf. Fechner 1860, foreword, p. v.

105 Cf. Byrne 1847, p. xvii: "For schools and other public places of instruction, dyed chalks will

answer to describe diagrams, &c. for private use coloured pencils will be found very convenient."

106 Id., p. vii.

107 Id., p. vii.

108 Id., p. xi.

109 Cf. Pestalozzi 1803, preface, p. v: "Die Anschauungslehre der Zahlenverhältnisse ist, als ein Theil der Methode, eine Kunst-übung, den Menschen auf eine, mit der Natur seines Geistes und mit der Art, wie sich seine Denk-kraft in ihm entwickelt, übereinstimmende Weise zählen und rechnen zu lehren."

110 Cf. Pico della Mirandola 1532, p. 137: "Conclusiones de mathematicis secundum opiniorum propriam numero lxxxv."

111 Cf. Borelli 1679, "Ad lectorem geometram" (introduction), n.p.

112 Ibid.: "progressus Intellectualis ex notis ad ignota".

113 Cf. Ashe 1684, p. 672 seqq.

114 Ibid.: "it rejects all trifling in words and Rhetorical schemes, all conjectures, authorities, prejudices and passion".

115 Cf. Early Letters of the Royal Society EL/A/36 (St. George Ashe, 27 April 1686); cf. AHRB Centre for Editing Lives and Letters, 2005. Cf. Pell 1668. Pell's algebra is an expanded and altered translation of the algebra of Johann Heinrich Rahn, Landvogt zu Kyburg.

116 Cf. *The Elements or Principles of Geometrie*, London 1684. The copy kept at the Trinity College Library in Dublin is signed by St. George Ashe, for which reason the online edition (Ann Arbor) postulated that he had contributed to its authorship. Our copy differs from the text in Dublin.

117 Id., "Advertisement", fol. A3 recto and verso.

118 The brief "Advertisement" ends with the statement that "This Summary was thought sufficient for an Introduction". Inserted into our copy, however, is an additional introduction with its own pagination, A-(A4) verso.

119 Id., fol. A1 recto: "And by consequence nothing is so apt to strengthen our Reason to give us clear notion of things, and secure us from being imposed upon fallacies or shadows of proof, as conversing herein."

120 Id., fol. A1 recto: "Demonstration therefore serving (as we said) to enlighten the mind."

121 Cf. *The Elements or Principles of Geometrie*, London 1684, fol. B4 verso.

122 Cf. Byrne 1847, p. vii.

123 One shouldn't separate "science" and "didactics" quite as sharply as they've been here. In the old tradition, according to Duns Scotus's understanding of Aristotle, *scientia* is above all other considerations a *medium demonstrationis* (cited here after: Duns Scotus or: Johannes de Cornubia? 1512, fol. a2 verso).

124 Cf. Brodhagen 1792, p. vii.

125 Cf. Lambert 1764.

126 Cf. Feder 1793, p. 70.

127 Cf. Stephani 1814, p. 9. Stephani includes pictograms, for example, Egyptian hieroglyphs (prior to Champollion) in the category of "seen language".

128 Id., p. 12 seq.

129 Cf. Oechslin 2007, p. 62 seqq.

130 Cf. Whitehead 1927, p. 21.

131 Cf. Goethe 1812, p. xxi.

132 Ibid.

133 Cf. Kant 1793, p. 104 seqq.

134 Id., p. 105.

135 Byrne 1847, p. ix.

136 Wagner 1851 (a), p. 124.

137 Cf. Byrne 1847, p. ix: "... renders the process of reasoning more precise, and the attainment more expeditious ..."

138 Cf. Moritz 1794, p. 87 seqq.

139 Cf. Burja 1794, p. 265 seqq.

140 Cf. Trendelenburg 1828, p. 457 seqq., esp. p. 457.

141 Id., p. 457.

142 Id., pp. 458 and 473 seq.

143 Cf. Byrne 1847, p. ix.

144 Cf. Wagner 1803, p. 148. Wagner writes in retrospect that he had already intended to tackle this task in his youth, but first actually achieved it in his *Mathematische Philosophie* in 1811: cf. Wagner 1851 (b), pp. xl and xxxi. – On Wagner cf. Stock 1982, p. 262 seqq.

145 Cf. Wagner 1851 (b), p. xli (retrospective view of the *Organon* of 1830).

146 Ibid.

147 Cf. Wagner 1851 (b), p. 207 seqq. (III. Sprachsystem).

148 Id., p. 244 (§ 325).

149 Id., pp. 243 (§ 324) and 244 (§ 326).

150 Id., pp. 214 (§ 292) and 260 (§ 342).

151 Id., p. 337 (appendix, § 24).

152 Cf. Wagner 1851 (a), p. 1 seqq.

153 Id., p. 2.

154 Cf. Wagner 1839, p. 312 seqq., esp. p. 313 seq.

155 Cf. Wagner 1803, p. 149.

156 Ibid.

157 Id., p. 155.

158 Cf. Unger 1833, p. 6. But Unger then goes so far as to declare that "the point is not to pass along Euclid's words with philological exactness, but only to preserve their spirit"; id., p. 11.

159 Cf. Türk 1811. A comparable doctrine of forms, devoted to the teaching of sketching, was published in 1836 by Gustav Adolf Tobler, who taught sketching in Berne. Quotation from: Türk 1830, p. 1.

160 Cf. Türk 1811, preface, p. vii.

161 Cf. Byrne 1847, p. xi seq.

162 Cf. Eberhard 1776, p. 5.

163 Id., p. 8.

164 Id., p. 4.

165 Mondrian 1920, p. 1: "Logic desires art to be the three-dimensional expression of our entire existence."

166 Cf. Koyré/Cohen 1972, p. 15.

167 Ibid.: "Has lineas describere geometria non docet, sed postulat."

168 Cf. Hölder 1900, p. 6. – Cf. above.

169 Cf. Einstein 1921, p. 3.

170 Id., p. 2 seq.

171 Id., p. 2.

172 Cf. Simon 1901, p. 19. Simon begins his foreword (p. v) by referring to his practical contribution to the doctrine of mathematical education and teaching.

173 About the words "strict" and "exact", cf. Oechslin 2009, p. 363 seqq.

174 The "other thread of geometric thought", i.e. logistics – whose origins extend back to the time of Oliver Byrne and Augustus De Morgan! (see above) – still claimed this as its achievement as late as 1929: "Wenn jemand auf irgend einem Gebiet der Philosophie oder der Einzelwissenschaften sich um eine exakte Analyse der Aussagen und Begriffe bemüht, so sollen ihm hier die logistischen und insbesondere die relationstheoretischen Hilfsmittel als ein scharfes Werkzeug in die Hand gegeben werden. Diese Hilfsmittel sind bisher, besonders in Deutschland, noch sehr wenig bekannt; nur in logisch-mathematischen Untersuchungen werden sie zu-

175 weilen angewendet." Cf. Carnap 1929, foreword, p. iii.
175 Cf. Isaac Newton's foreword of 8 May 1686 to his *Philosophiae Naturalis Principia Mathematica*.
176 Cf. Steck 1942, p. 13 seqq.
177 Cf. Mondrian 1920, p. 5: "car l'abstrait reste l'expression plastique en fonction de l'universel: c'est l'intériorisation la plus approfondie de l'extérieur et l'extériosiration la plus pure de l'intérieur".
178 Cf. Byrne 1847, p. vii.
179 Cf. Mondrian 1920, p. 1: "Il atteint son expression plastique par le conscient. Par cela, l'apparition de l'art est l'expression plastique de l'inconscient et du conscient. Elle montre le rapport de l'un et de l'autre: elle change, mais l'art reste immuable."
180 Id., p. 5.
181 Ibid.
182 Cf. Dermée n.d., p. 29 seqq., esp. p. 30.
183 Cf. Rosenberg 1921, p. 1.
184 Cf. Dermée n.d., p. 37, "De même, pas de logique apparente, afin de rebuter les efforts de l'intelligence pour mordre sur le poème. Mot d'ordre: rebuter l'intelligence."
185 Cf. Ozenfant/Jeanneret n.d. (a), p. 38 seqq.
186 Cf. Byrne 1847, p. vii.
187 Cf. Le Roy 1960, p. 17.
188 Id., p. 19 (with regard to Kant).
189 Also cf. the formulation: "La pensée géométrique ainsi considérée n'est donc pas la pensée mathématique pure, mais la pensée mathématique tendant à s'incarner dans un corps d'intuition imaginative, bref la pensée mathématique au seuil immédiat de l'applicaton."; id., p. 21)
190 Gerhardt explains Leibniz's didactic orientation on the basis of the frustration Leibniz experienced with regard to the possibility of comprehension: "In Leipzig, wo Leibniz seine akademischen Studien begann, las ein gewisser Joh. Kühn über die Elemente Euclid's; die Vorträge desselben waren aber so dunkel, dass außer Leibniz keiner der Zuhörer folgen konnte. Es wird erzählt, dass er allein sich mit dem Docenten in Discussionen über den Vortrag einliess und alsdann seinen Mitzuhörern die Lehrsätze verständlich machte ..."; cf. Gerhardt 1848, p. 7.
191 Cf. Rosenberg 1921, p. 1: "La

192 peinture est le moyen et non le but."
192 Cf. Ozenfant/Jeanneret n.d. (b), p. 369 seqq., esp. p. 382: "marche parfois fantasque de l'intuition".
193 Ibid.
194 Ibid.
195 Id., p. 379.
196 Cf. Byrne 1847, p. vii.
197 Cf. Ozenfant/Jeanneret n.d. (b), p. 382.
198 Cf. Kepes (1944) 1951.
199 Id., p. 15.
200 Id., p. 35 seqq.
201 Cf. Schopenhauer 1816, p. 11 (Chapter 1: "Vom Sehn"): "Alle Anschauung ist eine intellektuale. Denn ohne den Verstand käme es nimmermehr zur Anschauung, zur Wahrnehmung, Apprehension von Objekten, sondern es bliebe bei der bloßen Empfindung, die allenfalls, als Schmerz oder Wohlbehagen, eine Bedeutung in Bezug auf den Willen haben könnte, übrigens aber ein Wechsel bedeutungsloser Zustände und nichts einer Erkenntniß Aehnliches wäre."
202 Cf. above and Oechslin 2005, p. 176 seqq.
203 Cf. Wundt 1862, p. xix.
204 Ibid.
205 Cf. Kant 1787, preface to second edition, p. xiii.
206 Ibid.
207 Ibid.
208 Cf. Fechner 1860, p. 1: Here the "more unfavourable conditions" that interested him at the time: "Einleitendes. I. Allgemeine Betrachtung über die Beziehung von Leib und Seele. Indess die Lehre von der Körperwelt in den verschiedenen Zweigen der Naturwissenschaft zu einer grossen Entwicklung gediehen ist, und sich scharfer Principien und Methoden erfreut, welche ihr einen erfolgreichen Fortschritt sichern, indess die Lehre vom Geiste in Psychologie und Logik wenigstens bis zu gewissen Gränzen feste Grundlagen gewonnen hat, ist die Lehre von den Beziehungen zwischen Körper und Geist und Geist oder Leib und Seele bis jetzt fast blos ein Feld philosophischen Streites ohne festes Fundament und ohne sichere Principien und Methoden für den Fortschritt der Untersuchung geblieben."
209 Id., foreword, p. v.
210 Cf. Helmholtz 1968, p. 38: "in der Geometrie stets mit idealen

Gebilden zu tun ... deren körperliche Darstellung in der Wirklichkeit immer nur eine Annäherung an die Forderungen des Begriffes ist, und wird darüber, ob ein Körper fest, ob seine Flächen eben, seine Kanten gerade sind, erst mittels derselben Sätze entscheiden, deren tatsächliche Richtigkeit durch die Prüfung zu erweisen wäre."
211 Cf. Adorno 1966, preface, p. 7.
212 Cf. Mondrian 1920, p. 5; cf. p. 30, note 177.
213 Cf. Mondrian 1918 (reprint, Amsterdam 1968), p. 29 seqq.
214 Cf. Oechslin 2009.
215 Cf. Byrne 1847, p. vii.

PLATE XI.

CHEMISTRY OF COMBUSTION AND ILLUMINATION;

STRUCTURE OF FLAME.

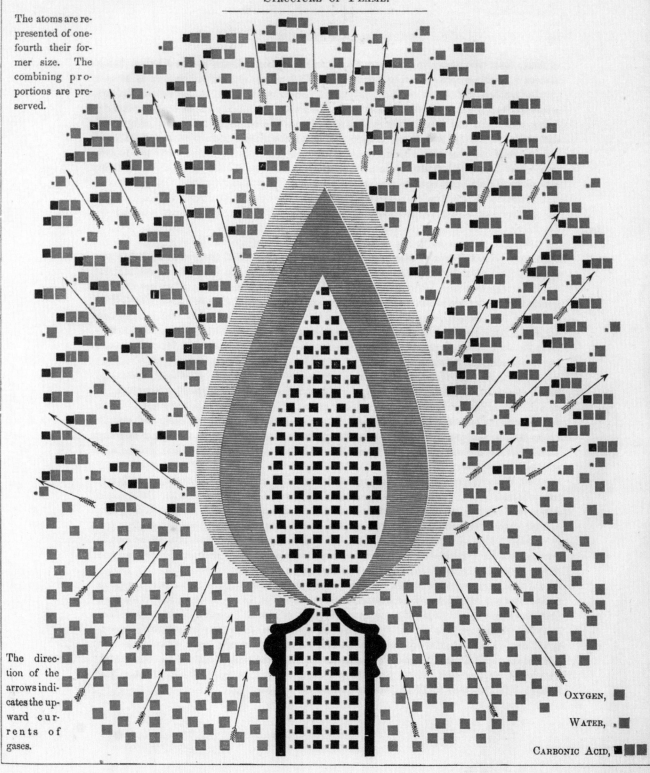

The atoms are represented of one-fourth their former size. The combining proportions are preserved.

The direction of the arrows indicates the upward currents of gases.

OXYGEN,

WATER,

CARBONIC ACID,

„To facilitate their acquirement"

Oliver Byrnes *The First Six Books of the Elements of Euclid*
– didaktisch, farbig und exzentrisch

Was treibt und bringt einen Surveyor of her Majesty's Settlements in the Falkland Islands dazu, die attraktivste Euklidausgabe aller Zeiten zu erfinden und veröffentlichen zu lassen? In mondrianschen Farben kommt sie uns, gleichsam avant la lettre, modern entgegen. Niemand, der dieses Buch in den Händen hält, kann sich der Faszination entziehen, die von diesen ‚Bildern‘ ausgeht, gerade weil damit das Verstehen schwierigster abstrakter mathematischer Gesetzmäßigkeiten auf einfachste Weise, wie es vorerst scheint, suggeriert und ganz konkret *ad oculos* demonstriert wird.

———

Die Crux mit der „anschaulichen Darstellung der Denkformen"

„Mathematiker, die sich ungerne in die Irrgänge
der Philosophie begeben, werden gebeten, hier
das Lesen des Vorworts abzubrechen."
– FREGE, *Grundgesetze der Arithmetik*, 1893[1]

Die Nachwelt ist mit Oliver Byrne eher unbarmherzig umgegangen. Das betrifft in erster Linie die Wissenschaft Mathematik und ihr Verhältnis zur eigenen Geschichte. Byrne kommt dort so gut wie gar nicht vor. Man sucht die spektakuläre Euklidausgabe vergebens in der *Bibliographia Euclideana* von Max Steck, obwohl doch gerade er sich der „mathematischen Gestalt" zugewandt und schon bei Proklus im Euklidkommentar die „Schaufähigkeit" aus-

gemacht hatte, um dann von hier aus über Nikolaus Cusanus zu Johannes Kepler, „unter Erneuerung pythagoräischer Motive", und zu Gottfried Wilhelm Leibniz einer Synthese nachzuforschen, bei der der *mundus intelligibilis* und der *mundus sensibilis*, das Abstrakte und das sinnlich Erfahrbare, zusammen gesehen und wieder zu einer Ganzheit geformt würden.[2]

So weit, weder in geschichtlicher noch in grundsätzlicher Hinsicht, wollte Byrne selbst allerdings nicht ausgreifen; seine Zielsetzung blieb didaktisch dem unmittelbaren Verstehen und Nutzen der Mathematik zugewandt, glaubte er. Und doch hätte sein *Euclid* zu jenen grundsätzlicheren Überlegungen führen können und müssen. Steck war davon überzeugt, dass sich die Mathematik „nicht gleich der reinen Logik" auf bloße Begriffe zurückführen ließe und dass stattdessen gelte: „Die Beteiligung der Anschauung an ihren Erkenntnissen läßt sich nicht bestreiten, weil die Mathemata eben nicht aus Begriffen, sondern nur durch deren ‚Konstruktion möglich sind‘.[3] Steck orientierte sich an Andreas Speiser und seiner *Mathematische[n] Denkweise* (1932) und – bezogen auf die wissenschaftliche Begriffsbildung – auch an Heinrich Rickert, der seinerseits darauf verwies, dass der Mathematik vorerst gar kein gegebenes Material vorliege und dass sie dieses selbst zu erschaffen habe. Das ist – gemäß Rickert – der Grund, weshalb sich Fragen nach weiterreichenden Definitionen der Geraden etwa (des „absolut Einfachen") als obsolet erweisen, so wie man mit den Versuchen, „blau oder rot definieren zu wollen", nur eine „Aufweisung" vornehmen würde.[4] Definitionen genügen sich selbst. Speiser verwies 1932 in seinem den „Abgrenzungen" gewidmeten ersten Kapitel auf den „Rechtsgrund", der bei allen denkbaren an-

Page/Seite/Page 38
Ill. 20
Edward L. Youmans, *Chemical Atlas*,
New York 1856, plate XI
– *Chemistry of Combustion and Illumination;
Structure of Flame.*
– *Verbrennungschemie und Lichtstärke: Struktur
der Flamme.*
– *Chimie de la combustion et intensité lumineuse :
structure de la flamme.*

derweitigen Interessen und Ausuferungen „für die Mathematik in der mathematischen Einsicht" läge.[5]

Speisers *Mathematische Denkweise* war 1932 Raoul La Roche, dem Bauherrn Le Corbusiers, gewidmet. Für ihn steht die Nähe mathematischer und künstlerischer Welten allein schon aufgrund der Beurteilungen ihrer Zuständigkeiten, ihrem „Rechtsgrund", außer Zweifel. Die Wissenschaften würden „durch ihre Rechtsgründe bestimmt und hier gehören die mathematische und die künstlerische Einsicht dem geistigen Gebiet an, dagegen das Experiment und die Ueberlieferung der äusseren Welt".[6] Das befördert natürlich die Ansicht, die mathematischen Formen und Figuren sollten spontanen menschlichen Erfindungen gleich – und nicht bloß als Resultat wissenschaftlicher Erfordernisse – philosophisch angesehen und beurteilt werden. Ein umfassenderes „System unsers Wissens (d.h. das System der gesamten Erfahrung)"[7] verlangte jedoch nach einem solchen „wissenschaftlichen Leistungszusammenhang", bei dem die „Anschaulichkeit der empirischen Welt" und insgesamt die Psychologie ihr Recht einfordert.[8] Rickert hat in seiner Erörterung der *Grenzen der naturwissenschaftlichen Begriffsbildung* den Gegensatz von „logischer Vollkommenheit" (eines Begriffes) und empirischer Anschauung herausgestellt, um ihn dann gleich in Anbetracht der tatsächlichen Wirksamkeit der Körperwelten wieder aufzuweichen. Nichts führt an diesen Schwierigkeiten vorbei.[9] Die kulturellen Aussichten, wenn etwa die mathematischen Feststellungen in ästhetische Wirksamkeiten hinein verlängert werden sollen, verschärfen den Gegensatz zusätzlich. Ernst Bloch hat schon 1908 – in seiner Würzburger Dissertation – bei Rickert methodische „Schwankungen" als Wesenszug seiner Philosophie ausgemacht und das auch just mit den um 1850 einsetzenden Veränderungen und divergierenden Interessen illustriert.[10]

Diese Fragen besitzen also in der spezifischen Akzentuierung und Zuspitzung ihren historischen Raum. Was bei Oliver Byrnes Kritiker Augustus De Morgan 1847 mit der „formal logic" begann[11], ist bei Edmund G. Husserl zur Krise ausgereift, die er unter den Begriff der „Mathematisierung" stellt und mit dem Verlust der Lebensbedeutsamkeit der Wissenschaft verbindet.[12] 1910/11 hatte Rickert festgestellt, die „objektivierende Weltanschauung" vermöge den Sinn unseres Lebens nicht zu deuten.[13] Husserl, damals mit den Idealen einer „strengen Wissenschaft" befasst, gestand sich ein, dass als „einzige reife Frucht" der „durch das Medium kritischer Reflexion" erfolgten Bemühungen die Begründung und Verselbstständigung der strengen Natur- und der Geisteswissenschaften „sowie neuer rein mathematischer Disziplinen" erreicht worden sei.[14] Für die dabei außen vorgebliebene Philosophie wünschte er sich – durchaus auf der Kritik der bei den „eindrucksvollsten Wissenschaften der Neuzeit, den mathematisch-physikalischen" unvermeidbaren „indirekten Methoden" aufbauend – eine Wissenschaft, „die ohne alle indirekt symbolisierenden und mathematisierenden Methoden, ohne den Apparat der Schlüsse und Beweise, doch eine Fülle strengster und für alle weitere Philosophie entscheidender Erkenntnisse gewinnt".[15] Sie sollte „im rechten Sinne philosophischer Intuition" einer „phänomenologischen Wesenserfassung" dienen.[16]

Die Gesichtspunkte und Interessen hatten sich längst auseinanderdividiert. Gottlob Frege hatte 1879 seine *Begriffsschrift, eine*

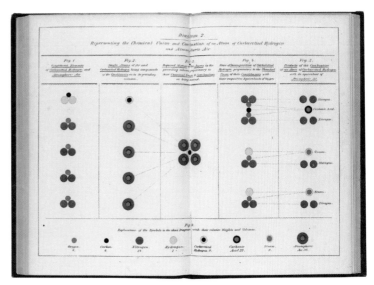

21

der arithmetischen nachgebildete Formelsprache des reinen Denkens publiziert, in deren Vorgeschichte im weitesten Sinne Byrnes *Euclid* durchaus einen Platz einnimmt. Frege hatte 1882 selbst die Bemerkung hinterhergeschickt, „eine anschauliche Darstellung der Denkformen" hätte eine „über die Mathematik hinausreichende Bedeutung".[17] Und er bat darum, Philosophen möchten doch „der Sache einige Bedeutung schenken".[18] Dass im Streit mit Husserl das Psychologische aller Wahrnehmung – beidseits – im Vordergrund stand, verwundert kaum. Man muss das bezogen auf Frege auch dahingehend lesen, dass er so unphilosophisch gar nicht war. Ganz im Gegenteil. Seinen ersten grundsätzlichen Erörterungen folgt 1893 im ersten Band der *Grundgesetze der Arithmetik* die Fußnote: „Mathematiker, die sich ungerne in die Irrgänge der Philosophie begeben, werden gebeten, hier das Lesen des Vorworts abzubrechen."[19] Danach geht es durchaus um die Frage, was gedacht und was dargestellt werden kann und soll. Natürlich argumentiert Frege gegen eine missbräuchliche „psychologische Verfälschung der Logik".[20] Er fordert andererseits Grenzen der „Erdichtungswillkür".[21] Und Arithmetik ist für ihn unzweifelhaft ein Zweig der Logik.[22] „Ich halte es für ein sicheres Anzeichen eines Fehlers, wenn die Logik Metaphysik und Psychologie nöthig hat, Wissenschaften, die selber der logischen Grundsätze bedürfen. Wo ist denn hier der eigentliche Urboden, auf dem Alles ruht? oder ist es wie bei Münchhausen, der sich am eigenen Schopfe aus dem Sumpfe zog?"[23]

Es geht immer wieder darum, was die Mathematik kann und soll, darf und nicht darf, was davon zum „Vorgestellten" gerät.[24] Wer Letzteres in den Vordergrund rückt, sei ein unverbesserlicher Idealist, so Frege gegen Benno Erdmann gerichtet.[25] Man erinnert sich, dass Bertrand A. W. Russell zu Beginn seines *An Essay on the Foundations of Geometry* (1897) bemerkte, die Geometrie wäre im 17. und 18. Jahrhundert im Kampf gegen den Empirizismus eine „impregable fortress of the idealists" geblieben.[26] So also sind die Fronten aufgebaut. Was bei Russell auf die Idealismus-Schelte folgt, ist die Darstellung der Wegentwicklung der Geometrie von Euklid, die mit der Infragestellung des Parallelenaxioms ansetzt und über Nikolai Iwanowitsch Lobatschewski und Johann Bolyai zu neuen Ufern führt.[27]

Gerade dies ging den Bemühungen Byrnes zeitlich voraus. Und später, 1854, waren zumindest einem engeren Zirkel Bernhard Riemanns *Ueber die Hypothesen, welche der Geometrie zu Grunde liegen* bekannt. Dessen Überlegungen gingen bekanntlich davon aus, dass die Geometrie den Begriff des Raumes voraussetzt und insgesamt die Begründungen der Axiome im Dunkeln blieben. So empfahl er, dass diese „von Euklid bis auf Legendre" weder von den Mathematikern noch von den Philosophen gelichtete Dunkelheit im Blick auf „das dem Raume zugrundeliegende Wirkliche", Erfahrungen und Tatsachen nutzend, allmählich umgearbeitet werde.[28] Das wies in die Physik. 1878 hielt Hermann von Helmholtz zum Stiftungsfest der Friedrich-Wilhelms-Universität in Berlin die Rede *Die Thatsachen in der Wahrnehmung* und erklärte den alten und neuen Widerspruch.[29] Dem „älteren Begriff der Anschauung", der sich auf das beziehe, was „sogleich mit dem sinnlichen Eindruck zum Bewusstsein kommt", stellte er seinen wissenschaftlichen Begriff entgegen: „Ich verlange für den Beweis der Anschaubarkeit nur, dass für jede Beobachtungsweise bestimmt und unzweideutig

Representing the Combustion of a given Volume

Fig. 1.

Volume of Carburetted Hydrogen to be
consumed and its equivalent of Oxygen

Required M
the preced
to their

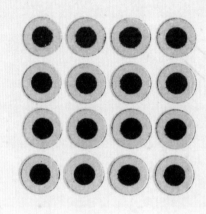

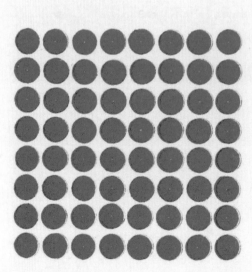

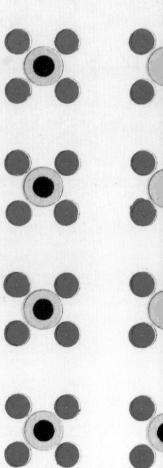

Atwood, del.

buretted Hydrogen and its equivalent of Oxygen.

2.

of the Atoms in

n preparatory

al Union.

Products of the Combustion of a given

Volume of Carburetted Hydrogen

and its equivalent of Oxygen

Carbonic Acid.

Fig. 3.

Steam

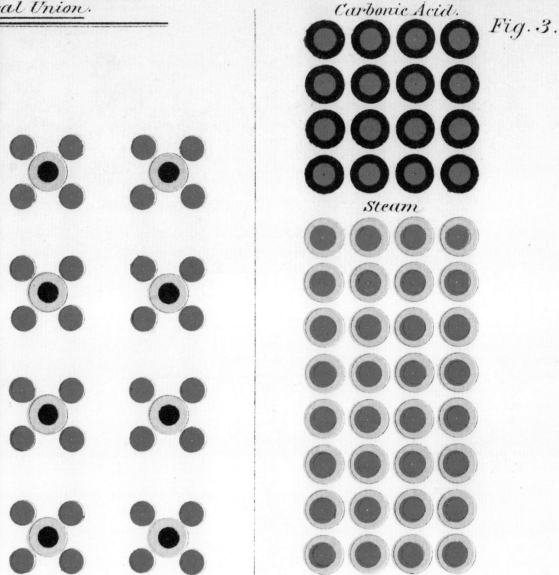

A. Meisel, Lith. Boston.

die entstehenden Sinneseindrücke anzugeben seien, nöthigenfalls unter Benutzung der wissenschaftlichen Kenntniss ihrer Gesetze, aus denen wenigstens für den Kenner dieser Gesetze hervorgehen würde, dass das betreffende Ding oder anzuschauende Verhältniss thatsächlich vorhanden sei."[30]

Helmholtz verzichtet bewusst auf jene „Leichtigkeit, Schnelligkeit, blitzähnliche Evidenz", die dem „älteren Begriff der Anschauung", dem unmittelbaren Sinneseindruck nämlich, zu eigen sind.[31] Die Abkoppelung ist erfolgt. Helmholtz hatte ja mit seiner Kritik schon dort angesetzt, wo Immanuel Kant die euklidischen Sätze als notwendig richtig und Abweichungen als gar nicht vorstellbar taxierte, um dann insofern klärend und ganz traditionell die Anschauungsform zu beschreiben. „Unser Auge sieht alles, was es sieht, als ein Aggregat farbiger Flächen im Gesichtsfeld; das ist seine Anschauungsform."[32] Aber darum ging es nun der Mathematik und Helmholtz erklärtermaßen gar nicht mehr. Husserl hatte später andererseits – durchaus auch mit Blick auf jene dem Sehsinn innewohnenden Vorzüge, wie dem der „blitzähnlichen Evidenz", auf die nun verzichtet werden sollte – Frege vorgeworfen, er würde sich „in unfruchtbare Hypersubtilitäten"[33] hineinbegeben, wogegen er selbst nun auf die „elementaren psychischen Daten" verweist. Begriffe wie „Qualität, Intensität, Ort, Zeit u. dgl. kann Niemand definiren".[34] Und das bezieht Husserl weiter auf „elementare Relationen" wie „Gleichheit, Aehnlichkeit, Steigerung, Ganzes und Theil, Vielheit und Einheit".[35] Die Phänomenologie bemüht sich um die abstrakten, reinen Vorstellungen! Husserl will sie bekanntlich als eine „Grundwissenschaft der Philosophie" etablieren und so (wieder) bei der „natürlichen Erkenntnis und Erfahrung", das was er „die Welt" nennt, anschließen.[36]

So weit reichte vormals der Anspruch der Geometrie. Jene „elementaren Relationen" gehörten insbesondere – gehören (!) – zur Domäne der Geometrie. Man kann sie weiterhin und in didaktischer Absicht in diesem Sinne verstehen und in jene (idealistische) Richtung hinein orientieren wollen. Wer das um 1850 tut, befindet sich insofern in einer kulturgeschichtlich bedeutsamen Tradition, ist aber nicht mehr Teil der *scientific community*, die sich auf dem Weg zu jenen „neuen rein mathematischen Disziplinen" befindet, deren Bedeutung ja Husserl durchaus anerkannt hat. Aber das macht die Krise nicht ungeschehen. „Was ist Wahrheit in unserm Anschauen und Denken? In welchem Sinne entsprechen unsere Vorstellungen der Wirklichkeit? Auf dieses Problem stossen Philosophie und Naturwissenschaft von zwei entgegengesetzten Seiten; es ist eine gemeinsame Aufgabe."[37] Diese Formulierung Helmholtz' bezeichnet 1879 den längst Tatsache gewordenen doppelten, getrennten Zugang zum Problem. Der Nachsatz zur „gemeinsamen Aufgabe" klingt in Anbetracht des unverkennbaren Auseinanderdriftens der Interessen und Bemühungen beschönigend. Für die euklidische Geometrie und ihre vermittelnde Tradition war es, zumindest in der einschlägigen Wissenschaft, ein Abschied.[38]

Oliver Byrne, der unzeitgemäße und exzentrische Mathematiker, und sein Kontrahent Augustus De Morgan

„Oliver Byrne's Euclid *in symbols and colored diagrams was not taken seriously, but was regarded a curiosity."*
– Cajori, *A History of Mathematical Notations*, 1928[39]

Man kann die Situation etwas zugespitzt auch so beschreiben: Byrne befindet sich 1847 mit seinen Farbdiagrammen („coloured diagrams") und dem blinden Zutrauen zu willkürlichen Darstellungsformen mathematisch in der Zeit vor 1850 und, wenn man will, künstlerisch in der Moderne. In jedem Fall steht ihm die alte Zielsetzung der *adaequatio rei ac intellectus*, der gesuchten Übereinstimmung von Erkenntnis und Sache, und die entsprechende sinnennahe Anschauungsform in erster Linie vor Augen. Dem will Byrne mit seinen didaktischen Mitteln von Figuren und Symbolen dienen, und das ist auch in seinem *Euclid*, unmissverständlich und unmittelbar ersichtlich, das erklärte Ziel. Erwähnung findet Byrnes *Euclid* deshalb nicht zufällig in der großartigen Darstellung, die Florian Cajori 1928 den in der Mathematik verwendeten Symbolen und Figuren gewidmet hat.[40] Doch tut er dies eher beiläufig und notiert, Byrnes *Euclid* sei mit seinen Symbolen und farbigen Diagrammen nicht ernst genommen und als Kuriosität gehandelt worden.[41] Als Kuriosität also wurde Byrnes *Euclid* wahrgenommen – und abgetan! Dabei hat gerade Cajori bemerkt, dass die Verwendung von Farbe bei der Darlegung geometrischer Probleme schon bei Heron von Alexandrien erwähnt ist, der seinerseits auf eine pythagoräische Tradition verweist.[42] Und er zitiert desweiteren Martianus Capella, der Fläche und Farbe einander zuordnet und der natürlich allen Aspekten der Figurenbildung gegenüber ohnehin offen ist. Die Tradition steht auf der Seite von Oliver Byrne.

Den tieferen Grund des Desinteresses an Byrnes *Euclid* sieht Cajori denn auch ganz offensichtlich in der Ansicht begründet, die gerade damals – 1849, zwei Jahre nach Erscheinen des Werkes – der wenig ältere Augustus De Morgan mit seiner ganzen Autorität vertrat. Die, die algebraische Symbole in die elementare Geometrie einführten, zerstörten deren eigentümlichen Charakter für jeden Studenten, der eine mechanische Beziehung zu jenen Symbolen besäße; für jeden, der jene aus der üblichen Algebra kennt. „Geometrical reasons, and arithmetical process, have each its own office; to mix the two in elementary instruction, is injurious to the proper acquisition of both."[43] Ein strenges Urteil, in Anbetracht der Tatsache, dass damals natürlich der Zusammenhang Arithmetik-Geometrie vielerorts sogar ausdrücklich Thema von Untersuchungen war und als nützliches Feld der Beobachtung diente, nicht zuletzt bei De Morgan selbst. Ob dieser mit seiner harschen Kritik gar Byrnes *Euclid* im Visier hatte? Dann würde dies wohl in erster Linie das den Größen und Zahlenverhältnissen gewidmete fünfte Buch Euklids betreffen.[44]

„Curiosity", Cajoris für die (mangelnde) Wertschätzung von Byrnes *Euclid* verwendete Umschreibung, gemahnt eher an ein bewusstes Ausweichen vor einer genaueren Bezeichnung der Qualität der von Byrne gewählten Zeichen und Symbole. Meint Cajori deren Unzeitgemäßheit oder Unbestimmtheit in einem weiteren Spektrum der Bildbeschreibung, gleichsam zwischen Ikonoklasmus und Idolatrie? Ist andererseits De Morgans Kritik der Vermengung geometrischer und arithmetischer Sprachen nicht eher ein Vorwand, um die grundsätzliche Abneigung auch gegen die Person zu kaschieren? Wir wissen es nicht. Immerhin ist bekannt, dass De Morgan Byrnes – unter dem Anagramm E. B. Revilo publiziertes – *The creed of St. Athanasius* von 1839 rezensiert und in sein *A Budget of Paradoxes* aufgenommen hat, in dem alles, was für ihn an mathematischen, pythagoräischen und kabalistischen Abwegigkeiten aufzuspüren war, Eingang fand. Das Urteil liest sich so: „This author really believed himself, and was in earnest. He is not the only person who has written nonsense by confounding the mathematical infinite (of quantity) with what speculators now more correctly express by the unlimited, the unconditionel, or the absolute."[45] In der späteren Bearbeitung durch David Eugene Smith findet sich dann auch noch, mit direktem Bezug auf den *Euclid*, die Zuordnung Byrnes zu den „minor mathematical writers".[46] Man lässt kein gutes Haar an Byrne! Die Anthologie randständiger mathematischer Ansichten und Theorien von Augustus De Morgan hat in einer jüngsten Ausgabe (1974) den Titel *The Encyclopedia of Excentrics* erhalten, und so hat Byrne nun in der Tat den Weg in die Rubrik mathematischer Kuriositäten und Exzentrizitäten gefunden![47]

Byrne ist natürlich Exzentriker, genauso wie De Morgan, dem man nachsagte, er hätte wegen seiner schon im ersten Lebensjahr in Indien erlittenen Behinderung (Einäugigkeit) Zeit seines Lebens nichts anderes als abstrakte Zahlen im Sinn gehabt. Aber natürlich reichen solche anekdotischen Hinweise nicht aus, um die Krise der Bildvorstellung in der damaligen Mathematik und bei De Morgan zu erklären. Vorerst aber gilt, dass Augustus De Morgan und Oliver Byrne sehr vieles, was die britische Welt bewegte, verband. De Morgan war seinerseits den Problemen von Didaktik und Unterricht ganz besonders zugetan. Er teilte die Ansicht, die sein Lehrer und Freund William Whewell 1836 schon im Buchtitel vertrat: *Thoughts on the study of mathematics, as part of a liberal education*.[48] Mathematik dient der Erziehung und ist eine gleicherweise moralische wie Vernunft befördernde Disziplin. Und es ist die pädagogische Ausrichtung, die die Mathematik formt und ihr auch einen gesellschaftlichen Status verleiht. Das ist durchaus konkret gemeint. De Morgans *Essay on Probabilities* von 1838 trägt den Untertitel *On their application to Life Contingencies and Insurance Offices* (Abb. 6) und soll auch konkret als Maßnahme gegen die allgemeine Ignoranz in Sachen Versicherungswesen verstanden und gelesen werden.[49] De Morgan war ein prominentes Mitglied der 1826 gegründeten Society for the Diffusion of Useful Knowledge und hat über 700 Beiträge für deren Organ, die *Penny Cyclopedia*, verfasst.[50] 1841 hat er dort einen kurzen Beitrag, *Proportion*, publi-

Representing the Combustion of a given Volu

Fig. 1.

Volume of Hydrogen to be consumed
and its equivalent of Atmospheric Air.

Required M
the precedi
to their

n 7.

Hydrogen and its equivalent of Atmospheric Air.

. 2 .

of the Atoms in
nn preparatory
l Union.

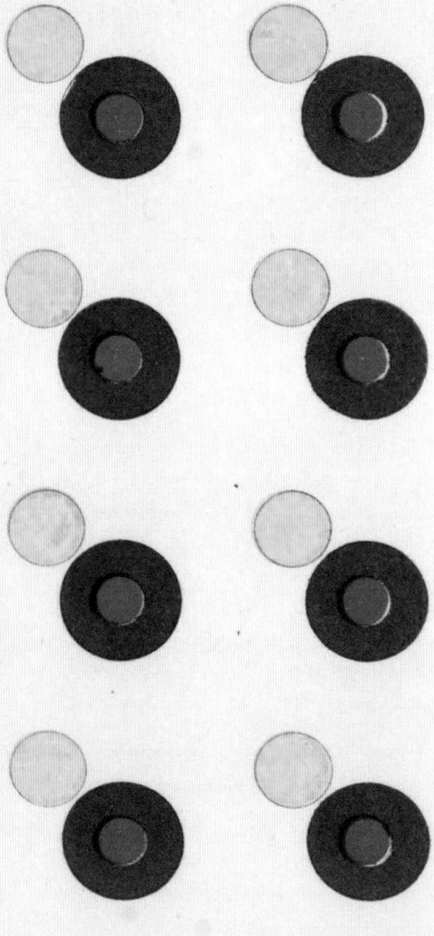

Products of the Combustion of a
given Volume of Hydrogen and its
equivalent of Atmospheric Air.

Steam.

Fig. 3.

Nitrogen.

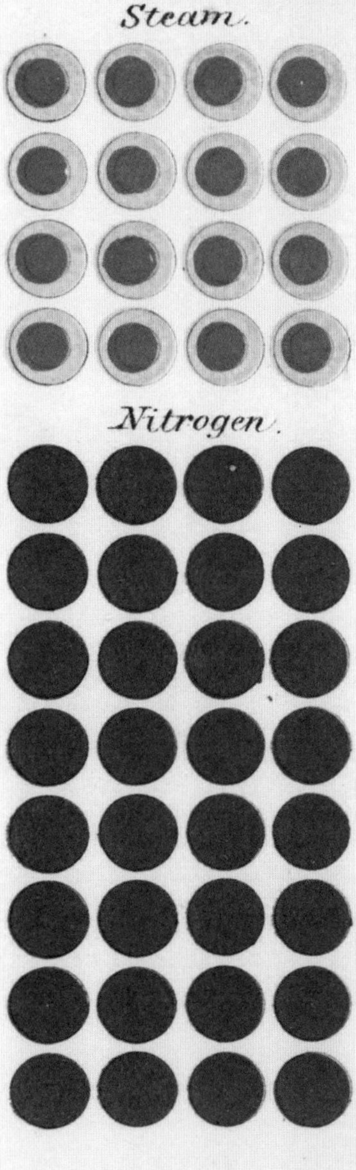

A.Meisel. Lith. Boston.

ziert und sich dabei mit Euklids fünftem Buch befasst.[51] Allein, es drängte ihn vermehrt zur Zahl, zur Arithmetik und Algebra, zur Logik und zu den Fragen der Wahrscheinlichkeit (Abb. 7). In dem Jahr, in dem Byrnes *Euclid* erschien, publizierte De Morgan seine *Formal Logic*, der eine ganze Reihe einschlägiger Untersuchungen folgte.[52] De Morgan und mit ihm die in die *symbolic logic* einmündende Mathematik scheinen ausschließen zu wollen, was Byrne mit seinem *Euclid* gerade umgekehrt zu seinem didaktischen Prinzip, nämlich der Erläuterung mittels Figuren und Symbolen, erhob. Das war natürlich lange vor ihm so oder anders oder zumindest im Ansatz praktiziert worden. So ganz isoliert war Oliver Byrne keineswegs. Auch die Farbe fand bald vermehrt in der wissenschaftlichen Illustration Verwendung.[53] Für die Mathematik soll gelten, es muss sauber getrennt werden, was getrennt sein will.[54] Für Byrnes Außenseitertum war wohl insgesamt ausschlaggebend, dass sich die Entwicklung der Geometrie – innerhalb der mathematischen Disziplin – längst von Euklid weg zu neuen Fragen wie gerade der formalen Logik hin entwickelte. Die Frage der Symbole ist dann vergleichsweise obsolet. Trotzdem scheint De Morgan jede sich ihm bietende Gelegenheit zu nutzen, um dagegen zu votieren und umso mehr der Logik zuzudienen. Jede sich entwickelnde Wissenschaft erschaffe ihre eigenen Symbole; und die Logik, die einzige Wissenschaft, die zugegebenermaßen über Jahrhunderte keinen wirklichen Fortschritt erzielt habe, sei die einzige, die keine Symbole in die Welt gesetzt hätte.[55]

Wie sehr hier letztlich generell Empirie – auch in der Mathematik! – gegen jegliches tatsächliche oder vermeintliche a priori durchgesetzt werden soll, steht noch auf einer ganz anderen Seite. John Stuart Mill äußert sich in seiner *Autobiography* in diesem Sinn und gegen die deutsche a-priori-Sicht menschlichen Wissens zu seinem *System of Logic* und dem Austausch mit Whewell: Dieses Buch hätte das geliefert, was sehr gefragt war, ein Textbuch der umgekehrten Auffassung, die alles Wissen aus der Erfahrung ableitet und alle moralischen und intellektuellen Qualitäten in erster Linie den damit verknüpften Ausrichtungen entnimmt.[56] Kein Platz für das alte *more geometrico* und auch nicht für deutschen Idealismus![57] Induktion war das Gebot der Stunde! Whewells *Philosophy of the Inductive Sciences, founded upon their history* (1840) hat nicht nur seine Schüler De Morgan und Mill nachhaltig beeinflusst, es hat den neuen Kurs der wissenschaftlichen Entwicklung mitsamt seiner moralischen Grundlegung wesentlich bestimmt. Als Byrnes *Euclid* 1847 aus der Chiswick Press kam, erschien gerade die zweite Auflage von Whewells *Philosophy of the Inductive Sciences*, der dann später, ganz britisch, auch noch ein *Novum Organum Renovatum* hinzugegeben wurde.[58] Das setzte die Akzente!

Mit der überkommenen Ansicht, die Elemente Euklids wären gemäß allgemeiner Überzeugung die Grundlage aller mathematischer Wissenschaft auf der ganzen Welt geworden, stand dagegen Byrne gleichsam auf der historischen Seite der Mathematik.[59] In Anbetracht der jüngsten Entwicklungen erschien es rückständig, hier zugunsten der Wahrheitssuche anzusetzen und dabei auch noch die (alten) Symbole und Figuren aus Euklid zu gewinnen und einzusetzen, um so die mathematischen Gesetze einsichtig zu gestalten, nämlich im Bereich der Sichtbarkeit zu belassen. Byrne dagegen schrieb in der Einleitung zu seinem *Euclid* 1847, jede Sprache bestünde aus repräsentativen Zeichen, und jene Zeichen wären die besten, die ihr Ziel mit der größten Präzision und Effizienz erreichen würden.[60] Das galt mit der *formal logic* als überholt. Cajori stellte übrigens fest, dass in der Folge insgesamt individuelle Ansätze ideographischer Darstellungen von einem in umgekehrte Richtung weisenden Konsens überrollt worden seien.[61]

Mit der scheinbar so rigiden Absage De Morgans an die Vermengung geometrischer und arithmetischer Sprachen oder anderweitiger Symbole ist klar, dass hier auch längst jene Tradition verlassen ist, die bei Proklus genauso wie bei Martianus Capella in ihrem ganzen, äußerst wirksamen Reichtum ausgebreitet war. Die Aussage, „Die Geometrie lehrt Sätze entdecken und beweisen, welche Eigenschaften der Figuren ausdrücken", verband man anderorts allerdings noch lange mit der notwendigen Mühe, „ohne welche man weder in der Wissenschaft noch in dem Leben Gewinn und Befriedigung hat".[62] Jemand wie der Heidelberger Professor Arthur Arneth setzte 1852 die Verdienste der Geometrie besonders hoch an: „Die Geometrie bietet uns unter allen Zweigen der Mathematik das lehrreichste Bild. Wir sehen, wie die Menschen vom Anfange des reinen Denkens an das Einzelne zu fassen suchten, und nur dieses mit Sicherheit erkennen wollten und konnten."[63] Byrne bezieht sich seinerseits ausdrücklich auf die Autorität all jener Philosophen in der Tradition Platos, die für diese Geschichte standen. Nun aber galt wohl, was Max Bense als „Ablösung der Mathematik von der Philosophie" beschrieb und mit der angestrengten Ausbildung der „facheigenen Präzisionssprache" erklärte.[64] Damit sollte, so die Deutung Benses, das „Vorauslaufen der mathematischen Probleme und Lösungen vor der eigentlichen mathematischen Bewältigung"[65] korrigiert werden; aber das ähnelt wohl eher dem Paradox vom Wettlauf des Herkules mit der Schildkröte!

Dieser zeitgebundene Fortschritt hat Byrne also offensichtlich aus der neueren Geschichte der Mathematik hinausgedrängt und dazu geführt, dass ihm das Hütchen der Kuriosität aufgesetzt wurde. Man sei auf andere Horizonte, auf die Kunst etwa, verwiesen, wo die Sprachen und die Figuren und deren vielfältige Bedeutungen weitergeführt werden. Die weniger erbauliche Konsequenz, die sich aus der Unzeitgemäßheit des *Euclid* ergibt, betrifft die Tatsache, dass Byrne scheinbar gerade noch aus typographischen und ästhetischen Gründen unser Interesse erregt.[66] Der Typograph und Designer Ruari McLean, der bei seiner Arbeit von Jan Tschichold ausging, ist auf diesem Weg auf den *Euclid* Byrnes aufmerksam geworden. Sein Urteil in seiner Darstellung *Victorian*

Book Design and Colour Printing (1963) setzt die Akzente in diesem Sinne: Er nennt das Buch eine absichtliche Komplizierung Euklids und weist andererseits den Triumph des 1851 auf der *Great Exhibition* in London gezeigten Buches Charles Whittingham zu, der es bei William Pickering in einer Auflage von 1000 Exemplaren erscheinen ließ. Daran knüpft sich dann auch noch die Anekdote, das aufwendige Buch hätte seinen Verleger in den Bankrott, zur Aufgabe der berühmten, von seinem gleichnamigen Onkel gegründeten Chiswick Press getrieben.[67]

Byrnes Weg und Argumentation – und das mit dem ‚farbigen' *Euclid* von 1847 erreichte Ziel

„This Work has a greater aim than mere illustration; we do not introduce colours for the purpose of entertainment, or to amuse by certain combinations of tint and form, but to assist the mind in its researches after truth, to increase the facilities of instruction, and to diffuse permanent knowledge. If we wanted authorities to prove the importance and usefulness of geometry, we might quote every philosopher since the days of Plato. Among the Greeks, in ancient, as in the school of Pestalozzi and others in recent times, geometry was adopted as the best gymnastic of the mind."
– BYRNE, *Euclid*, 1847[68]

Damit muss man sich abfinden, wir sind mit Byrne in den Zeiten des „überholten Euklid"[69] angekommen. Byrne und seine geometrischen Ansichten kommen in der einschlägigen logischen Literatur von Augustus De Morgan bis zu Willard Van Orman Quines *Philosophy of Logic* (1970) natürlich nicht vor. Aber das alte Bedürfnis vom Sichtbarmachen unserer Vorstellungen zu den Bedingungen von Plausibilität und der von Helmholtz entlassenen Vorzüge von „Leichtigkeit, Schnelligkeit, blitzähnlicher Evidenz" ist nicht vom Tisch. Sollen sich Künstler ihrer annehmen! Für Byrne und seinen *Euclid* gilt, dass er noch ganz der alten überkommenen Ansicht vertraut, wonach hier nicht nur Geometrie vermittelt, sondern im Sinne einer Denkschule Hilfeleistung bei der Wahrheitssuche, und zwar in grundsätzlicher Hinsicht, geboten wird.

Man muss also Oliver Byrne und Euklid dort nachgehen, wo die Mathematik gleichsam noch nicht der einschlägigen Geschichte der Disziplin und ihren Spezialisierungen nach 1850 folgt, sondern sich weiterhin, oder vielmehr erst recht, der großen kulturgeschichtlichen Tradition verpflichtet zeigt, wonach die später von Max Steck bemühte, zugegebenermaßen sehr pauschal gefasste Maxime passt: „Alle großen Mathematiker waren auch gleichzeitig Philosophen."[70] Dieser „universellen Sicht" fügte Steck

noch weitere, nicht minder allgemeine Sätze hinzu: „Alle großen Mathematiker hatten ein inniges Verhältnis zur Kunst und waren meist auch ausübende Künstler", und „Alle großen Mathematiker waren in der Geistes- und Kulturgeschichte, besonders in der ihres Volkes bis in die Mitte des 19. Jahrhunderts hinein, eigentlich zu Hause."[71]

Solche euphorischen Urteile machen es allerdings nicht leichter, Byrnes Unternehmung des *Euclid* einen angemessenen Platz in der langen Geschichte und Editionsgeschichte der *Elemente* Euklids zuzuweisen. Aber im Kern sind die Fragen gestellt. Es geht darum, den größeren kulturellen Zusammenhang zu bedenken. Für Byrne ist das unabdingbar, weil sich gerade daraus der tiefere Sinn und der größere Nutzen erhellen. Und dazu gehört, dass der Zusammenhang Geometrie-Figur-Form als eine wirkungsmächtige kulturelle Tradition respektiert wird. Dass dabei die Verankerung der Anschauung in der sinnlichen Wahrnehmung garantiert bleibt, ist wesentlich. Es stützt die didaktische Absicht seines *Euclid*, auch wenn dies vorerst eher in entschuldigender Weise vorgebracht wird. Bebilderung, wenn sie denn die Zeit des Lernens nicht verkürzt, ist so doch wenigstens unterhaltsam.[72] Man muss Byrnes eigenen Argumenten nachgehen.

Die didaktischen Vorbemerkungen, die Byrne in regelmäßiger Abfolge in seinen Büchern anbringt, sind auffällig genug. Dabei wird die Abgrenzung gegenüber der reinen Wissenschaft Mathematik stets betont. Viel sei von gelehrten und erfahrenen Mathematikern geschrieben worden; doch das richte sich mehr an die Fortgeschrittenen und Eingeweihten als an den noch unerfahrenen Studenten. Längliche Formeln, komplizierte Regeln und Beweisführungen würden den Anfänger eher verwirren als unterrichten, der dann enttäuscht das Erlernen jener Dinge aufgäbe, die er, wenn auf einfache Art zur Darstellung gebracht, schnell erworben hätte.[73] Byrne beruft sich auf seine eigene Erfahrung mit der abschreckenden Wirkung der Mathematik im eigenen Studium und in der Funktion des Vermittlers. Er will diese Situation korrigieren und verbessern. Er hätte deshalb seine Erklärungen in derselben Weise verfasst, wie er sie beim mündlichen Unterricht mit seinen Schülern verwendet hätte.[74] Unterrichtsnah, verständlich soll auch das Geschriebene sein. Mit dieser Absicht leitet Byrne 1835 die sphärische Trigonometrie ein, deren Untertitel auf die wenigen Regeln („few simple rules") und umgekehrt auf das Vermeiden größerer Schwierigkeiten ausdrücklich verweist.

Entsprechende Feststellungen und Empfehlungen ziehen sich wie ein roter Faden durch die zahlreichen, so deutlich didaktisch angelegten Publikationen Oliver Byrnes. Das *Handbook for the artisan, mechanic, and engineer* verspricht schon im ersten Satz der Einleitung, dass auch der noch nicht Eingeweihte binnen kürzester Zeit die schwierigsten Probleme verstehe.[75] Byrne scheut auch nicht den Vergleich mit den bekanntesten Größen seines Faches, ja fordert diese sogar heraus. Zu den Logarithmen-Tafeln im An-

24

hang zu seiner als „new art, designed for elementary instruction and the use of schools" (neue, für die Grundlagenbildung und den Schulgebrauch entwickelte Kunst) angepriesenen Publikation *The Young Dual Arithmetician* (1866) meinte er im Vorwort, sie wären ebenso effizient wie diejenigen von Babbage und Collet zusammen und benötigten weniger als ein Achtel von deren beanspruchtem Platz.[76] Immerhin haben Byrnes Bemühungen um die Logarithmen schon früh auch in Deutschland Beachtung gefunden, bezeichnenderweise dort, wo insbesondere der Nutzen oder gar die „Anwendung der Logarithmen auf das Leben" im Vordergrund standen. Solches las man im Untertitel zur Übernahme und Veröffentlichung des Eisenacher Schuldirektors Adolf Lorey, *Das Neueste und Interessanteste aus der Logarithmotechnik* (1852), deren Vorrede mit einem Verweis auf Oliver Byrne und M. Philippe Koralek begann und den Akzent auf die „technische Fertigkeit, besonders im augenblicklichen Berechnen der Logarithmen" legte.[77] Die Einleitung setzte mit dem Vergleich an: „Die Logarithmen sind eben so mächtig und wirksam in der Rechnung, als der Dampf in der Mechanik."[78]

Man erkennt in diesen Zeugnissen, dass Byrne zuvorderst die Vermittlung zu einfachsten Bedingungen angelegen war. Die Sehnsucht nach schnellem Verstehen steht im Vordergrund. Das hat ihn natürlich insbesondere auch in seinen geometrischen Arbeiten gelenkt. Den ersten wichtigen Akzent legt Byrne diesbezüglich mit seiner *The Doctrine of Proportion clearly developed, on a comprehensive, original, and very easy system; or, The Fifth Book of Euclid simplified*, die er als Mathematikprofessor des College of Civil Engineers in Putney 1841 vorlegt und den Leitern, Organen und

Studenten dieser Institution widmet (Abb. 8, 9).[79] Das „einfache System" und das auf das fünfte Buch Euklids bezogene Wörtchen „vereinfacht" stehen hier schon im Titel. Dort wird, schon 1841, in üblicher Manier neben anderen Werken des Autors auch *The First Six Books of the Elements of Euclid* angezeigt. Was in der *Doctrine of Proportion* folgt, ist denn auch in mancher Hinsicht ein Vorabdruck der entsprechenden Teile des *Euclid* von 1847, wobei dann die 1841 eingeführten Symbole teilweise in veränderter Form erscheinen. 1847 wird umgekehrt auf die vorausgegangene Publikation, insbesondere auf die dort ausgebreiteten und jetzt vernachlässigten algebraischen und arithmetischen Ausführungen verwiesen.[80]

Der Ausgangspunkt für Byrnes Werk ist klar. Er hält die einschlägige Forschung für lücken- und fehlerhaft und verfolgt dies über Adrien-Marie Legendre zurück bis zu Isaac Newton. Dem setzt er andererseits den alten Topos der in sich absolut stimmigen, fehlerfreien Logik Euklids gegenüber.[81] Für Byrne gilt dies insbesondere und uneingeschränkt für Euklids fünftes Buch, das er zum Meisterwerk menschlicher Vernunft erklärt.[82] Also gilt seine ganze Aufmerksamkeit dem Erklären und Darstellen, wobei er nun Symbole zur Hilfe nimmt, von denen er – im Widerspruch zu De Morgan und zur späteren Einschätzung Cajoris – sagt, die Einführung von Symbolen in geometrischen Abhandlungen würde mit jedem Tag gebräuchlicher.[83] Und weil dies und der Nutzen so evident seien, bedürfe es gar keiner weiteren Begründungen. 1841 ist es ihm allerdings noch ein Anliegen, die arithmetischen und algebraischen Darstellungsweisen mitzuführen; die Sache allein entscheide, ob man die Probleme auf Zahlen, Symbolen oder Linien aufbauen wolle.[84] Die Proportionslehre hat sich all dieser Mittel

Tabelle der Einheiten.

Erste Uebung.

Erste Reihe.

1 mal 1; 2 mal 1; 3 mal 1; 4 mal 1; 5 mal 1;
6 — 1; 7 — 1; 8 — 1; 9 — 1; 10 — 1.

Zweyte Reihe.
2 mal 1 ist 1 mal 2.

1 mal 2; 2 mal 2; 3 mal 2; 4 mal 2; 5 mal 2;
6 — 2; 7 — 2; 8 — 2; 9 — 2; 10 — 2.

Dritte Reihe.
3 mal 1 ist 1 mal 3.

1 mal 3; 2 mal 3; 3 mal 3; 4 mal 3; 5 mal 3;
6 — 3; 7 — 3; 8 — 3; 9 — 3; 10 — 3.

Vierte Reihe.
4 mal 1 ist 1 mal 4.

1 mal 4; 2 mal 4; 3 mal 4; 4 mal 4; 5 mal 4;
6 — 4; 7 — 4; 8 — 4; 9 — 4; 10 — 4.

Fünfte Reihe.
5 mal 1 ist 1 mal 5.

1 mal 5; 2 mal 5; 3 mal 5; 4 mal 5; 5 mal 5;
6 — 5; 7 — 5; 8 — 5; 9 — 5; 10 — 5.

A

in unterschiedlicher Weise und Verbindung ja immer wieder bedient.

Was folgt, sind Erklärungen, die die geometrischen Symbole an die Seite der bekannten algebraischen Formeln stellen und somit die sichtbaren Zeichen mit den entsprechenden Abstrahierungen vergleichen. Schließlich interessiert die Verwendung der Umgangssprache, was Byrne ja schon früher als Gradmesser einer erfolgreichen Methode angenommen hat.[85] Es kommt darauf an, die Unterschiede von Symbolen klar erkennen und mitteilen zu können; die Methode muss dementsprechend logisch, knapp und überzeugend ausfallen und den lästigen Ballast ausführlicher Details, der häufig anderen Methoden anhängt, vermeiden.[86] Es ist Byrne jetzt schon klar, dass farbliche Differenzierung diese klärende Unterscheidung unterstützen würde.[87] In seinem vom 19. November 1840 datierten Vorwort der *Doctrine of Proportion* wird dazu klar gesagt, es wäre dies beabsichtigt, jedoch aus Kostengründen verworfen worden.[88]

Byrne hat ganz offensichtlich schon damals Erfahrungen mit seiner Methode gesammelt, Zuspruch und Kritik erhalten. Es ging etwa darum, in der fünften Definition des fünften Buches, dort wo Euklid von den Vielfachen von Größen und deren proportionalen Identitäten handelt, das in der damals gebräuchlichsten englischen Euklidausgabe von Robert Simson verwendete „any equimultiples" (irgendein ‚Gleichvielfaches') durch „every equimultiples" (jedes ‚Gleichvielfache') zu ersetzen.[89] Die didaktische Absicht Byrnes ist selbst hier zu spüren. Er wolle nicht beliebige – und beliebig viele – Tests dieser Art folgen lassen, sondern einen Standard setzen. Niemand würde ihm widersprechen, dass Definitionen und auch einzelne ihrer Teile und Begriffe ohne weitere Erklärungen auskommen müssten. Das geht mit der didaktischen Zielsetzung einher, das Unterrichten müsse für jeden, der über elementare Dinge schreibt, das höchste Ziel sein.[90] Aber damit hatte Byrne sich auch einer eingehenderen Analyse und Deutung dieser schon immer als besonders schwierig erkannten euklidischen Definition enthalten. Es war ausgerechnet De Morgan, der sich damals mit dieser Frage und der Bedeutung von *ratio* und Proportionalität befasste und seine Überlegungen just 1841 in der *Penny Cyclopedia* publizierte.[91] Anders als Byrne hatte De Morgan Tests angesetzt, um so die Brauchbarkeit und Plausibilität der euklidischen Formel zu überprüfen, und er hatte sich zudem ausgerechnet der Vorstellung und Verbildlichung einer Säulenkolonnade bedient.[92]

Oliver Byrne war 1841 offensichtlich die Einsicht in die grundsätzliche Bedeutung Euklids vordringlich. Seine *Doctrine of Proportion* soll beweisen, dass Euklids fünftes Buch die einzig legitime Lehre geometrischer Proportionierung sei. Zudem will er an dieser Stelle auch aufzeigen, dass die Proportionen ebenso algebraisch, arithmetisch und geometrisch abgehandelt werden können, da sie ja in gleicher Weise diese Bereiche betreffen.[93] Die für die Illustration des fünften Buches Euklids gewählten – und

1847 leicht verändert und nunmehr farbig gestalteten – Symbole verfolgen einen Mittelweg und ähneln in der Tat am ehesten späteren Begriffsschriften. Sie heben sich von den geometrischen oder geometrisierenden Symbolen deutlich ab, mit denen Byrne die übrigen Bücher Euklids illustriert.

Byrne sieht durchaus die Schwierigkeiten, die bei diesem Vorgehen entstehen können. Vorsicht sei deshalb geboten, weil Farbe für sich genommen nichts zu tun habe mit Linien, Winkeln und Größen, außer diese zu benennen.[94] Wie soll man das in Anbetracht der doch gerade auf diese Hilfsmittel ausgerichteten didaktischen Maßnahmen erkennen respektive unterscheiden? Byrne stellt Punkt und Linie durch die Überlappung von Farbflächen symbolisch, auf Umwegen, muss man feststellen, dar. Man muss also gleichsam von den ins Bild gesetzten farbigen Flächen abstrahieren, um dann Punkt, Linie und Fläche zu entdecken.[95] Es geht dem in eher umständlicher Fassung die alte Erklärung voraus: Eine mathematische Linie ist Länge ohne Breite, deshalb könne sie keine Farbe besitzen, jedoch würde die Überlappung oder die Naht zweier Farbflächen eine gute Vorstellung davon geben, was mit einer mathematischen Linie gemeint sei. Wenn man gemeinhin von einer schwarzen oder roten Linie oder Linien sprechen würde, meine man eigentlich eine solche Nahtstelle.[96] Die Sache selbst findet sich also in der Berührung und Überlappung der Farbflächen dargestellt. Albrecht Dürer hatte in seiner *Underweysung der messung* 1525 die Not mangelnder Darstellungsmöglichkeit der abstrakten Linie durch das Reißen einer dicken, somit sichtbaren Linie auf direkte Weise gelindert, „Dann durch solche weyß muß der innerliche verstand im eussern werck angezeigt werden".[97] Byrne sieht durchaus die Risiken solcher Verweismethoden ein. Seine Farben und farbigen Diagramme würden vielleicht vorerst als eine etwas unbeholfene Methode erscheinen; dann aber verspricht er Vorkehrungen, die raffinierter und ausführlicher als alle je zuvor vorgestellten seien.[98] Das trifft zweifelsohne zu. Aber die „coloured diagrams", so scheint es, machen sich dabei selbständig. Man kann den Verdacht nicht ablegen, Byrne hätte zu dem euklidischen noch ein zweites, graphisches System hinzugegeben, dessen Nutzen zu beweisen, er nicht müde wird, indem er insbesondere darauf verweist, dass Farben sich weit besser einprägen würden als bloße, ohne besondere Merkzeichen versehene Sätze.[99]

„More easily fixed in the mind", besser einprägsam! Das also ist es, worauf es Byrne wirklich ankommt. Schon 1841 angekündigt, ist es ihm jetzt, 1847, gelungen, seinen *Euclid* farbig, merkfähig, allen Erfahrungen der Sinneswahrnehmung entsprechend zu gestalten. Das wird bald überall mit Erfolg praktiziert. 1856 wird, um nur zwei Beispiele zu nennen, in New York der *Chemical Atlas* von Edward Livingston Youmans publiziert, in dessen Titel ganz analog zu Byrnes Veröffentlichungen, die Darstellungsweise „in a series of beautifully colored diagrams" und auch die Intention „designed for the use of students" hervorgehoben erscheint (Abb. 18–20, 32, 39).

In Worcester veröffentlicht Ezekiel Webster Dimond 1867 *The Chemistry of Combustion* in einer möglichst einfachen und präzisen Sprache und natürlich unter Einsatz von Farbe an Stelle von chemischen Symbolen: Rot für Sauerstoff, Gelb für Wasserstoff, Blau für Stickstoff und Schwarz für Kohlenstoff (Abb. 21–23, 33).[100] Youmans schrieb seinerseits in seiner Einleitung, dass gerade in den Naturwissenschaften, da dort der Anspruch exakter Darstellung von Eigenschaften und Beziehungen besonders gefragt sei, die Verwendung sinnenhafter Diagramme ihren besonderen Nutzen unter Beweis stellen könnte.[101] Und er sah – heutigen Gewohnheiten weit vorauseilend – einen erhöhten Nutzen bildhafter Darstellung gerade dort, wo der Gegenstand erst gar nicht gesehen werden könne.[102] Als erstes Beispiel, das diese Bedingung erfüllt, zitiert er die Geometrie und umschreibt den entsprechenden Vorgang mit „diagramize geometrical conceptions", mit dem Umsetzen geometrischer Vorstellungen in Diagramme.[103]

Byrne hatte diese Diskussion schon 1841 aufgenommen und die besondere Bedeutung von Farbe bei der Illustration wissenschaftlicher Sachverhalte angezeigt. 1847 ist er ans Ziel gekommen. Wie sehr er sich mit dieser psychophysischen Frage avant la lettre befasst, belegt er 1847 mit Hinweisen aus der Poesie. Er zitiert Horaz und Aesop, um die Überlegenheit des Sehsinns zu dokumentieren. „Der Aufgabe nach uralt", läge das Neue nun eben in der „mathematischen Verknüpfung erfahrungsmässiger Thatsachen", wird Gustav Theodor Fechner 1860 im Vorwort zu *Elemente der Psychophysik* schreiben.[104] Was also liegt näher, als diese Tatsachen für die Darstellung wissenschaftlicher Sachverhalte einzusetzen. Solches liegt Byrnes Vorgehen zweifelsohne zugrunde. In Tat und Wahrheit verschiebt sich aber das Interesse vom wissenschaftlichen Gegenstand zu dessen Darstellung und didaktischer Vermittlung. Es drängt ihn, das in seiner Einleitung des *Euclid* zu betonen und genauso bildhaft und konkret herauszustreichen. Byrne empfiehlt farbige Kreide und für den privaten Gebrauch Farbstifte, um seinen *Euclid* lernend zu vertiefen.[105]

————

Der didaktische Impetus und die dazu notwendigen Maßnahmen

„Among the Greeks, in ancient, as in the school of Pestalozzi and others in recent times, geometry was adopted as the best gymnastic of the mind."
– BYRNE, *Euclid*, 1847[106]

Byrne erwähnt Johann Heinrich Pestalozzi gleich zu Beginn der Einleitung zu seinem *Euclid*. Es geht ihm um „the best gymnastic of the mind"[107], um eine Denkschule. Das didaktische Prinzip orientiert sich am Unterricht, an den „oral demonstrations" und am idealen Zusammenspiel von optischen und akustischen Eindrücken. Verstehen stellt sich ein, wenn letztendlich „reason, and fact, and proof" zusammenkommen und einen bleibenden Eindruck hinterlassen. Ob nun der Verweis vom Text zum Diagramm über Farbe und Form als den Zeichen oder über die entsprechenden Teile des Diagramms selbst verläuft, ist weniger wichtig, es zählt die Einfachheit, und es dient allemal der Zielstrebigkeit.[108] Mit seiner *Elementarlehre* und *Anschauungslehre der Zahlenverhältnisse* wollte Pestalozzi genau das erreichen, eine Methode oder „Kunstübung", um die Mathematik im Gleichgang mit der Entwicklung der „Denkkraft" zu erlernen (Abb. 24, 25). Und genau das strebte Byrne mittels Symbol, Figur und Farbe und zum Vorteil des Lernens an und für sich an.[109] „For the greater ease of learning" (Das Lernen zu erleichtern) ist also der Zweck, der letztlich Euklid unterlegt wird. Das steht in einer langen Tradition, in der der Mathematik in erster Linie eine Mittlerrolle zugewiesen wurde. Mathematik selbst wäre keine Wissenschaft, sagte Giovanni Pico della Mirandola in der ersten seiner eigenen Thesen zur Mathematik; sie führe nicht direkt zum Glück; sie sei eine Hilfswissenschaft, bilde den Weg, der zu anderweitigen Wissenschaften führt.[110] Es kommt auf die *medietas*, die Mittel- und Mittlerstellung an.

Wenn man die Dinge so angeht, so treten die mit Euklid verbundenen Unsicherheiten, die ihm zugeschriebene *obscuritas* zurück. Alle beschrieben dies rundum als äußerst dunkel, sagt Giovanni Alfonso Borelli zu Euklids Parallelenpostulat, weil ihm dazu die Grundlage, das Verständnis von Unendlichkeit, fehle.[111] Aber das lässt ihn nicht verzagen. Auch er beansprucht, neue Einsichten durch den – klassischen – Schluss von Bekanntem auf Unbekanntes zu gewinnen.[112] Und so publiziert er seinen *Euclides restitutus*.

Man richtet sich in dieser Situation ein und sucht nach Hilfsmitteln. Lange vor Oliver Byrne, 1684, hat St. George Ashe einen Beitrag zu Euklid für die *Philosophical Transactions* der Royal Society of London verfasst, dem er den Titel „A New and Easy Way of Demonstrating some Propositions in Euclid" gab.[113] Darin orientierte er sich am Vorrang des mathematischen Wissens, der „preeminence of Mathematical knowledge", um dann umso deutlicher auf der Bedeutung und Verlässlichkeit der mathematischen Methode zu insistieren. Im Vordergrund stehen die wenigen Axiome und Postulate, von denen jegliche Spielerei und mangelnde Präzision ferngehalten werden sollen.[114] Aus einem Brief von 1686 erfahren wir, dass er sich bei seinen Bemühungen der Darstellung des zweiten und fünften Buches Euklids der Methode aus John Pells *An Introduction to Algebra* bediente.[115] Wieweit diese Bemühungen mit dem 1684 in London anonym erschienenen *The Elements or Principles of Geometrie* zusammenhängen, muss offenbleiben (Abb. 26–28).[116] Tatsache ist, dass diesem in der Nachfolge Borellis verfassten Geometrie-Lehrbuch eine Einleitung mit Definitionen und Axiomen mitsamt der Erklärung der in der Folge verwendeten Zeichen folgt, wie sie teilweise Byrne noch 1847 benutzt. Die Ziel-

A=B=C

Elements
of
Geometry
Demonstrated
1684.

THE
ELEMENTS
OR
PRINCIPLES
OF
GEOMETRIE.

London, Printed by *J.P.* for *J. Seller* on the *Royal Exchange*, *R. Mount* on *Tower-Hill*, *A. Churchill* near *Amen-Corner*, and *J. Thornton* in the *Minories*. 1684.

Ill. 26
The Elements or Principles of Geometrie,
London 1684

setzungen sind ähnliche. Es geht um den schnellsten, effizientesten Weg, zu einem adäquaten Verständnis zu kommen, zum Vorteil all derer, die möglichst schnell zu den praktischen Fragen dieser Untersuchung gelangen möchten.[117] Dem sollen die einleitenden Definitionen dienen, wohl wissend, dass es sich natürlich bei Punkten, Linien und Winkeln um immaterielle Dinge handelt. Die Symbole erhalten umso mehr ihre Berechtigung. Aber die Erklärung reicht noch nicht aus; eine ausführlichere wird nachgereicht, in der der Akzent noch deutlicher auf den Wert der Demonstration gelegt wird: „Demonstration is the highest degree of Proof that any matter admits of." (Die Demonstration ist die höchste Beweisstufe, die ein jeder Gegenstand zulässt.)[118] Der grundsätzliche Nutzen der Geometrie, und mittelbar der Methode Euklids, zur Denkunterstützung und als Schutz gegen Irrtum und Täuschung wird hervorgehoben.[119] Der didaktische Nutzen wird umgehend notiert.[120] Deshalb ist es auch notwendig, die klärenden Voraussetzungen zu schaffen, zu denen letztlich nebst den Definitionen eben auch die Tabelle mit der Erklärung der Zeichen gehört, in der die graphischen Symbole für Funktion oder Bedeutungen wie „equal to" oder „like" oder „continued proportion" sowie für die Figuren von Dreieck oder Kreis aufgelistet sind.[121]

Die didaktischen Zielsetzungen scheinen, mitsamt den Bemühungen um entsprechende Methoden der Darstellung, von Euklid längst Besitz ergriffen zu haben. Ja, das scheint Euklid durch und durch inhärent zu sein. Byrnes beschwörende Worte in seiner Einleitung zum *Euclid* klingen nach, wonach die Farben eben nicht der Belustigung, sondern der Erleichterung auf dem Weg zur Wahrheit und zu nachhaltigem Wissen dienen sollen.[122] Man kann

es auch so sagen: Je mehr die sprichwörtliche *obscuritas* Euklids nachwirkt, desto wichtiger sind die Fragen der Methoden des Aufzeigens, der Demonstration und der didaktischen Mittel.[123] Und je deutlicher die Anwendung im Vordergrund steht, desto größer das Bedürfnis nach entsprechenden Modellen. „In der Mathematik muß der Lehrer alle Sätze durch Modelle erläutern, oder, wenn er diese nicht hat, den Vortrag durch deutliche und vollständige Zeichnungen zu ergänzen suchen."[124] Das gehört, wie Peter Heinrich Christoph Brodhagen in seiner *Anleitung zum gemeinnützigen Unterricht,* an Handwerker, Künstler und Fabrikanten gerichtet, 1792 schreibt, zu den absolut unverzichtbaren Voraussetzungen.

Mit Pestalozzi, auf den sich Byrne beruft, werden diese Anliegen verstärkt, die Methoden verfeinert und insbesondere die Frage der beteiligten Sinne vermehrt ins Auge gefasst. Ja, die Anpassung an die Sinne ist alsbald nicht nur begleitend, sondern sie diktiert. Das Angeschaute löst sich dann und bildet für sich selbst eine neue Logik, modern gesagt, einen Bilddiskurs. Das lässt sich bei Byrne durchaus beobachten. Sein *Euclid* richtet sich nach den Bemühungen seiner Zeit. „Auf die Beschaffenheit der Zeichen kömmt beim Denken viel an", hält beispielsweise 1793 Johann Georg Heinrich Feder fest und beruft sich natürlich auf Johann Heinrich Lamberts *Neues Organon*[125] (1764), das auch in Großbritannien bestens bekannt war und letztlich auch Byrne den Satz, dass alle Sprachen aus repräsentativen Zeichen bestehen, formulieren lässt.[126] Und noch mehr geht es jetzt um die Sinne, wie Byrne mit seiner wiederholt geäußerten Vorliebe für den mündlichen Unterricht bezeugt. Für Heinrich Stephani bildet der Kontrast zwischen der „Gehörsprache" und der „Gesichtssprache" den Ausgangspunkt seiner Be-

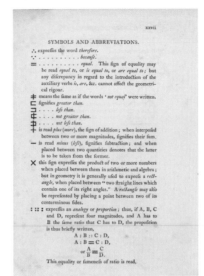

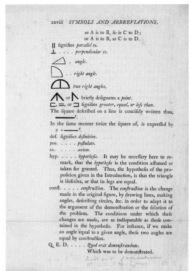

Ill. 29
Oliver Byrne, *The First Six Books of the Elements
of Euclid*, London 1847, p. xxvii
– *Symbols and Abbreviations.*
– *Symbole und Abkürzungen.*
– *Symboles et abréviations.*

Ill. 30
Oliver Byrne, *The First Six Books of the Elements
of Euclid*, London 1847, p. xxviii
– *Symbols and Abbreviations.*
– *Symbole und Abkürzungen.*
– *Symboles et abréviations.*

29

30

mühungen, die er 1814 unter dem Titel *Ausführliche Beschreibung
meiner einfachen Lese-Methode* in Erlangen erscheinen ließ.[127] Die
Buchstaben seien eigentlich „nur für das Auge willkürlich ange-
nommene Zeichen der verschiedenen Sprachlaute"; er möchte sie
jedoch als „die eigentlichen Noten für unser Sprachinstrument"
verstehen.[128] Um das zu beflügeln, bemüht er das Gedächtnis, das
schneller und nicht nur buchstabenweise, sondern vom Buchstaben zur Silbe zu ganzen Wörtern die Dinge einprägen und gleichsam mechanisch abrufen lässt. „Auf einen Blick" erkennbar soll es
sein.[129] Stephani beruft sich zwar auf Pestalozzi, folgt aber auch
noch alten mnemotechnischen Vorgehensweisen, bei denen man
über den Laut, von Tul(pe) auf das ‚p' und von Fich(te) auf das
‚t' schließen soll. Rasch fällt auf, dass das Ganze weniger einfach
ist, als der Titel des Buches verspricht. Man befindet sich noch im
Stadium des Experimentierens.

   Aber an der Ernsthaftigkeit der didaktischen Versprechungen
kann man nicht zweifeln. Das Prinzip „auf einen Blick", das was
beispielsweise Alfred North Whitehead (1927), auf eine Optimie-
rung der Sinneswahrnehmung („sense-perception") bezogen, mit
der Unmittelbarkeit des Vorzeigens („presentational immediacy")
bezeichnet, ist gar nicht so einfach zu bewerkstelligen und in seiner Wirkung zu garantieren.[130] Skepsis gegenüber unkonventio-
nellen optischen Hilfsmitteln ist übrigens durchaus an der Tages-
ordnung. Johannn Wolfgang von Goethe wundert sich im Vorwort
zu seiner *Farbenlehre* (1812) über die Manier, naturgeschichtlichen
Werken Tafeln hinzuzufügen:

   „Ein höchst unzulängliches Surrogat sind hierzu die Tafeln,
die man dergleichen Schriften beyzulegen pflegt. Ein freyes phy-

sisches Phänomen, das nach allen Seiten wirkt, ist nicht in Linien
zu fassen, und im Durchschnitt anzudeuten. Niemand fällt es ein,
chemische Versuche mit Figuren zu erläutern; bey den physischen
nah verwandten ist es jedoch hergebracht, weil sich eins und das
andre dadurch leisten lässt. Aber sehr oft stellen diese Figuren nur
Begriffe dar; es sind symbolische Hülfsmittel, hieroglyphische
Ueberlieferungsweisen, welche sich nach und nach an die Stelle
des Phänomens, an die Stelle der Natur setzen und die wahre Erkenntnis hindern, anstatt sie zu befördern."[131] Auch Goethe sieht
also die Gefahr der Verselbständigung solcher Symbole und kann
sich den Nutzen, etwa für den chemischen Bereich, gar nicht erst
vorstellen. Und doch konzediert er im nächsten Satz aus gege-
benem Anlass einen gewissen Sinn solcher Tafeln und Symbole:
„Entbehren konnten auch wir der Tafeln nicht; doch haben wir sie
so einzurichten gesucht, daß man sie zum didaktischen und pole-
mischen Gebrauch getrost zur Hand nehmen, ja gewisse derselben als einen Theil des nöthigen Apparats ansehen kann."[132] Auch
Goethe redet sich also mit didaktischen Argumenten heraus.

   Schließlich lässt sich auch Kant zu diesem Sachverhalt ver-
nehmen, als er die Frage „Was heißt: sich im Denken orientieren?"
zu beantworten suchte: „Wir mögen unsre Begriffe noch so hoch
anlegen, und dabei noch so sehr von der Sinnlichkeit abstrahiren,
so hängen ihnen doch noch immer bildliche Vorstellungen an,
deren eigentliche Bestimmung es ist, sie, die sonst nicht von der
Erfahrung abgeleitet sind, zum Erfahrungsgebrauche tauglich zu
machen."[133] Kant kommt auf diese Weise auf die Anschauung zu
sprechen und findet für das, was auch er mit Moses Mendelssohn
der „Evidenz der Demonstration" zuordnen oder auch nur einer

Orientierung zuweisen möchte, gleichsam als minimale Bedingung „ein gewisses Leitungsmittel".[134] Wie wir unsere Vorstellungen dem Erfahrungsgebrauche zuweisen, treibt auch ihn um.

———

Zeichen und Symbole zu einer mathematischen Philosophie

„Such for all common purposes are the audible signs called words, which are still considered as audible, whether addressed immediately to the ear, or through the medium of letters to the eye. Geometrical diagrams are not signs, but the materials of geometrical science, the object of which is to show the relative quantities or their parts by a process of reasoning called Demonstration."
– Byrne, *Euclid*, 1847[135]

„Das Schema der Reflexion ist also auch Schema der Reproduktion."
– Wagner, *Mathematische Philosophie*, 1851 (a)[136]

Zeichen zum „Erfahrungsgebrauche", „symbolische Hülfsmittel" oder auch generell nur „Leitungsmittel"! Man will wissen, wie es sich mit den Vorstellungen und mit der Anschauung verhält, und man sucht nach den Vorteilen der Präzision in der Demonstration und nach dem kürzesten Weg. Das sind die Sprachprobleme, für die das Interesse in der Zeit groß ist. Die Überlegung, die Oliver Byrne mit der Feststellung der Sprache als Zeichensystem beginnt, beendet er in der Überzeugung, dass in seinem Fall die Verwendung von farbigen Symbolen, Zeichen und Diagrammen die Denkprozesse präziser und schneller mache.[137]

Es liegt in der Luft, man muss an der Sprache arbeiten. Auf deutscher Seite bemüht sich Karl Philipp Moritz um das, was er in einer Rede in der Königlichen Akademie der Wissenschaften in Berlin „die Bildsamkeit der Deutschen Sprache" nennt.[138] Es fällt dort beispielsweise auf, dass „Mangel an deutschen Kunstwörtern in der Grössenlehre" herrscht.[139] „Wenn das gemeinsame Leben neue Zweige treibt, so treibt es auch neue Worte", schreibt Friedrich Adolf Trendelenburg, der Verfechter einer *lingua rationalis*.[140] Der Forscher ringt „das bleibende Gepräge für sein Ergebnis der Sprache ab".[141] Und da ja gilt, dass „auch das abstracteste Denken mit und in der Sprache ist", und es zudem drängt, die „Zurückführung auf einen einfachen Begriff durch eine einfache Bezeichnung" zu leisten, soll in dieser „aufsteigenden Linie" und aus der „Selbstbewegung der inneren Anschauung" heraus das Begreifen und der Begriff zusammengeführt werden.[142]

Oliver Byrne hat für sich die Vorteile der geometrischen, figürlichen – und farbgestützten – Sprache entdeckt und so bei-spielsweise den Zeitgewinn bei der Wahrnehmung demonstrativ quantifiziert.[143] Es fehlte nicht an Versuchen, die unterschiedlichen Sprachen mit ihren je eigenen Vorteilen zu vergleichen und zusammenzuführen. Johann Jakob Wagner sprach schon 1803 in seiner *Philosophie der Erziehungskunst* von der „Leichtigkeit, Mathematik in Philosophie zu übersetzen".[144] Die Logik wäre ihm dagegen schon immer als ungenügend erschienen, und er „suchte die Architektur der Welt und der Erkenntnis immer in der Mathematik".[145] In ihr erkannte er „die Form der Objektivierung des Geistigen d. h. die Sprache". Schließlich hätte ihn der „Dualismus" von Arithmetik und Geometrie dazu gebracht, von einem höher liegenden Gemeinsamen – der „Anschauung" – auszugehen.[146] In seinem erstmals 1830 und 1851 neu erschienenen *Organon* breitet Wagner das ganze Spektrum unterschiedlicher Sprachen und Sprachformen aus.[147] Er unterscheidet Zahlen- und Linienschrift, die Linien, Figuren, „Trigonometrie d.h. Wechselbeziehungen", „Körper d.h. Gestalten" und auch noch die Zusammensetzung von Linien und Figuren umfasst.[148] Er nennt die Geometrie, die ja die „Grundzüge zu einer Theorie der Gestalten" liefere, eine „Beziehungsschrift" und eine „Abstraktion von der Bilderschrift".[149] Er legt der „Construktion der Sprache" das Schema Wort-Zahl-Figur-Bild zugrunde und bildet daraus Analogien zu Poesie-Musik-Malerei-Plastik oder Mensch-Tier-Pflanze-Mineral.[150] Und er verweist auf die „Parallelreihe" Idee-Begriff-Wahrnehmung-Vorstellung respektive Symbol-Exempel-Zeichen-Bild.[151] Zudem stellt er das Ganze in seiner *Mathematische[n] Philosophie* in eine historische Perspektive, wonach sich das „spekulative Wissen" pythagoräisch als Zahl und Figur darstellte, die dann, unter der Dominanz des Wortes, in ein „mechanisches" Wesen überführt wurden „und Mathematik genannt werden".[152] Das Bild hingegen sei „zum zufälligen Spiele" herabgesunken; „unsere Kunst producirt nur den Schein."[153] So bleibt im Hinblick auf die wissenschaftliche Fragestellung das Verhältnis Wort-Zahl-Figur im Mittelpunkt des Interesses stehen. Und das beschäftigt Wagner insbesondere bei seinem Vorhaben, Mathematik in Philosophie zu übersetzen. Aus dem Zustand eines „todten Mechanismus" will er die Mathematik herausholen und als „die natürliche Ideensprache oder Sprache des Geistes" sowie als „die einzige allgemeine Wissenschaft oder Philosophie" rehabilitieren.[154]

Man muss dem Duktus der Darstellung – der Sprache! – gemäß diesem mathematisch-philosophischen Verständnis folgen. Als erstes Beispiel wählt Wagner 1803 in der *Philosophie der Erziehungskunst* symbolhaft den Pythagorassatz, der ja auch 1847 auf dem Titel von Byrnes *Euclid* erscheint. „Jede Linie ist Ausdruck von Bewegung, Bahn eines bewegten Körpers, zwar fixirt im Raume für die äußere Anschauung, aber doch nur construirbar durch den innern Sinn und in der Zeit beweglich."[155] Nun wird die Figur konstruiert: „Es sey nun eine Linie als Bahn gegeben; es komme dieser Linie von einer andern Seite auf gleichem Wege aber in entgegengesetzter Richtung eine andere entgegen, so werden beide Linien ... sich treffen, und falls ihre Kraft gleich ist, sich in einem Punkte aufs Zero der Bewegung reduciren."[156] Solcherlei Darlegung bedarf eines gewissen Aufwandes; es sind ja bildliche Vorstellungen, Erweiterungen ins Physikalische (des Vergleichs einer Linie mal mit „Hebel", mal mit „Pendul"), die den Vorgang unterstützen sollen, auf dass „unser Zögling Geist und Natur in ihrer gegenseitigen Spiegelung kennen lernen" kann.[157] Die „Sacherklärung" ist längst in eine „Worterklärung", „durch welche Begriffe erst gebildet werden", überführt worden, so wie das Ephraim Salomon Unger 1833 in seiner Einführung zum Lehrgebäude Euklids vorsieht.[158] Die Erklärungen sind durch die didaktischen Absichten eingeholt, wodurch sie auch begründet sind.

Auf diese Weise entsteht bei Wilhelm von Türk, dem Anhänger Pestalozzis, umfassender eine „Formen-Lehre", die im Stile der Zeit, in klar didaktischer Ausrichtung in einem Frage- und Antwortspiel zwischen Lehrer und Schüler ausgebreitet wird.[159]

„Lehrer: (Indem er einen Punkt, eine gerade Linie, und eine krumme Linie an die Tafel zeichnet.) Wie nennt man (auf 1 zeigend) dies Zeichen hier?
Kinder: Einen Punkt.
Lehrer: (auf 2 und 3 zeigend) Und diese beide Zeichen hier?
Kinder: Linien."

Der Reihe nach werden diese Übungen an den fünf Sinnen erprobt und auf Form, Farbe und Richtung ausgelegt; es soll letztlich die „Sprache für die innere Anschauung" gefunden und gebildet werden.[160] Es trifft sich alles wieder mit den Empfehlungen, die später auch Oliver Byrne mit seiner Privilegierung der Auge und Ohr gleichzeitig bemühenden mündlichen Demonstrationen verbindet.[161] Und unter dem Strich sind es, wie im Titel des Handbuches von Türk, die sinnlichen Wahrnehmungen, die als Ausgangspunkt im Zentrum der Diskussion stehen. Schließlich galt ja auch in aufklärerischen Zeiten, folgt man der Allgemeine[n] Theorie des Denkens und Empfindens, mit der Johann August Eberhard 1776 den Preis der Königlichen Akademie der Wissenschaften gewann, dass in der „neuesten spekulativen Philosophie" die „Entdeckungen in der Theorie der Empfindungen" insbesondere als Fortschritt aufgefallen wären.[162] Eberhard hob das in einem besonderen ersten Punkt hervor und zitiert „die Entdeckungen, die man über die Natur einiger abgeleiteter Eigenschaften ... der Körper nämlich der Farben, machte".[163] Es ging damals, in Übereinstimmung mit so vielen anderen Bemühungen, darum, „die Weltweisheit aus dem Himmel der Schulen herabzuziehen, und in die menschliche Gesellschaft einzuführen".[164]

Byrnes *Euclid* – doch ein Kunstwerk!

„La logique veut que l'art soit l'expression plastique de tout notre être."
– MONDRIAN, *Néo-Plasticisme*, 1920[165]

In der Nachfolge Pestalozzis und seiner *Anschauungslehre der Zahlenverhältnisse* drängt ohnehin alles, auch das Abstrakteste, in die physische, in die plastische Welt zurück. Byrnes Bild der euklidischen Geometrie als Gehirngymnastik deutet dies ebenso unfreiwillig wie überdeutlich an. Auch das entspricht einer alten Einsicht. In der Einleitung zu den *Philosophiae Naturalis Principia Mathematica* schreibt Isaac Newton am 8. Mai 1686, die Beschreibungen der geraden und krummen Linien, auf denen die Geometrie beruht, gehörten zur Mechanik.[166] Zudem, die Geometrie setze voraus; man müsse anderweitig nach Erklärung suchen.[167] Und andererseits bedarf die Geometrie der Erweiterungen jeglicher Art, um einsehbar und verstanden zu werden. Newton fordert das mit seinem Verweis, die Geometrie sei ja nur ein Teil einer sehr viel umfassenderen *mechanica universalis*, geradezu heraus. Man gelangt empirisch zu einer solchen „physischen Geometrie", so wie man aus der Beobachtung heraus zu Sätzen gelangen kann.[168] Man darf auch Albert Einstein mit seinem berühmten Vortrag zur „Geometrie und Erfahrung" bemühen, der seinerseits die „praktische Geometrie" als eine Naturwissenschaft, ja als den ältesten Zweig der Physik betrachtet.[169] Dem ging die Feststellung voraus, es sei „doch sicher, dass die Mathematik überhaupt und im speziellen auch die Geometrie ihre Entstehung dem Bedürfnis verdankt, etwas zu erfahren über das Verhalten wirklicher Dinge".[170] Das mindert nichts am hohen Wert jener „freien Schöpfungen des menschlichen Geistes", als die Einstein die Axiome erinnerte, wobei er dann – dem Entwicklungsgange im Umgang mit Symbolen entsprechend – beifügt: „Unter ,Punkt', ,Gerade' usw. sind in der axiomatischen Geometrie nur inhaltsleere Begriffsschemata zu verstehen.[171] Ein befriedigender Zustand ist das nicht und der Zusammenhang mit der Wirklichkeit ausdrücklich gefragt. Die Brisanz liegt in der Verbindung, worauf sie es alle – mit unterschiedlicher Akzentuierung – abgesehen haben.

Hierin treffen sich der Mathematiker und der Künstler. Und beim wechselseitigen Interesse und Einsatz der Mittel verschwindet von Zeit zu Zeit die eindeutige Kontur. Doch, weshalb sollte man dem Mathematiker weniger Kreativität zugestehen als dem Künstler und umgekehrt? Das mystische Dunkel ist Euklid nicht weniger fremd als dem modernen Bilderfinder, zumal wenn man sich der Anfänge der großen Tradition der Figuren- und Symbolbildung besinnt. Max Simon hatte 1901 auf die vorausgegangene Frage und Publikation Hubert Müllers *Besitzt die heutige*

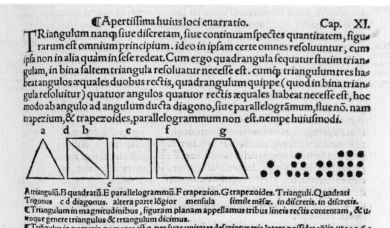

A triangulū. B quadratū. E parallelogrammū. F trapezion. G trapezoides. Trianguli. Quadrati
Trigonus c d diagonus. altera parte lōgior mensula simile mēsæ. in discretis. in discretis.
ℂTriangulum in magnitudinibus , figuram planam appellamus tribus lineis rectis contentam , & u=
troque genere triangulū & trtangulum dicimus.
ℂTriāgulus in numeris. numerus est q per suas unitates descriptus tria latera possidet gꝗlia, ut 1 5. 9. 6. ꝗ
ℂQuadratum, quatuor angulos & quatuor latera possidet æqualia.

2   ℂQuadran=

31

Schulgeometrie noch die Vorzüge des Euclid-Originals? geantwortet:
„Die deutsche Schulgeometrie hat sie nie besessen."[172] Vieles ist
Wunschdenken, idealtypische Vorstellung mathematisch strin-
genter Denkweise. Der Ruf nach einer strengen Wissenschaft,
weit in die Geisteswissenschaften hineinreichend,[173] und das
Bedürfnis eines „scharfen Werkzeuges"[174] hat immer wieder die
tatsächlichen physischen Schwierigkeiten vergessen lassen. Dass
nach dieser Maßgabe alles Präzise der Geometrie und alle Abwei-
chung davon der Mechanik, gleichbedeutend mit Praxis, zugewiesen würde, hat Newton mit der Feststellung quittiert: Die Fehler
liegen nicht in der Sache, sondern beim Nutzer. („Attamen errores
non sunt artis, sed artificum.")[175]

Blickt man nun andererseits auf die Kunst, so kann von jener
„Gestalt-Krise", die Steck 1942 bezogen auf die Mathematik be-
schwor, keine Rede sein.[176] Es scheint schon eher, dass dem von ihm
gewählten Motto von Leibniz, *Mathesis est scientia imaginabilium*,
der Mathematik als Wissenschaft von den Vorstellungen, eine noch
viel weitere Bedeutung, als vielleicht vermutet, zukommt. Das
Mathematische ist zu diesem Zeitpunkt längst und wie nie zuvor
in den Bereich nicht nur der Vorstellungen, sondern in denjenigen
des Sichtbaren, des tatsächlichen Physischen und Mechanischen
getreten, und diesmal nicht aus Not, sondern in überzeugter Absicht. Seit Piet Mondrian, und darin von Amédée Ozenfant und Le
Corbusier gefolgt und in die Architektur übertragen, ist im Begriff
des Plastischen, demjenigen der Gestalt in mancher Hinsicht ähn-
lich, umschrieben, was aus dem entsprechenden Verständnis und
aus der Einsicht heraus mit Macht in ein Äußeres drängt. Es geht
dabei um Grundsätzliches, nicht bloß um Formanalogie oder um

geometrisierende und stilisierende Formfindung. Auch reicht der
bloße Hinweis auf Reinigung und Einfachheit nicht aus, denn das
Abstrakte soll der plastische Ausdruck des Universellen bleiben,
gemäß jenem Wechselspiel von innen und außen, bei dem die tiefs-
te Verinnerlichung des Äußeren sich mit der reinsten Veräußerlichung des Innern trifft („car l'abstrait reste l'expression plastique
en fonction de l'universel: c'est l'intériorisation la plus approfondie
de l'extérieur et l'extériosiration la plus pure de l'intérieur.")[177] Es
ist Mondrian, der 1920 diese dezidierte Absage an alle bloß ober-
flächlichen Geometrismen, die doch nur außen vor bleiben, trifft.
Nur im tiefsten Verstehen und Begreifen lässt sich das Abstrakte,
das Mathematische und Geometrische, an die Wirklichkeit ziehen und – notgedrungen – in eine künstlerische Form bringen. Es
ist klar, dass sich die Verbindungen dort am ehesten ergeben, wo
dieser notwendige Bezug zur Wahrnehmung im Sinne einer physi-
kalischen Geometrie als Problem gesehen und wo er – zwecks Demonstration – ausdrücklich angestrebt, gesucht wurde, wie auch
bei Oliver Byrne. Insofern wird die Sonderstellung und Einzigar-
tigkeit des Byrne'schen *Euclid* erst – a posteriori – richtig bewusst.

Byrnes 1847 an den Anfang seiner Einleitung zum *Euclid*
gestellte Präzisierung, es ginge ihm eben nicht um irgendwelche
angenehmen Unterhaltungen, sondern um Wahrheitssuche und
Wissen, trifft sich mit den analogen Aussagen eines Mondrian.[178]
Mondrian geht es um ein universelles plastisches Mittel. Einleitend zu seinem Manifest *Le Néo-Plasticisme* (Abb. 42) unter-
streicht er seine Auffassung, wonach der Künstler den plastischen
Ausdruck über das Bewusste erreiche. Die Erscheinung der Kunst
sei so insgesamt der plastische Ausdruck des Unbewussten und

PLATE V.

EXAMPLES OF ISOMERISM.

Metamerism.

Polymerism.

OIL OF LEMONS.

OIL OF BERGAMOT.

ALDEHYDE.

OIL OF TURPENTINE.
(*Spirits of Turpentine.*)

OIL OF BLACK PEPPER.

ACETIC ETHER.

OIL OF JUNIPER.

OIL OF ORANGES.

OIL OF PEPPERMINT.

OIL OF COPAIBA.

OIL OF ROSES.

OIL OF LIMES.

OLEFIANT GAS.

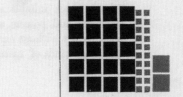

OIL OF LAVENDER.

des Bewussten; sie zeige die Beziehung zwischen den beiden auf, ändert sich, aber die Kunst selbst bleibt unveränderlich.[179] So wird gleichsam die didaktisch vermittelnde, sichtbar machende Seite, wie sie dem *Euclid* von 1847 beigegeben war, in der neuen Kunstauffassung in vergleichbarer Weise verdeutlicht, und die entsprechende Zielsetzung erklärt. Auch bei Mondrian geht es nicht primär um die bei diesem Prozess entstehende (Erscheinungs-) Form. Form als generelle Festlegung einer Erscheinung im Bild soll, umgekehrt, vermieden werden und stattdessen der Prozess hin zu Präzision und Abstraktion als universales plastisches Mittel im Vordergrund stehen.[180] Um dies zu verdeutlichen, kritisiert Mondrian ausdrücklich den – bloß äußerlichen – Reinigungs- und Vereinfachungsprozess, der sich in der Architektur zuweilen beobachten ließe. Nur wenige würden die plastische Wirkung des Abstrakten erreichen.[181]

Die Moderne kündigt sich auf dem neuen und alten Sockel des umstrittenen Leib-Seele-Konfliktes an. Man sucht die *raison* neu. Paul Dermée schreibt im ersten Heft von *L'Esprit Nouveau*, in Sachen Intelligenz geschehe alles im Bewusstsein und in einem hellen Zimmer.[182] Licht! Und gleichwohl sieht er den notwendigen Ausgleich und das erstrebte Gleichgewicht von Intelligenz und „lyrisme", wie das neue Stichwort nun lautet. Léonce Rosenberg bringt dazu zwei Formeln ins Gespräch, eine von Georges Braque zitierte und eine veränderte eigene: „J'aime la règle qui corrige l'émotion." (Ich liebe die Regel, die die Emotion korrigiert.) und Rosenbergs humanisierte Version: „J'aime le sentiment qui humanise la Règle." (Ich liebe das Gefühl, das die Regel humanisiert.)[183] Waren es früher im Großbritannien Byrnes insbesondere Ethik und Moral, die der Mathematik ihren tieferen Sinn erschließen sollten, so macht jetzt die Psychologie ihre Aufwartung, immer im Bestreben, die reinen Gedanken in die Welt zu bringen. Doch Zurückhaltung war gefordert. Zum Gebot der Stunde, „rebuter l'intelligence" (weg mit der Intelligenz), setzte Dermée auch die Empfehlung „pas de logique apparente" (keine Vorzeigelogik).[184] Nein, allzu offensichtlich sollte sich der neue Hang zur Gesetzmäßigkeit nicht äußern. Und Amédée Ozenfant und Charles-Edouard Jeanneret, der spätere Le Corbusier, die auf der nächstfolgenden Seite des ersten Heftes von *L'Esprit Nouveau* vom mechanischen Ursprung der plastischen Empfindung, Verlässlichkeit, Konstanten und Universalität für ihre künstlerische Arbeit ableiten wollten, kamen sehr schnell zur Einsicht, dass das nicht mehr als Grundlage und Ausgangspunkt sein konnte.[185]

Vermittlung und Klärung und die Besinnung auf das Wesentliche sind allerdings wieder einmal notwendig. Die Künste und die Wissenschaften wären so sehr angewachsen, dass die Erleichterung ihres Erwerbs nunmehr genauso wichtig sei wie deren Wachstum, so der erste, hier aus dem Zusammenhang gerissene Satz aus Byrnes *Euclid*.[186] Edouard Le Roy unternimmt es in *La pensée mathématique pure*, die auf seinen in den Jahren 1914/15 und

1918/19 am Collège de France gehaltenen Vorlesungen beruht, seine Vorstellung der reinen Mathematik als imaginative, das Sinnliche mit dem Intellektuellen verbindende Sichtweise zu charakterisieren.[187] Und das bezieht sich insbesondere auf die Geometrie, weshalb er von der spezifischen „intuition géométrique" spricht. Immer wieder drängt die Geometrie zur Wirklichkeit und in die sensible Welt hinein.[188] Le Roy trägt so der Wechselwirkung und der Tatsache einer physischen Geometrie Rechnung. Die Geometrie erscheint ihm als eine sensibilisierte Mathematik; sie ist von dieser Welt.[189] Die eigentliche reine Mathematik findet er in der Analyse. Das war schon Leibniz' Weg.[190]

Die Geometrie und Euklid sind dem Kompromiss mit dem Sinnlichen also stärker ausgesetzt. Und dies ist längst Teil ihrer Geschichte und Kultur. De Stijl und Mondrian waren diesbezüglich näher an der Sache, als die bloßen Bildermacher. Die Malerei ist das Mittel und nicht das Ziel, schrieb auch Léonce Rosenberg.[191] Und selbst, wenn es um die Farbe geht, scheinen die Argumente bei Byrne und bei Ozenfant und Le Corbusier vergleichbar. „Quand on parle peinture, on parle forcément couleur" (Wer Malerei sagt, meint zwangsläufig Farbe), liest man im programmatischen Text zum *Purisme*, der dort ansetzt, wo zu Beginn der Argumentation Logik aus den menschlichen Konstanten abgeleitet und als Kontrollinstanz gegen den zuweilen phantastischen Gang der Intuition eingesetzt erscheint.[192] Für sich allein genommen, wären Farben riskant, ja gefährlich.[193] Sie müssten der Sache dienen, sie sollen im Wesentlichen konstruktiv sein.[194] Malerei, so liest man weiterhin zum *Purisme*, sei die Verbindung gereinigter, angeordneter und architektonisierter Elemente.[195] Die Parallelen zu Byrne[196] sind nicht zu übersehen. Selbst die schon von ihm betonte größere Geschwindigkeit bei der optischen Aufnahme von Farben ist hier mitgedacht. Der Farbe sei gemäß der Ordnung in der Wahrnehmung die Eigenschaft von Schock eigen, indem sie dank der unmittelbaren optischen Wahrnehmung der Erkenntnis der Form, die zumindest teilweise bereits eine Kreation des Gehirns sei, vorangehe.[197]

Nimmt man hinzu, wieviel Gewicht Byrne der didaktischen Seite seines *Euclid* zukommen ließ, so findet sich eine noch deutlichere Parallele bei Gyorgy Kepes, der in der Tradition von De Stijl und unter dem direkten Einfluss der Gestaltpsychologie 1944 sein *Language of Vision* publizierte (Abb. 34, 35, 37, 41).[198] Der Gesichtspunkt der Sprache, der Vermittlung, ist hier gleichermaßen eingekehrt. In der Nachfolge Mondrians spricht Kepes von plastischer Organisation, wobei er zur Klärung die Umschreibung der Formung von Sinneseindrücken zu organischem Ganzen verwendet.[199] Der Gestaltungsprozess steht im Vordergrund, aber natürlich geht es hier vermehrt auch um visuelle Darstellung und natürlich um das geschaffene Bild. Gleichwohl ist verblüffend, wie sehr auch Kepes der Überlappung von Farbflächen seine Beachtung schenkt. Das dient nicht mehr der Darstellung

Ill. 33
Ezekiel W. Dimond, *The Chemistry of Combustion*,
Worcester 1867
– *Diagram 1. Elements employed and compounds
formed in the process of Combustion.*
– *Diagramm 1. Im Verbrennungsprozess entstehende
Verbindungen und verwendete Elemente.*
– *Diagramme 1. Eléments employés et composés formés
dans le procès de la combustion.*

Ill. 34
Gyorgy Kepes, *Language of Vision*, Chicago 1944,
p. 51
– Illustration of the "laws of visual organization".
– Illustration zu den „Gesetzen der Wahrneh-
mungsorganisation".
– Illustration des « lois de l'organisation visuelle ».

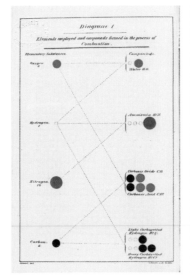

33   34

geometrischer Grundformen, wie bei Byrne, dafür umso mehr der Farbabgleichung und generell den visuellen Phänomenen.[200] Kepes' historischer Rückblick reicht bis zu Helmholtz, er erwähnt flüchtig Leonardo da Vinci, natürlich Goethe, aber auch Arthur Schopenhauer. Der hatte in seiner frühen Studie *Ueber das Sehn und die Farben* 1816 schon im ersten Satz den größeren Rahmen mitsamt den inhärenten Problemen beschrieben: „Alle Anschauung ist eine intellektuale. Denn ohne den Verstand käme es nimmermehr zur Anschauung, zur Wahrnehmung, Apprehension von Objekten, sondern es bliebe bei der bloßen Empfindung, die allenfalls, als Schmerz oder Wohlbehagen, eine Bedeutung in Bezug auf den Willen haben könnte, übrigens aber ein Wechsel bedeutungsloser Zustände und nichts einer Erkenntniß Aehnliches wäre."[201] Goethes *Farbenlehre* wollte und konnte er nicht den Status einer Theorie zuweisen. Andererseits werden seine Überlegungen der Psychophysik die entscheidenden Argumente liefern.

In Großbritannien schien – zu Byrnes und De Morgans Zeiten – jeder Versuch und jede Notwendigkeit, die engeren Grenzen der Mathematik zu verlassen, in die Ethik und die Moral zu führen. In modernen Zeiten ist es die Psychologie, die sich insbesondere der Grenzbereiche und aller mit dem Leib-Seele-Problem verbundenen Schwierigkeiten annimmt. Die Psychophysik hat die Künste gerade in jenem Moment direkt betroffen, als sie sich nach festen Gesetzen und Regeln – auch in besonderer Weise der Geometrie – entsann.[202] Und natürlich zeigt sich die Gestaltpsychologie an Fragen wie derjenigen von den sensorischen Prägnanzmomenten oder an den Wirkungsweisen der Farbe besonders interessiert. Alles hat in Byrnes *Euclid* eine wichtige Rolle gespielt.

In seiner den Methoden gewidmeten Einleitung zu *Beiträge zur Theorie der Sinneswahrnehmung* schreibt Wilhelm Wundt 1862: „Der Versuch die psychologischen Thatsachen auf metaphysischem Grund aufzubauen, hängt auf's innigste zusammen mit der mathematischen Behandlungsweise der Psychologie. Diese ist eine fast nothwendige Folge davon, dass die metaphysische Psychologie die deduktive Methode in sich einschliesst."[203] Das weist in geradezu imperativer Weise darauf hin, wie sehr auch die Geometrie und deren Versinnlichung gefragt sein könnte und ist. Wundt fährt fort: „Wo in einer Wissenschaft eine grössere Zahl von Thatsachen aus einigen Axiomen durch eine Reihe mehr oder minder verwickelter Schlüsse sich ableiten lässt, ohne dass doch zu dieser Ableitung die einfachen Verfahrungsweisen der formalen Logik genügen, da wird die Wissenschaft genöthigt die mathematische Zeichensprache zu Hülfe zu nehmen."[204] Dass die Natur zuweilen genötigt werden müsse, auf die Fragen der Vernunft zu antworten, hatte schon Kant postuliert.[205] Es bedarf solcher Unterstützung menschlicher Erkenntnismöglichkeit. Nach dieser Maßgabe formulierte Wundt: „Diese (=Zeichensprache) ist nur ein wirksames Hülfsmittel des Denkens, nur eine vervielfältigte Anwendung der logischen Gesetze, welche die Denkresultate auf jeder einzelnen Stufe der Schlussreihe durch bestimmte Zeichen fixirt."[206]

An dieser Stelle hatte Wundt noch eine Fußnote hinzugesetzt, die seine Einschätzung vom diesbezüglichen Entwicklungsstand der Mathematik enthielt: „Der Mathematiker dürfte diese Definition leicht zu weit finden, weil die Mathematik in der That bis jetzt eine so allgemeine Anwendung noch nicht gefunden hat. Aber es lässt sich, wie mir scheint, nicht verkennen, dass die ganze neuere Mathematik dieser Verallgemeinerung des Calküls, die sie lediglich zu einer erweiterten Logik macht, zustrebt.“[207]

Von hier aus sind die Entwicklungsstränge häufig genug getrennte Wege gegangen. Man kann es offenlassen, wie genau Byrnes mondrianscher *Euclid* zu dieser Entwicklung oder zu einer dieser Entwicklungen passt. Jene Mathematiker haben sich für ihn jedenfalls sehr wenig oder überhaupt nicht interessiert, nicht einmal die Euklidianer. Andererseits haben sich die Wissenschaften schon immer vornehmlich mit sich selbst beschäftigt und ihre „scharfen Principien und Methoden“ nur allzu gerne gegen die weniger potente Philosophie (in ihrem eigenen Kreis), was immer man darunter verstand, ausgespielt.[208] Auch die Fechner'sche Psychophysik, jene auf eine uralte Sache gesetzte neue Wissenschaft, die mit so umfassender Fragestellung ansetzte, sollte gemäß einer ersten Definition von 1860 „kurz eine exacte Lehre von den Beziehungen zwischen Leib und Seele“ bieten.[209] Exakt, wissenschaftlich sollte es werden!

Oliver Byrnes *Euclid* bleibt ein Solitär. Deshalb sind die potentiellen Verbindungen zu Pestalozzi oder zur mathematischen Philosophie eines Wagner, zum Gesichtspunkt der Sprache genauso wie zu dem der Geometrie umso interessanter und aufschlussreicher. Byrne stand den Tatsachen eines Helmholtz näher, als man vielleicht auf den ersten Blick vermutet. Man habe es „in der Geometrie stets mit idealen Gebilden zu tun … deren körperliche Darstellung in der Wirklichkeit immer nur eine Annäherung an die Forderungen des Begriffes ist, und wird darüber, ob ein Körper fest, ob seine Flächen eben, seine Kanten gerade sind, erst mittels derselben Sätze entscheiden, deren tatsächliche Richtigkeit durch die Prüfung zu erweisen wäre“.[210] Annäherungen an jene universalen Wahrheiten sind es, zu denen es Byrne, den Mathematiker, genauso hinzog wie Mondrian, den Künstler. Vielleicht ist Geometrie gar nicht jenes, mangels anderweitiger sicherer Grundlagen als unerschütterlich und konklusiv beschriebene Gebilde, dessen Erfindung man Euklid zuschreiben will, sondern doch vielmehr pythagoräischer, eine Vorstellung der Welt in Formen und Figuren, die nach dieser Maßgabe weniger konklusiv, stattdessen auf einen Blick erfahrbar sind. Oliver Byrne hat dieser Vorstellung Farbe verliehen und damit einer Sprache vorgegriffen, die sich in moderner Zeit *Neue Gestaltung*, so der bekannte Titel eines Buches von Theo van Doesburg, nannte.

Theodor W. Adorno setzte seiner *Negative[n] Dialektik* ein Diktum Walter Benjamins voran: „… man müsse durch die Eiswüste der Abstraktion hindurch, um zu konkretem Philosophieren bündig zu gelangen.“[211] Eine Eiswüste, die man schnellstmöglich hinter sich lassen möchte, ist das keineswegs! Alles dreht sich um diese Abstraktion und deren Drängen hinein in die sichtbare Welt, bei Byrne und Mondrian in jedem Falle. Man will sie nicht aufgeben, sondern sichtbar machen! „L'abstrait reste l'expresssion plastique en fonction de l'universel: c'est l'intériorisation la plus approfondie de l'extérieur et l'extériorisation la plus pure de l'intérieur.“[212] Bei diesem Satz aus dem Manifest *Le Néo-Plasticisme* von 1920 hatte Mondrian sich auf den dritten Teil seiner im *De Stijl* publizierten Bemerkungen „De Nieuwe Beelding in de Schilderkunst“ berufen, wo er sich dem Verhältnis „abstrakt/mathematisch“ in besonderer Weise gewidmet hatte.[213] Auf Aristoteles ginge die entsprechende Gleichsetzung zurück. In Tat und Wahrheit steht hier Mondrian noch ganz deutlich in jener, ihm insbesondere auch von Mathieu Schoenmaekers vermittelten[214] Tradition, in der das Interesse an universalen Vorstellungen lebendig gehalten wurde, und der die Geometrie schon immer als Ausgangspunkt und Euklid als Kronzeuge diente, noch viel umfassender in den Worten Oliver Byrnes: „If we wanted authorities to prove the importance and usefulness of geometry, we might quote every philosopher since the days of Plato.“[215]

Anmerkungen

1 Frege 1893, S. xiv, Anm. 1.
2 Vgl. Steck 1981, S. 179 f. Vgl. auch insbesondere Steck 1943, S. 131 ff.: passim u. S. 133 („Schaufähigkeit").
3 Zitat nach Knittermeyer 1939, S. 59 f., in: Steck 1943, Anm. 24, S. 148.
4 Vgl. Steck 1981, S. 180.
5 Vgl. Speiser 1932, S. 14.
6 Ibidem. Damit steht er in einer Tradition, die bis auf Schelling 1797 (Vorrede, S. iii f.) zurückreicht, der ja gegen die „bisherige ... Vermischung ganz heterogener Principien" in der Philosophie argumentierte und sie nun in eine „reine" und eine „angewandte" schied: „Die reine theoretische Philosophie beschäftigt sich bloß mit der Untersuchung über die Realität unsers Wissens überhaupt."
7 Vgl. Schelling 1797, S. iv.
8 Vgl. Rickert 1913, S. 189 u. 188.
9 Rickert 1913, S. 191, ergänzt hier: „... so lange eine mechanische Theorie fehlt", äußert aber kurz zuvor, dass auf dem Weg ihrer Vervollkommung „eine naturwissenschaftliche, d. h. eine mechanische Erklärung eines physischen Vorganges geradezu mit einer Veranschaulichung identifiziert werden müsse".
10 Vgl. Bloch 1909.
11 Vgl. unten.
12 Vgl. Husserl 1936, S. 77 ff. Entscheidend für unseren Zusammenhang (vgl. auch unten) ist die Analyse der Bedeutung der Geometrie vor und nach Galilei (S. 103 ff.), was vorlag, „ohne dass er, und wohlbegreiflich, das Bedürfnis empfand, in die Art, wie die idealisierende Leistung ursprünglich erwuchs (nämlich wie sie erwuchs aus dem Untergrunde der vorgeometrischen sinnlichen Welt und ihrer praktischen Künste), einzugehen und sich in Fragen zu vertiefen nach dem Ursprung der apodiktischen mathematischen Evidenz".
13 Vgl. Rickert 1910/11, S. 1 ff.: S. 7.
14 Vgl. Husserl 1910/11, S. 289 ff.: S. 289.
15 Id., S. 341.
16 Ibidem.
17 Vgl. Frege 1882, S. 48 ff.: S. 56; id., in: Frege 1964, S. 106 ff.: S. 114.
18 Ibidem.
19 Vgl. Frege 1893, Vorwort, S. xiv.

20 Id., S. xxv.
21 Id., S. 3.
22 Id., S. 1 ff. mit Verweis auf die vorausgegangene Publikation *Grundlagen der Arithmetik*, Breslau 1884.
23 Id., S. xix. Andererseits wehrt er sich (S. xii) natürlich gegen Annahmen wie „metaphysica sunt, non leguntur" und „mathematica sunt, non leguntur".
24 Id., S. xvii f. u. xx.
25 Id., S. xxi.
26 Vgl. Russell 1897, S. 1.
27 Id., S. 10 ff.
28 Vgl. Riemann 1892, S. 272 ff.: S. 272 u. 286. Die am Raumbegriff ansetzende Kritik der Geometrie ist dann besser verständlich, wenn man sich des Wolff'schen Verständnisses der Mathematik entsinnt; die erste Definition der Anfangsgründe der Geometrie lautet: „Die Geometrie ist eine Wissenschaft des Raumes, den die körperlichen Dinge nach ihrer Länge, Breite und Dicke einnehmen." (Hier zit. nach der späten Ausgabe: Wolff 1755, S. 65.) Gleichzeitig findet man aber auch die übliche Definition der „Geometrie, das ist, die Wissenschaft der Massen, oder der Grössen, in so fern sie als an einander hangend können gemessen werden ...", also der ‚Messkunst' (vgl. Fabricius 1752, S. 454).
29 Dem war in direktem Bezug zu Riemann der Beitrag „Über die Tatsachen, die der Geometrie zugrunde liegen" vorausgegangen (in: *Nachrichten von der Königlichen Gesellschaft der Wissenschaften und der Georg-August-Universität aus dem Jahre 1868*, Nr. 9, S. 193 ff.; abgedruckt in: Helmholtz 1968, S. 32 ff.).
30 Vgl. Helmholtz 1879, S. 25.
31 Ibidem.
32 Id., S. 23.
33 Vgl. Husserl 1891, S. 131: „Das Ziel, das sich Frege setzt, ist also ein chimärisches zu nennen."
34 Id., S. 130.
35 Ibidem.
36 Vgl. dazu insbesondere: Husserl 1913, Einleitung, S. 1 u. 7 ff.
37 Vgl. Helmholtz 1879, S. 7.
38 Wie unzeitgemäß auch die Frege'sche Begriffsschrift war, betont Lothar Kreiser in der Einleitung zu Frege, 1973, S. viii.
39 Cajori 1928, S. 429.
40 Vgl. Cajori 1928, S. 429.
41 Ibidem.

42 Id., Anm. 4, mit Bezug auf Heiberg 1912, S. 20.
43 Hier zit. nach Cajori, 1928, S. 429 f. (nach: De Morgan 1849, S. 92 f.): „Geometrisches Denken und arithmetische Methoden haben ihre jeweils eigene Funktion. Sie in der Grundlagenbildung zu vermischen, schadet dem ordentlichen Erwerb beider."
44 Vgl. auch unten.
45 Vgl. De Morgan 1872, S. 199: „Dieser Autor war wirklich von seiner Sache überzeugt und meint es ernst. Er ist nicht der Einzige, der Unsinn schreibt, weil er das mathematische Unendliche (der Größe) mit dem verwechselt hat, was Theoretiker heute richtiger mit dem Unbegrenzten, dem Uneingeschränkten oder dem Absoluten ausdrücken."
46 Vgl. De Morgan 1915, S. 329, Anm. 1. Daselbst, S. 344, die Kritik von Oliver Byrnes *Theory of Parallels* (1840).
47 Allzu oft ist das der größere Rahmen, in dem auch von mathematischer Seite Mathematikgeschichte betrieben wird! Vgl. Casselman 2000, S. 1257 ff. (S. 1260 zu Byrne).
48 Vgl. Phillips 2005, S. 105 ff.
49 Vgl. De Morgan 1838, Vorwort, S. xvi.
50 Vgl. Grattan-Guinness 1992, S. 1 ff.; Phillips 2005, S. 105 ff.
51 De Morgans Definitionen von *ratio* und Proportion werden noch von Thomas L. Heath für die besten gehalten (vgl. Heath 1956, S. 116 ff.). Die Diskussion zu Eutocius und den Begriffen *pelikotes* resp. *pelikos* ist allerdings lange vor De Morgan bei Meibomius 1655, S. 11, differenzierend geführt worden.
52 In demselben Jahr erschien auch die Publikation, die De Morgans besondere arithmetische Grundlegung seiner mathematischen Forschungen und Interessen belegt; vgl. De Morgan 1847.
53 Vgl. unten.
54 Solchen Äußerungen lag in erster Linie methodische Absicht zugrunde. Natürlich war das Interesse an Überlappungen von Geometrie und Arithmetik damals groß. 1846 publizierte Hermann Scheffler, ausgehend von einer Gauss'schen Beobachtung, seine Arbeit *Über das Verhältniß der Arithmetik zur Geometrie, ins-*

besondere über die geometrische Bedeutung der imaginären Zahlen, wobei dann eben einleitend die unterschiedliche Zuordnung zu „bildlicher" Darstellung respektive zum „ungeteilten Akt des Denkvermögens" in „abstrakten Begriffen" betont wurde. Natürlich würde De Morgan in einem falschen Licht erscheinen, wollte man ihn allein auf diese, von Cajori zitierte Aussage festlegen.
55 Aus den Akten der Cambridge Philosophical Society, Bd. 10, 1864, S. 173 ff.; hier zit. nach Church 1936, S. 121 ff.: S. 128.
56 Vgl. Mill 1873, S. 225.
57 Um dieses Bild zu vervollständigen, muss man sich Mills gemischte Reaktionen auf Auguste Comte zu Gemüte führen (vgl. id., S. 209 ff.).
58 Vgl. Whewell 1840 und 1847; Whewell 1849; Whewell 1858.
59 Vgl. Byrne 1847, Einleitung, S. vii.
60 Ibidem.
61 Vgl. Cajori 1928, S. 431: „Individual workers who in elementary fields proposed to express practically everything in ideographic form have been overruled." Cajori interpretiert es als Trend zu „conservatism" bezüglich der Verwendung von Symbolen und scheint es durch Gruppenzwang zu erklären: „by large groups or by representatives of large groups". Und er beendet diese Überlegungen sibyllinisch: „The problem requires a consensus of opinion, the wisdom of many minds. That wisdom discloses itself in the history of science. The judgement of the past calls for moderation."
62 Vgl. Hesse 1865, Vorrede.
63 Vgl. Arneth 1852, S. 288.
64 Vgl. Bense 1946, S. 53.
65 Ibidem.
66 Weit darüber hinaus reicht auch die wohl einzige neuere Behandlung von einigem Gewicht des Byrne'schen *Euclid* nicht: vgl. Tufte 1990, S. 84 ff.
67 Vgl. Casselman 2000.
68 Byrne 1847, Einleitung, S. vii: „Dieses Werk will mehr als nur illustrieren; wir verwenden Farben nicht zum Zwecke der Belustigung oder um mit bestimmten Kombinationen von Farbe und Form zu unterhalten, sondern um den Geist bei seiner Suche nach Wahrheit zu unterstützen, die Hilfsmittel der

Pädagogik zu mehren und bleibendes Wissen zu verbreiten. Bräuchten wir Autoritäten, um die Wichtigkeit und Nützlichkeit der Geometrie zu beweisen, könnten wir jeden Philosophen seit Plato zitieren. Unter den alten Griechen wie auch bei Pestalozzi und anderen Schulen der jüngeren Zeit galt die Geometrie als die beste Geistesübung."

69 Das Stichwort bei Krbek 1954, S. 205 ff. Dort als Untertitel das Motto: „Form ist die sichtbare Schwester der Zahl".

70 Vgl. Steck 1946, S. 17.

71 Ibidem.

72 Vgl. Byrne 1847, Einleitung, S. vii.

73 Vgl. Byrne 1835, 2002, Vorwort.

74 Ibidem.

75 Vgl. Byrne 1853, Vorwort, S. vii: „Although this work is written to guide the experienced and accomplished artisan, yet the descriptions and directions are of so practical a nature, that any mechanic or amateur, previously unacquainted with the subjects treated of, may, by following its pages as a text-book, succeed in his earliest attempts to accomplish even the most difficult processes inscribed."

76 Vgl. Byrne 1866, Vorwort, S. vi: „They are equal in power to Babbage's and Collet's combined, and take up less than one eighth part of their space."

77 Vgl. Lorey 1852, S. iii.

78 Id., Einleitung, S. 1.

79 Vgl. Byrne 1841.

80 Vgl. Byrne 1847, S. 210.

81 Vgl. Byrne 1841, S. viii: „... while there is not one mistake, oversight, or logical objection in the whole of Euclid's Fifth Book."

82 Ibidem: „... in fact, Euclid's Fifth Book is a master-piece of human reasoning."

83 Id., S. xv.

84 Id., S. xiv: „whether the structure be raised upon numbers, symbols, or lines, &c.".

85 Vgl. Anm. 74.

86 Vgl. Byrne 1841, S. xvi: „logical, strict, and convincing [...] without being attended with that tediousness and circuitous detail which frequently accompany other methods".

87 Ibidem.

88 Ibidem.

89 Vgl. dazu die spätere Übersetzung bei der „the same equimultiples" zur Klärung herangezo-

gen wird. Heath 1956, S. 120.

90 Vgl. Byrne 1841, S. xviii: „To teach should be the highest aim of a writer on elementary subjects, and not to adopt (which is too often the case) that stiff and formal manner so prejudicial to and inconsistent with the ideas of a learner; every thing likely to embarrass should be explained, and that authorial kind of scientific dignity should be set aside when the object is to instruct others."

91 Vgl. oben.

92 Vgl. Heath 1956, S. 122 f.

93 Byrne 1841, S. xviii.

94 Byrne 1847, S. xiii.

95 Die entsprechenden beweisführenden Darstellungen: Id., S. xiii u. xiv.

96 Id., S. xiii.

97 Vgl. Dürer 1525, fol. A ij recto.

98 Vgl. Byrne 1847, S. xiii: „a clumsy method [...] means more refined and extensive than any that has been hitherto proposed".

99 Id., S. xii: „The experience of all who have formed systems to impress facts on the understanding, agree in proving that coloured representations, as pictures, cuts, diagrams, &c. are more easily fixed in the mind than mere sentences unmarked by any peculiarity."

100 Dazu der Kommentar im Vorwort: „Technical terms always present a formidable obstacle to practical men in the investigation of any scientific subject." Vgl. Dimond 1867, S. vi.

101 Vgl. Youmans 1856, Einleitung, S. 9: „It is especially in natural science, where definite and exact ideas of properties and relations are to be communicated to the mind, that the employment of visible diagrams is most useful."

102 Ibidem: „Whenever the object to be contemplated cannot itself be seen, and consists of such fixed elements or qualities as are capable of being represented or delineated to the eye, pictorial illustrations become indispendable."

103 Ibidem.

104 Vgl. Fechner 1860, Vorwort, S. v.

105 Vgl. Byrne 1847, S. xvii: „For schools and other public places of instruction, dyed chalks will answer to describe diagrams, &c. for private use coloured pencils will be found very convenient."

106 Byrne 1847, Einleitung, S. vii: „Unter den alten Griechen wie

auch bei Pestalozzi und anderen Schulen der jüngeren Zeit galt die Geometrie als die beste Geistesübung."

107 Id., S. vii.

108 Id., S. xi.

109 Vgl. Pestalozzi 1803, Vorrede, S. v: „Die Anschaungslehre der Zahlenverhältnisse ist, als ein Theil der Methode, eine Kunstübung, den Menschen auf eine, mit der Natur seines Geistes und mit der Art, wie sich seine Denkkraft in ihm entwickelt, übereinstimmende Weise zählen und rechnen zu lehren."

110 Vgl. Pico della Mirandola 1532, S. 137: „Conclusiones de mathematicis secundum opinionem propriam numero lxxxv".

111 Vgl. Borelli 1679, „Ad lectorem geometram" (Einleitung), o. S.

112 Ibidem: „progressus Intellectualis ex notis ad ignota".

113 Vgl. Ashe 1684, S. 672 ff.

114 Ibidem: „it rejects all trifling in words and Rhetorical schemes, all conjectures, authorities, prejudices and passion".

115 Vgl. Early Letters of the Royal Society EL/A/36 (St. George Ashe, 27. April 1686); vgl. AHRB Centre for Editing Lives and Letters, 2005. Vgl. Pell 1668. Pells Algebra ist eine erweiterte veränderte Übersetzung der Algebra von Johann Heinrich Rahn, Landvogt zu Kyburg.

116 Vgl. The Elements or Principles of Geometrie, London 1684. Das Exemplar der Trinity College Library in Dublin weist die Signatur von St. George Ashe auf, zur Online-Ausgabe (Ann Arbor) wird wohl aus diesem Grunde eine Beteiligung postuliert. Unser Exemplar weist Abweichungen auf.

117 Id., „Advertisement", fol. A3 recto und verso.

118 Das kurze „Advertisement" endet mit der Feststellung: „This Summary was thought sufficient for an Introduction." Unserem Exemplar ist jedoch eine zusätzliche Einleitung mit eigener, unabhängiger Blattfolge, A-(A4) verso, eingerückt.

119 Id., fol. A1 recto: „And by consequence nothing is so apt to strengthen our Reason to give us clear notion of things, and secure us from being imposed upon fallacies or shadows of proof, as conversing herein."

120 Id., fol. A1 recto: „Demonstra-

tion therefore serving (as we said) to enlighten the mind."

121 Vgl. The Elements or Principles of Geometrie, London 1684, fol. B4 verso.

122 Vgl. Byrne 1847, S. vii.

123 Man sollte ‚Wissenschaft' und ‚Didaktik' nicht so sehr trennen, wie das hier eben geschehen ist. In alter Tradition, so bei Duns Scotus, ist scientia gemäß seinem Verständnis von Aristoteles allen andern Überlegungen voran ein medium demonstrationis. (Hier zit. nach: Duns Scotus (oder: Johannes de Cornubia?) 1512, fol. a 2 verso.)

124 Vgl. Brodhagen 1792, S. vii.

125 Vgl. Lambert 1764.

126 Vgl. Feder 1793, S. 70.

127 Vgl. Stephani 1814, S. 9. Unter „Gesichtssprache" fallen bei Stephani die Piktogramme, also beispielsweise – vor Champollion – die ägyptischen Hieroglyphen.

128 Id., S. 12 f.

129 Vgl. Oechslin 2007, S. 62 ff.

130 Vgl. Whitehead 1927, S. 21.

131 Vgl. Goethe 1812, S. xxi.

132 Ibidem.

133 Vgl. Kant 1793, S. 104 ff.

134 Id., S. 105.

135 Byrne 1847, S. ix: „Dergestalt sind die akustischen Zeichen für den allgemeinen Gebrauch, die wir Wörter nennen, dass sie stets als hörbar aufgefasst werden, ob nun direkt an das Ohr gerichtet oder, über den Umweg der Buchstaben, an das Auge. Geometrische Diagramme sind keine Zeichen, sondern Rohstoffe der geometrischen Wissenschaft, deren Ziel es ist, die relativen Größen oder ihre Teile durch den Denkprozess der Demonstration sichtbar zu machen."

136 Wagner 1851 (a), S. 124.

137 Vgl. Byrne 1847, S. ix: „... renders the process of reasoning more precise, and the attainment more expeditious ..."

138 Vgl. Moritz 1794, S. 87 ff.

139 Vgl. Burja 1794, S. 265 ff.

140 Vgl. Trendelenburg 1828, S. 457 ff.: S. 457.

141 Id., S. 457.

142 Id., S. 458 u. 473 f.

143 Vgl. Byrne 1847, S. ix.

144 Vgl. Wagner 1803, S. 148. Im Rückblick schreibt Wagner, diese Aufgabe hätte er sich schon als Jüngling vorgenommen, um sie dann in der Mathematische[n] Philosophie erstmals 1811 zu realisieren. Vgl. Wagner 1851 (b), S. xl

u. xxxi. – Vgl. zu Wagner: Stock 1982, S. 262 ff.

145 Vgl. Wagner 1851 (b), S. xli. (Rückblick auf das *Organon* von 1830).

146 Ibidem.

147 Vgl. Wagner 1851 (b), S. 207 ff. (III. Sprachsystem).

148 Id., S. 244 (§ 325).

149 Id., S. 243 (§ 324) und S. 244 (§ 326).

150 Id., S. 214 (§ 292) und S. 260 (§ 342).

151 Id., S. 337 (Anhang, § 24).

152 Vgl. Wagner 1851 (a), S. 1 ff.

153 Id., S. 2.

154 Vgl. Wagner 1839, S. 312 ff.: S. 313 f.

155 Vgl. Wagner 1803, S. 149.

156 Ibidem.

157 Id., S. 155.

158 Vgl. Unger 1833, S. 6. Unger geht dann allerdings so weit festzustellen, es käme „hier nicht darauf an, mit philologischer Genauigkeit die Worte des Euklid wieder zu geben, sondern nur der Geist desselben soll beibehalten" werden; id., S. 11.

159 Vgl. Türk 1811. Eine vergleichbare, dem Zeichenunterricht gewidmete Formenlehre hat der Berner Zeichenlehrer Gustav Adolf Tobler 1836 veröffentlicht. Das Zitat nach: Türk 1830, S. 1.

160 Vgl. Türk 1811, Vorrede, S. vii.

161 Vgl. Byrne 1847, S. xi f.

162 Vgl. Eberhard 1776, S. 5.

163 Id., S. 8.

164 Id., S. 4.

165 Mondrian 1920, S. 1: „Die Logik will, dass die Kunst der plastische Ausdruck unseres gesamten Daseins sei."

166 Vgl. Koyré/Cohen 1972, S. 15.

167 Ibidem: „Has lineas describere geometria non docet, sed postulat."

168 Vgl. oben und: Hölder 1900, S. 6.

169 Vgl. Einstein 1921, S. 3.

170 Id., S. 2 f.

171 Id., S. 2.

172 Vgl. Simon 1901, S. 19. Simon beginnt sein Vorwort (S. v) mit dem Hinweis auf seinen praktischen Beitrag zur mathematischen Erziehungs- und Unterrichtslehre.

173 Zu den Wörtchen ‚streng' und ‚exakt' vgl. Oechslin 2009, S. 363 ff.

174 Das hat der ,andere Strang geometrischen Denkens', die Logistik, deren Ursprünge in die Zeit Oliver Byrnes und Augustus De Morgans! zurückreichen (vgl.

oben) auch noch 1929 als seine Errungenschaft reklamiert: „Wenn jemand auf irgend einem Gebiet der Philosophie oder der Einzelwissenschaften sich um eine exakte Analyse der Aussagen und Begriffe bemüht, so sollen ihm hier die logistischen und insbesondere die relationstheoretischen Hilfsmittel als ein scharfes Werkzeug in die Hand gegeben werden. Diese Hilfsmittel sind bisher, besonders in Deutschland, noch sehr wenig bekannt; nur in logisch-mathematischen Untersuchungen werden sie zuweilen angewendet." Vgl. Carnap, 1929, Vorwort, S. iii.

175 Vgl. Vorwort vom 8. Mai 1686 zu den *Philosophiae Naturalis Principia Mathematica* von Isaac Newton.

176 Vgl. Steck 1942, S. 13 ff.

177 Vgl. Mondrian 1920, S. 5.

178 Vgl. Byrne 1847, S. vii.

179 Vgl. Mondrian 1920, S. 1: „Il atteint son expression plastique par le conscient. Par cela, l'apparition de l'art est l'expression plastique de l'inconscient et du conscient. Elle montre le rapport de l'un et de l'autre: elle change, mais l'art reste immuable."

180 Id., S. 5.

181 Ibidem.

182 Vgl. Dermée o. J., S. 29 ff., S. 30: „Dans l'intelligence, tout se passe avec l'accompagnement de conscience, dans une chambre claire."

183 Vgl. Rosenberg 1921, S. 1.

184 Vgl. Dermée o. J., S. 37: „De même, pas de logique apparente, afin de rebuter les efforts de l'intelligence pour mordre sur le poème. Mot d'ordre: rebuter l'intelligence."

185 Vgl. Ozenfant/Jeanneret o. J. (a), S. 38 ff.

186 Vgl. Byrne 1847, S. vii: „The arts and sciences have become so extensive, that to facilitate their acquirement is of as much importance as to extend their boundaries."

187 Vgl. Le Roy 1960, S. 17.

188 Id., S. 19 (mit Bezug auf Kant).

189 Vgl. auch die Formulierung: „La pensée géométrique ainsi considérée n'est donc pas la pensée mathématique pure, mais la pensée mathématique tendant à s'incarner dans un corps d'intuition imaginative, bref la

pensée mathématique au seuil immédiat de l'applicaton." (Id., S. 21.)

190 Gerhardt erklärt den Bildungsgang Leibniz' gleichsam aus der erlebten Frustration bezüglich der Möglichkeit des Verstehens: „In Leipzig, wo Leibniz seine akademischen Studien begann, las ein gewisser Joh. Kühn über die Elemente Euclid's; die Vorträge desselben waren aber so dunkel, dass außer Leibniz keiner der Zuhörer folgen konnte. Es wird erzählt, dass er allein sich mit dem Docenten in Discussionen über den Vortrag einliess und alsdann seinen Mitzuhörern die Lehrsätze verständlich machte ...". Vgl. Gerhardt 1848, S. 7.

191 Vgl. Rosenberg 1921, S. 1.

192 Vgl. Ozenfant/Jeanneret o. J. (b), S. 369 ff., S. 382: „marche parfois fantasque de l'intuition".

193 Ibidem.

194 Ibidem.

195 Id., S. 379.

196 Vgl. Byrne 1847, S. vii.

197 Vgl. Ozenfant/Jeanneret o. J. (b), S. 382: „Mais la couleur a des propriétés de choc (ordre sensoriel) précédant optiquement celui de la forme (qui est une création déjà partiellement cérébrale)."

198 Vgl. Kepes (1944) 1951.

199 Id., S. 15.

200 Id., S. 35 ff.

201 Vgl. Schopenhauer 1816, S. 11 (Erstes Kapitel: „Vom Sehn").

202 Vgl. oben und: Oechslin 2005, S. 176 ff.

203 Vgl. Wundt 1862, S. xix.

204 Ibidem.

205 Vgl. Kant 1787, Vorrede zur 2. Aufl., S. xiii.

206 Ibidem.

207 Ibidem.

208 Vgl. Fechner 1860, S. 1: Hier die Darstellung der „ungünstigeren Verhältnisse", die sich seinen Interessen vorerst boten: „Einleitendes. I. Allgemeiner Betrachtung über die Beziehung von Leib und Seele. Indess die Lehre von der Körperwelt in den verschiedenen Zweigen der Naturwissenschaft zu einer grossen Entwicklung gediehen ist, und sich scharfer Principien und Methoden erfreut, welche ihr einen erfolgreichen Fortschritt sichern, indess die Lehre vom Geiste in Psychologie und Logik wenigstens bis zu gewissen Grän-

zen feste Grundlagen gewonnen hat, ist die Lehre von den Beziehungen zwischen Körper und Geist und Geist oder Leib und Seele bis jetzt fast blos ein Feld philosophischen Streites ohne festes Fundament und ohne sichere Principien und Methoden für den Fortschritt der Untersuchung geblieben."

209 Id., Vorwort, S. v.

210 Vgl. Helmholtz 1968, S. 38.

211 Vgl. Adorno 1966, Vorrede, S. 7.

212 Vgl. Mondrian 1920, S. 5: „Das Abstrakte bleibt plastischer Ausdruck nach Maßgabe des Universellen: die tiefgreifendste Verinnerlichung des Äußeren und die reinste Veräußerlichung des Inneren."

213 Vgl. Mondrian 1918 (Nachdruck, Amsterdam 1968), S. 29 ff.

214 Vgl. Oechslin 2009.

215 Vgl. Byrne 1847, S. vii: „Bräuchten wir Autoritäten, um die Wichtigkeit und Nützlichkeit der Geometrie zu beweisen, könnten wir jeden Philosophen seit Plato zitieren."

GYORGY KEPES

LANGUAGE OF VISION

Painting, Photography, Advertising–Design

Paul Theobald and Company

« To facilitate their acquirement »

The First Six Books of the Elements of Euclid d'Oliver Byrne
– didactique, coloré et excentrique

Qu'est-ce qui peut inciter un Surveyor of her Majesty's Settlements aux îles Malouines à inventer l'édition d'Euclide la plus séduisante de tous les temps et à la publier? Avec ces couleurs à la Mondrian elle nous semble moderne avant la lettre. Celui qui tient ce livre entre ses mains ne peut se soustraire à la fascination qu'exercent ses «images» et ce, justement, parce que la compréhension des règles mathématiques abstraites les plus difficiles y est suggérée, comme il y paraît un temps, le plus simplement du monde, et démontrée tout à fait concrètement *ad oculos*.

***

Le point sensible :
La « représentation parlante des formes de pensée »

« Les mathématiciens qui entrent de mauvaise grâce dans les labyrinthes de la philosophie sont priés d'abandonner ici la lecture de l'avant-propos. »
– FREGE, *Grundgesetze der Arithmetik*, 1893[1]

La postérité s'est montrée plutôt féroce avec Oliver Byrne. Cela concerne en premier lieu la science des mathématiques et sa relation avec sa propre histoire. Oliver Byrne n'y apparaît pratiquement pas. On cherche vainement la spectaculaire édition d'Euclide dans la *Bibliographia Euclideana* de Max Steck, bien que celui-ci se soit justement intéressé à la «forme mathématique» («mathematische Gestalt») et qu'il ait déjà découvert la «qualité visible» de l'interprétation d'Euclide de Proclus, passant ensuite par Nicolas

de Cuse pour aller à Johannes Kepler, «en renouvelant les motifs pythagoriciens», et à Gottfried Wilhelm Leibniz, à la recherche d'une synthèse dans laquelle le *mundus intelligibilis* et le *mundus sensibilis*, l'abstraction et la perception à travers les sens, seraient vus ensemble et formeraient à nouveau un tout. [2]

Oliver Byrne lui-même ne voulait toutefois pas aller aussi loin, ni au point de vue historique ni fondamentalement: son objectif, croyait-il, restait de manière didactique orienté vers la compréhension immédiate et l'utilité des mathématiques. Et pourtant son *Euclid* aurait pu et dû mener à ces réflexions fondamentales. Steck était convaincu que les mathématiques, «ce qui n'est pas le cas de la pure logique», ne se laissaient pas ramener à de simples concepts et qu'il convenait de dire: «La participation de la contemplation à ses connaissances ne peut être contestée, parce que les mathématiques ne sont justement pas possibles d'après des concepts mais seulement ‹par leur construction›.»[3] Steck s'alignait sur Andreas Speiser et sa *Mathematische Denkweise* (1932) et, en relation avec la formation des concepts scientifiques, aussi sur Heinrich Rickert qui fit remarquer de son côté qu'aucun matériau donné n'existait pour le moment pour les mathématiques et qu'elles devaient le créer elles-mêmes. Selon Rickert, c'est la raison pour laquelle des questions touchant par exemple à des définitions plus larges des lignes droites (l'«absolument simple») s'avèrent obsolètes, tout comme on ne ferait qu'une «monstration» si l'on tentait de «définir le bleu ou le rouge».[4] Les définitions se suffisent à elles seules. En 1932, dans son premier chapitre consacré aux «Délimitations», Andreas Speiser fit référence au «fondement de droit» qui existerait quels que soient tous les autres intérêts et ce qui va au-delà «dans l'intuition mathématique pour les mathématiques».[5]

Publiée en 1932, *Die Mathematische Denkweise* de Speiser était dédiée à Raoul La Roche, un amateur d'art qui se fit construire une villa par Le Corbusier. Pour lui, il ne fait aucun doute que le monde mathématique et le monde artistique sont proches, rien qu'en raison des appréciations de leurs sphères de compétence, de leur «fondement de droit». Les sciences seraient «définies de par leurs fondements de droit, et l'intuition mathématique et artistique appartient ici au domaine mental, en revanche l'expérience et la transmission au monde extérieur».[6] Cela nourrit évidemment l'idée selon laquelle les formes et figures mathématiques devraient être considérées et jugées philosophiquement comme des inventions humaines spontanées – et non seulement comme le résultat d'exigences scientifiques. Un «système de notre savoir» (c'est-à dire le système de l'expérience totale) plus complet[7] demandait cependant une telle «relation d'accomplissement» («wissenschaftlicher Leistungszusammenhang») dans laquelle l'«intelligibilité du monde empirique», et la psychologie dans l'ensemble, réclame son dû.[8] Dans son livre *Grenzen der naturwissenschaftlichen Begriffsbildung* où il étudie les limites de la conceptualisation dans les sciences de la nature, Heinrich Rickert a mis en évidence l'opposition entre la «perfection logique» (d'un concept) et l'intuition empirique, pour l'atténuer d'emblée en considération de l'effet réel des mondes des corps. Impossible de faire l'impasse sur ces difficultés.[9] Les perspectives culturelles, lorsque les constatations mathématiques doivent être prolongées dans des effets esthétiques par exemple, ne font qu'accentuer l'opposition. Dès 1908, dans sa Dissertation de Wurtzbourg, Ernst Bloch a identifié chez Rickert des «fluctuations» méthodiques caractérisant sa philosophie, ce qu'il a aussi illustré précisément avec les changements intervenant vers 1850 et des intérêts divergents.[10]

Accentuées de manière spécifique et précisées, ces questions possèdent donc leur espace historique. Ce qui a commencé avec la «logique formelle» chez le critique d'Oliver Byrne, Augustus De Morgan en 1847[11], a mûri chez Edmund G. Husserl jusqu'à atteindre le point critique qu'il associe au concept de «mathématisation» et qu'il relie à la perte de signification vitale de la science.[12] En 1910/1911, Rickert avait constaté que la «conception objectivisante du monde» n'était pas susceptible d'expliquer le sens de notre vie.[13] Husserl, qui se penchait à l'époque sur les idéaux d'une «science rigoureuse», dut admettre que le «seul fruit mûr» des efforts faits «par le médium de la réflexion critique» n'aurait été que la justification et l'autonomisation des rigoureuses sciences naturelles et humaines «ainsi que de nouvelles disciplines purement mathématiques».[14] Pour la philosophie restée ce faisant ignorée, il désirait – se basant sur la critique des «méthodes indirectes» inévitables dans le cas des «sciences impressionnantes de l'ère moderne, les sciences mathématiques-physiques» – une science

qui, «dénuée de toutes les méthodes symbolisant indirectement et mathématisant, sans l'appareil des conclusions et des preuves, acquiert une profusion de connaissances les plus rigoureuses et décisives pour le reste de la philosophie».[15] Elle devait servir une «saisie de l'essence phénoménologique» dans le «sens de l'intuition philosophique».[16]

Les points de vue et les intérêts divergeaient depuis longtemps. En 1879, Gottlob Frege avait publié *L'idéographie (Begriffsschrift, eine der arithmetischen nachgebildete Formelsprache des reinen Denkens)*, dans l'antécédent de laquelle, au sens large, l'*Euclid* d'Oliver Byrne a sa place. Frege avait lui-même fait remarquer en 1882 qu'«une représentation parlante des formes de pensée» aurait une «signification dépassant les mathématiques».[17] Et il pria les philosophes «d'accorder quelque importance à la chose».[18] Il n'est pas étonnant que dans la dispute qui l'oppose à Husserl, l'aspect psychologique de toute perception ait été des deux côtés au premier plan. En ce qui concerne Frege, il faut le lire en se disant qu'il n'était au fond pas si aphilosophique. Au contraire. Ses premiers propos fondamentaux sont suivis en 1893, dans le premier volume des *Fondements de l'arithmétique (Grundgesetze der Arithmetik)*, de la note en bas de page suivante: «Les mathématiciens qui entrent de mauvaise grâce dans les labyrinthes de la philosophie sont priés d'abandonner ici la lecture de l'avant-propos.»[19] Ensuite il se penche sur la question de savoir ce qui peut et doit être pensé, ce qui peut et doit être représenté, apportant évidemment des arguments pour lutter contre une «falsification psychologique de la logique» abusive.[20] Il réclame d'un autre côté que des limites soient imposées au «despotisme de la fiction».[21] Et l'arithmétique est pour lui indubitablement une discipline relevant de la logique.[22] «Cela représente pour moi un signe certain d'erreur, lorsque la logique a besoin de la métaphysique et de la psychologie, des sciences qui nécessitent elles-mêmes les principes logiques. Où est donc ici le sol véritablement premier sur lequel tout repose? Où bien est-ce que c'est comme chez Münchhausen qui s'extirpa du marécage en se tirant par les cheveux?»[23]

Il est sans cesse question de ce que les mathématiques sont capables et doivent faire, de ce qui leur est permis ou non, de ce qui se retrouve «présenté».[24] Celui qui place ce dernier point au premier plan, serait un incorrigible idéaliste, dixit Frege, à l'adresse de Benno Erdmann.[25] On se souvient qu'au début de son *Essai sur les fondements de la géométrie (An Essay on the Foundations of Geometry*, 1897) Bertrand A. W. Russell remarquait qu'au XVIIe et au XVIIIe siècle, durant le combat contre l'empirisme, la géométrie serait restée une «forteresse imprenable des idéalistes».[26] C'est donc ainsi que les fronts sont édifiés. Russell fait suivre la semence sur l'idéalisme de la représentation du développement de la géométrie se distançant d'Euclide qui commence avec la remise en question de l'axiome des parallèles et mène à de nouveaux rivages en passant par Nikolaï Ivanovitch Lobatchevski et Johann Bolyai.[27]

Page/Seite/Page 68
Ill. 35
Gyorgy Kepes, *Language of Vision*, Chicago 1944

Ill. 36
Oliver Byrne, *The First Six Books of the Elements
of Euclid*, London 1847, p. 236
– Example of the pictorial organization.
– Beispiel der Bildorganisation.
– Exemple d'organisation de l'image.

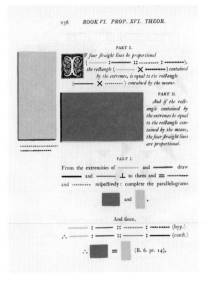

36

Ceci précédait justement dans le temps les études d'Oliver Byrne. Et plus tard, en 1854, un cercle étroit connaissait au moins l'exposé *Sur les hypothèses sous-jacentes à la géométrie (Ueber die Hypothesen, welche der Geometrie zu Grunde liegen)* de Bernhard Riemann. On sait que le point de départ de ses réflexions était que la géométrie présuppose le concept d'espace et que, dans l'ensemble, les fondements des axiomes restaient dans l'ombre. Il recommandait que cette obscurité que n'ont éclairée ni les mathématiciens ni les philosophes «d'Euclide à Legendre» soit progressivement remaniée en regard du «réel sous-jacent à l'espace», en utilisant des expériences et des faits.[28] Cela allait en direction de la physique. En 1878, à l'occasion de la fête commémorative de la fondation de l'université Friedrich-Wilhelm à Berlin, Hermann von Helmholtz fit une conférence intitulée *Les faits dans la perception (Die Thatsachen in der Wahrnehmung)* et expliqua l'ancienne et la nouvelle contradiction.[29] Au «concept plus ancien d'intuition» qui se rapporterait à «ce qui arrive immédiatement à la conscience par l'impression des sens», il oppose son concept scientifique: «Je réclame seulement comme preuve de la représentation intuitive (‹ Anschaubarkeit ›) que les impressions des sens émergeant soient précisées, de manière certaine et sans équivoque, pour chaque mode d'observation en utilisant si c'est nécessaire la connaissance scientifique de leurs lois, desquelles ressortiraient, au moins pour le connaisseur de ces lois, que la chose en question ou la relation à examiner existe effectivement.»[30]

Helmholtz renonce consciemment à cette «facilité, vitesse, évidence fulgurante» propres à l'«ancien concept d'intuition», à savoir l'impression immédiate des sens.[31] Le décrochage a eu lieu.

La critique de Helmholtz s'amorçait à vrai dire déjà là où Immanuel Kant estimait les propositions euclidiennes nécessairement exactes et les divergences inimaginables, pour décrire ensuite, dans cette mesure de manière clarifiante et tout à fait traditionnelle, la forme d'intuition («Anschaungsform»). «Notre œil voit tout ce qu'il voit comme un agrégat de surfaces colorées dans le champ visuel; c'est sa forme d'intuition.»[32] Mais il ne s'agissait plus du tout de cela pour les mathématiques et Helmholtz, ainsi qu'il l'explique. D'un autre côté, Husserl avait plus tard – et aussi en considération de ces qualités, telle celle de l'«évidence fulgurante», qui habitent le sens visuel, à laquelle il fallait maintenant renoncer – reproché à Frege de s'égarer «dans des hypersubtilités stériles»,[33] alors que lui-même renvoie maintenant aux «données psychiques élémentaires». «Nul ne peut définir» des concepts comme «la qualité, l'intensité, le lieu, le temps et d'autres choses semblables».[34] Et Husserl continue de rapporter cela à des «concepts élémentaires» comme «l'égalité, l'analogie, la gradation, le tout et les parties, la quantité et l'unité».[35] La phénoménologie étudie les notions abstraites et pures! On sait que Husserl veut l'établir comme une «science fondamentale de la philosophie» et ainsi enchaîner (une fois encore) avec la «cognition et expérience naturelles», ce qu'il nomme «le monde».[36]

Le champ d'action de la géométrie était jadis aussi vaste. Ces «relations élémentaires» faisaient notamment partie – font partie (!) – de son domaine. On peut continuer, et dans une intention didactique, à les comprendre dans ce sens et vouloir les orienter dans cette direction (idéaliste). Celui qui procède ainsi vers 1850 fait partie sur ce point d'une tradition significative sur le plan historico-culturel mais il n'est plus membre de la communauté scientifique qui se trouve sur la voie de ces «nouvelles disciplines mathématiques pures» dont Husserl a reconnu l'importance. Il n'empêche que la crise a eu lieu. «Qu'est-ce que la vérité dans notre regard et notre pensée? En quel sens nos idées correspondent-elles à la réalité? La philosophie et les sciences naturelles butent sur ce problème de deux côtés opposés; c'est une tâche commune.»[37] Formulée par Helmholtz en 1879, cette phrase désigne l'accès double, dissocié, au problème, devenu un fait depuis longtemps. La remarque sur la «tâche commune» semble euphémique face à cet éloignement progressif des intérêts et des efforts, sur lesquels il était impossible de se méprendre. Pour la géométrie euclidienne et sa tradition de transmission, il s'agissait d'un adieu, du moins dans la science correspondante.[38]

Oliver Byrne, le mathématicien dont les idées insolites ne sont pas en phase avec son époque, et son adversaire Augustus De Morgan

« Oliver Byrne's Euclid *in symbols and colored diagrams was not taken seriously, but was regarded a curiosity. »*
– CAJORI, *A History of Mathematical Notations*, 1928[39]

En forçant un peu le trait, on peut décrire ainsi la situation: en 1847, avec ses «diagrammes colorés» et sa confiance aveugle dans les formes de représentations arbitraires, Byrne se trouve, mathématiquement parlant, dans les années avant 1850 et, si l'on veut, dans l'ère moderne sur le plan artistique. En tout cas, il vise en premier lieu l'ancien objectif de l'*adaequatio rei ac intellectus*, la conformité de la compréhension avec le fait, et la correspondance de la forme intuitive avec la perception à travers les sens. C'est à cette fin qu'il crée ses figures et symboles didactiques et c'est aussi, de manière immédiatement visible et sans ambiguïté, le but déclaré dans son *Euclid*. Ce n'est pas un hasard si l'ouvrage est mentionné dans l'œuvre magistrale que Florian Cajori a consacrée en 1928 aux symboles et aux figures utilisés en mathématiques.[40] Mais il le fait plutôt incidemment et note qu'avec ses symboles et ses diagrammes colorés, l'*Euclid* de Byrne n'a pas été pris sérieusement mais regardé comme une curiosité.[41] Ainsi l'*Euclid* de Byrne a été perçu comme une bizarrerie – et nul n'en a fait cas! Ceci dit, c'est justement Cajori qui fait remarquer qu'Héron d'Alexandrie mentionne déjà l'utilisation de la couleur pour exposer des problèmes géométriques, renvoyant de son côté à une tradition pythagoricienne.[42] Et il cite par ailleurs Martianus Capella qui associe surface et couleur et dont l'esprit est de toute façon ouvert à tous les aspects de la formation de figures. Oliver Byrne a la tradition de son côté.

Cajori voit manifestement aussi la raison plus profonde du manque d'intérêt suscité par l'*Euclid* dans le point de vue que soutenait justement avec toute son autorité en 1849, deux ans après la parution de l'ouvrage, Augustus De Morgan à peine plus âgé que Byrne. Selon lui, ceux qui introduisent des symboles algébriques dans la géométrie élémentaire détruiraient ce qu'elle a de particulier pour l'étudiant qui possède une relation mécanique avec ces symboles; pour celui qui les connaît de l'algèbre courante. «La pensée géométrique et les méthodes arithmétiques ont chacune leurs fonctions propres. Mélanger les deux dans l'instruction primaire nuit à l'acquisition correcte des deux.»[43] Un jugement sévère si l'on considère qu'à cette époque la relation entre l'arithmétique et la géométrie était le thème explicite de recherches en de nombreux endroits et servait de précieux champ d'observation, Augustus De Morgan lui-même n'étant pas le dernier à l'utiliser.[44] De Morgan visait-il l'*Euclid* de Byrne en formulant cette âpre critique? Alors cela concernerait probablement en premier lieu le Livre V des Eléments d'Euclide consacré aux grandeurs et aux proportions arithmétiques.

En utilisant le terme «curiosity», pour montrer le manque de considération dont jouissait l'*Euclid* de Byrne, Cajori semble plutôt éluder consciemment la question de la caractérisation exacte de la qualité des signes et symboles choisis par celui-ci. Cajori veut-il parler de leur caractère inactuel ou indéterminé dans un spectre plus vaste de la description de l'image, pour ainsi dire entre l'iconoclasme et l'idolâtrie? D'un autre côté, la critique que fait De Morgan du mélange des langages de la géométrie et de l'arithmétique n'est-elle pas plutôt un prétexte qui dissimule une aversion fondamentale et aussi personnelle? Nous l'ignorons. Nous savons toutefois que De Morgan a critiqué *The creed of St. Athanasius* écrit par Byrne en 1839 sous le pseudonyme anagrammatique d'E. B. Revilo, et qu'il l'a incorporé à son livre *A Budget of Paradoxes* dans lequel il a recensé tout ce qu'il a pu découvrir d'absurdités mathématiques, pythagoriciennes et cabalistiques. La sentence tombe: «Cet auteur croit vraiment à ce qu'il dit, et il est très sincère. Il n'est pas le seul à avoir écrit des absurdités en confondant l'infini mathématique (notion de quantité) avec ce que les spéculateurs appellent maintenant plus correctement l'illimité, l'inconditionnel ou l'absolu.»[45] Sans compter que dans l'édition ultérieure revue par David Eugene Smith, il est même fait mention de Byrne dans la rubrique «minor mathematical writers», en relation directe avec l'*Euclid*.[46] Décidément, on ne passe rien à Byrne! L'édition la plus récente (1974) de l'anthologie des théories et points de vue marginaux d'Augustus De Morgan a été intitulée *The Encyclopedia of Excentrics*, et Oliver Byrne est ainsi effectivement entré dans la rubrique des curiosités et excentricités mathématiques![47]

Bien sûr que Byrne est un excentrique, exactement comme Augustus De Morgan dont on disait qu'il n'aurait eu de toute sa vie rien d'autre en tête que des chiffres abstraits, et ce à cause de son infirmité – il avait perdu l'usage d'un œil alors qu'il n'avait que quelques mois. Mais de telles mentions anecdotiques ne suffisent évidemment pas à expliquer la crise de la représentation en mathématiques à l'époque et chez De Morgan. On considérera pour le moment que nombre de choses qui intéressaient le monde britannique reliaient Augustus De Morgan et Oliver Byrne. De Morgan était tout particulièrement attaché aux problèmes de la didactique et de l'enseignement et partageait les idées que son professeur et ami William Whewell soutenait déjà en 1836 dans le titre de l'ouvrage : *Thoughts on the study of mathematics, as part of a liberal education.*[48] Les mathématiques servent à éduquer, elles sont une discipline à la fois morale et contribuant au développement de la raison. Et c'est l'orientation pédagogique qui forme les mathématiques et leur prête aussi un statut social. Il s'agit d'une pensée absolument concrète. En 1838, son *Essay on Probabilities* porte le sous-titre *On their application to Life Contingencies and Insurance Offices* (ill. 6) et doit aussi être lu et compris concrètement comme une mesure contre l'ignorance généralisée en matière d'assurances.[49] De Morgan était un membre éminent de la Society for the Diffusion of Useful Knowledge fondée en 1826 et il a rédigé plus de sept cents contributions pour leur organe, la *Penny Cyclopedia*[50], y publiant en 1841 un court article intitulé *Proportion* qui traite du Livre V d'Euclide.[51] Il portait néanmoins une attention accrue au nombre, à l'arithmétique et l'algèbre, à la logique et aux questions de probabilité (ill. 7) qui l'attiraient. L'année où parut l'*Euclid* de Byrne, De Morgan publie sa *Formal Logic*, qui sera suivie de toute une série de recherches correspondantes.[52] De Morgan – et avec lui les mathématiques débouchant sur la logique symbolique – semble vouloir exclure ce que Byrne a élevé justement dans son *Euclid* en principe didactique, notamment l'explication à l'aide de figures et de symboles.

Cela avait évidemment été pratiqué ainsi ou autrement longtemps avant lui, ou du moins on s'en était approché. Oliver Byrne n'était en aucun cas complètement isolé. La couleur trouva bientôt, elle aussi, une utilisation plus poussée dans l'illustration scientifique.[53] Il n'y a que pour les mathématiques que l'on considère qu'il faut séparer proprement ce qui veut être séparé.[54] Ce qui a probablement été dans l'ensemble décisif pour le caractère marginal de Byrne, c'est que la géométrie – à l'intérieur de la discipline mathématique – évoluait depuis longtemps, s'éloignant d'Euclide pour aborder de nouvelles questions telles, justement, celle de la logique formelle. En comparaison, la question des symboles est alors obsolète. Il n'empêche que De Morgan semble profiter de toute occasion qui se présente pour s'y opposer et servir d'autant plus la logique : chaque science en développement élaborerait ses propres symboles ; et la logique, la seule science dont il faut bien avouer qu'elle n'a fait aucun progrès réel au cours des siècles, serait la seule qui n'aurait pas généré de symboles.[55]

A quel point finalement l'empirisme en général – et même en mathématiques ! – doit être imposé contre tout a priori réel ou présumé, c'est une tout autre histoire. Dans son autobiographie, John Stuart Mill s'exprime en ce sens et contre le savoir allemand ou a priori, se prononçant pour son *System of Logic* et l'échange avec Whewell : cet ouvrage aurait fourni ce qui était très demandé, un livret d'une conception inverse, qui déduit tout savoir de l'expérience et puise toutes les qualités morales et intellectuelles en premier lieu dans les orientations qui y sont attachées.[56] Pas de place ici pour l'ancien *more geometrico* et pour l'idéalisme allemand non plus![57] L'induction est à l'ordre du jour ! La *Philosophy of the Inductive Sciences, founded upon their history* (1840) de Whewell n'a pas seulement influencé durablement ses élèves De Morgan et Mill, elle a défini de manière essentielle la nouvelle direction du développement scientifique, y compris son fondement moral. C'est au moment où l'*Euclid* de Byrne sortait de la Chiswick Press en 1847 qu'apparut la seconde édition de la *Philosophy of the Inductive Sciences* de Whewell – plus tard, de manière bien britannique, on lui ajouta encore un *Novum Organum Renovatum*.[58] Voilà qui donnait le ton !

En revanche, ayant adopté l'idée traditionnelle selon laquelle les Eléments d'Euclide seraient devenus selon la conviction générale le fondement de toute science mathématique de par le monde, Byrne se trouvait pour ainsi dire du côté historique des mathématiques.[59] Face aux développements récents, il semblait arriéré de tenter ici une approche au profit de la quête de la vérité et, ce faisant, de puiser en plus dans Euclide les figures et symboles (anciens) et de les employer pour présenter les lois mathématiques de manière évidente, en les laissant dans le domaine de la visibilité. Byrne écrit en revanche dans l'introduction de son *Euclid* en 1847 : « Chaque langue est composée de signes représentatifs et les meilleurs signes sont ceux qui atteignent leur but avec la plus grande précision et la plus grande efficience. »[60] Avec la logique formelle, ceci était considéré comme dépassé. D'ailleurs Cajori constata que des approches individuelles de représentations idéographiques auraient par la suite généralement été submergées par un consensus orienté dans le sens contraire.[61]

Ce refus apparemment si rigide du mélange de langages géométriques et arithmétiques ou d'autres symboles de la part d'Augustus De Morgan montre clairement que cette tradition qui, chez Proclus autant que chez Martianus Capella se déployait dans toute sa richesse et son extrême vigueur, est ici aussi révolue depuis longtemps. Toutefois on associa encore un long moment ailleurs l'assertion « La géométrie apprend à découvrir des propositions et à prouver quelles qualités les figures expriment » avec l'effort nécessaire « sans lequel on ne trouve profit et satisfaction ni dans la science ni dans la vie ».[62] En 1852, un homme comme le professeur Arthur Arneth de Heidelberg plaçait particulièrement haut les mérites de la géométrie : « De toutes les branches des mathé-

Study of the advancing and receding qualities of colors

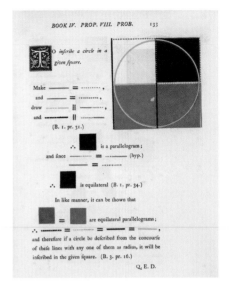

38

matiques, la géométrie nous offre l'image la plus instructive. Nous voyons comment les hommes, dès le départ de la pensée pure, ont tenté d'appréhender le particulier, et ne pouvaient et voulaient reconnaître avec certitude que celui-ci ».[63] De son côté, Byrne se réfère expressément à l'autorité de tous les philosophes de la tradition platonicienne, qui représentaient cette histoire. Mais ce qui avait cours maintenant, c'est ce que Max Bense décrivait comme le « détachement des mathématiques de la philosophie » et expliquait avec la formation assidue du « langage de précision spécifique ».[64] Il était ainsi possible, selon l'interprétation de Bense, de corriger le fait que les « problèmes et solutions mathématiques devançaient la véritable maîtrise mathématique »[65] ; mais cela ressemble plutôt au paradoxe d'Hercule et de la tortue !

Ce progrès lié à l'époque a donc manifestement écarté Oliver Byrne de l'histoire plus récente des mathématiques et lui a valu d'être regardé comme une bête curieuse. On est renvoyé à d'autres domaines, l'art par exemple, qui continue de traiter les langages et les figures et leurs multiples significations. La conséquence moins édifiante du manque d'actualité de l'*Euclid* était en rapport avec le fait que Byrne semble n'éveiller notre intérêt que pour des raisons typographiques et esthétiques.[66] C'est de cette manière que l'*Euclid* a attiré l'attention du typographe et designer Ruari McLean, qui avait pris Jan Tschichold comme point de départ de son travail. Le jugement qu'il émet dans sa description *Victorian Book Design and Colour Printing* (1963) va dans ce sens : il estime que le livre complique volontairement Euclide et attribue d'un autre côté le triomphe de l'ouvrage présenté en 1851 à l'Exposition universelle de Londres à Charles Whittingham, qui le fit paraître

en mille exemplaires chez William Pickering. Et puis le bruit courut que les frais de publication du livre auraient acculé Whittingham à la ruine, l'obligeant à céder la célèbre imprimerie Chiswick Press, fondée par son oncle qui portait le même nom.[67]

La démarche et l'argumentation de Byrne – et le but atteint avec l'*Euclid* « en couleur » de 1847

*« This Work has a greater aim than mere illustration;
we do not introduce colours for the purpose of entertainment,
or to amuse by certain combinations of tint and form, but to
assist the mind in its researches after truth, to increase the
facilities of instruction, and to diffuse permanent knowledge.
If we wanted authorities to prove the importance and usefulness
of geometry, we might quote every philosopher since the
days of Plato. Among the Greeks, in ancient, as in the
schoolof Pestalozzi and others in recent times, geometry
was adopted as the best gymnastic of the mind. »*
– Byrne, *Euclid*, 1847[68]

Il faut donc se faire une raison : avec Byrne nous entrons dans l'époque où Euclide est « dépassé ».[69] Byrne et ses représentations géométriques n'apparaissent évidemment pas dans la littérature correspondante, des travaux de logique d'Augustus De Morgan à la *Philosophy of Logic* (1970) de Willard Van Orman Quine. Mais le besoin de rendre visibles nos conceptions de manière plausible et la

« facilité, la rapidité, l'évidence fulgurante » décrites par Helmholtz reste bien vivace. Aux artistes de prendre les choses en main!

Pour ce qui est d'Oliver Byrne et de son *Euclid*, on considère qu'il fait encore entièrement confiance à l'idée traditionnelle selon laquelle ce n'est pas seulement la géométrie qui sert d'intermédiaire ici, mais que, dans le sens d'une école de la pensée, une assistance est proposée dans la recherche de la vérité, et ce fondamentalement.

Il faut donc se pencher sur Oliver Byrne et Euclide, là où les mathématiques ne suivent pour ainsi dire pas encore l'histoire de la discipline et ses spécialisations après 1850 mais où elles continuent de se montrer, ou même se montrent plus que jamais, tributaires de la grande tradition historico-culturelle, la maxime formulée plus tard par Max Steck, de manière très générale il est vrai, étant parfaitement adaptée ici : « Tous les grands mathématiciens étaient aussi en même temps des philosophes. »[70] A cette vision universelle, Steck ajoute d'autres formules, non moins générales : « Tous les grands mathématiciens entretenaient avec l'art une relation fervente et étaient aussi la plupart du temps des artistes en activité » et « Tous les grands mathématiciens étaient à vrai dire chez eux dans l'histoire culturelle et l'histoire des idées, et particulièrement dans celle de leur peuple jusqu'au milieu du XIXe siècle. »[71]

Ces jugements optimistes ne nous aident néanmoins pas à assigner à l'entreprise de Byrne une place adéquate dans la longue histoire et l'histoire de l'édition des *Eléments d'Euclide*. Mais fondamentalement les questions sont posées. Il s'agit d'examiner le contexte culturel plus étendu, ce qui est indispensable pour Byrne, parce que c'est à partir de cela que l'on peut éclaircir le sens plus profond et l'utilité plus grande de l'œuvre. Et le fait que le rapport géométrie-figure-forme soit respecté comme une tradition de grande influence en fait partie. Il est essentiel ici que l'ancrage de l'intuition dans la perception des sens reste garantie afin de soutenir l'intention didactique de son *Euclid*, même si ceci est en un premier temps présenté comme pour s'excuser : « Si l'illustration ne raccourcit pas le temps d'apprentissage, elles le rend au moins plus agréable. »[72] Il faut se pencher sur les propres arguments de Byrne.

Les remarques préliminaires que Byrne formule à intervalles réguliers dans ses livres sont suffisamment frappantes. Il y souligne toujours la distinction avec la pure science mathématique. Beaucoup de choses auraient été écrites par des mathématiciens érudits et expérimentés; mais ces travaux s'adresseraient davantage aux étudiants avancés et aux initiés qu'aux étudiants manquant encore d'expérience. Les longues formules, les règles compliquées et les démonstrations rebuteraient le débutant plus qu'elles ne l'instruiraient et celui-ci, déçu, cesserait d'apprendre ces choses qu'il aurait vite acquises si elles avaient été représentées avec simplicité.[73] Byrne se réfère à son expérience personnelle de l'effet dissuasif des mathématiques durant ses propres études et dans sa

fonction d'intermédiaire. Il veut corriger cette situation et l'améliorer. C'est pour cette raison qu'il aurait formulé ses explications de la même manière que dans le cours oral avec ses élèves.[74] L'écrit doit lui aussi être proche de la pratique et compréhensible. C'est l'intention de Byrne lorsqu'il introduit en 1835 la trigonométrie sphérique, dont le sous-titre renvoie expressément aux quelques règles simples (« few simple rules ») et, inversement, à l'évitement de difficultés plus grandes.

Des observations et recommandations correspondantes s'étirent comme un fil rouge à travers les nombreuses publications, agencées de manière clairement didactiques, d'Oliver Byrne. La première phrase de l'introduction du *Handbook for the artisan, mechanic, and engineer* promet que même le non-initié comprendra les problèmes les plus ardus en moins de temps qu'il n'en faut pour le dire.[75] Byrne ne craint pas non plus la comparaison avec les plus grands noms de sa discipline, on peut même dire qu'il les défie. A propos des tables de logarithmes dans l'annexe de sa publication *The Young Dual Arithmetician* (1866), vantée comme « new art, designed for elementary instruction and the use of schools » (un art nouveau, créé pour l'instruction élémentaire et l'usage dans les écoles), il écrira dans l'avant-propos qu'elles seraient aussi efficaces que celles de Babbage et Collet prises ensemble et ne nécessiteraient que moins d'un huitième de la place que celles-ci exigeaient.[76] Quoi qu'il en soit, l'attention que Byrne portait aux logarithmes a suscité de bonne heure un vif intérêt et ce aussi en Allemagne, là où primait l'avantage ou même l'« application des logarithmes à la vie », ce qui est révélateur. On pouvait lire ceci dans le sous-titre de la publication intitulée *Das Neueste und Interessanteste aus der Logarithmotechnik* (1852) du directeur d'école d'Eisenach, Adolf Lorey, dont la préface s'ouvrait sur une référence à Byrne et M. Philippe Koralek et soulignait la « dextérité technique, particulièrement en ce qui concerne le calcul instantané des logarithmes ».[77] L'introduction s'ouvre sur une comparaison: « Les logarithmes sont aussi puissants et efficaces en calcul que la vapeur en mécanique. »[78]

Ces témoignages indiquent que pour Byrne il y va en premier lieu de la transmission dans les conditions les plus simples. Le désir d'une compréhension rapide est au premier plan. Cela l'a évidemment aussi particulièrement guidé dans ses travaux géométriques. Byrne pose le premier accent important à ce sujet avec *The Doctrine of Proportion clearly developed, on a comprehensive, original, and very easy system; or, The Fifth Book of Euclid simplified*, qu'il soumet en 1841 tant que professeur de mathématiques du College of Civil Engineers à Putney et dédie aux directeurs, organes et étudiants de cette institution (ill. 8, 9).[79] Le titre de l'ouvrage évoque déjà le « système très commode » et le mot « simplifié » se référant au Livre V d'Euclide. Dès 1841, *The First Six Books of the Elements of Euclid* y est aussi indiqué, comme cela se fait couramment, à côté d'autres ouvrages de l'auteur. Ce qui suit dans la *Doctrine of Pro-*

portion est donc aussi, à plus d'un point de vue, une pré-impression des parties correspondantes de l'*Euclid* de 1847, les symboles introduits en 1841 apparaissant en partie sous une forme modifiée. Inversement, en 1847, il est fait mention de la publication précédente, en particulier des explications algébriques et arithmétiques qui y sont présentées et sont maintenant négligées.[80]

Le point de départ de l'ouvrage d'Oliver Byrne est clair. Pour l'auteur, la recherche correspondante est lacunaire et pleine d'inexactitudes et il observe ceci jusqu'à Isaac Newton en passant par Adrien-Marie Legendre.[81] Il lui oppose le vieux topique selon lequel la logique d'Euclide est absolument cohérente et exempte d'erreurs. Pour Byrne ceci vaut en particulier et sans réserve pour le Livre V d'Euclide qu'il déclare être le chef-d'œuvre de la raison humaine.[82] Il concentre donc son attention sur l'explication et l'illustration, s'appuyant sur des symboles dont il dit – ce qui est en contradiction avec De Morgan et l'estimation ultérieure de Cajori – que leur introduction dans les traités géométriques serait chaque jour plus usitée.[83] Face à l'évidence de ceci et l'utilité de la méthode, d'autres raisons ne seraient pas nécessaires. En 1841, toutefois, son objectif est encore de conserver les modes de représentation arithmétiques et algébriques; selon le cas on peut décider si la structure peut être édifiée sur des nombres, des symboles ou des lignes.[84] Ne s'est-on pas toujours servi de ces moyens de manière diverse et dans d'autres relations pour calculer les proportions?

Suivent alors des explications qui placent les symboles géométriques aux côtés des formules algébriques connues et comparent ainsi les signes visibles aux abstractions correspondantes («visible symbols with the abstractions for which they stand»). Finalement on remarque l'utilisation du langage familier, ce qu'il considérait déjà autrefois comme l'indicateur d'une méthode portant ses fruits.[85] Il s'agit de pouvoir reconnaître clairement et de transmettre les différences des symboles; en conséquence, la méthode doit être logique, stricte et convaincante et éviter ces détails ennuyeux et interminables qui accompagnent souvent d'autres méthodes.[86] Byrne a déjà compris que la différenciation par les couleurs appuierait cette distinction qui cherche à rendre les choses plus claires.[87] Dans son avant-propos à la *Doctrine of Proportion*, daté du 19 novembre 1840, il dit clairement à ce sujet que cela était l'intention à laquelle il a fallu renoncer pour des raisons financières.[88]

Byrne a manifestement déjà expérimenté sa méthode à l'époque, il a reçu des encouragements et des critiques. Il s'agissait par exemple, dans la cinquième définition du Livre V des *Eléments*, là où Euclide traite des multiples de grandeurs et de leurs identités proportionnelles, de remplacer la notion de «any equimultiples» (n'importe quels équimultiples) utilisée par Robert Simson dans l'édition d'Euclide anglaise la plus courante par «every equimultiples» (tous les équimultiples).[89] Même ici on remarque l'intention didactique de Byrne. Il ne cherche pas à faire suivre des tests quelconques et en quantité illimitée de ce genre mais à établir une

norme. Personne ne le contredirait s'il déclarait que les définitions et aussi quelques-uns de leurs parties et concepts doivent se passer d'explications supplémentaires. Cela est inséparable de l'objectif didactique; pour celui qui écrit sur des choses élémentaires, enseigner doit être le but le plus élevé.[90] Mais en procédant ainsi, Byrne s'était aussi abstenu d'offrir une analyse plus détaillée et d'expliquer cette définition euclidienne jugée particulièrement difficile depuis toujours. Et c'est Augustus De Morgan, qui s'intéressait à cette époque à cette question et à la signification du *ratio* et de la proportionnalité, qui publia ses réflexions justement en 1841 dans la *Penny Cyclopedia*.[91] Contrairement à Byrne, De Morgan avait mis au point des tests visant à contrôler l'utilité et la plausibilité de la formule euclidienne et il s'était en outre précisément servi d'une colonnade pour représenter et visualiser.[92]

En 1841, la connaissance de la signification fondamentale d'Euclide ne souffrait manifestement aucun retard pour Oliver Byrne. Sa *Doctrine of Proportion* doit prouver que le Livre V des *Eléments* d'Euclide représente le seul enseignement légitime de la proportionnalisation géométrique. Il veut en outre montrer à cet endroit que les proportions peuvent être traitées aussi bien de manière algébrique, arithmétique et géométrique vu qu'elles concernent pareillement ces domaines.[93] Les symboles choisis pour illustrer le Livre V des *Eléments* d'Euclide – ils seront modifiés légèrement en 1847 et sont désormais en couleur – empruntent la voie intermédiaire et ressemblent effectivement plutôt aux idéographies ultérieures. Ils se démarquent clairement des symboles géométriques ou géométrisants avec lesquels Byrne illustre les autres Livres des *Eléments* d'Euclide.

Byrne voit très bien les difficultés que peut générer cette approche: «La prudence est de règle parce que la couleur prise isolément n'a rien à voir avec les lignes, les angles et les grandeurs, sinon le fait de les nommer.»[94] Comment reconnaître voire distinguer cela face aux mesures didactiques orientées justement sur ces aides? Byrne représente le point et la ligne symboliquement, indirectement ainsi qu'on le constate, par des surfaces coloriées qui se chevauchent. Il faut donc pour ainsi dire «soustraire» quelque chose aux surfaces de couleur montrées dans l'illustration pour découvrir le point, la ligne et la surface.[95] L'ancienne explication mène la marche sous une forme plutôt compliquée: «Une ligne mathématique qui est une longueur sans largeur ne peut posséder de couleur, néanmoins le chevauchement de deux surfaces de couleur donne une bonne idée de ce qu'on entend par ligne mathématique... Lorsqu'on parle couramment de ligne noire ou rouge ou de lignes noires ou rouges, on pense en général à un tel accolage.»[96] On peut donc représenter la chose en question par le contact ou le chevauchement de surfaces coloriées. Dans son *Underweysung der messung* (Instructions pour la mesure à la règle et au compas; titre de l'édition française «L'art de la mesure» ou «Géométrie») de 1525, Albrecht Dürer avait éludé plus directement la difficulté de la

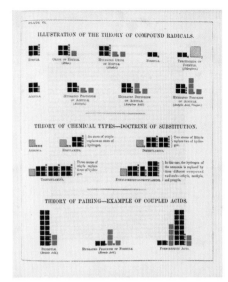

Ill. 39
Edward L. Youmans, *Chemical Atlas*, New York 1856, plate VI
– Example of colour and form, pictorial design: *Illustration of the Theory of Compound Radicals.*
– Beispiel von Farbe und Form, Bildgestaltung: *Bildliche Darstellung der Radikaltheorie.*
– Exemple de couleur et de forme : *Illustration de la théorie des radicaux composés.*

Ill. 40
Oliver Byrne, *The First Six Books of the Elements of Euclid*, London 1847, p. xiv
– Example of coloured plane and line: Depiction of a line (without breadth) by overlapping coloured planes.
– Beispiel von Farbfläche und Linie: Darstellung der Linie (ohne Breite) durch Überlappung von Farbflächen.

– Exemple de surface de couleur et de ligne : Représentation de la ligne (sans largeur) par le chevauchement de surfaces de couleur.

Ill. 41
Gyorgy Kepes, *Language of Vision*, Chicago 1944, p. 35
– Example of coloured planes, adjacency, and effects: *Adjacent color surfaces modify each other in hue and brightness.*
– Beispiel von Farbflächen, Berührung und Effekten: *Benachbarte Farbflächen modifizieren einander in Farbton und Helligkeit.*
– Exemple de surfaces de couleur, contact et effets : *Des surfaces de couleur adjacentes se modifient mutuellement sur le plan de la teinte et de la clarté.*

représentation de la ligne abstraite en traçant une ligne plus épaisse et ainsi visible, « car de cette manière, la raison intérieure doit être montrée dans l'œuvre extérieure ».[97] Byrne est bien conscient des risques que présentent de telles méthodes référentielles. Ses couleurs et ses diagrammes colorés sembleraient peut-être d'abord un peu maladroits ; mais il promet ensuite des garanties plus affinées et détaillées que toutes celles proposées à ce jour.[98] Ce qui est sans nul doute exact. Mais il semble que, ce faisant, les « coloured diagrams » s'émancipent. On ne peut s'empêcher de penser que Byrne a ajouté au système euclidien un second système, graphique celui-là, dont il ne se lasse pas de prouver l'utilité en indiquant en particulier que les couleurs se laisseraient beaucoup mieux mémoriser que de simples phrases dénuées de particularités.[99]

« More easily fixed in the mind » ! Voilà donc ce qui importe vraiment à Byrne. Il a maintenant réussi en 1847 ce qu'il a annoncé en 1841 : agencer son *Euclid* en couleur, facile à retenir, et adapté à toutes les expériences de la perception sensible. Ceci est bientôt pratiqué partout avec succès. En 1856, pour ne citer que deux exemples, est publié à New York le *Chemical Atlas* d'Edward Livingston Youmans, dans le titre duquel, de manière tout à fait comparable aux publications de Byrne, le mode de représentation « in a series of beautifully colored diagrams » et aussi l'intention, « designed for the use of students » semblent mis en avant (ill. 18–20, 32, 39). A Worcester, Ezekiel Webster Dimond publie en 1867 *The Chemistry of Combustion* dont la langue est la plus simple et la plus précise possible et évidemment en utilisant des couleurs au lieu de symboles chimiques : rouge pour l'oxygène, jaune pour l'hydrogène, bleu pour l'azote et noir pour le carbone (ill. 21–23, 33).[100]

Dans son introduction, Youmans écrit que c'est justement dans le domaine des sciences naturelles où la présentation exacte des propriétés et des relations est indispensable, que l'utilisation de diagrammes lisibles s'avère la plus profitable.[101] Et il voit – précédant de loin les habitudes d'aujourd'hui – une utilisation accrue de la représentation par l'image là où l'objet ne peut pas être vu du tout.[102] A titre d'exemples remplissant ces conditions, il cite en premier la géométrie et décrit l'opération correspondante comme « diagramize geometrical conceptions », la transformation de conceptions géométriques en diagrammes.[103]

Byrne avait entamé cette discussion dès 1841 et montré l'importance particulière de la couleur lorsqu'il s'agit d'illustrer des faits scientifiques. Il atteint son but en 1847. La même année, des allusions qu'il fait à la poésie montrent combien il s'intéresse à cette question psychologique avant la lettre. Il cite Horace et Esope pour documenter la supériorité du sens visuel. « Vieux comme le monde si l'on considère la tâche », le nouveau se trouverait maintenant dans la « combinaison mathématique de faits empiriques », écrira Gustav Theodor Fechner en 1860 dans son avant-propos aux *Elemente der Psychophysik*.[104] Il semble bien que le plus simple soit d'utiliser cela pour représenter des faits scientifiques. Et c'est sans aucun doute ce qui est sous-jacent à la démarche de Byrne. Dans les faits et en vérité, l'intérêt se déplace de l'objet scientifique à sa représentation et à sa transmission didactique. Il se sent poussé à souligner cela dans son introduction d'*Euclid* et à le mettre en avant de manière aussi imagée et concrète. Byrne recommande la craie de couleur et, pour l'usage privé, des crayons de couleur pour approfondir son *Euclid* en l'étudiant.[105]

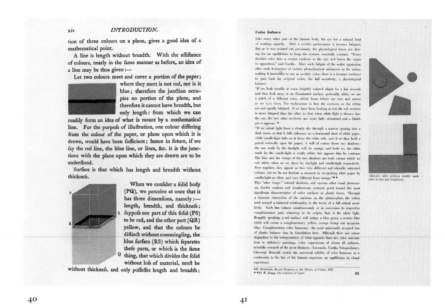

L'impetus didactique et les mesures qui lui sont nécessaires

« Among the Greeks, in ancient, as in the school of Pestalozzi and others in recent times, geometry was adopted as the best gymnastic of the mind. »
– Byrne, *Euclid*, 1847[106]

Byrne mentionne Johann Heinrich Pestalozzi dès le début de son introduction à *Euclid*. Il y est question de la « meilleure gymnastique de l'esprit »[107], d'une école de la pensée. Le principe didactique est orienté sur l'enseignement, les « démonstrations orales » et sur l'interaction idéale des impressions visuelles et acoustiques. La compréhension apparaît quand « la raison et le fait et la preuve » sont finalement réunis et laissent une impression durable. L'important n'est pas de savoir si la référence du texte au diagramme passe en tant que signe par la couleur et la forme ou si elle passe elle-même par les parties correspondantes du diagramme, c'est la simplicité qui compte et tout ce qui favorise la détermination.[108] C'est exactement cela que Pestalozzi voulait atteindre avec son *Elementarlehre* et son *Anschauungslehre der Zahlenverhältnisse*, une méthode ou un « exercice artistique » (« Kunstübung ») pour apprendre les mathématiques au même rythme que les « capacités cognitives » se développent (ill. 24, 25). Et c'est précisément cela qu'ambitionnait Byrne au moyen du symbole, de la figure et de la couleur et pour rendre l'étude plus facile.[109] « For the greater ease

of learning » – voilà donc en fin de compte la visée de l'auteur. Cela fait partie d'une longue tradition dans laquelle on a attribué en premier lieu un rôle d'intermédiaire aux mathématiques. Les mathématiques elles-mêmes ne sont pas une science, écrivait Jean Pic de la Mirandole dans la première de ses thèses sur les mathématiques ; elles ne mènent pas directement au bonheur ; elles sont des sciences auxiliaires, créent la voie qui mène à d'autres sciences.[110] Tout dépend de la *medietas*, de la position moyenne et intermédiaire.

Si on aborde les choses ainsi, on voit réapparaître les incertitudes liées à Euclide, l'obscurité qu'on lui attribuait. Tout le monde trouverait ceci extrêmement obscur, dit Giovanni Alfonso Borelli, évoquant le cinquième postulat d'Euclide, l'axiome des parallèles, parce qu'il lui manquerait les fondements, la compréhension de l'infini.[111] Mais il ne se laisse pas abattre. Lui aussi demande à acquérir de nouvelles connaissances – de manière classique – en déduisant ce qui est inconnu de ce qui est connu.[112] Et c'est ainsi qu'il publie son *Euclides restitutus*.

On s'arrange avec cette situation et on cherche des instruments susceptibles de rendre la tâche plus aisée. Longtemps avant Oliver Byrne, en 1684, St. George Ashe avait écrit pour les *Philosophical Transactions* de la Royal Society of London un article sur Euclide qu'il avait intitulé « A New and Easy Way of Demonstrating some Propositions in Euclid ».[113] Il s'y oriente sur la prééminence du savoir mathématique, « preeminence of Mathematical knowledge », pour insister d'autant plus clairement sur l'importance et la fiabilité de la méthode mathématique. Au premier plan, on trouve les quelques rares axiomes et postulats desquels il faut éloigner tout ce qui pourrait être ludique et toute absence de précision.[114] Une lettre de 1686 nous apprend que pour tenter de représenter le Livre II et le Livre V des *Eléments* d'Euclide, il s'est servi de la méthode préconisée par John Pell dans *An Introduction to Algebra*.[115] On ignore dans quelle mesure ses efforts sont en relation avec *The Elements or Principles of Geometrie*, un ouvrage anonyme paru en 1684 (ill. 26–28).[116] Ce qui est certain, c'est que ce manuel de géométrie rédigé postérieurement à Borelli suit une introduction avec des définitions et des axiomes accompagnés de l'explication des signes utilisés ensuite, signes en partie identiques à ceux qu'Oliver Byrne utilisait encore en 1847. Les objectifs sont similaires. Il s'agit de trouver la voie la plus rapide et la plus efficiente menant à une compréhension adéquate, pour le profit de tous ceux qui désireraient arriver le plus promptement possible aux questions pratiques de cette recherche.[117] C'est à cela que doivent servir les définitions de l'introduction, étant bien entendu que les points, les lignes et les angles sont des choses immatérielles. Les symboles en conservent d'autant plus leur légitimité. Mais l'explication ne suffit pas ; elle est suivie d'une autre explication plus détaillée, dans laquelle l'accent est mis encore plus distinctement sur la valeur de la démonstration : « Demonstration is the highest degree of Proof that any matter admits of » (la démonstration est le plus haut degré de preuve admise par une matière quelconque).[118] L'avantage fondamental de la géométrie, et indirectement de la méthode d'Euclide, est mis en évidence, pour aider l'homme à réfléchir et à le protéger de l'erreur et de l'illusion.[119] L'avantage didactique est noté sur le champ.[120] C'est la raison pour laquelle il est aussi nécessaire de créer les conditions préalables visant plus de clarté, dont fait aussi partie finalement, à côté des définitions, le tableau expliquant les signes, dans lequel les symboles graphiques indiquant la fonction ou les significations de « equal to » ou « like » ou « continued proportion » ainsi que des figures du triangle ou du cercle sont présentés dans une liste.[121]

Il semble que les objectifs didactiques, et avec eux les tentatives de trouver les méthodes correspondantes de représentation, aient depuis longtemps pris possession d'Euclide. Oui, cela semble être complètement inhérent à Euclide. Les mots formulés avec insistance par Oliver Byrne dans son introduction à *Euclid*, selon lesquels le but des couleurs n'était pas d'amuser ou de divertir mais de faciliter la recherche de la vérité et de propager un savoir durable, sonnent à nos oreilles.[122] On peut aussi le dire ainsi : plus l'effet de l'*obscuritas* proverbiale d'Euclide se prolonge, plus les questions de l'indication, de la démonstration et des instruments didactiques sont importantes.[123] Et plus l'utilisation est mise au premier plan, plus le besoin de modèles correspondants est grand. « En mathématiques, l'enseignant doit expliquer toutes les propositions par des modèles ou, s'il ne dispose pas de ceux-ci, chercher à compléter ce qu'il énonce par des dessins clairs et complets. »[124] Cela fait partie des conditions absolument indispensables, ainsi que l'écrit Peter Heinrich Christoph Brodhagen en 1792 dans son *Anleitung zum gemeinnützigen Unterricht*, destinée aux artisans, aux artistes et aux fabricants.

Avec Pestalozzi, auquel Byrne se réfère, ces demandes sont renforcées, les méthodes affinées et la question de la participation des sens est examinée de plus près. Oui, l'adaptation aux sens n'est bientôt plus accessoire mais essentielle. Ce qui est regardé se détache alors et construit pour lui-même une nouvelle logique, ou exprimé de manière moderne, un discours imagé. On l'observe très bien chez Byrne. Son *Euclid* est orienté vers les préoccupations de son temps. Ainsi Johann Georg Heinrich Feder constate en 1793 : « Beaucoup de choses dépendent de la configuration des signes lorsque l'on pense » et se réfère évidemment au *Neues Organon* de Johann Heinrich Lambert[125] (1764), qui était aussi très connu en Grande-Bretagne et qui est aussi finalement à l'origine de la phrase de Byrne selon laquelle toutes les langues seraient composées de signes représentatifs.[126] Et les sens sont plus que jamais au centre de l'attention, ainsi qu'en témoigne Byrne avec sa prédilection maintes fois exprimée pour l'enseignement oral. Pour Heinrich Stephani, le contraste entre la « langue entendue » et la « langue regardée » est le point de départ d'études qu'il publie en 1814 à Erlangen sous le titre *Ausführliche Beschreibung meiner einfachen Lese-Methode*.[127] Les lettres seraient à vrai dire « des signes des divers sons vocaux acceptés arbitrairement seulement pour l'œil » ; il désirerait cependant les considérer comme « les véritables notes de notre instrument linguistique ».[128] Pour le stimuler, il a recours à la mémoire qui peut retenir et consulter quasi mécaniquement de manière plus rapide les choses, et pas seulement les lettres, mais les lettres en syllabes et les mots entiers. Cela doit être reconnaissable du premier coup d'œil.[129] Si Stephani se réfère à Pestalozzi, il reste néanmoins fidèle aux anciennes méthodes mnémotechniques dans lesquelles on peut déduire la fin du mot – par exemple le « p » de Tul(pe), la tulipe, et le « t » de Fich(te), l'épicéa. On remarque vite que tout cela est moins simple que ne le laisse supposer le titre du livre. On en est encore au stade de l'expérimentation.

Mais nul ne peut douter du sérieux des promesses didactiques. Le principe « au premier coup d'œil », ce que par exemple Alfred North Whitehead (1927), en relation avec une optimisation des perceptions des sens (« sense-perception »), appelle l'immédiateté de la présentation (« presentational immediacy »), n'est pas si simple à mettre en œuvre et son effet n'est pas garanti.[130] Il n'empêche que face aux aides visuelles non-conventionnelles, un certain scepticisme est tout à fait à l'ordre du jour.

Dans l'avant-propos de son *Traité des couleurs* (*Farbenlehre*, 1812), Johann Wolfgang von Goethe s'étonne de la manière qui consiste à ajouter des planches aux ouvrages d'histoire naturelle : « Les planches que l'on a l'habitude de joindre à ce genre d'écrits sont un substitut extrêmement insuffisant. On ne peut cerner par des lignes ni esquisser en coupe un phénomène naturel qui exerce ses effets en tous sens. Il ne vient à l'idée de personne d'expliquer des expériences de chimie avec des figures ; pour tout ce qui est physiquement proche, c'est cependant l'usage parce qu'une chose ou l'autre peut être ainsi expliquée. Mais très souvent ces figures ne représentent que des concepts ; ce sont des moyens de fortune symboliques, des modes de transmission hiéroglyphiques qui peu à peu prennent la place du phénomène et de la nature, et entravent la véritable connaissance au lieu de la favoriser. »[131] Goethe voit donc aussi le danger de l'autonomisation de tels symboles et qu'ils puissent être utiles, par exemple en chimie, ne lui vient même pas à l'esprit. Et pourtant il leur accorde en l'occurrence dans la phrase suivante un certain sens : « Nous ne pouvons nous non plus nous passer des planches ; mais nous avons tenté de les agencer de telle manière que l'on puisse assurément s'en servir de manière didactique et polémique et même en regarder certaines comme faisant partie de l'appareil nécessaire. »[132] Où l'on voit que Goethe lui aussi se sert d'arguments didactiques pour se dérober.

Finalement Kant lui aussi s'intéresse à la thématique lorsqu'il tente de répondre à la question « Qu'est-ce que s'orienter dans la pensée ? » : « Nous pouvons placer nos concepts aussi haut et les abstraire autant que nous voulons des sens, il n'en reste pas moins que des idées figuratives leur restent attachées, dont la véritable détermination est de rendre aptes à l'usage empirique ceux qui ne se sont pas écartés de l'expérience. »[133] Kant en arrive de cette manière à parler de l'intuition (« Anschauung ») et trouve pour ce qu'il attribue, à l'instar de Moses Mendelssohn, à l'« évidence de la démonstration » ou à quoi il voudrait seulement donner une direction, pour ainsi dire en tant que condition minimale, « une certaine orientation ».[134] La manière dont nous attribuons nos idées à l'usage empirique le hante lui aussi.

————

Signes et symboles d'une philosophie mathématique

« Such for all common purposes are the audible signs called words, which are still considered as audible, whether addressed immediately to the ear, or through the medium of letters to the eye. Geometrical diagrams are not signs, but the materials of geometrical science, the object of which is to show the relative quantities or their parts by a process of reasoning called Demonstration. »
– Byrne, *Euclid*, 1847[135]

« Le schéma de la réflexion est donc aussi le schéma de la reproduction. »
– Wagner, *Mathematische Philosophie*, 1851 (a)[136]

« Usage empirique », « aides symboliques » ou en général seulement « orientation » ! On veut savoir ce qu'il en est des idées et de l'intui-

tion (« Anschauung ») et on cherche les avantages de la précision dans la démonstration et la voie la plus courte. Ce sont les problèmes linguistiques auxquels on s'intéresse beaucoup à l'époque. La réflexion amorcée par Oliver Byrne lorsqu'il identifie la langue à un système de signes s'achève dans la conviction que, dans son cas, l'utilisation de symboles colorés, de signes et de diagrammes rendrait les processus cognitifs plus précis et plus rapides.[137]

C'est dans l'air du temps, il faut travailler la langue. Du côté allemand, Karl Philipp Moritz consacre ses efforts à ce qu'il appelle, dans un discours à l'Académie royale des Sciences de Berlin , « la formabilité (‹ Bildsamkeit ›) de la langue allemande ».[138] On est par exemple frappé par le fait qu'il règne un « manque de termes artificiels allemands dans la théorie des grandeurs ».[139] « Quand la vie commune fait pousser de nouvelles branches, elle fait aussi pousser de nouveaux mots », écrit Friedrich Adolf Trendelenburg, le défenseur d'une *lingua rationalis*.[140] Le chercheur arrache « à la langue l'empreinte permanente pour son résultat »[141]. Et comme on considère que, « la pensée la plus abstraite est aussi avec et dans la langue » et qu'il est en outre urgent de « revenir à un concept simple en passant par une désignation simple », il faut, dans cette « ligne ascendante » et à partir de l'« auto-mouvement de l'intuition intérieure, réunir le concevoir et le concept ».[142]

Oliver Byrne a découvert les avantages du langage géométrique figuratif – en s'appuyant sur la couleur – et a ainsi par exemple quantifié de manière démonstrative le temps gagné pendant la perception.[143] Les essais visant à comparer les langues diverses avec leurs qualités particulières et à les réunir ne manquaient pas. Johann Jakob Wagner évoquait dès 1803 dans sa *Philosophie der Erziehungskunst* la « facilité de traduire les mathématiques en philosophie ».[144] En revanche, la logique lui aurait toujours semblé insuffisante et c'est dans les mathématiques qu'il a « toujours cherché l'architecture du monde et la connaissance ».[145] Il a reconnu en elles « la forme de l'objectivisation du mental, c'est-à-dire le langage ». Finalement, le « dualisme » de l'arithmétique et de la géométrie l'aurait conduit à prendre comme point de départ un élément commun situé plus haut, l'« intuition » (« Anschauung »).[146] Dans son *Organon* paru pour la première fois en 1830 et réédité en 1851, Wagner déploie toute la gamme des différentes langues et formes linguistiques.[147] Il distingue l'écriture des nombres et l'écriture des lignes qui comprend les lignes, les figures, « la trigonométrie c'est-à-dire les relations réciproques », « les corps c'est-à-dire les formes » et en plus la configuration de lignes et de figures.[148] Il nomme la géométrie qui livrerait les « traits fondamentaux d'une théorie des formes », une « écriture de relations » et une « abstraction de l'écriture imagée ».[149] Il prend pour base de la « construction de la langue » le schéma mot-nombre-figure-image, créant à partir de cela des analogies à poésie-musique-peinture-sculpture ou être humain-animal-plante-minéral.[150] Et il renvoie à la « série parallèle » idée-concept-perception-représentation respectivement symbole-exemple-signe-image.[151] En outre, dans sa *Mathematische Philosophie,* il place le tout dans une perspective historique, selon laquelle le « savoir spéculatif » pythagoricien était représenté sous forme de nombre et de figure, lesquels, sous la domination du mot, ont ensuite été transformés en une entité « mécanique », « et sont nommés mathématiques ».[152] L'image, en revanche, serait tombée en l'état de « jeux fortuits » ; « notre art ne produit que du paraître. »[153] Au regard du questionnement scientifique, la relation mot-nombre-figure reste donc au centre de l'intérêt. Et cela le préoccupe, en particulier dans son projet de traduire la mathématique en philosophie. Il veut sortir les mathématiques de l'état de « mécanisme mort » et les réhabiliter en tant que « langage naturel des idées ou langue de l'esprit » ainsi qu'« unique science générale ou philosophie ».[154]

Il faut suivre les traits caractéristiques de la représentation – du langage ! – en vertu de cette compréhension mathématico-philosophique. Dans sa *Philosophie der Erziehungskunst* de 1803, Wagner choisit de manière symbolique le théorème de Pythagore, qui apparaît d'ailleurs aussi en 1847 sous forme de figure sur la page-titre de l'*Euclid* d'Oliver Byrne. « Toute ligne est l'expression du mouvement, la trajectoire d'un corps en déplacement, fixée il est vrai dans l'espace pour être vue de l'extérieur mais qui ne peut être construite que par le sens intérieur et se meut dans le temps. »[155] Maintenant on construit la figure : « Soit une ligne donnée comme trajectoire ; qu'une autre ligne vienne vers elle d'un autre côté, sur la même voie mais en sens inverse, les deux lignes vont alors [...] se rencontrer, et si leur force est identique se réduire en un point, au zéro du mouvement. »[156] Ce genre d'énoncé demande un certain travail ; nous avons affaire ici à des représentations figura-tives, des extensions dans le domaine de la physique (la comparaison d'une ligne, ici avec une « poulie », là avec un « pendule »), qui doivent soutenir l'opération afin que « notre élève apprenne à connaître l'esprit et la nature dans le reflet qu'elles se donnent l'une de l'autre ».[157] La « définition réelle » (« Sacherklärung ») a été transformée depuis longtemps en « définition nominale » (« Worterklärung ») à travers laquelle les concepts sont formés, ainsi que l'observe Ephraim Salomon Unger en 1833 dans son introduction au système théorique d'Euclide.[158] Les explications sont rattrapées par les intentions didactiques, ce qui les justifie aussi.

De cette manière voit le jour chez Wilhelm von Türk, disciple de Pestalozzi, un « enseignement des formes » plus détaillé, qui, dans le style de l'époque et orienté de manière clairement didactique, est déployé sous forme de jeu de questions-réponses entre le maître et l'élève.[159]

« Le maître : (Il dessine un point, une droite, une courbe sur le tableau.)

Comment nomme-t-on (désignant 1) ce signe ?

Les enfants : Un point.

Le maître : (désignant 2 et 3) Et ces deux signes-ci ?

Les enfants : Des lignes. »

Ces exercices sont expérimentés à tour de rôle aux cinq sens et étendus à la forme, la couleur et l'orientation ; il s'agit en fin de compte de trouver et de former le « langage pour l'observation intérieure » (« Sprache für die innere Anschauung »).[160] Tout cela rejoint de nouveau les recommandations qu'Oliver Byrne associe

P. MONDRIAN

LE NÉO-PLASTICISME

Editions de l'EFFORT MODERNE
Léonce ROSENBERG
19, Rue de la Baume, 19
PARIS (8ᵉ)

1920

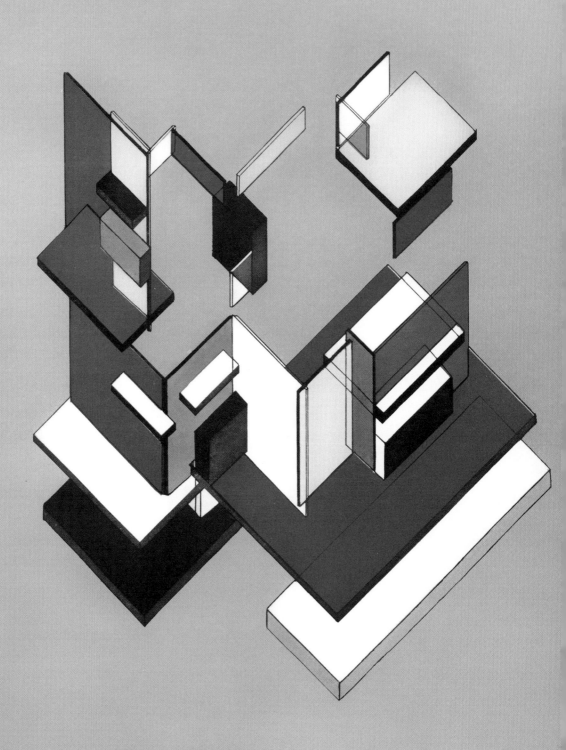

de stijl

the museum of modern art bulletin

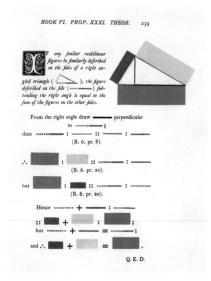

44

plus tard aussi à ses démonstrations orales privilégiant simultanément la vue et l'ouïe.[161] En fin de compte ce sont, comme l'indique le titre du manuel de Wilhelm von Türk, les perceptions des sens qui sont le point de départ au cœur de la discussion. Finalement, si l'on en croit la *Allgemeine Theorie des Denkens und Empfindens* qui a valu à Johann August Eberhard le prix de l'Académie royale des sciences de Berlin en 1776, on considérait aussi à l'époque des Lumières que dans la « plus récente philosophie spéculative », les « découvertes dans la théorie des sensations » auraient été remarquées en particulier comme un progrès.[162] Eberhard le souligne dans un premier point particulier et cite « les découvertes que l'on a faites sur la nature de quelques qualités dérivées […] des corps, notamment des couleurs ».[163] Il s'agissait à l'époque, en accord avec tant d'autres études, « de faire descendre la sagesse universelle du ciel des écoles et de l'introduire dans la société humaine ».[164]

L'*Euclid* de Byrne – si, c'est une œuvre d'art !

*« La logique veut que l'art soit l'expression plastique
de tout notre être. »*
– MONDRIAN, *Néo-Plasticisme*, 1920[165]

A la suite de Pestalozzi et de son *Anschauungslehre der Zahlenverhältnisse*, tout, même le plus abstrait, est repoussé dans le monde physique, le monde des formes. L'image que donne Oliver Byrne de la géométrie euclidienne qu'il voit comme une gymnastique mentale l'indique, aussi involontairement que très distinctement. Cela aussi correspond à une interprétation ancienne. Dans l'introduction à la *Philosophiae Naturalis Principia Mathematica*, Isaac Newton écrit le 8 mai 1686 que les descriptions des lignes droites et courbes sur lesquelles repose la géométrie feraient partie de la mécanique.[166] De plus, la géométrie postulant, il faudrait chercher ailleurs une explication.[167] Et d'un autre côté, la géométrie a besoin d'expansions en tout genre pour être accessible et être comprise. Et Newton de faire remarquer que la géométrie ne serait qu'une partie d'une *mechanica universalis* beaucoup plus vaste. On atteint empiriquement une telle « géométrie physique » de la même façon que l'on peut arriver aux phrases à partir de l'observation.[168] On peut aussi avoir recours à Albert Einstein et son célèbre exposé intitulé « Géométrie et expérience ». Lui considère la « géométrie pratique » comme une science de la nature, et même comme la branche la plus ancienne de la physique[169] – il avait constaté plus haut qu'il n'était « pas moins sûr que les mathématiques en général et tout particulièrement la géométrie sont nées de notre besoin d'apprendre quelque chose sur le comportement des choses réelles ».[170] Cela ne diminue en rien la valeur de ces « créations libres de l'esprit humain » que sont les axiomes ainsi qu'il le rappelle, ajoutant alors – ce qui correspond à l'évolution dans le maniement des symboles : « Par ‹ point ›, ‹ droite ›, etc., il ne faut entendre en géométrie axiomatique que des schèmes conceptuels vides de tout contenu. »[171] Ce n'est pas une situation satisfaisante et le rapport avec la réalité est expressément demandé. C'est la relation, sur laquelle – avec une accentuation différente – ils ont tous des vues, qui recèle la force explosive.

C'est ici que se croisent le mathématicien et l'artiste. Et les contours s'estompent de temps en temps avec les intérêts mutuels et l'emploi des moyens. Mais pourquoi devrait-on accorder moins de créativité au mathématicien qu'à l'artiste et vice-versa ? L'obscurité mystique n'est pas moins étrangère à Euclide qu'à l'inventeur d'images moderne, surtout si l'on se souvient des débuts de la grande tradition de la création des figures et des symboles. En 1901, Max Simon avait répondu à la question précédente et à la publication de Hubert Müller, *Besitzt die heutige Schulgeometrie noch die Vorzüge des Euclid-Originals?* (La géométrie scolaire allemande possède-t-elle encore les qualités de l'original d'Euclide ?) : « La géométrie scolaire allemande ne les a jamais possédées. »[172] On voit beaucoup d'illusions, un type idéal de pensée mathématique stricte. La demande d'une science rigoureuse, allant loin dans les sciences humaines,[173] et le besoin d'un « outil tranchant »[174] ont sans cesse fait oublier les difficultés physiques effectives. Que tout ce qui était précis ait été attribué à la géométrie et tout ce qui s'en écartait à la mécanique, synonyme de pratique, Newton en a pris connaissance en constatant que les erreurs ne sont pas dans la chose mais chez l'utilisateur (« Attamen errores non sunt artis, sed artificum »).[175]

D'un autre côté, si on regarde ce qui se passe dans le domaine de l'art, il ne peut être question de cette « crise de la forme » (« Gestalt-Krise ») que Max Steck invoquait en 1942 en ce qui concerne les mathématiques.[176] Il semble plutôt que la devise choisie par lui, *Mathesis est scientia imaginabilium* (Leibniz), qui considère les mathématiques comme une science des choses imaginables, ait une signification beaucoup plus large qu'on ne le supposerait. A ce moment-là, les mathématiques ont pénétré depuis longtemps, et plus que jamais auparavant, dans le domaine non seulement des idées mais dans celui du visible, du physique et du mécanique, et cette fois non par nécessité mais intentionnellement. Depuis Mondrian, et suivi en cela par Amédée Ozenfant et Le Corbusier et transposé dans l'architecture, est réécrit dans le concept « plastique », semblable à maints point de vue à celui de la forme, ce qui, issu de la compréhension correspondante et du discernement, est poussé avec force vers l'extérieur. Il s'agit ici de choses fondamentales, pas seulement d'analogie formelle ou de recherches tendant à géométriser et styliser les formes. La seule indication d'épuration et de simplicité ne suffit pas non plus, « car l'abstrait reste l'expression plastique en fonction de l'universel : c'est l'intériorisation la plus approfondie de l'extérieur et l'extériorisation la plus pure de l'intérieur ». [177] C'est Piet Mondrian qui, en 1920, rejette ainsi résolument tous les géométrismes purement superficiels qui resteraient de toute façon à l'écart. Seule une prise de conscience et une compréhension profondes permettent de tirer l'abstrait, le mathématique et le géométrique vers la réalité et – par nécessité – de le mettre dans une forme artistique. Il va de soi que les rapports apparaissent le plus là où cette référence nécessaire à la perception, dans le sens

d'une géométrie physique, a été vue comme un problème et là où – dans le but de la démonstration – elle a été expressément visée, recherchée, comme c'est aussi le cas chez Oliver Byrne. Dans cette mesure, on ne prend vraiment conscience qu'a posteriori de la position particulière et du caractère unique de l'*Euclid* de Byrne.

La précision que donne Byrne en 1847 au début de son introduction à *Euclid* – l'ouvrage n'aurait pas pour but l'agréable divertissement mais la quête de la vérité et le savoir – rejoint les propos similaires de Mondrian.[178] Celui-ci est à la recherche d'« un moyen plastique universel ». En préliminaire à son manifeste intitulé *Le Néo-Plasticisme* (ill. 42), il souligne sa façon de voir selon laquelle l'artiste « atteint son expression plastique par le conscient. Par cela, l'apparition de l'art est l'expression plastique de l'inconscient et du conscient. Elle montre le rapport de l'un et de l'autre : elle change, mais l'art reste immuable. »[179] C'est ainsi que l'aspect de transmission didactique, la manière de rendre visible, que possédait l'*Euclid* de 1847 est quasiment mis en lumière par la comparaison dans la nouvelle conception de l'art et l'objectif correspondant expliqué. Chez Mondrian non plus il ne s'agit pas en premier lieu de la forme qui apparaît lors de ce processus. Il faut, au contraire, éviter la forme en tant que fixation générale d'une apparence dans une image et mettre au premier plan le processus vers la précision et l'abstraction en tant que « moyen plastique universel ».[180] Afin de rendre ceci explicite, Mondrian critique expressément le processus de simplification et de purification – purement extérieur – que l'on peut observer parfois dans le domaine de l'architecture. Rares seraient ceux qui atteindraient l'effet plastique de l'abstrait.[181]

L'ère moderne s'annonce sur le fondement ancien et actuel du conflit entre le corps et l'âme, qui fait l'objet d'une controverse. On cherche à nouveau la *raison*. Paul Dermée écrit dans le premier cahier de *L'Esprit Nouveau* : « Dans l'intelligence, tout se passe avec l'accompagnement de conscience, dans une chambre claire. »[182] Lumière ! Il voit néanmoins l'ajustement nécessaire et l'équilibre recherché d'intelligence et de « lyrisme », le nouveau mot-clé. Léonce Rosenberg apporte ici deux formules qui vont animer les débats, une de Georges Braque qu'il cite : « J'aime la règle qui corrige l'émotion », et une autre, modifiée, qui lui est propre : « J'aime le sentiment qui humanise la règle. »[183] Si autrefois, en Grande-Bretagne, l'éthique et la morale d'Oliver Byrne, en particulier, devaient aider à comprendre le sens profond des mathématiques, c'est maintenant la psychologie qui offre ses services, toujours dans le souci d'apporter au monde des pensées pures. Mais la réserve est de rigueur. Au mot d'ordre qui est de « rebuter l'intelligence », Paul Dermée joint la recommandation « pas de logique apparente ».[184] Non, le nouveau penchant au conformisme ne devait pas trop se manifester. Et Amédée Ozenfant ainsi que Charles-Edouard Jeanneret, futur Le Corbusier, qui, sur la page suivante du premier cahier de *L'Esprit Nouveau* voulaient faire dériver de l'« origine mécanique de la sensation plastique » la fiabilité, les constantes et l'universalité pour leur travail artistique, comprendront très vite que cela ne pouvait être plus que fondement et point de départ.[185]

La transmission et l'élucidation et un retour à l'essentiel sont assurément une fois de plus nécessaires. Les arts et les sciences auraient pris tant d'ampleur que faciliter leur acquisition serait maintenant aussi important que faire reculer leurs limites – ainsi la première phrase, ôtée de son contexte, de l'*Euclid* de Byrne.[186] Edouard Le Roy entreprend dans *La pensée mathématique pure* qui repose sur les cours magistraux qu'il a donnés au Collège de France au cours des années 1914/15 et 1918/19, de caractériser son idée de mathématique pure de «vue imaginative intermédiaire entre le sensible et l'intellectuel».[187] Et ceci se réfère particulièrement à la géométrie, raison pour laquelle il parle de l'«intuition géométrique» spécifique. La géométrie s'immisce sans cesse dans la réalité et le monde sensible.[188] C'est ainsi que Le Roy prend en compte l'interaction et la réalité d'une géométrie physique. La géométrie lui apparaît comme une «mathématique sensibilisée»; elle est de ce monde.[189] C'est dans l'analyse qu'il trouve la mathématique vraiment pure. Leibniz avait lui aussi emprunté cette voie.[190]

La géométrie et Euclide sont donc exposés plus massivement au compromis avec le monde sensible, ce qui fait depuis longtemps partie de leur histoire et de la culture. De Stijl et Mondrian étaient à cet égard plus proches de la chose que les simples créateurs d'images. «La peinture est le moyen et non le but», écrivit aussi Léonce Rosenberg.[191] Et même lorsqu'il s'agit de la couleur, les arguments qu'utilisent Oliver Byrne, Ozenfant et Le Corbusier semblent comparables. «Quand on parle peinture, on parle forcément couleur», peut-on lire dans le texte programmatique du *Purisme* qui commence là où, au début de l'argumentation, la logique apparaît, dérivée des «constantes humaines», et utilisée en tant qu'instance de contrôle contre la «marche parfois fantasque de l'intuition».[192] Prises isolément, les couleurs seraient problématiques, voire dangereuses.[193] Elles devraient servir la cause, elles doivent être «essentiellement constructives».[194] «Une peinture est l'association d'éléments épurés, associés, architecturés».[195] Impossible de ne pas remarquer les parallèles à Byrne[196]. Même la plus grande rapidité de la perception visuelle des couleurs, qu'il soulignait déjà, est prise en compte ici: «Mais la couleur a des propriétés de choc (ordre sensoriel) précédant optiquement la connaissance de la forme (qui est une création déjà partiellement cérébrale).»[197]

Si l'on considère en outre le poids que Byrne a donné à l'aspect didactique de son *Euclid*, on observe un parallèle encore plus net chez Gyorgy Kepes qui, dans la tradition de De Stijl et sous l'influence directe de la Gestalt, a publié en 1944 son *Language of Vision* (ill. 34, 35, 37, 41).[198] L'aspect de la langue, de la transmission, est ici rétabli de la même façon. A la suite de Mondrian, Kepes parle d'organisation plastique, utilisant à des fins explicatives la paraphrase du modelage d'impressions des sens devenant des touts organiques.[199] Le processus de formation est au premier plan mais il s'agit ici aussi évidemment de manière accrue de présentation visuelle et évidemment de l'image créée. On est néanmoins stupéfait lorsqu'on remarque à quel point Kepes accorde lui aussi de l'attention au chevauchement des surfaces de couleur. Celui-ci ne sert plus la représentation de formes géométriques élémentaires comme chez Byrne mais d'autant plus l'équilibre chromatique et en général les phénomènes visuels.[200] La rétrospective historique de Kepes va jusqu'à Helmholtz, il mentionne brièvement Léonard de Vinci, Goethe bien sûr mais aussi Arthur Schopenhauer qui, dans la première phrase de son étude de 1816 intitulée *De la vue (Ueber das Sehn und die Farben)*, avait déjà décrit le cadre plus large avec les problèmes inhérents: «Toute intuition (‹ Anschauung ›) est intellectuelle. Car sans l'entendement (‹ Verstand ›), on ne parviendrait jamais à l'intuition, à la perception, à l'appréhension des objets; mais on en resterait à la simple sensation qui tirerait bien quelque signification de son rapport à la volonté, comme douleur ou plaisir, mais qui n'en demeurerait pas moins un changement d'états vides de sens et non pas quelque chose qui ressemblerait à une connaissance.»[201] Il ne voulait et ne pouvait pas accorder au *Traité des couleurs (Zur Farbenlehre)* de Goethe le statut de théorie. D'un autre côté, ses réflexions livreront les arguments décisifs à la psychophysique.

En Grande-Bretagne – du temps d'Oliver Byrne et d'Augustus De Morgan –, toute tentative visant à sortir des limites plus étroites des mathématiques semblait mener à l'éthique et à la morale. A l'époque moderne, celles-ci ont cédé la place à la psychologie qui se charge en particulier des zones limitrophes et de toutes les difficultés associées au problème corps-âme. C'est au moment où elle se souvenait des lois et des règles fixes – et aussi en particulier de celles de la géométrie – que la psychophysique a concerné les arts.[202] Et évidemment la psychologie gestaltienne s'intéresse particulièrement à des questions comme celles des moments de prégnance sensorielle ou au mode d'action de la couleur. Tout cela a joué un rôle important dans l'*Euclid* d'Oliver Byrne.

En 1862, dans son introduction aux *Beiträge zur Theorie der Sinneswahrnehmung*, consacrée aux méthodes, 'Wilhelm Wundt écrit: «La tentative de construire des faits psychologiques sur une base métaphysique, est très étroitement attachée au traitement mathématique de la psychologie. Celle-ci est une conséquence presque nécessaire du fait que la psychologie métaphysique englobe la méthode déductive.»[203] Cela indique quasi impérativement combien la géométrie, et sa transposition sensible, pourrait, elle aussi, être demandée et l'est. Wundt poursuit: «Si, dans une science, les simples procédures de la logique formelle ne suffisent pas à faire dériver un nombre plus élevé de faits de quelques axiomes, à travers une série de conclusions plus ou moins compliquées, le langage des signes mathématique devra venir à l'aide de la science.»[204] Kant avait déjà postulé que, de temps à autre, la nature devrait être forcée de répondre aux questions de la raison.[205] Un tel soutien de l'intelligibilité humaine est nécessaire. Et Wundt de formuler après cette demande : « Ce [langage des signes] n'est qu'une aide efficace de la pensée, il n'est qu'une utilisation multipliée des lois de la logique, qui fixe les résultats de la pensée sur chaque degré de la série de conclusions à l'aide de signes déterminés. »[206]

Wundt avait ajouté à cet endroit une note en bas de page indiquant ce qu'il pensait du stade de développement des mathématiques à cet égard : « Le mathématicien devrait trouver cette définition un peu trop vaste, parce que les mathématiques n'ont effectivement pas encore trouvé jusqu'ici une utilisation aussi générale. Mais il me semble qu'il est impossible de méconnaître que les toutes nouvelles mathématiques aspirent à cette nouvelle généralisation du calcul qui fait seulement d'elles une logique élargie. »[207]

A partir d'ici, les choses ont assez souvent évolué dans des voies différentes. La question de savoir avec quelle précision l'Euclide mondrianesque de Byrne est adapté à ce développement, ou à l'un de ces développements, reste ouverte. Ce qui est sûr, c'est que les mathématiciens se sont très peu ou pas du tout intéressés à lui, même les euclidiens. D'un autre côté, le domaine des sciences est depuis toujours un domaine fermé sur lui-même et les scientifiques n'ont que trop volontiers fait jouer leurs « principes et méthodes précis » contre la philosophie moins puissante (dans ses propres cercles), quoi que cela ait pu signifier.[208] Nouvelle science basée sur une chose fort ancienne, la psychophysique de Fechner qui commençait avec un questionnement si complet, devait offrir, elle aussi, selon une première définition de 1860 « brièvement un enseignement exact des relations entre le corps et l'âme ».[209] De l'exactitude, un caractère scientifique, voilà ce qu'on attendait !

L'*Euclid* d'Oliver Byrne reste unique en son genre. C'est la raison pour laquelle les relations potentielles avec Pestalozzi ou avec la philosophie mathématique de Wagner, que ce soit sous l'aspect du langage ou de la géométrie, n'en sont que plus intéressantes et révélatrices. Il était plus proche des faits de Helmholtz qu'il n'y paraît peut-être de prime abord. On aurait « constamment affaire en géométrie à des figures idéales [...] dont la représentation physique n'est en réalité toujours qu'une approche des exigences du concept, et on ne décidera si un corps est solide, si ses surfaces sont planes, si ses angles sont droits qu'à l'aide des mêmes propositions dont la justesse effective resterait à prouver par l'examen. »[210] Approcher ces vérité universelles, voilà ce qui a attiré Byrne, le mathématicien, autant que Piet Mondrian, l'artiste. Peut-être que la géométrie n'est pas du tout ce que l'on décrit, en l'absence d'autres bases sûres, comme une structure inébranlable et conclusive dont on veut attribuer l'invention à Euclide, mais bien davantage une création pythagoricienne, une représentation du monde en formes et en figures qui sont conformément à ceci moins conclusives mais au lieu de cela appréhensibles au premier coup d'œil. Oliver Byrne a habillé cette idée de couleurs et anticipé ainsi un langage qui sera

nommé à l'époque moderne *Neue Gestaltung*, ainsi le titre connu d'un livre de Theo van Doesburg.

Theodor W. Adorno a précédé sa *Dialectique négative (Negative Dialektik)* d'une sentence de Walter Benjamin : « ... Il faut traverser les déserts glacés de l'abstraction pour parvenir au point où il est possible de philosopher concrètement. »[211] Il ne s'agit en aucun cas d'un désert glacé que l'on désirerait quitter le plus vite possible ! Tout tourne autour de cette abstraction et de sa pénétration dans le monde visible, en tout cas chez Byrne et Mondrian. Il n'est pas question de l'abandonner mais de la rendre visible ! « L'abstrait reste l'expression plastique en fonction de l'universel : c'est l'intériorisation la plus approfondie de l'extérieur et l'extériorisation la plus pure de l'intérieur. »[212] Dans cette phrase du manifeste *Le Néo-Plasticisme* de 1920, Mondrian s'était référé à la troisième partie de ses remarques « De Nieuwe Beelding in de Schilderkunst » publiées dans *De Stijl*, où il concentrait son attention sur la relation « abstraite/mathématique ».[213] L'équation correspondante remonterait à Aristote.[214] En vérité et concrètement, Mondrian se trouve ici encore clairement dans la tradition qui lui a été en particulier transmise aussi par Mathieu Schoenmaekers, dans laquelle l'intérêt porté aux idées universelles était maintenu vivace et dans laquelle la géométrie servait depuis toujours de point de départ et Euclide de témoin capital. Pour le formuler plus globalement avec les mots d'Oliver Byrne : « Si nous avions besoin d'autorités pour prouver l'importance et l'utilité de la géométrie, nous pourrions citer chaque philosophe depuis l'époque de Platon. »[215]

Ill. 45
Piet Mondrian
*Composition with Red, Yellow, and Blue/Komposition mit Rot,
Gelb und Blau/Composition avec rouge, jaune et bleu*, 1927
Oil on canvas, 51.1 x 51.1 cm (20 1/8 x 20 1/8 inches)
Cleveland, The Cleveland Museum of Art, Contemporary
Collection of the Cleveland Museum of Art 1967.215
© 2010 Mondrian/Holtzman Trust c/o HCR International,
Virginia, USA

Annotations

1   Frege 1893, p. xiv, note 1.
2   Cf. Steck 1981, p. 179 et suiv. Cf. en particulier aussi : Steck 1943, S. 131 et suiv.: passim et. p. 133 (« Schaufähigkeit »).
3   Citation d'après Knittermeyer 1939, p. 59 et suiv. in : Steck 1943, note 24, p. 148.
4   Cf. Steck 1981, p. 180.
5   Cf. Speiser 1932, p. 14.
6   Ibidem. Il se trouve ainsi dans la tradition qui remonte à Schelling 1797, préface, p. iii et suiv., qui argumentait contre le « mélange [...] jusqu'ici de principes tout à fait hétérogènes » en philosophie et faisait maintenant une distinction entre la philosophie « pure » et la philosophie « appliquée » : « La philosophie purement théorique ne s'occupe que de l'analyse de la réalité de notre savoir . »
7   Cf. Schelling 1797, p. iv.
8   Cf. Rickert 1913, p. 189 et 188.
9   Rickert 1913, p. 191, complète ici : «... tant qu'une théorie mécanique fait défaut », mais déclare un peu plus haut que sur la voie de son perfectionnement « une explication scientifique, c'est-à-dire mécanique d'un processus naturel devrait pratiquement être identifiée à une démonstration ».
10 Cf. Bloch 1909.
11 Cf. ci-dessous.
12 Cf. Husserl 1936, p. 77 et suiv. Déterminante pour notre contexte (cf. aussi ci-dessous), l'analyse de la signification de la géométrie avant et après Galilée (p. 103 et suiv.), « sans qu'il ressente le besoin, ce que l'on conçoit aisément, d'aborder la manière dont cette activité idéalisante naquit initialement (notamment du substrat du monde sensible pré-géométrique et de ses arts pratiques) et d'approfondir les questions de l'origine de l'évidence mathématique apodictique ».
13 Cf. Rickert 1910/11, p. 1 et suiv. : p. 7.
14 Cf. Husserl 1910/11, p. 289 et suiv. : p. 289.
15 Id., p. 341.
16 Ibidem.
17 Cf. Frege 1882, p. 48 et suiv. : p. 56 ; id., in : Frege 1964, p. 106 et suiv. : p. 114.
18 Ibidem.
19 Cf. Frege 1893, avant-propos, p. xiv.

20 Id., p. xxv.
21 Id., p. 3.
22 Id., p. 1 et suiv. avec référence à la précédente publication *Grundlagen der Arithmetik*, Breslau 1884.
23 Id., p. xix. D'un autre côté il se défend évidemment (p. xii) contre des suppositions telles que « metaphysica sunt, non leguntur » et « mathematica sunt, non leguntur ».
24 Id., p. xvii et suiv. et xx.
25 Id., p. xxi.
26 Cf. Russell 1897, p. 1.
27 Id., p. 10 et suiv.
28 Cf. Riemann 1892, p. 272 et suiv. : p. 272 et 286. La critique de la géométrie qui commence avec le concept d'espace est plus compréhensible si on se souvient de la manière dont Wolff concevait les mathématiques ; la première définition des principes fondamentaux de la géométrie est la suivante : « La géométrie est une science de l'espace que les objets physiques occupent selon leur longueur, leur largeur et leur épaisseur. » (Cité ici d'après l'édition tardive : Wolff 1755, p. 65.) Mais on trouve aussi en même temps la définition courante « La géométrie, c'est la science des mesures ou des grandeurs dans la mesure où elles peuvent être mesurées en étant attachées l'une à l'autre [...] », donc de l'« art de la mesure » (cf. Fabricius 1752, p. 454).
29 Précédé, en référence directe à Riemann, de la contribution « Über die Tatsachen, die der Geometrie zugrunde liegen » (in : *Nachrichten von der Königlichen Gesellschaft der Wissenschaften und der Georg-August-Universität aus dem Jahre 1868*, n° 9, p. 193 et suiv. ; reproduit dans : Helmholtz 1968, p. 32 et suiv.).
30 Cf. Helmholtz 1879, p. 25.
31 Ibidem.
32 Id., p. 23.
33 Cf. Husserl 1891, p. 131 : « Le but que se fixe Frege doit donc être nommé chimérique. »
34 Id., p. 130.
35 Ibidem.
36 Cf. ici en particulier : Husserl 1913, introduction, p. 1 et 7 et suiv.
37 Cf. Helmholtz 1879, p. 7.
38 Lothar Kreiser souligne dans son introduction à Frege, 1973, p. viii, à quel point l'idéographie de ce dernier était, elle aussi, démodée.

39 Cajori 1928, p. 429.
40 Cf. Cajori 1928, p. 429.
41 Ibidem.
42 Id., note 4, avec référence à Heiberg 1912, p. 20.
43 Cité ici d'après Cajori, 1928, p. 429 et suiv. (d'après : De Morgan 1849, p. 92 et suiv.). « Geometrical reasons, and arithmetical process, have each its own office ; to mix the two in elementary instruction, is injurious to the proper acquisition of both. »
44 Cf. aussi ci-dessous.
45 Cf. De Morgan 1872, p. 199, « This author really believed himself, and was in earnest. He is not the only person who has written nonsense by confounding the mathematical infinite (of quantity) with what speculators now more correctly express by the unlimited, the unconditionel, or the absolute. »
46 Cf. De Morgan 1915, p. 329, note 1. Op. cit. p. 344 la critique de la *Theory of Parallels* (1840) d'Oliver Byrne.
47 Ceci est par trop souvent le cadre plus vaste dans lequel on fait aussi l'histoire des mathématiques du côté des mathématiques ! Cf. Casselman 2000, p. 1257 et suiv. (p. 1260 à propos de Byrne).
48 Cf. Phillips 2005, p. 105 et suiv.
49 Cf. De Morgan 1838, avant-propos, p. xvi.
50 Cf. Grattan-Guinness 1992, p. 1 et suiv. ; Phillips 2005, p. 105 et suiv.
51 Les définitions que donne De Morgan de la *ratio* et de la proportion sont encore considérées comme les meilleures par Thomas L. Heath (cf. Heath 1956, p. 116 et suiv. La discussion à propos d'Eutocius et des concepts *pelikotes* voire *pelikos* a néanmoins été menée bien avant De Morgan de manière différenciée chez Meibomius 1655, p. 11.
52 La même année parut aussi la publication, qui prouve le fondement arithmétique particulier des recherches et intérêts mathématiques de De Morgan ; cf. De Morgan 1847.
53 Cf. ci-dessous.
54 De telles déclarations sont basées en premier lieu sur une intention méthodique. On s'intéressait évidemment beaucoup à l'époque aux chevauchements de la géométrie et de l'arithmétique. En 1846, Hermann Scheffler, par-

tant d'une observation de Gauss, a publié son travail intitulé *Über das Verhältniß der Arithmetik zur Geometrie, insbesondere über die geometrische Bedeutung der imaginären Zahlen*, soulignant dans l'introduction le classement différent sous la rubrique représentation « figurative » voire « acte entier de la capacité intellectuelle » en « concepts abstraits » . On se ferait bien sûr une idée fausse de De Morgan si on voulait le réduire à cette déclaration citée par Cajori.
55 Des actes de la Cambridge Philosophical Society, vol. 10, 1864, p. 173 et suiv. ; cité ici d'après : Church 1936, p. 121 et suiv. : p. 128.
56 Cf. Mill 1873, p. 225.
57 Pour compléter cette image, il faut prendre le temps de lire les réactions mitigées de Mill à Auguste Comte (et suiv. id., p. 209 et suiv.).
58 Cf. Whewell 1840 et 1847 ; Whewell 1849 ; Whewell 1858.
59 Cf. Byrne 1847, introduction, p. vii.
60 Ibidem.
61 Cf. Cajori 1928, p. 431 : « Individual workers who in elementary fields proposed to express practically everything in ideographic form have been overruled. » Cajori l'interprète comme une tendance au conservatisme en ce qui concerne l'utilisation de symboles et semble l'expliquer par la pression du groupe : « by large groups or by representatives of large groups ». Et il clôt ces réflexions de manière sibylline : « The problem requires a consensus of opinion, the wisdom of many minds. That wisdom discloses itself in the history of science. The judgement of the past calls for moderation. »
62 Cf. Hesse 1865, préface.
63 Cf. Arneth 1852, p. 288.
64 Cf. Bense 1946, p. 53.
65 Ibidem.
66 Ce qui est probablement la seule étude récente de quelque importance sur l'*Euclid* de Byrne ne va pas beaucoup plus loin : cf. Tufte 1990, p. 84 et suiv.
67 Cf. Casselman 2000.
68 Byrne 1847, introduction, p. vii, « Le but de cet ouvrage est plus que l'illustration ; nous n'utilisons pas les couleurs pour divertir ou pour amuser avec certaines combinaisons de couleur et de

forme, mais pour aider l'esprit dans sa recherche de vérité, accroître les facilités de l'instruction et diffuser un savoir durable. Si nous avions besoin d'autorités pour prouver l'importance et l'utilité de la géométrie, nous pourrions citer chaque philosophe depuis l'époque de Platon. Chez les anciens Grecs comme à l'école de Pestalozzi et d'autres plus récentes, la géométrie était considérée comme la meilleure gymnastique de l'esprit. »

69 Le mot-clé chez : Krbek 1954, p. 205 et suiv. Ici en sous-titre la devise : « La forme est la sœur visible du nombre. »

70 Cf. Steck 1946, p. 17.

71 Ibidem.

72 Cf. Byrne 1847, introduction, p. vii.

73 Cf. Byrne 1835, 2002, avant-propos.

74 Ibidem.

75 Cf. Byrne 1853, avant-propos, p. vii : « Although this work is written to guide the experienced and accomplished artisan, yet the descriptions and directions are of so practical a nature, that any mechanic or amateur, previously unacquainted with the subjects treated of, may, by following its pages as a text-book, succeed in his earliest attempts to accomplish even the most difficult processes inscribed. »

76 Cf. Byrne 1866, avant-propos, p. vi, « They are equal in power to Babbage's and Collet's combined, and take up less than one eighth part of their space. »

77 Cf. Lorey 1852, p. iii.

78 Id., introduction, p. 1.

79 Cf. Byrne 1841.

80 Cf. Byrne 1847, p. 210.

81 Cf. Byrne 1841, p. viii, « ...while there is not one mistake, oversight, or logical objection in the whole of Euclid's Fifth Book. »

82 Ibidem. « ...in fact, Euclid's Fifth Book is a master-piece of human reasoning. »

83 Id., p. xv.

84 Id., p. xiv, « whether the structure be raised upon numbers, symbols, or lines, &c. ».

85 Cf. Ci-dessus note 74.

86 Cf. Byrne 1841, p. xvi, « logical, strict, and convincing... without being attended with that tediousness and circuitous detail which frequently accompany other methods ».

87 Ibidem.

88 Ibidem.

89 Cf. la traduction ultérieure qui met à contribution « the same equimultiples » à des fins explicatives. Heath 1956, p. 120.

90 Cf. Byrne 1841, p. xviii : « To teach should be the highest aim of a writer on elementary subjects, and not to adopt (which is too often the case) that stiff and formal manner so prejudicial to and inconsistent with the ideas of a learner; every thing likely to embarrass should be explained, and that authorial kind of scientific dignity should be set aside when the object is to instruct others. »

91 Cf. ci-dessus.

92 Cf. Heath 1956, p. 122 et suiv.

93 Byrne 1841, p. xviii.

94 Byrne 1847, p. xiii.

95 Les démonstrations correspondantes : id., p. xiii et xiv.

96 Id., p. xiii.

97 Cf. Dürer 1525, fol. A ij recto : « Dann durch solche weyß muß der innerliche verstand im eussern werck angetzeigt werden. »

98 Cf. Byrne 1847, p. xiii, « a clumsy method ... means more refined and extensive than any that has been hitherto proposed ».

99 Id., p. xii, « The experience of all who have formed systems to impress facts on the understanding, agree in proving that coloured representations, as pictures, cuts, diagrams, &c. are more easily fixed in the mind than mere sentences unmarked by any peculiarity. »

100 A ce sujet, le commentaire dans l'avant-propos : « Technical terms always present a formidable obstacle to practical men in the investigation of any scientific subject. » Cf. Dimond 1867, p. vi.

101 Cf. Youmans 1856, introduction, p. 9, « It is especially in natural science, where definite and exact ideas of properties and relations are to be communicated to the mind, that the employment of visible diagrams is most useful. »

102 Ibidem. « Whenever the object to be contemplated cannot itself be seen, and consists of such fixed elements or qualities as are capable of being represented or delineated to the eye, pictorial illustrations become indispendable. »

103 Ibidem.

104 Cf. Fechner 1860, introduction, p. v.

105 Cf. Byrne 1847, p. xvii, « For

schools and other public places of instruction, dyed chalks will answer to describe diagrams, &c. for private use coloured pencils will be found very convenient. »

106 Byrne 1847, introduction, p. vii, « Chez les anciens Grecs comme à l'école de Pestalozzi et d'autres plus récentes, la géométrie était considérée comme la meilleure gymnastique de l'esprit. »

107 Id., p. vii.

108 Id., p. xi.

109 Cf. Pestalozzi 1803, préface, p. v : « La théorie des rapports arithmétiques est, en tant que partie de la méthode, un exercice artistique visant à enseigner à l'homme à compter et à calculer, d'une manière correspondant à la nature de son esprit et à la manière dont sa force mentale se développe en lui. »

110 Cf. Pic de la Mirandole 1532, p. 137; « Conclusiones de mathematicis secundum opinionem propriam numero lxxxv. »

111 Cf. Borelli 1679, « Ad lectorem geometram » (introduction), s. p.

112 Ibidem : « progressus Intellectualis ex notis ad ignota. »

113 Cf. Ashe 1684, p. 672 et suiv.

114 Ibidem : « it rejects all trifling in words and Rhetorical schemes, all conjectures, authorities, prejudices and passion. »

115 Cf. Early Letters of the Royal Society EL/A/36 (St. George Ashe, 27 avril 1686) ; Cf. AHRB Centre for Editing Lives and Letters, 2005. Cf. Pell 1668. L'Algèbre de Pell est une traduction élargie et modifiée de l'Algèbre de Johann Heinrich Rahn, bailli de Kyburg.

116 Cf. *The Elements or Principles of Geometrie*, Londres 1684. L'exemplaire de la Trinity College Library à Dublin montre la signature de St. George Ashe, c'est sans doute la raison pour laquelle une participation est postulée dans l'édition en ligne (Ann Arbor). Notre exemplaire présente des divergences.

117 Id., « Advertisement », fol. A3 recto et verso.

118 Le bref « Advertisement » s'achève sur la constatation : « This Summary was thought sufficient for an Introduction ». Une introduction supplémentaire présentant une succession de feuilles indépendantes A–(A4) verso, est pourtant insérée dans notre exemplaire.

119 Id., fol. A1 recto : « And by consequence nothing is so apt to strengthen our Reason to give us clear notion of things, and secure us from being imposed upon fallacies or shadows of proof, as conversing herein. »

120 Id., fol. A1 recto : « Demonstration therefore serving (as we said) to enlighten the mind. »

121 Cf. *The Elements or Principles of Geometrie*, Londres 1684, fol. B4 verso.

122 Cf. Byrne 1847, p. vii.

123 On de devrait pas séparer la « science » et la « didactique » comme cela vient d'être le cas ici. Dans l'ancienne tradition, chez Jean Duns Scot par exemple, la « scientia » est, selon sa compréhension d'Aristote, avant toutes les autres réflexions un *medium demonstrationis*. (Cité ici d'après : Jean Duns Scot (ou : Johannes de Cornubia?) 1512, fol. a 2 verso.)

124 Cf. Brodhagen 1792, p. vii.

125 Cf. Lambert 1764.

126 Cf. Feder 1793, p. 70.

127 Cf. Stephani 1814, p. 9. Pour Stephani les pictogrammes, par exemple – avant Champollion – les hiéroglyphes égyptiens, font partie du « langage regardé ».

128 Id., p. 12 et suiv.

129 Cf. Oechslin 2007. p. 62 et suiv.

130 Cf. Whitehead 1927, p. 21.

131 Cf. Goethe 1812, p. xxi.

132 Ibidem.

133 Cf. Kant 1793, p. 104 et suiv.

134 Id., p. 105.

135 Byrne 1847, p. ix, « Tels les signes acoustiques d'usage courant que nous nommons mots, toujours considérés comme audibles qu'ils soient immédiatement adressés a l'oreille, ou à l'œil par le biais des lettres. Les diagrammes géométriques ne sont pas des signes mais des matériaux de la science géométrique dont le but est de montrer les grandeurs relatives ou leurs parties par un processus de raisonnement nommé Démonstration. »

136 Wagner 1851 (a), p. 124.

137 Cf. Byrne 1847, p. ix. (« ... renders the process of reasoning more precise, and the attainment more expeditious... »)

138 Cf. Moritz 1794, p. 87 et suiv.

139 Cf. Burja 1794, p. 265 et suiv.

140 Cf. Trendelenburg 1828, p. 457 et suiv. : p. 457.

141 Id., p. 457.

142 Id., p. 458 et 473 et suiv.

143 Cf. Byrne 1847, p. ix.

144 Cf. Wagner 1803, p. 148. Wagner écrit rétrospectivement, qu'adolescent il se serait déjà promis d'entreprendre cette tâche, qu'il réalisera pour la première fois en 1811 dans la *Mathematische[n] Philosophie*: cf. Wagner 1851 (b), p. xl et xxxi. – Cf. pour Wagner: Stock 1982, p. 262 et suiv.

145 Cf. Wagner 1851 (b), p. xli. (Vue rétrospective sur l'*Organon* de 1830).

146 Ibidem.

147 Cf. Wagner 1851 (b), p. 207 et suiv. (III. Système linguistique).

148 Id., p. 244 (§ 325).

149 Id., p. 243 (§ 324) et p. 244 (§ 326).

150 Id., p. 214 (§ 292) et p. 260 (§ 342).

151 Id., p. 337 (annexe, § 24).

152 Cf. Wagner 1851 (a), p. 1 et suiv.

153 Id., p. 2.

154 Cf. Wagner 1839, p. 312 et suiv.: p. 313 et suiv.

155 Cf. Wagner 1803, p. 149.

156 Ibidem.

157 Id., p. 155.

158 Cf. Unger 1833, p. 6. Unger va néanmoins jusqu'à constater qu'il ne « s'agirait pas ici de rendre avec une exactitude philologique les mots d'Euclide mais seulement de conserver leur esprit. »; id., p. 11.

159 Cf. Türk 1811. Le professeur de dessin bernois Gustav Adolf Tobler a publié en 1836 une étude des formes similaire, consacrée à l'enseignement du dessin. Citation dans: Türk 1830, p. 1.

160 Cf. Türk 1811, préface, p. vii.

161 Cf. Byrne 1847, p. xi et suiv.

162 Cf. Eberhard 1776, p. 5.

163 Id., p. 8.

164 Id., p. 4.

165 Mondrian 1920, p. 1.

166 Cf. Koyré/Cohen 1972, p. 15.

167 Ibidem: « Has lineas describere geometria non docet, sed postulat. »

168 Cf. Hölder 1900, p. 6. – Cf. ci-dessus.

169 Cf. Einstein 1921, p. 3.

170 Id., p. 2 et suiv.

171 Id., p. 2.

172 Cf. Simon 1901, p. 19. Simon ouvre son avant-propos (p. v) en signalant sa contribution pratique à la théorie de l'enseignement et la théorie de l'éducation mathématiques.

173 A propos des mots « strict » et « exact », cf.: Oechslin 2009, p. 363 et suiv.

174 L'autre « ligne de pensée géomé-trique », la logistique, dont les origines remontent à l'époque d'Oliver Byrne et Augustus De Morgan (cf. ci-dessus), l'a encore réclamé en 1929 comme son ac-quis : « Lorsque, dans un domaine quelconque de la philosophie ou des sciences, quelqu'un cherche à analyser exactement les déclarations et les concepts, il faut lui donner ici les instruments logistiques et relevant en particulier de la théorie des relations, qui lui serviront d'outil tranchant. Ces instruments sont jusqu'ici encore très peu connus, en particulier en Allemagne ; ils ne sont utilisés de temps à autre que pour des recherches logico-mathématiques. » Cf. Carnap, 1929, avant-propos, p. iii.

175 Cf. avant-propos du 8 mai 1686 aux *Philosophiae Naturalis Principia Mathematica* d'Isaac Newton.

176 Cf. Steck 1942, p. 13 et suiv.

177 Cf. Mondrian 1920, p. 5.

178 Cf. Byrne 1847, p. vii.

179 Cf. Mondrian 1920, p. 1.

180 Id., p. 5.

181 Ibidem.

182 Cf. Dermée non daté, p. 29 et suiv.: p. 30.

183 Cf. Rosenberg 1921, p. 1.

184 Cf. Dermée non daté, p. 37, « De même, pas de logique apparente, afin de rebuter les efforts de l'intelligence pour mordre sur le poème. Mot d'ordre: rebuter l'intelligence. »

185 Cf. Ozenfant/Jeanneret, non daté (a) p. 38 et suiv.

186 Cf. Byrne 1847, p. vii, « The arts and sciences have become so extensive, that to facilitate their acquirement is of as much importance as to extend their boundaries ».

187 Cf. Le Roy 1960, p. 17.

188 Id., p. 19 (avec référence à Kant).

189 Cf. aussi la formulation: « La pensée géométrique ainsi considérée n'est donc pas la pensée mathématique pure, mais la pensée mathématique tendant à s'incarner dans un corps d'intuition imaginaire, bref la pensée mathématique au seuil immédiat de l'application. » (id., p. 21.)

190 Gerhardt explique la formation de Leibniz pour ainsi dire par la frustration qu'il a connue en ce qui concerne la possibilité de comprendre les cours: « A Leipzig, où Leibniz commença ses études universitaires, un certain Joh. Kühn commentait les Elé-ments d'Euclide ; ses conférences étaient si obscures qu'aucun des auditeurs ne pouvait suivre hormis Leibniz. On raconte qu'il fut le seul à s'engager dans des discussions avec le professeur à propos de cette conférence et qu'il rendit ensuite les enseignements compréhensibles aux autres membres de l'auditoire ». Cf. Gerhardt 1848, p. 7.

191 Cf. Rosenberg 1921, p. 1.

192 Cf. Ozenfant/Jeanneret non daté (b), p. 369 et suiv.: p. 382.

193 Ibidem.

194 Ibidem.

195 Id., p. 379.

196 Cf. Byrne 1847, p. vii.

197 Cf. Ozenfant/Jeanneret non daté (b), p. 382.

198 Cf. Kepes (1944) 1951.

199 Id., p. 15.

200 Id., p. 35 et suiv.

201 Cf. Schopenhauer 1816, p. 11 (premier chapitre: De la vue): « Alle Anschauung ist eine intellektuale. Denn ohne den Verstand käme es nimmermehr zur Anschauung, zur Wahrnehmung, Apprehension von Objekten, sondern es bliebe bei der bloßen Empfindung, die allenfalls, als Schmerz oder Wohlbehagen, eine Bedeutung in Bezug auf den Willen haben könnte, übrigens aber ein Wechsel bedeutungsloser Zustände und nichts einer Erkenntniß Aehnliches wäre. »

202 Cf. Ci-dessus et: Oechslin 2005, p. 176 et suiv.

203 Cf. Wundt 1862, p. xix.

204 Ibidem.

205 Cf. Kant 1787, préface à la seconde édition, p. xiii.

206 Ibidem.

207 Ibidem.

208 Cf. Fechner 1860, p. 1: Ici la description de la « situation défavorable », qui se présenta d'abord à lui : « Introduction. I. Observation générale de la relation entre l'âme et le corps. Alors que l'enseignement du monde physique s'est bien développé dans les différentes branches de la science et s'est doté de principes stricts et de méthodes lui assurant un progrès promis au succès, alors que l'enseignement de l'esprit en psychologie et en logique a obtenu des bases solides, du moins jusqu'à certaines limites, l'enseignement des relations entre les corps et l'esprit et l'esprit ou le corps et l'âme n'est resté jusqu'ici qu'un champ de débats philoso-phiques sans fondement solide et sans principes ou méthodes assurant le progrès de la recherche. »

209 Id., avant-propos, p. v.

210 Cf. Helmholtz 1968, p. 38: « in der Geometrie stets mit idealen Gebilden zu tun ... deren körperliche Darstellung in der Wirklichkeit immer nur eine Annäherung an die Forderungen des Begriffes ist, und wird darüber, ob ein Körper fest, ob seine Flächen eben, seine Kanten gerade sind, erst mittels derselben Sätze entscheiden, deren tatsächliche Richtigkeit durch die Prüfung zu erweisen wäre. »

211 Cf. Adorno 1966, préface, p. 7.

212 Cf. Mondrian 1920, p. 5.

213 Cf. Mondrian 1918 (réimpression Amsterdam 1968), p. 29 et suiv.

214 Cf. Oechslin 2009.

215 Cf. Byrne 1847, p. vii, « If we wanted authorities to prove the importance and usefulness of geometry, we might quote every philosopher since the days of Plato. »

Bibliography – Bibliografie – Bibliographie

Adorno, Theodor W., *Negative Dialektik*, Frankfurt am Main 1966.

Arneth, Arthur, *Die Geschichte der reinen Mathematik in ihrer Beziehung zur Geschichte der Entwicklung des menschlichen Geistes*, Stuttgart 1852.

Ashe, St. George, "A New and Easy Way of Demonstrating Some Propositions in Euclid [...]", *Philosophical Transactions of the Royal Society of London* 14, 1684, p. 672 seqq.

Bense, Max, *Konturen einer Geistesgeschichte der Mathematik*, Hamburg 1946.

Bloch, Ernst, *Kritische Erörterungen über Rickert und das Problem der modernen Erkenntnistheorie*, Ludwigshafen 1909.

Borelli, Giovanni Alfonso, *Euclides restitutus*, 3rd ed., Rome 1679.

Brodhagen, Peter Heinrich Christoph, *Anleitung zum gemeinnützigen Unterricht für Handwerker, Künstler und Fabrikanten über die praktischsten Grundsätze mathematischer, physischer, chemischer und technologischer Kenntnisse*, Hamburg 1792.

Burja, Abel, "Von deutschen Kunstwörtern die zur Grössenlehre (Mathematik) gehören", *Beiträge zur Deutschen Sprachkunde*, lecture held at the Royal Academy of Sciences, Berlin, First Collection, Berlin 1794, p. 265 seqq.

Byrne, Oliver, *The Doctrine of Proportion clearly developed, on a comprehensive, original, and very easy system; or, The Fifth Book of Euclid simplified*, London 1841.

Byrne, Oliver, *The First Six Books of the Elements of Euclid, in which coloured diagrams and symbols are used instead of letters for the greater ease of learners*, London 1847.

Byrne, Oliver, *The Handbook for the artisan, mechanic, and engineer [...]*, Philadelphia, Penn., 1853.

Byrne, Oliver, *The Young Geometrician*, London 1865.

Byrne, Oliver, *The Young Dual Arithmetician; or, Dual Arithmetic: A new art, designed for elementary instruction and the use of schools [...]*, London 1866.

Byrne, Oliver, *The Geometry of Compasses*, London 1877.

Byrne, Oliver, *A short practical treatise on Spherical Trigonometry; containing a few simple rules, by which the great difficulties to be encountered by the student in this branch of mathematics are effectually obviated*, originally published London 1835, n. p. 2002.

Cajori, Florian, *A History of Mathematical Notations, Vol. I, Notations in elementary mathematics*, La Salle, Ill., 1928.

Carnap, Rudolf, *Abriss der Logistik*, Vienna 1929.

Casselman, Bill, "Pictures and Proofs", *Notices of the AMS*, November 2000, p. 1257 seqq.

Church, Alonzo, "A Bibliography of Symbolic Logic", *The Journal of Symbolic Logic* 1, no. 4, December 1936, p. 121 seqq.

De Morgan, Augustus, *An Essay on Probabilities, and on their Application to Life Contingencies and Insurance Offices*, London 1838.

De Morgan, Augustus, *Formal Logic: or, the calculus of inference, necessary and probable*, London 1847.

De Morgan, Augustus, *Arithmetical Books from the invention of printing to the present time, being brief notices of a large number of works drawn up from actual inspection*, London 1847.

De Morgan, Augustus, *Trigonometry and Double Algebra*, London 1849.

De Morgan, Augustus, *A Budget of Paradoxes, reprinted, with the Author's Additions from the "Athenaeum"*, London 1872.

De Morgan, Augustus, *A Budget of Paradoxes, reprinted with the author's additions from the "Athenäum"*, 2nd ed., Chicago/London 1915.

Dermée, Paul, "Découverte du Lyrisme", *L'Esprit Nouveau* 1 (n. d.), p. 29 seqq.

Dimond, Ezekiel Webster, *The Chemistry of Combustion, applied to the economy of fuel with special reference to the construction of fire chambers, for steam boilers*, Worcester 1867.

Diogenes Laertius, *Delle Vite de' Filosofi ... accresciute, & migliorate ... da Gio. Felice Astolfi ... Abbellite pur' hora di figure bellissime di Gioseffo Salviati ...*, Venice 1611.

Duns Scotus, John, *Questiones utiles subtilissimi Doctoris Joannis Scoti Super Libros priorum: Eiusdem questiones super Libros posteriorum*, Venice 1512.

Dürer, Albrecht, *Underweysung der messung, mit dem zirckel und richtscheyt, in Linien ebnen unnd gantzen corporen [...]*, Nuremberg 1525.

Early Letters of the Royal Society EL/A/36, issued by the AHRB Centre for Editing Lives and Letters (St. George Ashe, 27 April 1686), London 2005.

Eberhard, Johann August, *Allgemeine Theorie des Denkens und Empfindens*, Berlin 1776.

Einstein, Albert, *Geometrie und Erfahrung*, Sitzungsberichte der Preussischen Akademie der Wissenschaften. 27. Januar. Öffentliche Sitzung zur Feier des Jahrestages König Friedrichs II., Sonderdruck, Berlin 1921.

The Elements or Principles of Geometrie, London 1684.

Fabricius, Johann Andrea, *Abriss einer allgemeinen Historie der Gelehrsamkeit*, vol. I, Leipzig 1752.

Fechner, Gustav Theodor, *Elemente der Psychophysik*, Leipzig 1860.

Feder, Johann Georg Heinrich, *Logik und Metaphysik*, Frankfurt am Main/Leipzig 1793.

Frege, Gottlob, "Über die wissenschaftliche Berechtigung einer Begriffsschrift", *Zeitschrift für Philosophie und philosophische Kritik* 81, 1882, p. 48 seqq.

Frege, Gottlob, *Grundlagen der Arithmetik*, Breslau 1884.

Frege, Gottlob, *Grundgesetze der Arithmetik. Begriffsschriftlich abgeleitet*, vol. I, Jena 1893.

Frege, Gottlob, *Begriffsschrift und andere Aufsätze*, 2nd ed., Hildesheim 1964.

Frege, Gottlob, *Schriften zur Logik: Aus dem Nachlass*, with an introduction by Lothar Kreiser, Berlin 1973.

Gerhardt, C. J., *Die Entdeckung der Differentialrechnung durch Leibniz*, Halle 1848.

Goethe, Johann Wolfgang von, *Zur Farbenlehre*, vol. 1, Vienna 1812.

Grattan-Guinness, Ivor, "An eye for method: Augustus de Morgan and mathematical education", *Paradigm* 9, December 1992, p. 1 seqq.

Heath, Thomas L. (ed.), *The thirteen books of Euclid's Elements [...]* with introduction and commentary by Thomas L. Heath, vol. 2, 2nd rev. ed., New York 1956.

Heiberg, J. L., *Heron Alexandrinus, Opera IV*, Leipzig 1912.

Helmholtz, Hermann von, *Die Thatsachen in der Wahrnehmung*, Berlin 1879.

Helmholtz, Hermann von, "Ueber die Thatsachen, die der Geometrie zum Grunde liegen", in id., *Über Geometrie*, Darmstadt 1968, p. 32 seqq.

Hesse, Ludwig Otto, *Vorlesungen aus der analytischen Geometrie der geraden Linie, des Punktes und des Kreises in der Ebene*, Leipzig 1865.

Hölder, Otto, *Anschauung und Denken in der Geometrie*, Akademische Antrittsvorlesung, Leipzig 1900.

Husserl, Edmund G., *Philosophie der Arithmetik. Psychologische und logische Untersuchungen*, Leipzig 1891.

Husserl, Edmund G., "Philosophie als strenge Wissenschaft", *Logos* I, 1910/11, p. 289 seqq.

Husserl, Edmund G., *Ideen zu einer reinen Phänomenologie und phänomenologischen Philosophie*, Halle 1913.

Husserl, Edmund G., "Die Krisis der europäischen Wissenschaften und die transcendentale Phänomenologie: Eine Einleitung in die phänomenologische Philosophie", *Philosophia* I, 1936, p. 77 seqq.

Kant, Immanuel, *Critik der reinen Vernunft, Zweyte hin und wieder verbesserte Auflage*, Riga 1787.

Kant, Immanuel, "Was heißt: sich im Denken orientieren?", in id., *Kleine Schriften*, Neuwied 1793, p. 104 seqq.

Kepes, Gyorgy, *Language of Vision*, Chicago 1944.

Knittermeyer, Hinrich, *Immanuel Kant*, Bremen 1939.

Koyré, Alexander/Cohen, I. Bernhard (eds.), *Isaac Newton's Philosophiae Naturalis Principia Mathematica*, vol. 1, Cambridge, Mass., 1972.

Krbek, Franz von, *Eingefangenes Unendlich: Bekenntnis zur Geschichte der Mathematik*, Leipzig 1954.

Lambert, Johann Heinrich, *Neues Organon oder Gedanken über die Erforschung und Bezeichnung des Wahren und dessen Unterscheidung von Irrthum und Schein*, Leipzig 1764.

Le Roy, Edouard, *La pensée mathématique pure*, Paris 1960.

Lorey, Adolf, *Das Neueste und Interessanteste aus der Logarithmotechnik und der Anwendung der Logarithmen auf das Leben: Nach den englischen und französischen Schriften von Byrne und Koralek [...]*, Weimar 1852.

Meibomius, Marc, *De Proportionibus*, Hafniae 1655.

Michelsen, Johann Andreas Christian, *Euclides Elemente, für den gegenwärtigen Zustand der Mathematik bearbeitet, erweitert und fortgesetzt*, Berlin 1791.

Mill, John Stuart, *Autobiography*, 2nd ed., London 1873.

Mondrian, Piet, "De Nieuwe Beelding in de Schilderkunst: 3. De nieuwe beelding als abstract-reelle schilderkunst; Beeldingsmiddel en compositie", *De Stijl* I, no. 4, 1918 (repr. Amsterdam 1968), p. 29 seqq.

Mondrian, Piet, *Le Néo-Plasticisme. Principe général de l'équivalence plas-*

tique. Aux hommes futurs, Paris 1920.

Moritz, Karl Philipp, "Über die Bildsamkeit der Deutschen Sprache", *Beiträge zur Deutschen Sprachkunde*, speech held at the Royal Academy of Sciences, Berlin, First Collection, Berlin 1794, p. 87 seqq.

Oechslin, Werner, "Ozenfant und Le Corbusier: die neue, systematische Grundlegung der Kunst und die Psychophysik", in Karin Gimmi, et al. (eds.), *SvM Die Festschrift für Stanislaus von Moos*, Zurich 2005, p. 176 seqq.

Oechslin, Werner, "Auf einen Blick", in Heike Gfrereis/Marcel Lepper (eds.), *Deixis: Vom Denken mit dem Zeigefinger*, Göttingen 2007, p. 62 seqq.

Oechslin, Werner, "[...] und die Geschichte macht selbst wieder Geschichte [...]. Geschichtliches und Anderes zur 'Historismus'-Frage", in Hannes Böhringer/Arne Zerbst (eds.), *Die tätowierte Wand: Über Historismus in Königslutter*, Munich 2009, p. 363 seqq.

Oechslin, Werner "'God werkt geometrisch' – 'Holländereien' einmal anders: kosmologisch, theosophisch und architektonisch", *SCHOLION*, 2009.

Ozenfant, Amedée/Jeanneret, Charles-Edouard, "Sur la Plastique", *L'Esprit Nouveau* 1 (n.d.; a), p. 38 seqq.

Ozenfant, Amedée/Jeanneret, Charles-Edouard, "Le Purisme", *L'Esprit Nouveau* 4 (n.d.; b), p. 369 seqq.

Pell, John, *An Introduction to Algebra*, London 1668.

Pestalozzi, Johann Heinrich, *Pestalozzis Elementar-Bücher: Anschauungslehre der Zahlenverhältnisse*, first booklet, Zurich/Berne and Tübingen 1803.

Phillips, Christopher, "Augustus De Morgan and the propagation of moral mathematics", *Studies in History and Philosophy of Science*, part A, 36, no. 1, March 2005, p. 105 seqq.

Pico della Mirandola, Giovanni, *Conclusiones nongentae, in omni genere scientiarum [...]*, Nuremberg 1532.

Quine, Willard Van Orman, *Philosophy of Logic*, Englewood Cliffs, New Jersey, 1970.

Rickert, Heinrich, "Vom Begriff der Philosophie", *Logos* I, 1910/11, p. 1 seqq.

Rickert, Heinrich, *Die Grenzen der naturwissenschaftlichen Begriffsbildung*, 2nd newly rev. ed., Tübingen 1913.

Riemann, Bernhard, "Ueber die Hypothesen, welche der Geometrie zu Grunde liegen" (*Habilitation*

lecture held on 10 June 1854), in id., *Gesammelte mathematische Werke und wissenschaftlicher Nachlass*, 2nd ed., Leipzig 1892, p. 272 seqq.

Rosenberg, Léonce, *Cubisme et Empirisme*, Paris 1921.

Russell, Bertrand A. W., *An Essay on the Foundations of Geometry*, Cambridge 1897.

Scheffler, Hermann, *Über das Verhältniß der Arithmetik zur Geometrie, insbesondere über die geometrische Bedeutung der imaginären Zahlen*, Brunswick 1846.

Schelling, Friedrich Wilhelm Joseph, *Ideen zu einer Philosophie der Natur*, Leipzig 1797.

Schopenhauer, Arthur, *Ueber das Sehn und die Farben*, Leipzig 1816.

Simon, Max, *Euclid und die sechs planimetrischen Bücher*, Leipzig 1901.

Speiser, Andreas, *Die mathematische Denkweise*, Zurich 1932.

Steck, Max, *Mathematik als Begriff und Gestalt*, Halle 1942.

Steck, Max, "Proklus Diadochus und seine Gestaltlehre der Mathematik", *Nova Acta Leopoldina*, n. s., 13, no. 93, Halle 1943, p. 131 seqq.

Steck, Max, *Grundgebiete der Mathematik*, Heidelberg 1946.

Steck, Max, *Bibliographia Euclideana*, Hildesheim 1981.

Stephani, Heinrich, *Ausführliche Beschreibung meiner einfachen Lese-Methode*, Erlangen 1814.

Stock, Wolfgang G., "Die Philosophie Johann Jakob Wagners", *Zeitschrift für Philosophische Forschung*, 1982, p. 262 seqq.

Tartaglia, Nicola, *Euclide Megarense Philospho: Solo Introduttore delle Scientie Mathematice: diligentemente reassettato, et alla integrità ridotto ...*, Venice 1543.

Tobler, Gustav Adolf, *Die Formenlehre in Verbindung mit den reinen Elementen des freien Handzeichnens [...]*, Burgdorf 1836.

Trendelenburg, Friedrich Adolf, "Das to eni einai, to agatho einai etc. etc. und das to ti en einai bei Aristoteles: Ein Beitrag zur aristotelischen Begriffsbestimmung und zur griechischen Syntax", *Rheinisches Museum für Philologie, Geschichte und griechische Philosophie* 2, no. 4, 1828, p. 457 seqq.

Tufte, Edward R., *Envisioning Information*, Cheshire, Conn., 1990.

Türk, C.C. Wilhelm von, *Die sinnlichen Wahrnehmungen, als Grundlage des Unterrichts in der Muttersprache: Ein Handbuch für Mütter und Lehrer*, Winterthur 1811.

Türk, C.C. Wilhelm von, *Leitfaden*

für den Unterricht in der Formen- und Grössen-Lehre. Vierte verbesserte und bedeutend vermehrte Auflage ..., Potsdam 1830.

Unger, Ephraim Salomon, *Die Geometrie des Euklid und das Wesen derselben [...] Für Alle, die eine gründliche Kenntniß dieser Wissenschaft in kurzer Zeit erwerben wollen*, Erfurt 1833.

Valla, Giorgio, *Aristotelis Magnorum Moralium Liber primus*, in *Ethicorum Aristotelis ad Nicomachum Libri Decem: Et Tres eorundem Conversiones*, Freiburg im Breisgau 1541.

Wagner, Johann Jakob, *Philosophie der Erziehungskunst*, Leipzig 1803.

Wagner, Johann Jakob, "Mathematische Philosophie", in Philipp Ludwig Adam (ed.), *Johann Jakob Wagner's Kleine Schriften*, part 1, Ulm 1839, p. 312 seqq.

Wagner, Johann Jakob, *Mathematische Philosophie, Neue wohlfeile Ausgabe*, Ulm 1851 (a).

Wagner, Johann Jakob, *Organon der menschlichen Erkenntnis: Neue wohlfeile Ausgabe*, Ulm 1851 (b).

Whewell, William, *The Philosophy of the Inductive Sciences, founded upon their history*, London 1840, 2nd ed., London 1947.

Whewell, William, *Of Induction, with special reference to Mr. J. Stuart Mill's System of Logic*, London 1849.

Whewell, William, *Novum Organum Renovatum, Being the second part of the Philosophy of the Inductive Sciences*, London 1858.

Whitehead, Alfred North, *Symbolism: Its Meaning and Effect*, Barbour-Page Lectures, University of Virginia 1927, New York 1927.

Wolff, Christian, *Auszug aus den Anfangs-Gründen aller Mathematischen Wissenschaften, Zu Bequemerem Gebrauche der Anfänger*, Frankfurt am Main/Leipzig 1755.

Wundt, Wilhelm, *Beiträge zur Theorie der Sinneswahrnehmung*, Leipzig/Heidelberg 1862.

Youmans, Edward L., *Chemical Atlas; or, The Chemistry of Familiar Objects: Exhibiting the General Principles of the Science in a series of beautifully colored diagrams, and accompanied by Explanatory Essays, embracing the latest views of the subjects illustrated. Designed for the use of students and pupils in all schools where chemistry is taught*, New York 1856.

Acknowledgements
Danksagung
Remerciements

This facsimile of Oliver Byrne's *The First Six Books of the Elements of Euclid* was photographed from a copy in the possession of John Windle Antiquarian Bookseller, San Francisco. The original volume was digitally imaged by 42–line, Oakland; our thanks go to E. M. Ginger at 42–line for her valuable collaboration.

Der vorliegende Nachdruck von Oliver Byrnes *The First Six Books of the Elements of Euclid* erfolgte auf Grundlage des Exemplars von John Windle Antiquarian Bookseller, San Francisco. Die digitale Reproduktion des Originals wurde von 42–line, Oakland, durchgeführt, und unser Dank geht an E. M. Ginger von 42–line für die gute Zusammenarbeit.

La présente réimpression des *The First Six Books of the Elements of Euclid* d'Oliver Byrne a été réalisée à partir de l'exemplaire en possession de John Windle Antiquarian Bookseller, San Francisco. La numérisation du volume de l'édition originale a été réalisée par 42–line, Oakland, et nous remercions E. M. Ginger du 42–line pour son excellente collaboration.

Credits
Fotonachweis
Crédits

Bibliothek Werner Oechslin, Einsiedeln: pp. 4, 6, 9, 11, 13, 14, 17, 31–33, 38, 41–43, 46/47, 50, 51, 54–57, 60, 61, 63, 68, 71, 74, 75, 78, 79, 83–85; © British Library Board, London: pp. 18, 20, 23, 24, 26; © 2010 Mondrian/Holtzman Trust c/o HCR International, Virginia, USA: p. 89.

The author
Der Autor
L'auteur

WERNER OECHSLIN, born 1944, studied art history, archaeology, philosophy, and mathematics, completed his doctoral studies in Zurich in 1970, and began teaching at MIT in 1975. Prior to his *Habilitation* in 1980, he taught in Berlin and Geneva and at Harvard University. He has been professor in Bonn, from 1980 to 1984, and since 1985, in Zurich at the Swiss Federal Institute of Technology, where he headed the Institute for the History and Theory of Architecture from 1986 to 2006. The focus of his research is architectural theory and the cultural history of architecture. His most recent publication is *Palladianismus: Andrea Palladio – Werk und Wirkung*, Zurich 2008. He is the founder of the Bibliothek Werner Oechslin (Werner Oechslin Library) in Einsiedeln.

WERNER OECHSLIN, geboren 1944, studierte Kunstgeschichte, Archäologie, Philosophie und Mathematik, promovierte 1970 in Zürich und begann seine Lehrtätigkeit am MIT 1975. Bis zu seiner Habilitation 1980 unterrichtete er in Berlin, Genf und an der Harvard University. Von 1980–1984 lehrte er in Bonn und ist seit 1985 Professor an der ETH Zürich, wo er von 1986–2006 das Institut gta leitete. Sein Forschungsschwerpunkt bildet die Architekturtheorie und Kulturgeschichte der Architektur. Zuletzt erschien von ihm der Band *Palladianismus. Andrea Palladio – Werk und Wirkung*, Zürich 2008. Er ist Gründer der Bibliothek Werner Oechslin in Einsiedeln.

WERNER OECHSLIN, né en 1944, a étudié l'histoire de l'art, l'archéologie, la philosophie et les mathématiques. Il a reçu son doctorat en 1970 à Zurich et a commencé sa carrière d'enseignant au MIT en 1975. Avant de passer son agrégation en 1980, il a enseigné à Berlin, à Genève et à la Harvard University. De 1980 à 1984, il a enseigné à Bonn et depuis 1985, il est professeur à l'EPF (Ecole polytechnique fédérale) de Zurich où il a dirigé l'Institut gta (Institut d'histoire et de théorie de l'architecture) de 1986 à 2006. La théorie de l'architecture et l'histoire culturelle de l'architecture constituent les axes principaux de son travail de recherche. Il a publié dernièrement l'ouvrage *Palladianismus. Andrea Palladio – Werk und Wirkung*, Zurich 2008. Il est le fondateur de la bibliothèque Werner Oechslin à Einsiedeln.

Imprint

Cover and Box
Oliver Byrne, *The First Six Books of the Elements of Euclid*, London 1847
Figure illustrating the Pythagorean Theorem.

Booklet
Oliver Byrne, *The First Six Books of the Elements of Euclid*, London 1847, p. 133 (detail)

Page 2
Oliver Byrne, *The First Six Books of the Elements of Euclid*, London 1847
Title page with a figure illustrating the Pythagorean Theorem.

Page 4
Oliver Byrne, *The First Six Books of the Elements of Euclid*, London 1847
Book I. Proposition I. Problem.

To stay informed about upcoming TASCHEN titles, please request our magazine at www.taschen.com/magazine or write to TASCHEN America, 6671 Sunset Boulevard, Suite 1508, Los Angeles, CA 90028, USA; contact-us@taschen.com; Fax: +1-323-463-4442. We will be happy to send you a free copy of our magazine which is filled with information about all of our books.

© 2010 TASCHEN GmbH
Hohenzollernring 53, D–50672 Köln
www.taschen.com

Project management: Petra Lamers-Schütze, Cologne
Editorial collaboration: Nicole Bilstein, Malmö; Mahros Allamezade, Cologne
English translation: Howard Fine, Munich
French translation: Michèle Schreyer, Cologne
Design: Sense/Net Art Direction, Andy Disl and Birgit Eichwede, Cologne
Production: Horst Neuzner, Cologne

ISBN 978-3-8365-1775-1
Printed in China

BYRNE'S EUCLID

THE FIRST SIX BOOKS OF

THE ELEMENTS OF EUCLID

WITH COLOURED DIAGRAMS

AND SYMBOLS

THE FIRST SIX BOOKS OF
THE ELEMENTS OF EUCLID
IN WHICH COLOURED DIAGRAMS AND SYMBOLS
ARE USED INSTEAD OF LETTERS FOR THE
GREATER EASE OF LEARNERS

BY OLIVER BYRNE

SURVEYOR OF HER MAJESTY'S SETTLEMENTS IN THE FALKLAND ISLANDS
AND AUTHOR OF NUMEROUS MATHEMATICAL WORKS

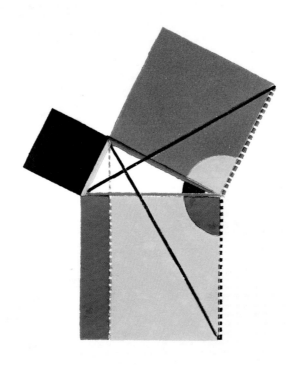

LONDON
WILLIAM PICKERING
1847

TO THE

RIGHT HONOURABLE THE EARL FITZWILLIAM,

ETC. ETC. ETC.

THIS WORK IS DEDICATED

BY HIS LORDSHIP'S OBEDIENT

AND MUCH OBLIGED SERVANT,

OLIVER BYRNE.

INTRODUCTION.

THE arts and fciences have become fo extenfive, that to facilitate their acquirement is of as much importance as to extend their boundaries. Illuftration, if it does not fhorten the time of ftudy, will at leaft make it more agreeable. THIS WORK has a greater aim than mere illuftration; we do not introduce colours for the purpofe of entertainment, or to amufe *by certain combinations of tint and form*, but to affift the mind in its refearches after truth, to increafe the facilities of inftruction, and to diffufe permanent knowledge. If we wanted authorities to prove the importance and ufefulnefs of geometry, we might quote every philofopher fince the days of Plato. Among the Greeks, in ancient, as in the fchool of Peftalozzi and others in recent times, geometry was adopted as the beft gymnaftic of the mind. In fact, Euclid's Elements have become, by common confent, the bafis of mathematical fcience all over the civilized globe. But this will not appear extraordinary, if we confider that this fublime fcience is not only better calculated than any other to call forth the fpirit of inquiry, to elevate the mind, and to ftrengthen the reafoning faculties, but alfo it forms the beft introduction to moft of the ufeful and important vocations of human life. Arithmetic, land-furveying, menfuration, engineering, navigation, mechanics, hydroftatics, pneumatics, optics, phyfical aftronomy, &c. are all dependent on the propofitions of geometry.

Much however depends on the firſt communication of any ſcience to a learner, though the beſt and moſt eaſy methods are ſeldom adopted. Propoſitions are placed before a ſtudent, who though having a ſufficient underſtanding, is told juſt as much about them on entering at the very threſhold of the ſcience, as gives him a prepoſſeſſion moſt unfavourable to his future ſtudy of this delightful ſubject; or " the formalities and paraphernalia of rigour are ſo oſtentatiouſly put forward, as almoſt to hide the reality. Endleſs and perplexing repetitions, which do not confer greater exactitude on the reaſoning, render the demonſtrations involved and obſcure, and conceal from the view of the ſtudent the confecution of evidence." Thus an averſion is created in the mind of the pupil, and a ſubject ſo calculated to improve the reaſoning powers, and give the habit of cloſe thinking, is degraded by a dry and rigid courſe of inſtruction into an uninterefting exerciſe of the memory. To raiſe the curioſity, and to awaken the liſtleſs and dormant powers of younger minds ſhould be the aim of every teacher; but where examples of excellence are wanting, the attempts to attain it are but few, while eminence excites attention and produces imitation. The object of this Work is to introduce a method of teaching geometry, which has been much approved of by many ſcientific men in this country, as well as in France and America. The plan here adopted forcibly appeals to the eye, the moſt ſenſitive and the moſt comprehenſive of our external organs, and its pre-eminence to imprint it ſubject on the mind is ſupported by the incontrovertible maxim expreſſed in the well known words of Horace :—

Segnius irritant animos demiſſa per aurem
Quàm quæ ſunt oculis ſubjeɛ̃ta fidelibus.
A feebler impreſs through the ear is made,
Than what is by the faithful eye conveyed.

All language confifts of reprefentative figns, and thofe figns are the beft which effect their purpofes with the greateft precifion and difpatch. Such for all common purpofes are the audible figns called words, which are ftill confidered as audible, whether addreffed immediately to the ear, or through the medium of letters to the eye. Geometrical diagrams are not figns, but the materials of geometrical fcience, the object of which is to fhow the relative quantities of their parts by a procefs of reafoning called Demonftration. This reafoning has been generally carried on by words, letters, and black or uncoloured diagrams; but as the ufe of coloured fymbols, figns, and diagrams in the linear arts and fciences, renders the procefs of reafoning more precife, and the attainment more expeditious, they have been in this inftance accordingly adopted.

Such is the expedition of this enticing mode of communicating knowledge, that the Elements of Euclid can be acquired in lefs than one third the time ufually employed, and the retention by the memory is much more permanent; thefe facts have been afcertained by numerous experiments made by the inventor, and feveral others who have adopted his plans. The particulars of which are few and obvious; the letters annexed to points, lines, or other parts of a diagram are in fact but arbitrary names, and reprefent them in the demonftration; inftead of thefe, the parts being differently coloured, are made to name themfelves, for their forms in correfponding colours reprefent them in the demonftration.

In order to give a better idea of this fyftem, and

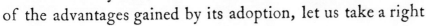

of the advantages gained by its adoption, let us take a right angled triangle, and exprefs fome of its properties both by colours and the method generally employed.

Some of the properties of the right angled triangle ABC, *expreffed by the method generally employed.*

1. The angle BAC, together with the angles BCA and ABC are equal to two right angles, or twice the angle ABC.

2. The angle CAB added to the angle ACB will be equal to the angle ABC.

3. The angle ABC is greater than either of the angles BAC or BCA.

4. The angle BCA or the angle CAB is lefs than the angle ABC.

5. If from the angle ABC, there be taken the angle BAC, the remainder will be equal to the angle ACB.

6. The fquare of AC is equal to the fum of the fquares of AB and BC.

The fame properties expreffed by colouring the different parts.

1.

That is, the red angle added to the yellow angle added to the blue angle, equal twice the yellow angle, equal two right angles.

2.

Or in words, the red angle added to the blue angle, equal the yellow angle.

3.

The yellow angle is greater than either the red or blue angle.

4.  or

Either the red or blue angle is lefs than the yellow angle.

5. 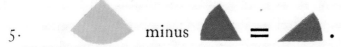 minus

In other terms, the yellow angle made lefs by the blue angle equal the red angle.

6. $\underline{\hspace{2cm}}^2 = \underline{\hspace{2cm}}^2 + \underline{\hspace{1.5cm}}^2.$

That is, the fquare of the yellow line is equal to the fum of the fquares of the blue and red lines.

In oral demonftrations we gain with colours this important advantage, the eye and the ear can be addreffed at the fame moment, fo that for teaching geometry, and other linear arts and fciences, in claffes, the fyftem is the beft ever propofed, this is apparent from the examples juft given.

Whence it is evident that a reference from the text to the diagram is more rapid and fure, by giving the forms and colours of the parts, or by naming the parts and their colours, than naming the parts and letters on the diagram. Befides the fuperior fimplicity, this fyftem is likewife confpicuous for concentration, and wholly excludes the injurious though prevalent practice of allowing the ftudent to commit the demonftration to memory; until reafon, and fact, and proof only make impreffions on the underftanding.

Again, when lecturing on the principles or properties of figures, if we mention the colour of the part or parts referred to, as in faying, the red angle, the blue line, or lines, &c. the part or parts thus named will be immediately feen by all in the clafs at the fame inftant; not fo if we fay the angle ABC, the triangle PFQ, the figure EGKt, and fo on;

for the letters muſt be traced one by one before the ſtudents arrange in their minds the particular magnitude referred to, which often occaſions confuſion and error, as well as loſs of time. Alſo if the parts which are given as equal, have the ſame colours in any diagram, the mind will not wander from the object before it; that is, ſuch an arrangement preſents an ocular demonſtration of the parts to be proved equal, and the learner retains the data throughout the whole of the reaſoning. But whatever may be the advantages of the preſent plan, if it be not ſubſtituted for, it can always be made a powerful auxiliary to the other methods, for the purpoſe of introduction, or of a more ſpeedy reminiſcence, or of more permanent retention by the memory.

The experience of all who have formed ſyſtems to impreſs facts on the underſtanding, agree in proving that coloured repreſentations, as pictures, cuts, diagrams, &c. are more eaſily fixed in the mind than mere ſentences unmarked by any peculiarity. Curious as it may appear, poets ſeem to be aware of this fact more than mathematicians; many modern poets allude to this viſible ſyſtem of communicating knowledge, one of them has thus expreſſed himſelf:

> Sounds which addreſs the ear are loſt and die
> In one ſhort hour, but theſe which ſtrike the eye,
> Live long upon the mind, the faithful ſight
> Engraves the knowledge with a beam of light.

This perhaps may be reckoned the only improvement which plain geometry has received ſince the days of Euclid, and if there were any geometers of note before that time, Euclid's ſucceſs has quite eclipſed their memory, and even occaſioned all good things of that kind to be aſſigned to him; like Æſop among the writers of Fables. It may alſo be worthy of remark, as tangible diagrams afford the only medium through which geometry and other linear

arts and fciences can be taught to the blind, this vifible fyftem is no lefs adapted to the exigencies of the deaf and
dumb.

Care muft be taken to fhow that colour has nothing to
do with the lines, angles, or magnitudes, except merely to
name them. A mathematical line, which is length without breadth, cannot poffefs colour, yet the junction of two
colours on the fame plane gives a good idea of what is
meant by a mathematical line; recollect we are fpeaking
familiarly, fuch a junction is to be underftood and not the
colour, when we fay the black line, the red line or lines, &c.

Colours and coloured diagrams may at firft appear a
clumfy method to convey proper notions of the properties
and parts of mathematical figures and magnitudes, however they will be found to afford a means more refined and
extenfive than any that has been hitherto propofed.

We fhall here define a point, a line, and a furface, and
demonftrate a propofition in order to fhow the truth of this
affertion.

A point is that which has pofition, but not magnitude;
or a point is pofition only, abftracted from the confideration
of length, breadth, and thicknefs. Perhaps the following defcription is better calculated to explain the nature of
a mathematical point to thofe who have not acquired the
idea, than the above fpecious definition.

Let three colours meet and cover a
portion of the paper, where they meet
is not blue, nor is it yellow, nor is it
red, as it occupies no portion of the
plane, for if it did, it would belong
to the blue, the red, or the yellow
part; yet it exifts, and has pofition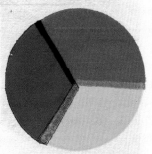
without magnitude, fo that with a little reflection, this junc-

tion of three colours on a plane, gives a good idea of a mathematical point.

A line is length without breadth. With the affiftance of colours, nearly in the fame manner as before, an idea of a line may be thus given :—

Let two colours meet and cover a portion of the paper;

where they meet is not red, nor is it blue; therefore the junction occupies no portion of the plane, and therefore it cannot have breadth, but only length: from which we can readily form an idea of what is meant by a mathematical line. For the purpofe of illuftration, one colour differing from the colour of the paper, or plane upon which it is drawn, would have been fufficient; hence in future, if we fay the red line, the blue line, or lines, &c. it is the junctions with the plane upon which they are drawn are to be underftood.

Surface is that which has length and breadth without thicknefs.

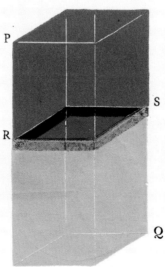

When we confider a folid body (**PQ**), we perceive at once that it has three dimenfions, namely :— length, breadth, and thicknefs; fuppofe one part of this folid (**PS**) to be red, and the other part (**QR**) yellow, and that the colours be diftinct without commingling, the blue furface (**RS**) which feparates thefe parts, or which is the fame thing, that which divides the folid without lofs of material, muft be without thicknefs, and only poffeffes length and breadth;

this plainly appears from reafoning, fimilar to that juft employed in defining, or rather defcribing a point and a line.

The propofition which we have felected to elucidate the manner in which the principles are applied, is the fifth of the firft Book.

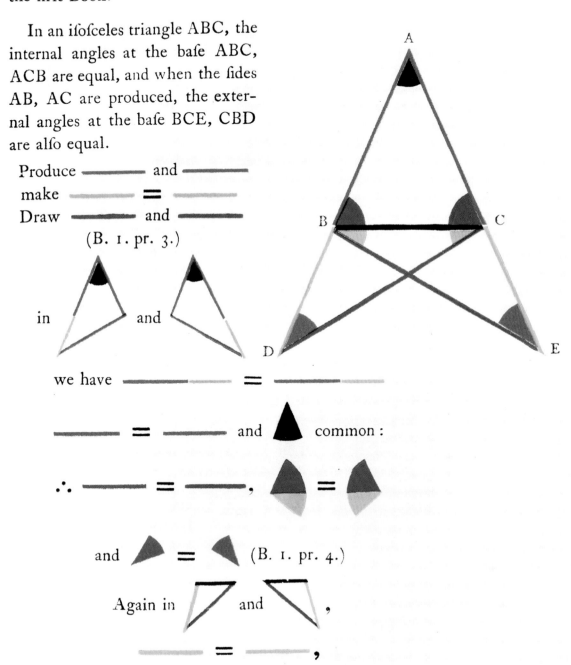

In an ifofceles triangle ABC, the internal angles at the bafe ABC, ACB are equal, and when the fides AB, AC are produced, the external angles at the bafe BCE, CBD are alfo equal.

Produce ——— and ———
make ——— = ———
Draw ——— and ———
(B. 1. pr. 3.)

in   and

we have ——— = ———

——— = ——— and ▲ common :

∴ ——— = ———, ◣ = ◢

and ◤ = ◥ (B. 1. pr. 4.)

Again in ◺ and ◿ ,

——— = ——— ,

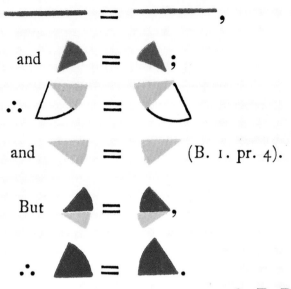

Q. E. D.

By annexing Letters to the Diagram.

LET the equal fides AB and AC be produced through the
extremities BC, of the third fide, and in the produced part
BD of either, let any point D be affumed, and from the
other let AE be cut off equal to AD (B. 1. pr. 3). Let
the points E and D, fo taken in the produced fides, be connected by ftraight lines DC and BE with the alternate extremities of the third fide of the triangle.

In the triangles DAC and EAB the fides DA and AC
are refpectively equal to EA and AB, and the included
angle A is common to both triangles. Hence (B. 1. pr. 4.)
the line DC is equal to BE, the angle ADC to the angle
AEB, and the angle ACD to the angle ABE; if from
the equal lines AD and AE the equal fides AB and AC
be taken, the remainders BD and CE will be equal. Hence
in the triangles BDC and CEB, the fides BD and DC are
refpectively equal to CE and EB, and the angles D and E
included by thofe fides are alfo equal. Hence (B. 1. pr. 4.)

the angles DBC and ECB, which are thofe included by the third fide BC and the productions of the equal fides AB and AC are equal. Alfo the angles DCB and EBC are equal if thofe equals be taken from the angles DCA and EBA before proved equal, the remainders, which are the angles ABC and ACB oppofite to the equal fides, will be equal.

Therefore in an ifofceles triangle, &c.

Q. E. D.

Our object in this place being to introduce the fyftem rather than to teach any particular fet of propofitions, we have therefore felected the foregoing out of the regular courfe. For fchools and other public places of inftruction, dyed chalks will anfwer to defcribe diagrams, &c. for private ufe coloured pencils will be found very convenient.

We are happy to find that the Elements of Mathematics now forms a confiderable part of every found female edu-cation, therefore we call the attention of thofe interefted or engaged in the education of ladies to this very attractive mode of communicating knowledge, and to the fucceeding work for its future developement.

We fhall for the prefent conclude by obferving, as the fenfes of fight and hearing can be fo forcibly and inftanta-neoufly addreffed alike with one thoufand as with one, *the million* might be taught geometry and other branches of mathematics with great eafe, this would advance the pur-pofe of education more than any thing that *might* be named, for it would teach the people how to think, and not what to think; it is in this particular the great error of education originates.

THE ELEMENTS OF EUCLID.

BOOK I.

DEFINITIONS.

I.

A *point* is that which has no parts.

II.

A *line* is length without breadth.

III.

The extremities of a line are points.

IV.

A ftraight or right line is that which lies evenly between its extremities.

V.

A furface is that which has length and breadth only.

VI.

The extremities of a furface are lines.

VII.

A plane furface is that which lies evenly between its extremities.

VIII.

A plane angle is the inclination of two lines to one another, in a plane, which meet together, but are not in the fame direction.

IX.

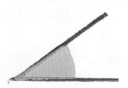

A plane rectilinear angle is the inclination of two ftraight lines to one another, which meet together, but are not in the fame ftraight line.

X.

When one ſtraight line ſtanding on another ſtraight line makes the adjacent angles equal, each of theſe angles is called a *right angle*, and each of theſe lines is ſaid to be *perpendicular* to the other.

XI.

An obtuſe angle is an angle greater than a right angle.

XII.

An acute angle is an angle leſs than a right angle.

XIII.

A term or boundary is the extremity of any thing.

XIV.

A figure is a ſurface encloſed on all ſides by a line or lines.

XV.

A circle is a plane figure, bounded by one continued line, called its circumference or periphery; and having a certain point within it, from which all ſtraight lines drawn to its circumference are equal.

XVI.

This point (from which the equal lines are drawn) is called the centre of the circle.

XVII.

A diameter of a circle is a ftraight line drawn through the centre, terminated both ways in the circumference.

XVIII.

A femicircle is the figure contained by the diameter, and the part of the circle cut off by the diameter.

XIX.

A fegment of a circle is a figure contained by a ftraight line, and the part of the circumference which it cuts off.

XX.

A figure contained by ftraight lines only, is called a rectilinear figure.

XXI.

A triangle is a rectilinear figure included by three fides.

XXII.

A quadrilateral figure is one which is bounded by four fides. The ftraight lines ━━━━ and ━━━━ connecting the vertices of the oppofite angles of a quadrilateral figure, are called its diagonals.

XXIII.

A polygon is a rectilinear figure bounded by more than four fides.

XXIV.

A triangle whofe three fides are equal, is faid to be equilateral.

XXV.

A triangle which has only two fides equal is called an ifofceles triangle.

XXVI.

A fcalene triangle is one which has no two fides equal.

XXVII.

A right angled triangle is that which has a right angle.

XXVIII.

An obtufe angled triangle is that which has an obtufe angle.

XXIX.

An acute angled triangle is that which has three acute angles.

XXX.

Of four-fided figures, a fquare is that which has all its fides equal, and all its angles right angles.

XXXI.

A rhombus is that which has all its fides equal, but its angles are not right angles.

XXXII.

An oblong is that which has all its angles right angles, but has not all its fides equal.

XXXIII.

A rhomboid is that which has its oppofite fides equal to one another,
but all its fides are not equal, nor its
angles right angles.

XXXIV.

All other quadrilateral figures are called trapeziums.

XXXV.

Parallel ftraight lines are fuch as are in
the fame plane, and which being produced continually in both directions,
would never meet.

POSTULATES.

I.

Let it be granted that a ftraight line may be drawn from
any one point to any other point.

II.

Let it be granted that a finite ftraight line may be produced to any length in a ftraight line.

III.

Let it be granted that a circle may be defcribed with any
centre at any diftance from that centre.

AXIOMS.

I.

Magnitudes which are equal to the fame are equal to
each other.

II.

If equals be added to equals the fums will be equal.

III.

If equals be taken away from equals the remainders will be equal.

IV.

If equals be added to unequals the fums will be unequal.

V.

If equals be taken away from unequals the remainders will be unequal.

VI.

The doubles of the fame or equal magnitudes are equal.

VII.

The halves of the fame or equal magnitudes are equal.

VIII.

Magnitudes which coincide with one another, or exactly fill the fame fpace, are equal.

IX.

The whole is greater than its part.

X.

Two ftraight lines cannot include a fpace.

XI.

All right angles are equal.

XII.

If two ftraight lines (⸺⸺) meet a third ftraight line (⸺⸺) fo as to make the two interior angles (▰ and ◗) on the fame fide lefs than two right angles, thefe two ftraight lines will meet if they be produced on that fide on which the angles are lefs than two right angles.

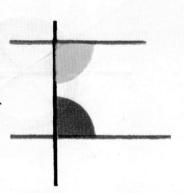

The twelfth axiom may be expreſſed in any of the following ways:

1. Two diverging ſtraight lines cannot be both parallel to the ſame ſtraight line.

2. If a ſtraight line interſect one of the two parallel ſtraight lines it muſt alſo interſect the other.

3. Only one ſtraight line can be drawn through a given point, parallel to a given ſtraight line.

Geometry has for its principal objects the expoſition and explanation of the properties of *figure*, and figure is defined to be the relation which ſubſiſts between the boundaries of ſpace. Space or magnitude is of three kinds, *linear, ſuperficial*, and *ſolid*.

Angles might properly be conſidered as a fourth ſpecies of magnitude. Angular magnitude evidently conſiſts of parts, and muſt therefore be admitted to be a ſpecies of quantity. The ſtudent muſt not ſuppoſe that the magni-

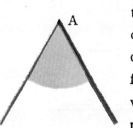

tude of an angle is affected by the length of the ſtraight lines which include it, and of whoſe mutual divergence it is the meaſure. The *vertex* of an angle is the point where the *ſides* or the *legs* of the angle meet, as A.

An angle is often deſignated by a ſingle letter when its legs are the only lines which meet together at its vertex. Thus the red and blue lines form the yellow angle, which in other ſyſtems would be called the angle A. But when more than two lines meet in the ſame point, it was neceſſary by former methods, in order to avoid confuſion, to employ three letters to deſignate an angle about that point,

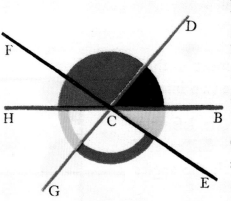

the letter which marked the vertex of the angle being always placed in the middle. Thus the black and red lines meeting together at C, form the blue angle, and has been ufually denominated the angle FCD or DCF. The lines FC and CD are the legs of the angle; the point C is its vertex. In like manner the black angle would be defignated the angle DCB or BCD. The red and blue angles added together, or the angle HCF added to FCD, make the angle HCD; and fo of other angles.

When the legs of an angle are produced or prolonged beyond its vertex, the angles made by them on both fides of the vertex are faid to be *vertically oppofite* to each other: Thus the red and yellow angles are faid to be vertically oppofite angles.

Superpofition is the procefs by which one magnitude may be conceived to be placed upon another, fo as exactly to cover it, or fo that every part of each fhall exactly coincide.

A line is faid to be *produced*, when it is extended, prolonged, or has its length increafed, and the increafe of length which it receives is called its *produced part*, or its *production*.

The entire length of the line or lines which enclofe a figure, is called its *perimeter*. The firft fix books of Euclid treat of plain figures only. A line drawn from the centre of a circle to its circumference, is called a *radius*. The lines which include a figure are called its *fides*. That fide of a right angled triangle, which is oppofite to the right angle, is called the *hypotenufe*. An *oblong* is defined in the fecond book, and called a *rectangle*. All the lines which are confidered in the firft fix books of the Elements are fuppofed to be in the fame plane.

The *ftraight-edge* and *compaffes* are the only inftruments, the use of which is permitted in Euclid, or plain Geometry. To declare this restriction is the object of the *postulates*.

The *Axioms* of geometry are certain general propositions, the truth of which is taken to be self-evident and incapable of being established by demonstration.

Propositions are those results which are obtained in geometry by a process of reasoning. There are two species of propositions in geometry, *problems* and *theorems*.

A *Problem* is a proposition in which something is proposed to be done; as a line to be drawn under some given conditions, a circle to be described, some figure to be constructed, &c.

The *solution* of the problem consists in showing how the thing required may be done by the aid of the rule or straight-edge and compasses.

The *demonstration* consists in proving that the process indicated in the solution really attains the required end.

A *Theorem* is a proposition in which the truth of some principle is asserted. This principle must be deduced from the axioms and definitions, or other truths previously and independently established. To show this is the object of demonstration.

A *Problem* is analogous to a postulate.

A *Theorem* resembles an axiom.

A *Postulate* is a problem, the solution of which is assumed.

An *Axiom* is a theorem, the truth of which is granted without demonstration.

A *Corollary* is an inference deduced immediately from a proposition.

A *Scholium* is a note or observation on a proposition not containing an inference of sufficient importance to entitle it to the name of a *corollary*.

A *Lemma* is a proposition merely introduced for the purpose of establishing some more important proposition.

SYMBOLS AND ABBREVIATIONS.

∴ expresses the word *therefore.*

∵ . . . . *because.*

= . . . . *equal.* This sign of equality may be read *equal to,* or *is equal to,* or *are equal to ;* but any discrepancy in regard to the introduction of the auxiliary verbs *is, are,* &c. cannot affect the geometrical rigour.

≠ means the same as if the words ' *not equal*' were written.

⊐ signifies *greater than.*

⊒ . . . . *less than.*

⊉ . . . . *not greater than.*

⊈ . . . . *not less than.*

+ is read *plus (more),* the sign of addition ; when interposed between two or more magnitudes, signifies their sum.

— is read *minus (less),* signifies subtraction ; and when placed between two quantities denotes that the latter is to be taken from the former.

× this sign expresses the product of two or more numbers when placed between them in arithmetic and algebra ; but in geometry it is generally used to express a *rectangle,* when placed between " two straight lines which contain one of its right angles." A *rectangle* may also be represented by placing a point between two of its conterminous sides.

: :: : expresses an *analogy* or *proportion ;* thus, if A, B, C and D, represent four magnitudes, and A has to B the same ratio that C has to D, the proposition is thus briefly written,

$$A : B :: C : D,$$
$$A : B = C : D,$$
$$\text{or } \frac{A}{B} = \frac{C}{D}.$$

This equality or sameness of ratio is read,

as A is to B, fo is C to D;

or A is to B, as C is to D.

‖ fignifies *parallel to.*

⊥ . . . . *perpendicular to.*

◿ . *angle.*

◜ . . *right angle.*

⌓ . *two right angles.*

⋀ or ⋀ briefly defignates a *point.*

⊏, =, or ⊐ fignifies *greater, equal, or lefs than.*

The fquare defcribed on a line is concifely written thus,

—————^{2}.

In the fame manner twice the fquare of, is expreffed by

2 ⋅ —————^{2}.

def. fignifies *definition.*

pos. . . . . *poftulate.*

ax. . . . . *axiom.*

hyp. . . . . *hypothefis.* It may be neceffary here to remark, that the *hypothefis* is the condition affumed or
taken for granted. Thus, the hypothefis of the propofition given in the Introduction, is that the triangle
is ifofceles, or that its legs are equal.

conft. . . . . *conftruction.* The *conftruction* is the change
made in the original figure, by drawing lines, making
angles, defcribing circles, &c. in order to adapt it to
the argument of the demonftration or the folution of
the problem. The conditions under which thefe
changes are made, are as indifputable as thofe contained in the hypothefis. For inftance, if we make
an angle equal to a given angle, thefe two angles are
equal by conftruction.

Q. E. D. . . . . . *Quod erat demonftrandum.*

Which was to be demonftrated.

Faults to be corrected before reading this Volume.

PAGE 13, line 9, *for* def. 7 *read* def. 10.

 45, laft line, *for* pr. 19 *read* pr. 29.

 54, line 4 from the bottom, *for* black and red line *read* blue and red line.

 59, line 4, *for* add black line fquared *read* add blue line fquared.

 60, line 17, *for* red line multiplied by red and yellow line *read* red line multiplied by red, blue, and yellow line.

 76, line 11, *for* def. 7 *read* def. 10.

 81, line 10, *for* take black line *read* take blue line.

 105, line 11, *for* yellow black angle add blue angle equal red angle *read* yellow black angle add blue angle add red angle.

 129, laft line, *for* circle *read* triangle.

 141, line 1, *for* Draw black line *read* Draw blue line.

 196, line 3, before the yellow magnitude infert M.

Euclid.

BOOK I.

PROPOSITION I. PROBLEM.

N *a given finite straight line* (——) *to defcribe an equilateral triangle.*

Defcribe 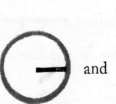 and

 (poftulate 3.); draw —— and —— (poft. 1.).

then will △ be equilateral.

For —— = —— (def. 15.);

and —— = —— (def. 15.),

∴ —— = —— (axiom. 1.);

and therefore △ is the equilateral triangle required.

Q. E. D.

B

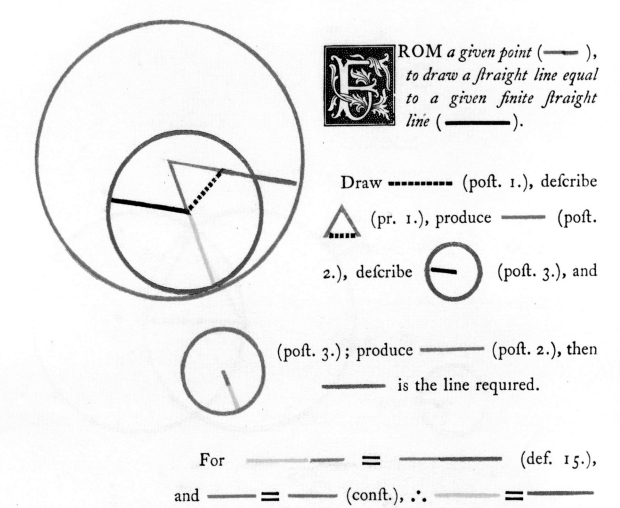

ROM *a given point* (——），
*to draw a ſtraight line equal
to a given finite ſtraight
line* (————）．

Draw ------------ (poſt. 1.), deſcribe
△ (pr. 1.), produce —————— (poſt.
2.), deſcribe ⊘ (poſt. 3.), and
(poſt. 3.); produce —————— (poſt. 2.), then
—————— is the line required.

For —————— = —————— (def. 15.),
and ——— = ——— (conſt.), ∴ —————— = ——————
(ax. 3.), but (def. 15.) ——— = ——— = ——— ;
∴ —————— drawn from the given point (——————),
is equal the given line —————— .

Q. E. D.

ROM *the greater* (——·····) *of two given ſtraight lines, to cut off a part equal to the leſs* (———).

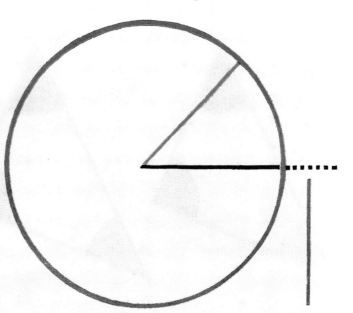

Draw ——— = ——— (pr. 2.); deſcribe

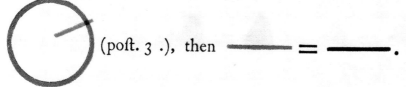

(poſt. 3 .), then ——— = ———.

For ——— = ——— (def. 15.),

and ——— = ——— (conſt.);

∴ ——— = ——— (ax. 1.).

Q. E. D.

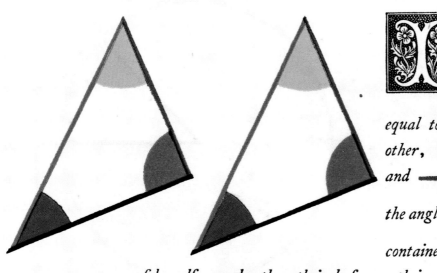

IF *two triangles have two fides of the one respectively equal to two fides of the other, (——— to ——— and ——— to ———) and the angles (* *and* *)*

contained by thofe equal fides alfo equal; then their bafes or their fides (——— and ———) are alfo equal: and the remaining and their remaining angles oppofite to equal fides are refpectively equal

(*=* *and* *=* *): and the triangles are equal in every refpect.*

Let the two triangles be conceived, to be fo placed, that the vertex of the one of the equal angles, or ; fhall fall upon that of the other, and ——— to coincide with ———, then will ——— coincide with ——— if applied: confequently ——— will coincide with ———, or two ftraight lines will enclofe a fpace, which is impoffible (ax. 10), therefore ——— = ———, =

and = , and as the triangles and

coincide, when applied, they are equal in every refpect.

Q. E. D.

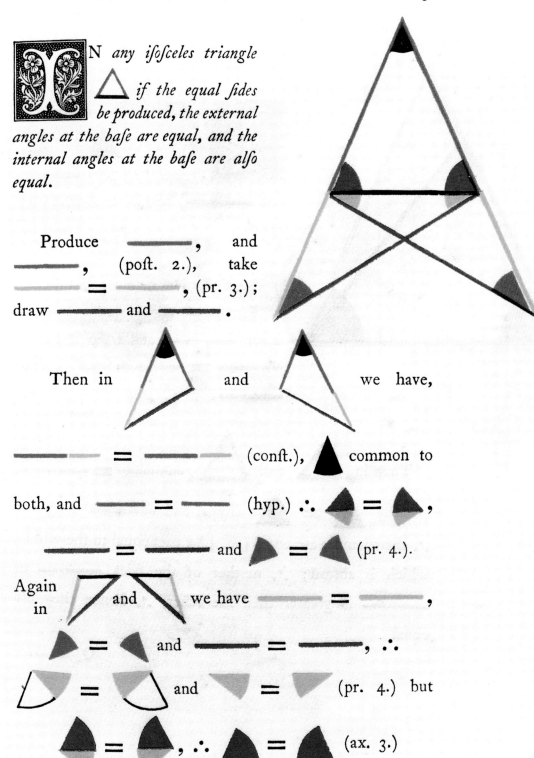

N *any iſoſceles triangle if the equal ſides be produced, the external angles at the baſe are equal, and the internal angles at the baſe are alſo equal.*

Produce ─────, and ─────, (poſt. 2.), take ───── = ─────, (pr. 3.); draw ───── and ─────.

Then in ⟨△⟩ and ⟨△⟩ we have,

───── = ───── (conſt.), ▲ common to both, and ─── = ─── (hyp.) ∴ ◣ = ◢,

─── = ─── and ◣ = ◢ (pr. 4.).

Again in ⟨△⟩ and ⟨△⟩ we have ───── = ─────,

◣ = ◢ and ─── = ───, ∴

◺ = ◿ and ▽ = ▽ (pr. 4.) but

◣ = ◢, ∴ ◣ = ◢ (ax. 3.)

Q. E. D.

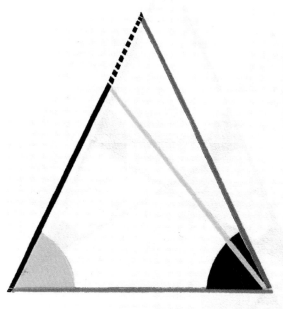

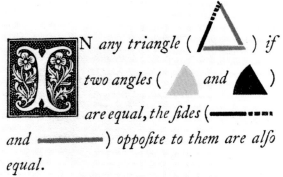

N *any triangle (* *) if two angles (* ▲ *and* ▲ *) are equal, the fides (*————••••— *and* ————*) oppofite to them are alfo equal.*

For if the fides be not equal, let one of them ————••••— be greater than the other ————, and from it cut off ———— = ————— (pr. 3.), draw ————— .

Then in △ and △ , ———— = —————, (conft.) ▲ = ▲ (hyp.) and ———— common, ∴ the triangles are equal (pr. 4.) a part equal to the whole, which is abfurd ; ∴ neither of the fides ————••••— or ————— is greater than the other, ∴ hence they are equal

Q. E. D.

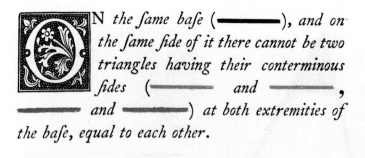

O N *the same base* (————), *and on the same side of it there cannot be two triangles having their conterminous sides* (———— *and* ————, ———— *and* ————) *at both extremities of the base, equal to each other.*

When two triangles ſtand on the ſame baſe, and on the ſame ſide of it, the vertex of the one ſhall either fall outſide of the other triangle, or within it; or, laſtly, on one of its ſides.

If it be poſſible let the two triangles be conſtructed ſo that $\left\{ \begin{array}{c} ———— = ———— \\ ———— = ———— \end{array} \right\}$, then

draw — — — — and,

◣ = ▼ (pr. 5.)

∴ ▼ ⊐ ▼ and

∴ ▼ ⊐ ◣ }

but (pr. 5.) ▼ = ◣ } which is abſurd,

therefore the two triangles cannot have their conterminous ſides equal at both extremities of the baſe.

Q. E. D.

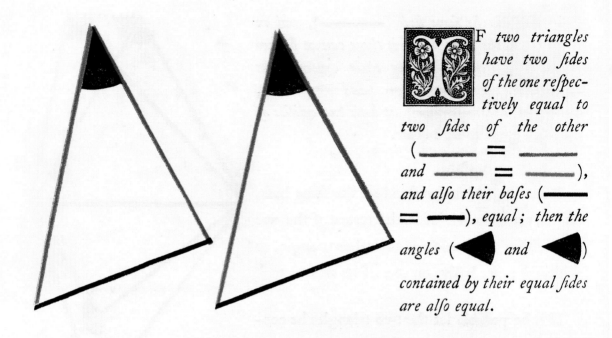

F *two triangles have two sides of the one respectively equal to two sides of the other* (———— = ———— *and* ———— = ————), *and also their bases* (—— = ——), *equal; then the angles* (◀ *and* ◀) *contained by their equal sides are also equal.*

If the equal bases ———— and ———— be conceived to be placed one upon the other, so that the triangles shall lie at the same side of them, and that the equal sides ———— and ————, ———— and ———— be con-terminous, the vertex of the one must fall on the vertex of the other; for to suppose them not coincident would contradict the last proposition.

Therefore the sides ———— and ————, being coin-cident with ———— and ————,

∴ ▲ = ▲ .

Q. E. D.

O *bifect a given rectilinear angle* (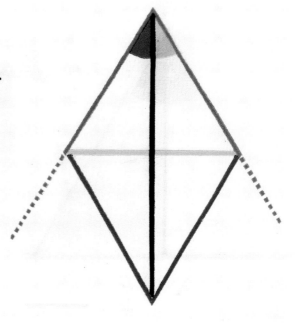).

Take ———— = ———— (pr. 3.)

draw ————, upon which

defcribe ∨ (pr. 1.),

draw ————.

Becaufe ———— = ———— (conft.)

and ———— common to the two triangles

and ———— = ———— (conft.),

∴ ◢ = ◣ (pr. 8.)

Q. E. D.

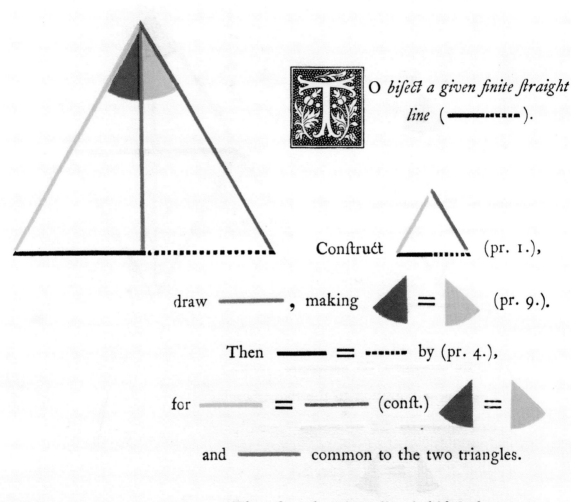

O *bifect a given finite ftraight line* (———·······).

Conftruct ◺ (pr. 1.),

draw ———, making ◣ = ◢ (pr. 9.).

Then ——— = ······· by (pr. 4.),

for ——— = ——— (conft.) ◣ = ◢

and ——— common to the two triangles.

Therefore the given line is bifected.

Q. E. D.

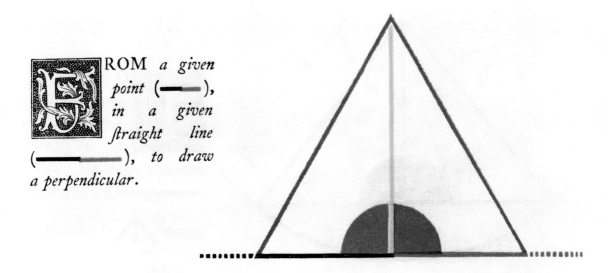

ROM *a given point* (———), *in a given ſtraight line* (———), *to draw a perpendicular.*

Take any point (———) in the given line,

cut off ——— = ——— (pr. 3.),

construct  (pr. 1.),

draw ——— and it ſhall be perpendicular to the given line.

For ——— = ——— (conſt.)

——— = ——— (conſt.)

and ——— common to the two triangles.

Therefore ◗ = ◖ (pr. 8.)

∴ ——— ⊥ ——— (def. 10.).

Q. E. D.

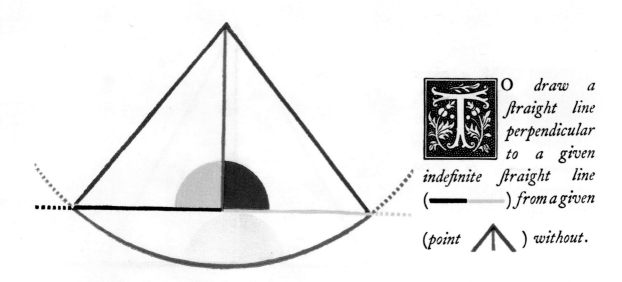

O *draw a straight line perpendicular to a given indefinite straight line* (━━━━━) *from a given*

(*point* ⋀) *without.*

With the given point ⋀ as centre, at one side of the line, and any diftance ━━━━ capable of extending to the other fide, defcribe ⌣ ,

Make ━━━━ ≡ ━━━━ (pr. 10.)

draw ━━━━ , ━━━━ and ━━━━ .

then ━━━━ ⊥ ━━━━ .

For (pr. 8.) fince ━━━━ ≡ ━━━━ (conft.)

━━━━ common to both,

and ━━━━ ≡ ━━━━ (def. 15.)

∴ ◗ ≡ ◖ , and

∴ ━━━━ ⊥ ━━━━ (def. 10.).

Q. E. D.

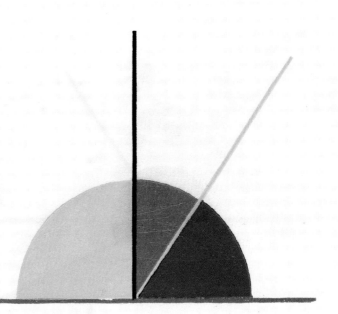

HEN *a straight line* (——) *standing upon another straight line* (——) *makes angles with it; they are either two right angles or together equal to two right angles.*

If —— be ⊥ to —— then,

and ▲ = ⬨ (def. 7.),

But if —— be not ⊥ to ——,

draw —— ⊥ —— ; (pr. 11.)

＋ = ⬨ (conſt.),

= = ＋

∴ ＋ = ＋ ＋ (ax. 2.)

= ＋ = ⬨.

Q. E. D.

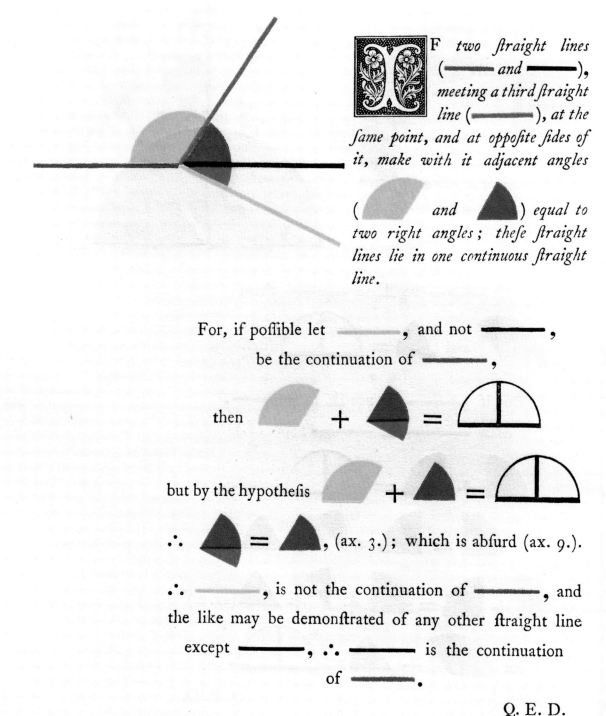

I F *two straight lines* (━━ *and* ━━), *meeting a third straight line* (━━), *at the same point, and at opposite sides of it, make with it adjacent angles* (◗ *and* ◤) *equal to two right angles; these straight lines lie in one continuous straight line.*

For, if possible let ━━, and not ━━, be the continuation of ━━,

then ◗ **+** ◤ **=** ⬖

but by the hypothesis ◗ **+** ◤ **=** ⬖

∴ ◤ **=** ◤ , (ax. 3.); which is absurd (ax. 9.).

∴ ━━, is not the continuation of ━━, and the like may be demonstrated of any other straight line except ━━, ∴ ━━ is the continuation of ━━.

Q. E. D.

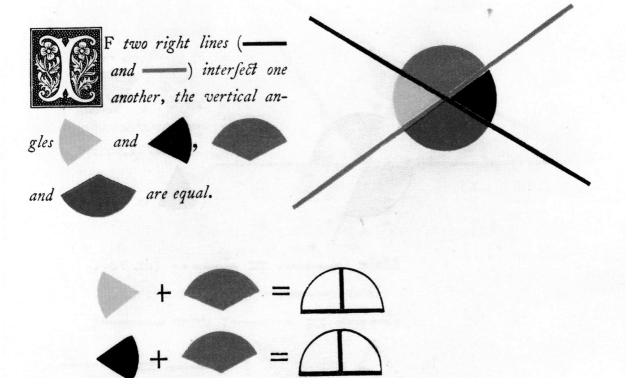

IF *two right lines* (———— *and* ————) *interſect one another, the vertical an-gles* and , and are equal.

In the ſame manner it may be ſhown that

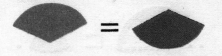

Q. E. D.

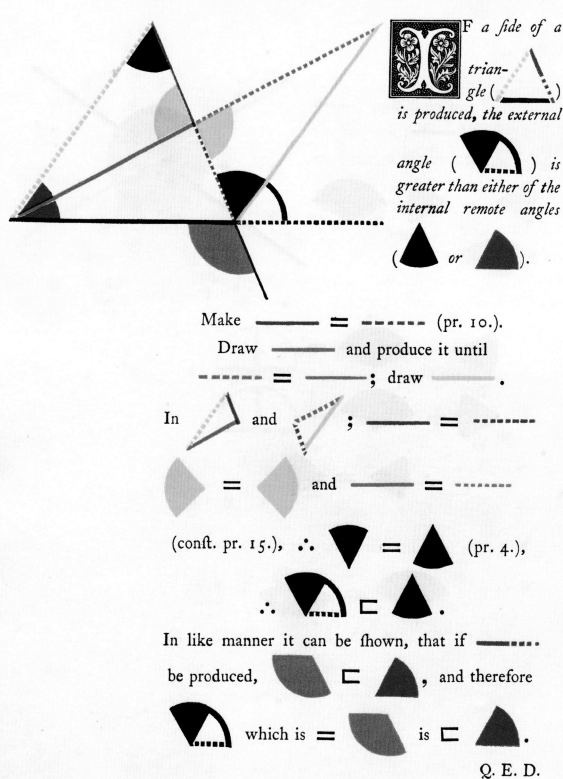

F *a fide of a* *trian-* *gle* (⎯⎯) *is produced, the external* *angle* ( ) *is greater than either of the* *internal remote angles* (or).

Make ⎯⎯ = ----- (pr. 10.).

Draw ⎯⎯ and produce it until

----- = ⎯⎯ ; draw .

In and ; ⎯⎯ = -----

= and ⎯⎯ = -----

(conſt. pr. 15.), ∴ = (pr. 4.),

∴ ⊏ .

In like manner it can be ſhown, that if ⎯⎯···

be produced, ⊏ , *and therefore*

which is = is ⊏ .

Q. E. D.

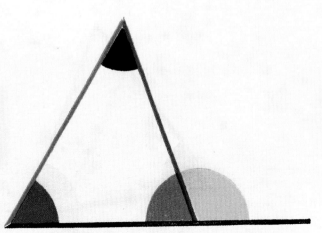

 NY *two angles of a tri-*

angle are to-

gether lefs than two right angles.

Produce ——————, then will

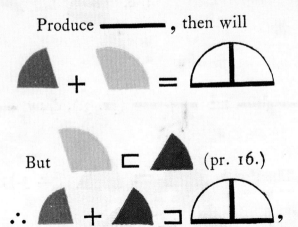

and in the fame manner it may be fhown that any other two angles of the triangle taken together are lefs than two right angles.

Q. E. D.

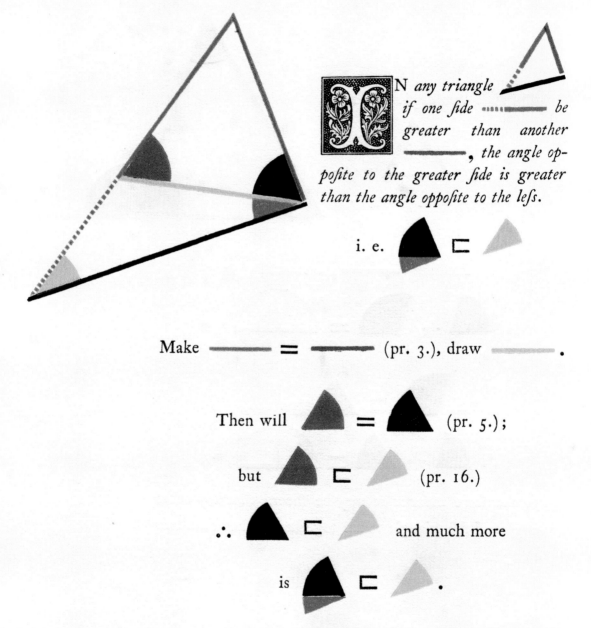

N *any triangle if one fide* ▪▪▪▪▪ *be greater than another* ━━━ , *the angle opposite to the greater fide is greater than the angle opposite to the lefs.*

i. e.   ◣ ⊏ ◢

Make ━━━ = ━━━ (pr. 3.), draw ━━━ .

Then will   ◣ = ◣ (pr. 5.);

but   ◣ ⊏ ◣ (pr. 16.)

∴   ◣ ⊏ ◢   and much more

is   ◣ ⊏ ◢ .

Q. E. D.

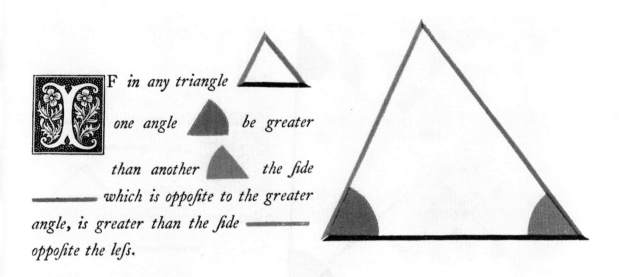

F *in any triangle* ▬ *one angle* ▲ *be greater than another* ▲ *the side* ▬ *which is oppofite to the greater angle, is greater than the fide* ▬ *oppofite the lefs.*

If ▬ be not greater than ▬ then muſt

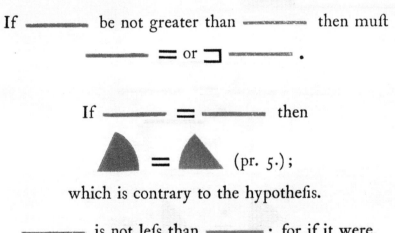

▬ = or ⊐ ▬ .

If ▬ = ▬ then

▲ = ▲ (pr. 5.);

which is contrary to the hypotheſis.

▬ is not leſs than ▬ ; for if it were,

▲ ⊐ ▲ (pr. 18.)

which is contrary to the hypotheſis:

∴ ▬ ⊏ ▬ .

Q. E. D.

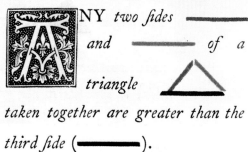

NY *two sides* ————— *and* ————— *of a triangle* △ *taken together are greater than the third side* (—————).

Produce —————, and

make ‑‑‑‑‑ = ————— (pr. 3.);

draw ————— .

Then becaufe ‑‑‑‑‑ = ————— (conft.),

◣ = ◤ (pr. 5.)

∴ ◣ ⊏ ◤ (ax. 9.)

∴ ————— + ‑‑‑‑‑ ⊏ ————— (pr. 19.)

and ∴ ————— + ————— ⊏ ————— .

Q. E. D

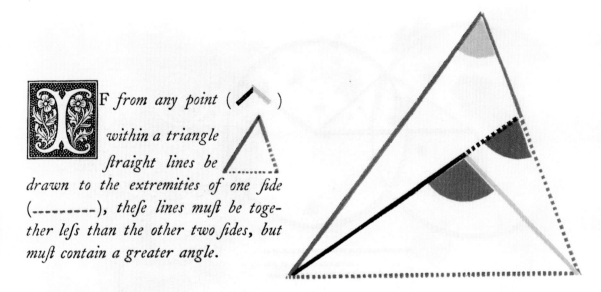

IF *from any point* ( ) *within a triangle ftraight lines be drawn to the extremities of one fide* (----------), *thefe lines muft be together lefs than the other two fides, but muft contain a greater angle.*

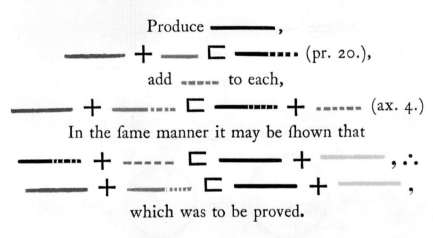

Produce ———,

——— + ——— ⊏ ———···· (pr. 20.),

add ------ to each,

——— + ———···· ⊏ ———···· + ------ (ax. 4.)

In the fame manner it may be fhown that

——···· + ------ ⊏ ——— + ———— , ∴

——— + ———···· ⊏ ——— + ———— ,

which was to be proved.

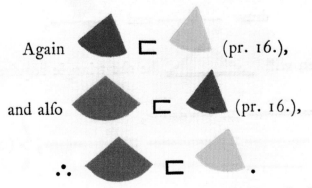

Again ◣ ⊏ ◣ (pr. 16.),

and alfo ◣ ⊏ ◣ (pr. 16.),

∴ ◣ ⊏ ◣ .

Q. E. D.

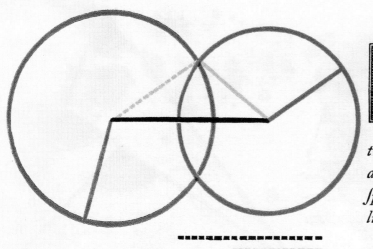

 IVEN *three right lines* $\Big\{$ ▬▬▬▬ ▬▬▬▬ *the ſum of any two greater than the third, to conſtruct a tri-angle whoſe ſides ſhall be re-ſpectively equal to the given lines.*

Aſſume ▬▬▬ = ▬▬▬▬ (pr. 3.).

Draw ▬▬▬ = ▬▬▬ $\Big\}$ (pr. 2.).

and ▬▬▬ = ▬▬

With ▬▬▬ and ▬▬▬ as radii,

deſcribe and (poſt. 3.);

draw ▬▬▬ and ▬▬▬ ,

then will be the triangle required.

For ▬▬▬ ≡ ▬▬▬ ,

▬▬▬ ≡ ▬▬▬ ≡ ▬▬▬ , $\Big\}$ (conſt.)

and ▬▬▬ ≡ ▬▬▬ ≡ ▬▬▬ .

Q. E. D.

T *a given point* (___) *in a*
given straight line (▬▬ ▪▪▪▪),
to make an angle equal to a
given rectilineal angle (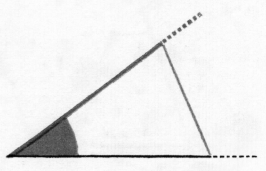).

Draw ▬▬▬ between any two points
in the legs of the given angle.

Conftruct ▱ (pr. 22.).

fo that ▬▬ = ▬▬ , ▬▬ = ▬▬

and ▬▬ ▬▬ .

Then ◢ = ◢ (pr. 8.).

Q. E. D.

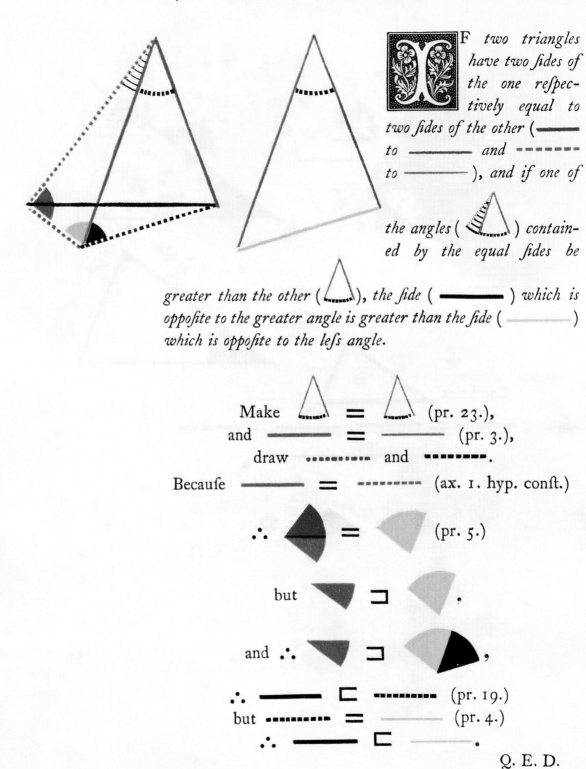

F *two triangles have two fides of the one respectively equal to two fides of the other* (————— *to* ————— *and* - - - - - - *to* —————), *and if one of the angles* (◁) *contained by the equal fides be greater than the other* (◁), *the fide* (—————) *which is oppofite to the greater angle is greater than the fide* (—————) *which is oppofite to the lefs angle.*

Make ◁ = ◁ (pr. 23.),

and ————— = ————— (pr. 3.),

draw - - - - - - and - - - - - - .

Becaufe ————— = - - - - - - (ax. 1. hyp. conft.)

∴ ◣ = ◣ (pr. 5.)

but ◣ ⊐ ◣ ,

and ∴ ◣ ⊐ ◣ ,

∴ ————— ⊏ - - - - - - (pr. 19.)

but - - - - - - = ————— (pr. 4.)

∴ ————— ⊏ ————— .

Q. E. D.

I F *two triangles have two sides* (———— *and* ————) *of the one respectively equal to two sides* (———— *and* ————) *of the other, but their bases unequal, the angle subtended by the greater base* (————) *of the one, must be greater than the angle subtended by the less base* (————) *of the other.*

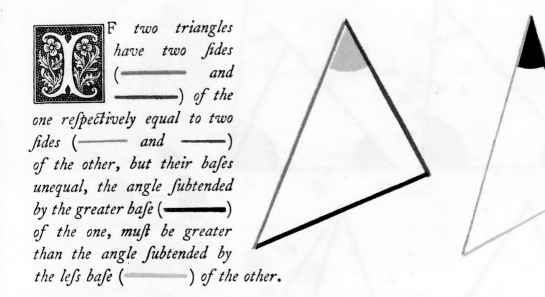

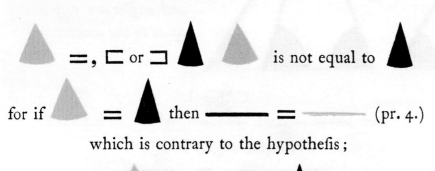

= , ⊏ or ⊐   is not equal to

for if   =   then ———— = ———— (pr. 4.)

which is contrary to the hypothesis;

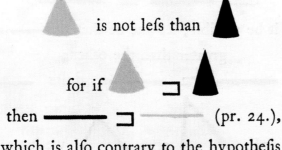

is not less than

for if   ⊐

then ———— ⊐ ———— (pr. 24.),

which is also contrary to the hypothesis:

∴   ⊏   .

Q. E. D.

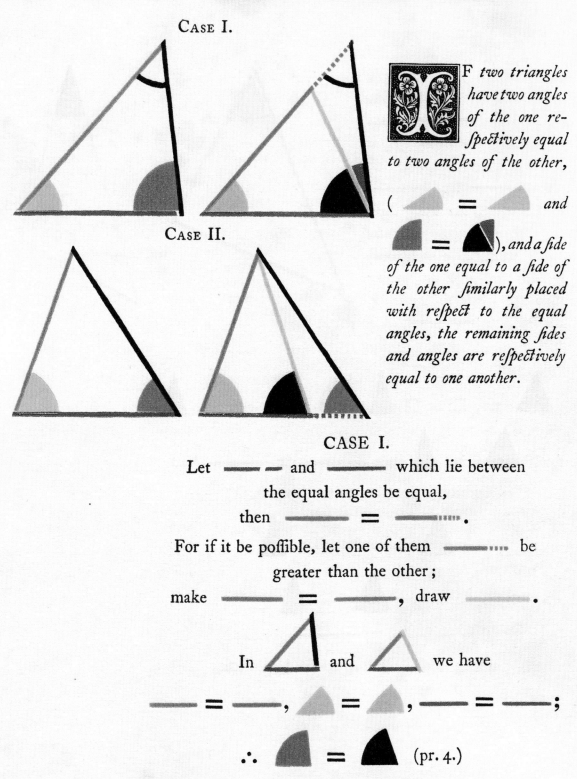

CASE I.

CASE II.

F *two triangles have two angles of the one respectively equal to two angles of the other,*

(▨ = ▨ *and*

◗ = ◗), *and a side of the one equal to a side of the other similarly placed with respect to the equal angles, the remaining sides and angles are respectively equal to one another.*

CASE I.

Let ——— and ——— which lie between
the equal angles be equal,

then ——— = ———.

For if it be possible, let one of them ——— be
greater than the other;

make ——— = ———, draw ———.

In △ and △ we have

——— = ———, ◤ = ◤, ——— = ———;

∴ ◗ = ◗   (pr. 4.)

but ▲ = ◣ (hyp.)

and therefore   ◣ = ◣ , which is abſurd;
hence neither of the ſides ▬▬ and ▬▬•••• is
greater than the other; and ∴ they are equal;

∴ ▬▬ = ▬▬ , and ◁ = ◁ , (pr. 4.).

CASE II.

Again, let ▬▬▬ = ▬▬▬ , which lie oppoſite

the equal angles ▲ and ▲ . If it be poſſible, let
▬▬•••• ⊏ ▬▬ , then take ▬▬ = ▬▬ ,
draw ▬▬ .

Then in △ and △ we have ▬▬ = ▬▬ ,

▬▬ = ▬▬ and ▲ = ▲ ,

∴ ▲ = ▲ (pr. 4.)

but   ▲ = ▲ (hyp.)

∴ ▲ = ▲ which is abſurd (pr. 16.).

Conſequently, neither of the ſides ▬▬ or ▬▬•••• is
greater than the other, hence they muſt be equal. It
follows (by pr. 4.) that the triangles are equal in all
reſpects.

Q. E. D.

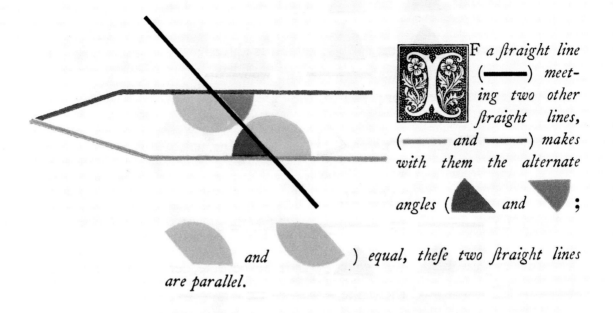

I F *a ſtraight line* (————) *meeting two other ſtraight lines,* (———— *and* ————) *makes with them the alternate angles* (▲ *and* ▼ ; and ◣ ◢) *equal, theſe two ſtraight lines are parallel.*

If ———— be not parallel to ———— they ſhall meet when produced.

If it be poſſible, let thoſe lines be not parallel, but meet when produced ; then the external angle ▼ is greater than ▲ (pr. 16), but they are alſo equal (hyp.), which is abſurd : in the ſame manner it may be ſhown that they cannot meet on the other ſide ; ∴ they are parallel.

Q. E. D.

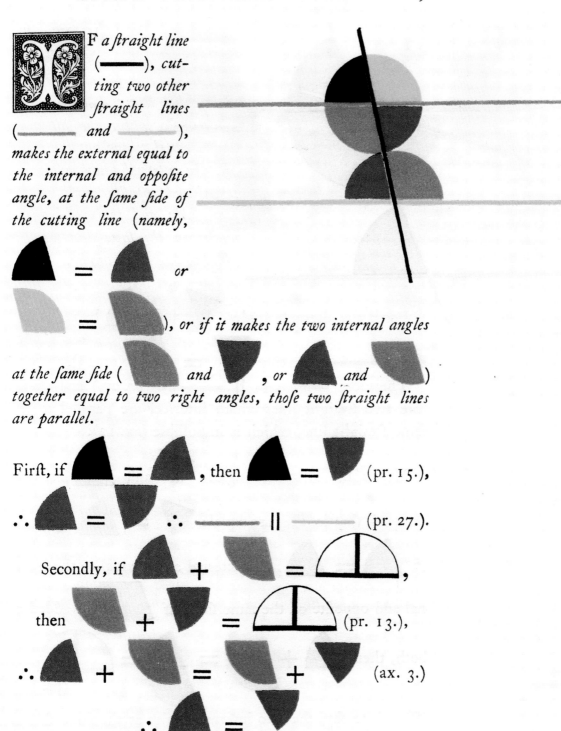

I F *a straight line* (———), *cut-ting two other straight lines* (———— *and* ————), *makes the external equal to the internal and oppofite angle, at the fame fide of the cutting line (namely,*

◢ = ◣ *or*

◣ = ◣), *or if it makes the two internal angles*

at the fame fide (◣ *and* ◢ *, or* ◣ *and* ◣ *) together equal to two right angles, thofe two ftraight lines are parallel.*

Firft, if ◢ = ◣ , then ◢ = ◣ (pr. 15.),

∴ ◣ = ◣ ∴ ———— ‖ ———— (pr. 27.).

Secondly, if ◣ + ◣ = ◠ ,

then ◣ + ◣ = ◠ (pr. 13.),

∴ ◣ + ◣ = ◣ + ◣ (ax. 3.)

∴ ◣ = ◣

∴ ———— ‖ ———— (pr. 27.)

Q. E. D.

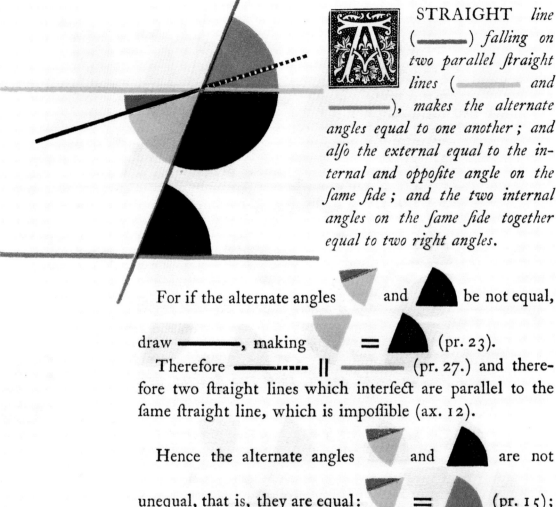

STRAIGHT *line* (———) *falling on two parallel straight lines* (——— *and* ———), *makes the alternate angles equal to one another; and also the external equal to the internal and opposite angle on the same side; and the two internal angles on the same side together equal to two right angles.*

For if the alternate angles and be not equal,

draw ———, making = (pr. 23).

Therefore ——— ‖ ——— (pr. 27.) and therefore two straight lines which interfect are parallel to the same straight line, which is impoffible (ax. 12).

Hence the alternate angles and are not

unequal, that is, they are equal: = (pr. 15);

∴ = , the external angle equal to the inter-

nal and oppofite on the fame fide: if be added to

both, then + = = (pr. 13).

That is to fay, the two internal angles at the fame fide of the cutting line are equal to two right angles.

Q. E. D.

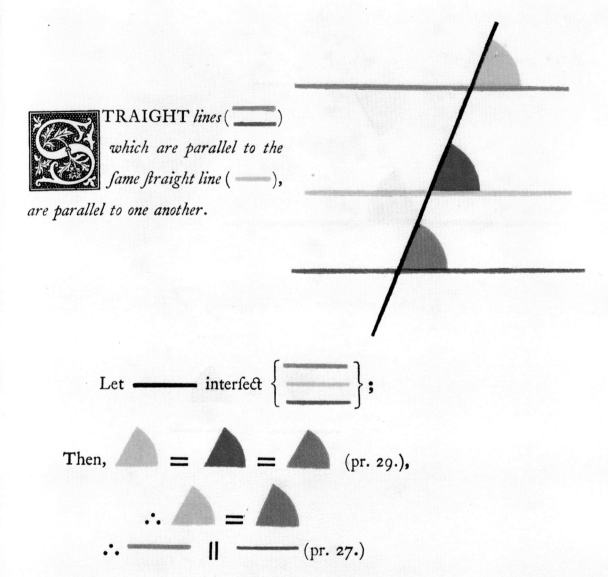

STRAIGHT *lines* (⸻)
which are parallel to the
same straight line (⸻),
are parallel to one another.

Let ⸻ interſect $\left\{ \begin{array}{c} ⸻ \\ ⸻ \\ ⸻ \end{array} \right\}$;

Then, △ = △ = △ (pr. 29.),

∴ △ = △

∴ ⸻ ∥ ⸻ (pr. 27.)

Q. E. D.

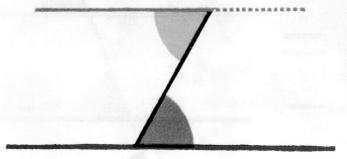

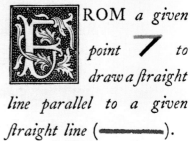

ROM *a given point* ⟋ *to draw a straight line parallel to a given straight line* (———).

Draw ——— from the point ⟋ to any point ∠

in ———,

make ▽ = ◣ (pr. 23.),

then ——— ‖ ——— (pr. 27.).

Q. E. D.

F *any side* (————)
*of a triangle be pro-
duced, the external*

angle (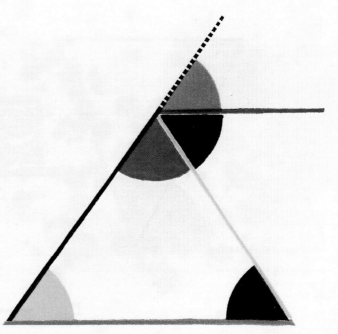) *is equal*

to the sum of the two internal and

opposite angles (▲ *and* ▲),
*and the three internal angles of
every triangle taken together are
equal to two right angles.*

Through the point ∕ draw

———— ‖ ———— (pr. 31.).

Then { ▲ = ▲
        ▲ = ▼ } (pr. 29.),

∴ ▲ + ▲ = ◖ (ax. 2.),

and therefore

▲ + ◣ + ▲ = ◖ = ⌓ (pr. 13.).

Q. E. D.

F

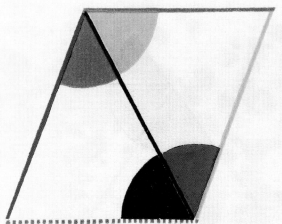

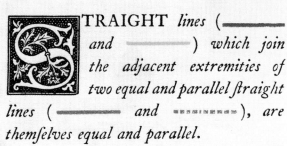

STRAIGHT *lines* (——— *and* ———) *which join the adjacent extremities of two equal and parallel ſtraight lines* (——— *and* ———), *are themſelves equal and parallel.*

Draw ——— the diagonal.

——— = ········· (hyp.)

▼ = ▲ (pr. 29.)

and ——— common to the two triangles;

∴ ——— = ———, and ▼ = ▲ (pr. 4.);

and ∴ ——— ‖ ——— (pr. 27.).

Q. E. D.

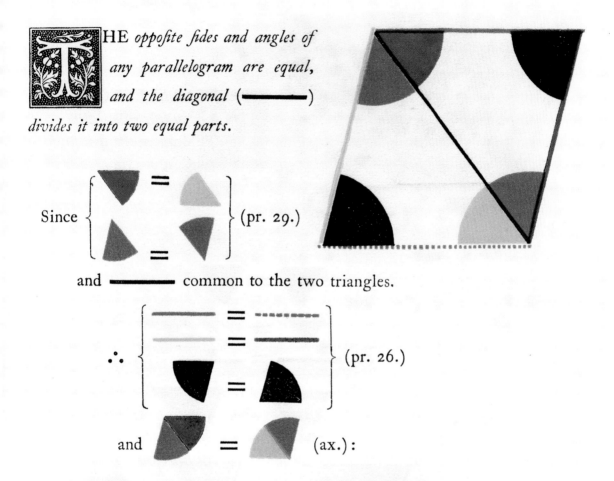

THE *oppofite fides and angles of any parallelogram are equal, and the diagonal* (———) *divides it into two equal parts.*

Since ⎰ ⎱ (pr. 29.)

and ——— common to the two triangles.

∴ ⎰ ⎱ (pr. 26.)

and = (ax.) :

Therefore the oppofite fides and angles of the parallelogram are equal: and as the triangles ◣ and ◺ are equal in every refpect (pr. 4,), the diagonal divides the parallelogram into two equal parts.

Q. E. D.

ARALLELOGRAMS *on the same base, and between the same parallels, are (in area) equal.*

On account of the parallels,

◣ = ◣ ;   ⎫ (pr. 29.)

▼ = ▽ ;   ⎬ (pr. 29.)

and ▬▬▬ = ▬▬▬ ⎭ (pr. 34.)

But, ◥ = ◤   (pr. 8.)

∴ ◤ minus ◣ = ◣ ,

and ◤ minus ◣ = ◥ ;

∴ ◥ = ◥ .

Q. E. D.

ARALLELO-
GRAMS

(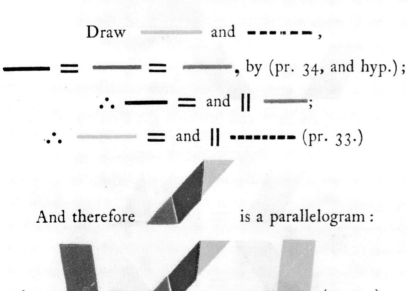 *and* 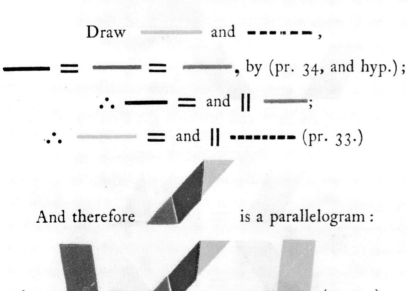) *on*
equal bafes, and between the
fame parallels, are equal.

Draw ———— and ━ ━ ━ ━ ,

━━━ = ———— = ———— , by (pr. 34, and hyp.);

∴ ━━━ = and ‖ ———— ;

∴ ———— = and ‖ ━ ━ ━ ━ (pr. 33.)

And therefore 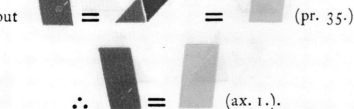 is a parallelogram :

but 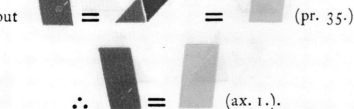 = 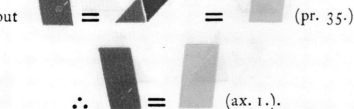 = 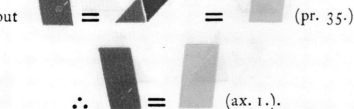 (pr. 35.)

∴ 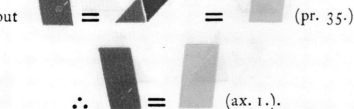 = 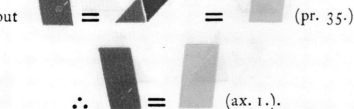 (ax. 1.).

Q. E. D.

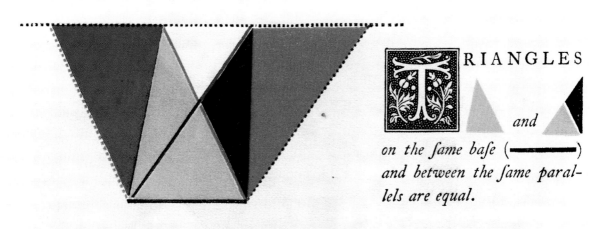

 RIANGLES *and*
on the fame bafe (———)
and between the fame paral-
lels are equal.

Draw ‒‒‒‒‒ || ——— ⎫
‒‒‒‒‒ || ——— ⎬ (pr. 31.)
⎭

Produce ‒‒‒‒‒‒‒‒‒ .

 and   are parallelograms

on the fame bafe, and between the fame parallels,

and therefore equal. (pr. 35.)

∴ ⎰ 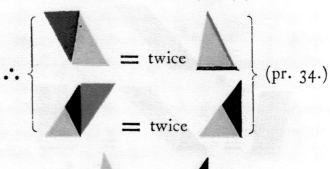 = twice   ⎱ (pr. 34.)
  ⎱ = twice   ⎰

∴   =   .

Q. E D.

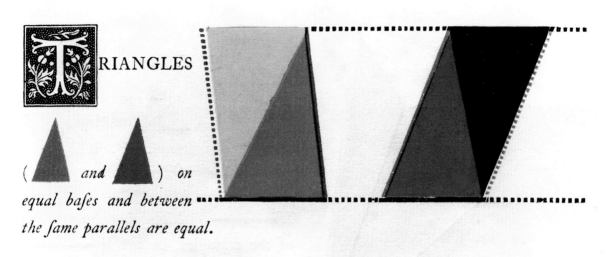

RIANGLES

(*and*   ) *on*
equal baſes and between
the ſame parallels are equal.

Draw   ‖   } (pr. 31.).
and   ‖

   =   (pr. 36.);

but   = twice   (pr. 34.),

and   = twice   (pr. 34.),

∴   =   (ax. 7.).

Q. E. D.

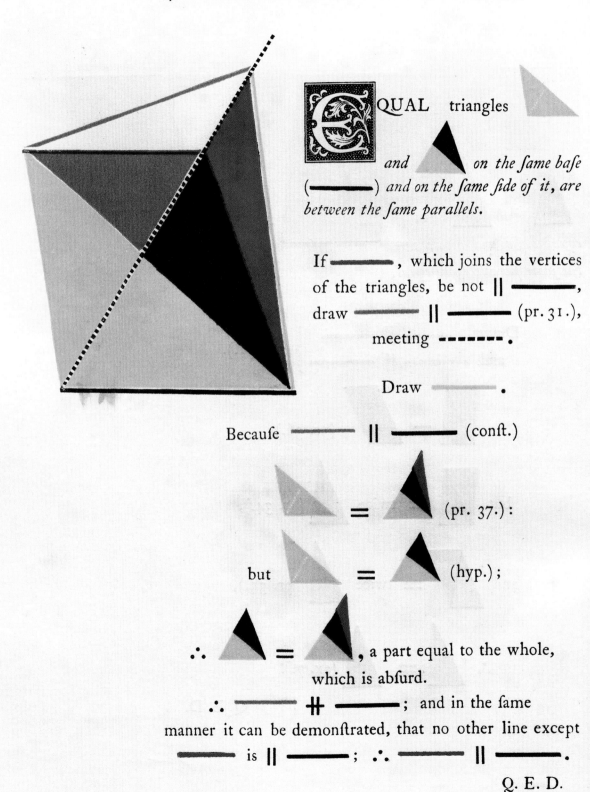

QUAL triangles and on the *same base*
(——————) *and on the same side of it, are
between the same parallels.*

If ——————, which joins the vertices
of the triangles, be not ‖ ——————,
draw —————— ‖ —————— (pr. 31.),
meeting ------- .

Draw —————— .

Becaufe —————— ‖ —————— (conſt.)

—————— = —————— (pr. 37.) :

but —————— = —————— (hyp.) ;

∴ —————— = —————— , a part equal to the whole,
which is abſurd.

∴ —————— ‖⃥ —————— ; and in the ſame
manner it can be demonſtrated, that no other line except
—————— is ‖ —————— ; ∴ —————— ‖ —————— .

Q. E. D.

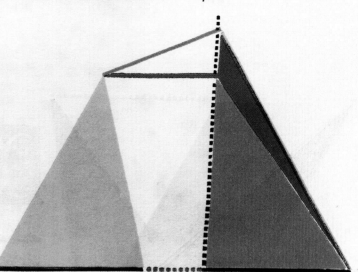

QUAL *triangles*

(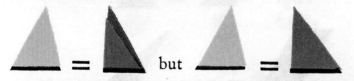 *and* _____)
*on equal bafes, and on the
fame fide, are between the
fame parallels.*

If _____ which joins the vertices of triangles

be not ‖ _____ ,

draw _____ ‖ _____ (pr. 31.),

meeting --------- .

Draw _____ .

Becaufe _____ ‖ _____ (conft.)

_____ = _____ but _____ = _____

∴ _____ = _____ , a part equal to the whole,

which is abfurd.

∴ _____ ╫ _____ : and in the fame manner it

can be demonftrated, that no other line except

_____ is ‖ _____ : ∴ _____ ‖ _____ .

Q. E. D.

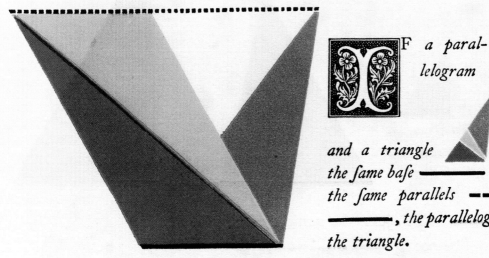

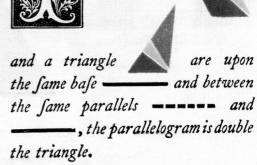

IF a parallelogram and a triangle are upon the same bafe ———— and between the same parallels ------ and ————, the parallelogram is double the triangle.

Draw ———— the diagonal;

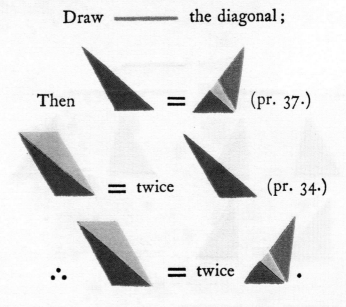

Then ◣ = ◤ (pr. 37.)

= twice ◥ (pr. 34.)

∴ ◥ = twice ◤ .

Q. E. D.

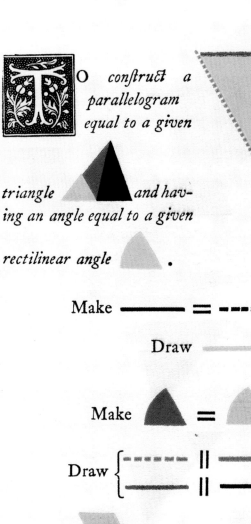

O *conftruct a parallelogram equal to a given* triangle *and hav-ing an angle equal to a given* rectilinear angle .

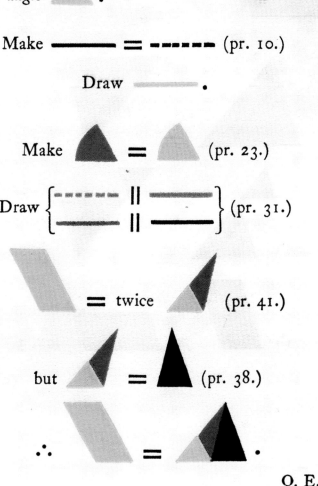

Make ———— = ------ (pr. 10.)

Draw ———— .

Make ⬥ = ⬥ (pr. 23.)

Draw { ------ ‖ ———— } (pr. 31.)
        { ———— ‖ ———— }

= twice (pr. 41.)

but = (pr. 38.)

∴ = .

Q. E. D.

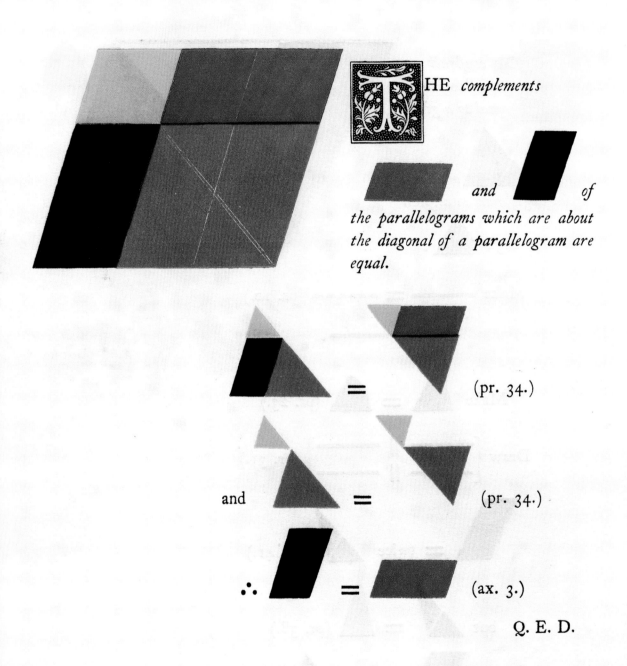

THE *complements* and of the parallelograms which are about the diagonal of a parallelogram are equal.

= (pr. 34.)

and = (pr. 34.)

∴ = (ax. 3.)

Q. E. D.

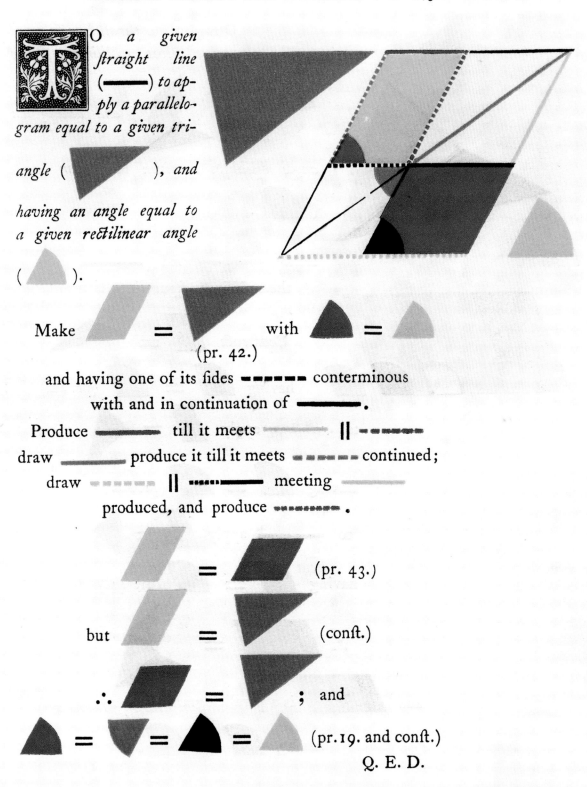

O a given *straight line* (———) to apply a parallelogram equal to a given triangle (   ), and

having an angle equal to a given rectilinear angle (   ).

Make   =   with   =   (pr. 42.)

and having one of its sides ▬ ▬ ▬ conterminous with and in continuation of ———.

Produce ——— till it meets ——— ‖ ▬ ▬ ▬

draw ——— produce it till it meets ▬ ▬ ▬ continued;

draw ▬ ▬ ▬ ‖ ▬▬▬ meeting ——— produced, and produce ▬▬▬.

    =   (pr. 43.)

but   =   (conft.)

∴   =   ; and

  =   =   =   (pr. 19. and conft.)

Q. E. D.

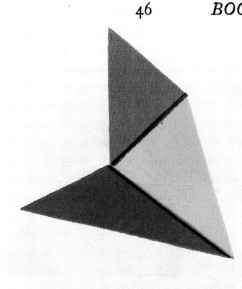

O *construct a parallelogram equal to a given rectilinear figure*

( ) *and having an*

angle equal to a given rectilinear angle

( ).

Draw ———— and ———— dividing the rectilinear figure into triangles.

Construct   =

having   =   (pr. 42.)

to ———— apply   =

having   =   (pr. 44.)

to ———— apply   =

having   =   (pr. 44.)

∴   =

and   is a parallelogram. (prs. 29, 14, 30.)

having   =   .

Q. E. D.

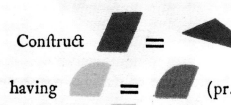

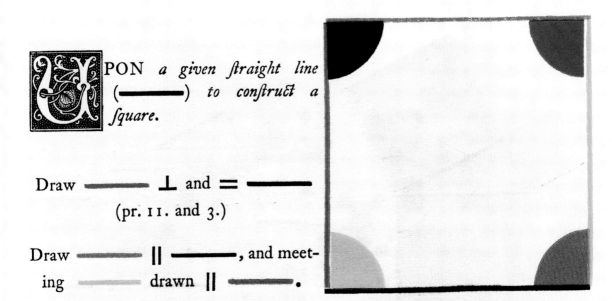

UPON *a given ſtraight line* ( ) *to conſtruct a ſquare.*

Draw ⊥ and =
(pr. 11. and 3.)

Draw || , and meeting drawn || .

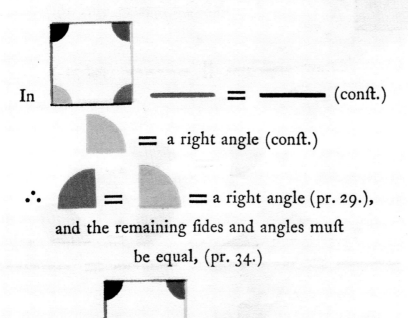

In  = (conſt.)

 = a right angle (conſt.)

∴  =  = a right angle (pr. 29.), and the remaining ſides and angles muſt be equal, (pr. 34.)

and ∴ 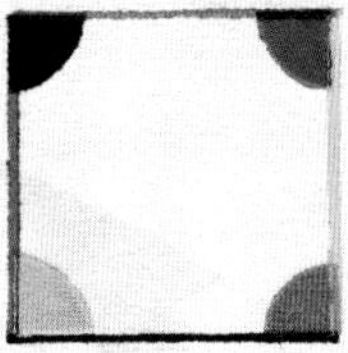 is a ſquare. (def. 27.)

Q. E. D.

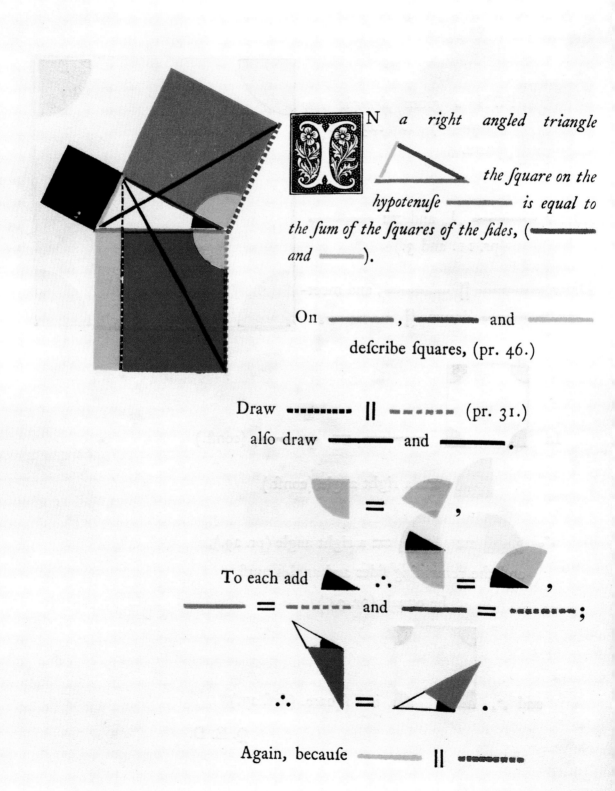

N a right angled triangle the *square on the hypotenuse* ━━━━ *is equal to the sum of the squares of the sides,* (━━━━ *and* ━━━━).

On ━━━━ , ━━━━ and ━━━━ describe squares, (pr. 46.)

Draw ▪▪▪▪▪▪▪ ‖ ▪ ▪ ▪ ▪ ▪ (pr. 31.)
also draw ━━━━ and ━━━━ .

∴ ━━━━ = ━ ━ ━ and ━━━━ = ▪▪▪▪▪▪▪ ;

Again, because ━━━━ ‖ ▪▪▪▪▪▪▪

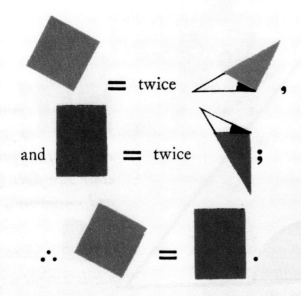

In the ſame manner it may be ſhown

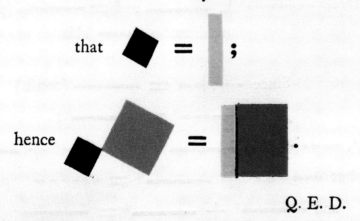

Q. E. D.

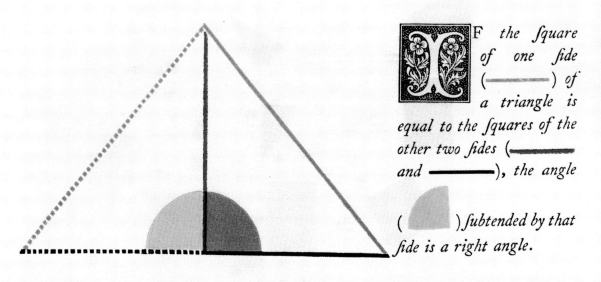

F the *square*
of one side
(————) *of*
a triangle is
equal to the squares of the
other two sides (————
and ————), *the angle*

( ) *subtended by that*
side is a right angle.

Draw ---------- ⊥ ———— and ═ ———— (prs. 11. 3.)
and draw ---------- also.

Since ---------- ═ ———— (conſt.)

---------- ^{2} ═ ———— ^{2};

∴ ----------^{2} + ————^{2} ═ ————^{2} + ————^{2},

but ----------^{2} + ————^{2} ═ ----------^{2} (pr. 47.),

and ————^{2} + ————^{2} ═ ————^{2} (hyp.)

∴ ----------^{2} ═ ————^{2},

∴ ---------- ═ ————;

and ∴   ═   (pr. 8.),

conſequently   is a right angle.

Q. E. D.

BOOK II.

DEFINITION I.

 RECTANGLE or a right angled parallelogram is faid to be contained by any two of its adjacent or conterminous fides.

Thus: the right angled parallelogram ▬ is faid to be contained by the fides ▬▬ and ▬▬ ;

or it may be briefly defignated by ▬▬ . ▬▬ .

If the adjacent fides are equal; i. e. ▬▬ = ▬▬ ,

then ▬▬ . ▬▬ which is the expreffion

for the rectangle under ▬▬ and ▬▬

is a fquare, and

is equal to $\left\{ \begin{array}{l} \text{▬▬} . \text{▬▬} \text{ or } \text{▬▬}^2 \\ \text{▬▬} . \text{▬▬} \text{ or } \text{▬▬}^2 \end{array} \right.$

DEFINITION II.

IN a parallelogram, the figure compofed of one of the parallelograms about the diagonal, together with the two complements, is called a *Gnomon*.

Thus 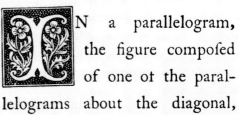 and are

called Gnomons.

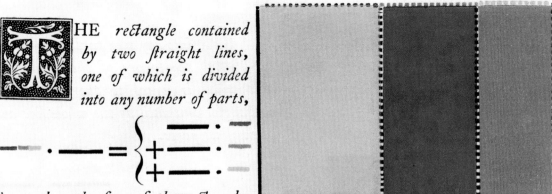

HE *rectangle contained by two straight lines, one of which is divided into any number of parts,*

is equal to the sum of the rectangles contained by the undivided line, and the several parts of the divided line.

Draw ▬ ⊥ ▬ and ═ ▬ (prs. 2. 3. B.1.);
complete the parallelograms, that is to say,

Draw { ∥ ∥ } (pr. 31. B. 1.)

= + +

= ▬ · ▬

= ▬ · ▬ , = ▬ · ▬ ,

= ▬ · ▬

∴ ▬ · ▬ = ▬ · ▬ +
▬ · ▬ + ▬ · ▬ .

Q. E. D.

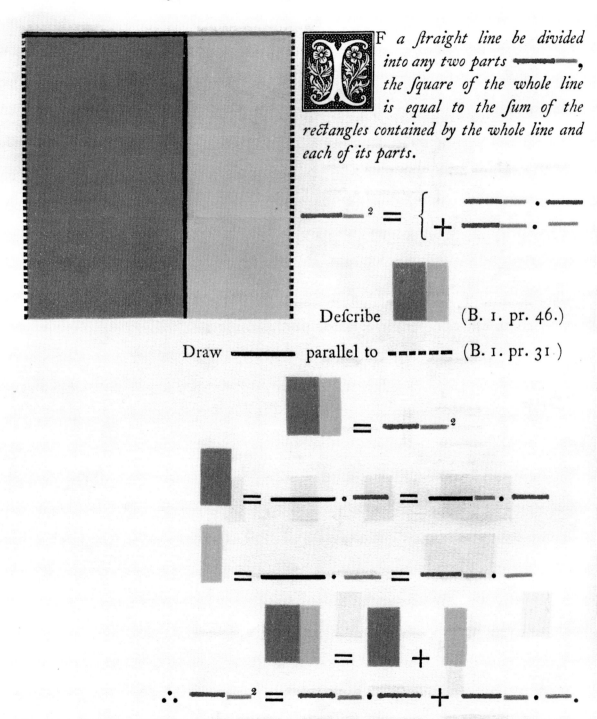

F *a straight line be divided into any two parts* ━━━━, *the square of the whole line is equal to the sum of the rectangles contained by the whole line and each of its parts.*

Defcribe (B. 1. pr. 46.)

Draw ━━━━ parallel to ━ ━ ━ (B. 1. pr. 31.)

Q. E. D.

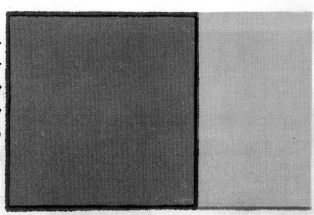

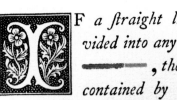F *a ſtraight line be di-*
vided into any two parts
——— , *the rectangle*
contained by the whole
line *and either of its parts, is equal to*
the *ſquare of that part, together with*
the *rectangle under the parts.*

$$ \underline{\quad} \cdot \underline{\ } = \underline{\ }^2 + \underline{\ } \cdot \underline{\ } \text{, or,} $$

$$ \underline{\quad} \cdot \underline{\ } = \underline{\ }^2 + \underline{\ } \cdot \underline{\ } . $$

Deſcribe ■ (pr. 46, B. 1.)

Complete ▮ (pr. 31, B. 1.)

Then ■ = ■ + ▮ , but

■ = ——— · ——— and

■ = ——^{2} , ▮ = —— · —— ,

∴ ——— · —— = ——^{2} + —— · —— :

In a ſimilar manner it may be readily ſhown

that ——— · —— = ——^{2} + ——— · —— .

Q. E. D

 F *a ſtraight line be divided into any two parts* ━━ ━━, *the ſquare of the whole line is equal to the ſquares of the parts, together with twice the rectangle contained by the parts.*

$$ \underline{\quad\quad\quad}^{2} = \underline{\quad\quad}^{2} + \underline{\quad}^{2} + $$

twice ━━•━━.

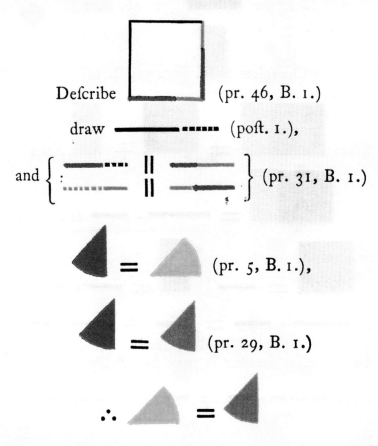

Deſcribe ▢ (pr. 46, B. 1.)

draw ━━ ▪▪▪▪ (poſt. 1.),

and $\left\{ \begin{array}{l} \text{━━ ▪▪ } \| \text{ ━━} \\ \text{━━ } \| \text{ ━━▶} \end{array} \right\}$ (pr. 31, B. 1.)

◤ = ◥ (pr. 5, B. 1.),

◤ = ◥ (pr. 29, B. 1.)

∴ ◤ = ◥

∴ by (prs. 6, 29, 34. B. 1.) ◰ is a square $= \underline{\qquad}^2.$

For the fame reafons ◰ is a fquare $= \underline{\quad}^2,$

$$\blacksquare = \blacksquare = \underline{\qquad} \cdot \underline{\quad} \quad \text{(pr. 43, b. 1.)}$$

but ◰ $=$ ◰ $+$ ▬ $+$ ▮ $+$ ◿ ,

$$\therefore \underline{\qquad}^2 = \underline{\qquad}^2 + \underline{\quad}^2 +$$

twice $\underline{\qquad} \cdot \underline{\quad}.$

Q. E. D.

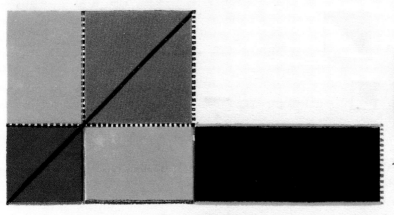

F   a ſtraight
line be divided

into two equal

parts and alſo

into two unequal parts,
the rectangle contained by

the unequal parts, together with the ſquare of the line between
the points of ſection, is equal to the ſquare of half that line

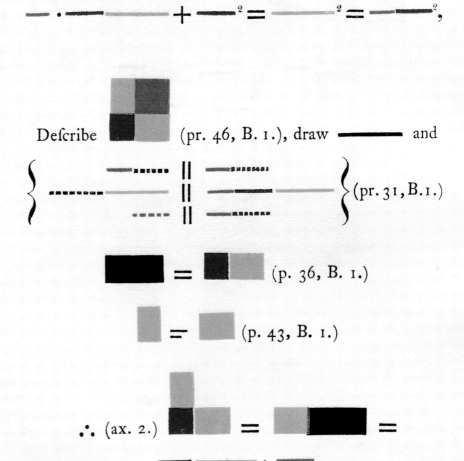

Defcribe ▦ (pr. 46, B. 1.), draw ──── and

⎰ ... ⎱ (pr. 31, B.1.)

∴ (ax. 2.)

but ■ = ⎯² (cor. pr. 4. B. 2.)

and ▦ = ⎯⎯² (conſt.)

∴ (ax. 2.) ▦ = ▦

∴ ⎯ · ⎯ + ⎯² =

⎯² = ⎯².

Q. E. D.

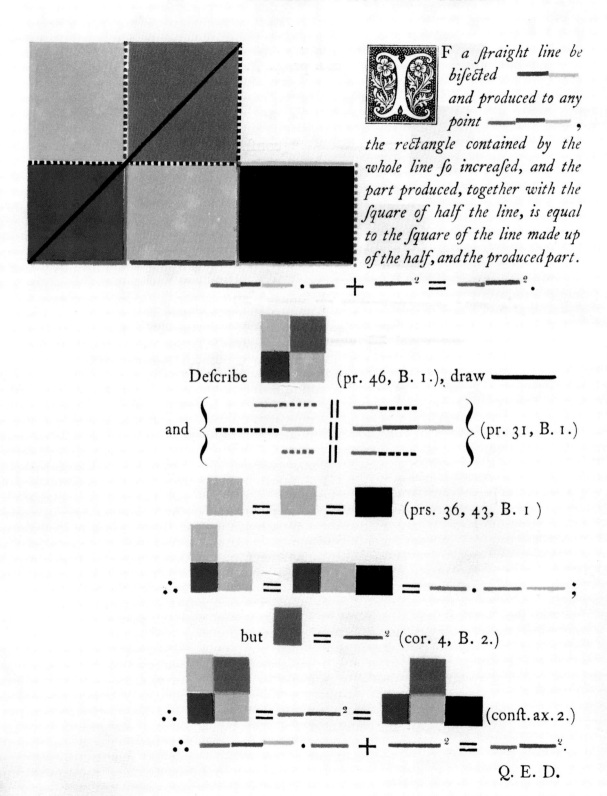

I F *a straight line be bisected* ━━ *and produced to any point* ━━ , *the rectangle contained by the whole line so increased, and the part produced, together with the square of half the line, is equal to the square of the line made up of the half, and the produced part.*

Describe ▦ (pr. 46, B. 1.), draw ━━

and { ━━ ‖ ━━ }

{ ━━ ‖ ━━ } (pr. 31, B. 1.)

{ ━━ ‖ ━━ }

■ = ■ = ■ (prs. 36, 43, B. 1)

∴ ▦ = ▦ = ━━ . ━━ ;

but ■ = ━━ ^{2} (cor. 4, B. 2.)

∴ ▦ = ━━ ^{2} = ▦ (const. ax. 2.)

∴ ━━ . ━━ + ━━ ^{2} = ━━ ^{2}.

Q. E. D.

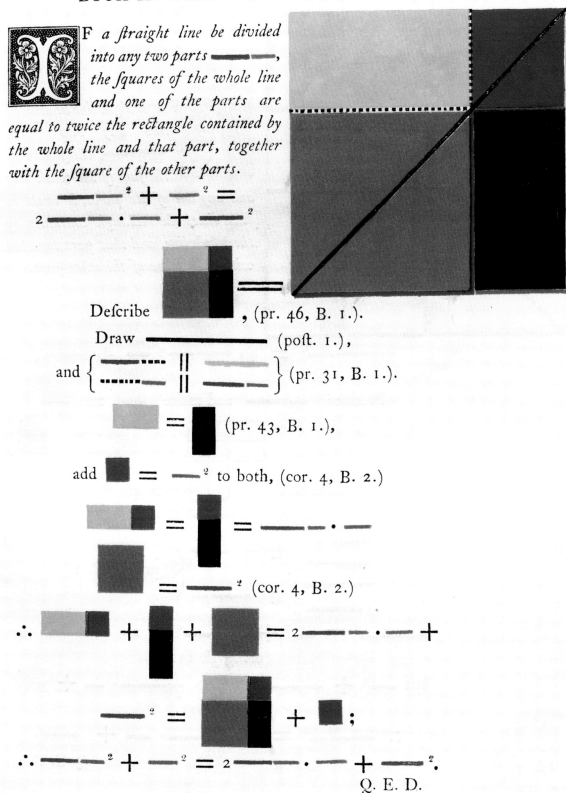

F *a ſtraight line be divided into any two parts* ▬▬ ▬, *the ſquares of the whole line and one of the parts are equal to twice the rectangle contained by the whole line and that part, together with the ſquare of the other parts.*

$$ \overline{}^2 + \overline{}^2 = $$
$$ 2\ \overline{}\ \cdot\ + \overline{}^2 $$

Deſcribe ▦ ═, (pr. 46, B. 1.).

Draw ▬▬▬▬▬ (poſt. 1.),

and $\left\{ \begin{array}{c} \blacksquare\text{--} \ \| \ \blacksquare\text{--} \\ \text{--}\blacksquare \ \| \ \text{--}\blacksquare \end{array} \right\}$ (pr. 31, B. 1.).

▬ = ▮ (pr. 43, B. 1.),

add ▪ = ▬² to both, (cor. 4, B. 2.)

▦ = ▮ = ▬▬ · ▬

▪ = ▬² (cor. 4, B. 2.)

∴ ▦ + ▮ + ▪ = 2 ▬▬ · ▬ +

▬² = ▦ + ▪ ;

∴ ▬▬² + ▬² = 2 ▬▬ · ▬ + ▬².

Q. E. D.

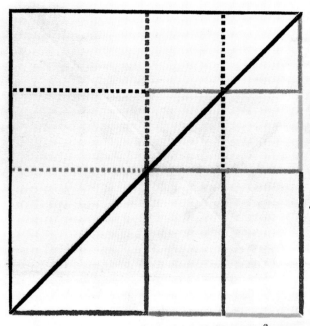

F *a straight line be divided into any two parts* ——— ———, *the square of the sum of the whole line and any one of its parts, is equal to four times the rectangle contained by the whole line, and that part together with the square of the other part.*

$$ \underline{\qquad}^2 = 4 \cdot \underline{\qquad} \cdot \underline{\quad} + \underline{\quad}^2, $$

Produce ——— and make ——— = ———

Construct ▦ (pr. 46, B. 1.);

draw ———,

$$\left.\begin{array}{c} \text{———} \\ \text{———} \end{array}\right\} \parallel \text{———} \quad \left.\begin{array}{c} \\ \end{array}\right\}$$

$$\left.\begin{array}{c} \text{———} \\ \text{———} \end{array}\right\} \parallel \text{———}$$ (pr. 31, B. 1.)

$$ \underline{\quad}^2 = \underline{\quad}^2 + \underline{\quad}^2 + 2 \cdot \underline{\quad} \cdot \underline{\quad} $$
(pr. 4, B. 11.)

but $\underline{\quad}^2 + \underline{\quad}^2 = 2 \cdot \underline{\quad} \cdot \underline{\quad} + \underline{\quad}^2$
(pr. 7, B. 11.)

$$ \therefore \underline{\quad}^2 = 4 \cdot \underline{\quad} \cdot \underline{\quad} + \underline{\quad}^2. $$

Q. E. D.

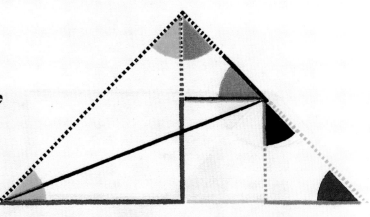

F a *ſtraight line be divided into two equal parts* ——— ———, *and alſo into two unequal parts* ——— ———, *the ſquares of the unequal parts are together double the ſquares of half the line, and of the part between the points of ſection.*

$$ \underline{\quad\quad}^2 + \underline{\quad}^2 = 2\,\underline{\quad\quad\quad}^2 + 2\,\underline{\quad}^2. $$

Make ————— ⊥ and = ————— or ———— ,

Draw ••••••••••• and •••••••••••• ,

————— ‖ ———— , —‖ ———— , and draw ——— .

 =   (pr. 5, B. 1.) = half a right angle.
(cor. pr. 32, B. 1.)

= (pr. 5, B. 1.) = half a right angle.
(cor. pr. 32, B. 1.)

∴ = a right angle.

= = = (prs. 5, 29, B. 1.).

hence ———— = ———— , •••••• = ——— = ——— (prs. 6, 34, B. 1.)

$$ \underline{\quad\quad}^2 = \begin{cases} \underline{\quad\quad}^2 + \underline{\quad\quad}^2, \text{ or } + \underline{\quad\quad}^2 \\ = \begin{cases} \text{••••••••}^2 = 2\,\underline{\quad\quad}^2 \\ \text{(pr. 47, B. 1.)} \\ \text{••••••}^2 = 2\,\underline{\quad}^2 \end{cases} \end{cases} $$

∴ ————^{2} + ———^{2} = 2 ————^{2} + 2 ——^{2}.

Q. E. D.

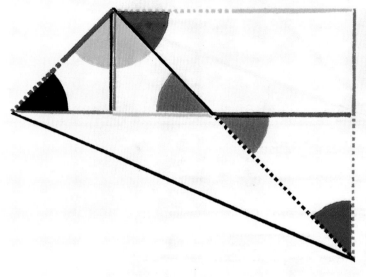

F *a ftraight line be bi-fected and pro-duced to any point* , *the fquares of the whole produced line, and of the produced part, are toge-ther double of the fquares of the half line, and of the line made up of the half and pro-duced part.*

$$ \underline{\qquad}^2 + \underline{\quad}^2 = 2\ \underline{\quad}^2 + 2\ \underline{\quad}^2. $$

Make ▬▬ ⊥ and ═ to ▬▬ or ▬▬ ,

draw ▬▬•• and ▬▬---- ,

and $\left\{ \begin{array}{c} \text{▬▬····} \ \| \ \text{▬▬} \\ \text{▬▬····} \ \| \ \text{▬▬} \end{array} \right\}$ (pr. 31, B. 1.);

draw ▬▬ alfo.

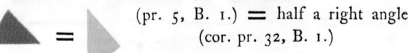 (pr. 5, B. 1.) ═ half a right angle.
(cor. pr. 32, B. 1.)

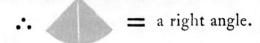 (pr. 5, B. 1.) ═ half a right angle
(cor. pr. 32, B. 1.)

∴ ═ a right angle.

▲ = ▲ = ◗ = ▼ = ◀ =

half a right angle (prs. 5, 32, 29, 34, B. 1.),

and ▬ = ▬ , ▬ = ▬ =

▬ , (prs. 6, 34, B. 1.).   Hence by (pr. 47, B. 1.)

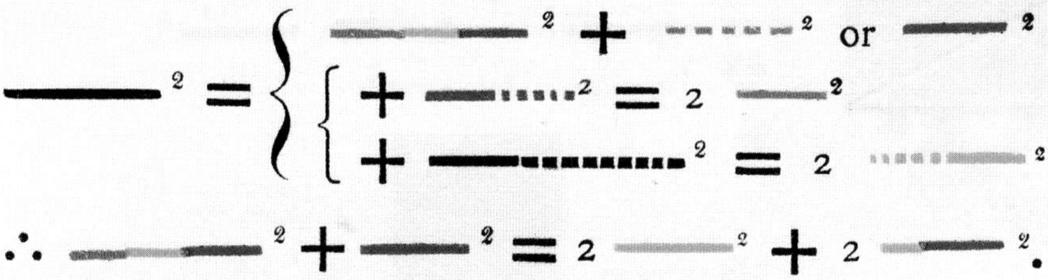

$$ \underline{\qquad}^2 = \left\{ \begin{array}{l} \underline{\qquad}^2 + \underline{\qquad}^2 \text{ or } \underline{\qquad}^2 \\ \left\{ \begin{array}{l} + \underline{\qquad}^2 = 2 \underline{\qquad}^2 \\ + \underline{\qquad}^2 = 2 \underline{\qquad}^2 \end{array} \right. \end{array} \right. $$

$$ \therefore \underline{\qquad}^2 + \underline{\qquad}^2 = 2 \underline{\qquad}^2 + 2 \underline{\qquad}^2 . $$

Q. E. D.

K

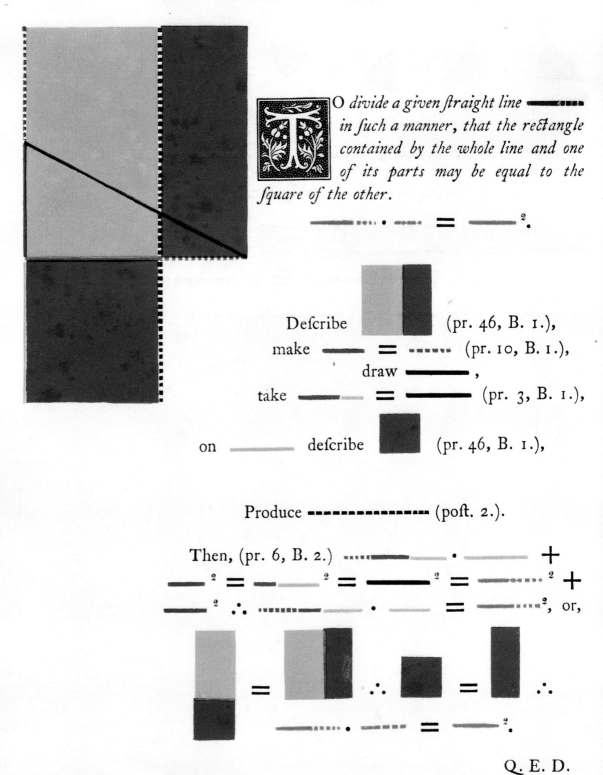

O *divide a given ſtraight line* ▬▬▬ *in ſuch a manner, that the rectangle contained by the whole line and one of its parts may be equal to the ſquare of the other.*

$$\text{▬▬} \cdot \text{▬▬} = \text{▬▬}^2.$$

Deſcribe   ▮▮   (pr. 46, B. 1.),

make   ▬▬ = ┄┄   (pr. 10, B. 1.),

draw ▬▬ ,

take ▬▬ = ▬▬   (pr. 3, B. 1.),

on ▬▬ deſcribe ▮   (pr. 46, B. 1.),

Produce ▬ ▬ ▬ ▬ (poſt. 2.).

Then, (pr. 6, B. 2.) ▬▬ · ▬▬ +

$$\text{▬▬}^2 = \text{▬▬}^2 = \text{▬▬}^2 = \text{▬▬}^2 +$$

$$\text{▬▬}^2 \therefore \text{▬▬} \cdot \text{▬▬} = \text{▬▬}^2, \text{ or,}$$

▮ = ▮▮ ∴ ▮ = ▮ ∴

$$\text{▬▬} \cdot \text{▬▬} = \text{▬▬}^2.$$

Q. E. D.

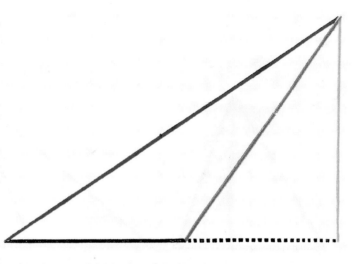

N *any obtuſe angled triangle, the ſquare of the ſide ſubtending the obtuſe angle exceeds the ſum of the ſquares of the ſides containing the obtuſe angle, by twice the rectangle contained by either of theſe ſides and the produced parts of the ſame from the obtuſe angle to the perpendicular let fall on it from the oppoſite acute angle.*

$$\text{———}^2 \; \sqsubset \; \text{———}^2 \; + \; \text{———}^2 \; \text{by}$$

$$2 \; \text{———} \cdot \text{------} .$$

By pr. 4, B. 2.

$$\text{———}^2 = \text{———}^2 + \text{--------}^2 + 2 \, \text{———} \cdot \text{-----} :$$

add ———^2 to both

$$\text{------}^2 + \text{———}^2 = \text{———}^2 \; (\text{pr. 47, B. 1.})$$

$$= 2 \cdot \text{———} \cdot \text{-------} + \text{———}^2 + \left\{ \begin{array}{c} \text{--------}^2 \\ \text{———}^2 \end{array} \right\} \text{or}$$

$$+ \text{———}^2 \; (\text{pr. 47, B. 1.}). \quad \text{Therefore,}$$

$$\text{———}^2 = 2 \cdot \text{———} \cdot \text{--------} + \text{———}^2 +$$

$$\text{———}^2 : \text{hence} \; \text{———}^2 \; \sqsubset \; \text{———}^2 + \text{———}^2$$

$$\text{by} \; 2 \cdot \text{———} \cdot \text{-------} .$$

Q. E. D.

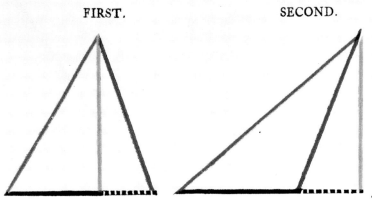

FIRST.   SECOND.

N *any tri-
angle, the
square of the
side subtend-
ing an acute angle, is
less than the sum of the
squares of the sides con-
taining that angle, by twice the rectangle contained by either
of these sides, and the part of it intercepted between the foot of
the perpendicular let fall on it from the opposite angle, and the
angular point of the acute angle.*

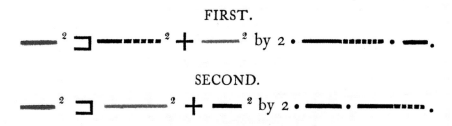

Firſt, ſuppoſe the perpendicular to fall within the

triangle, then (pr. 7, B. 2.)

add to each ⎯⎯⎯² then,

∴ (pr. 47, B. 1.)

and $\therefore$ ⸻^{2} ⊐ ⸺^{2} + ⸻^{2} by

$2 \cdot$ ⸻ $\cdot$ ⸻.

Next ſuppoſe the perpendicular to fall without the triangle, then (pr. 7, B. 2.)

⸺^{2} + ⸻^{2} = $2 \cdot$ ⸺ $\cdot$ ⸻ + ⸺^{2},

add to each ⸻^{2} then

⸺^{2} + ⸻^{2} + ⸻^{2} = $2 \cdot$ ⸺ $\cdot$ ⸻

+ ⸺^{2} + ⸻^{2} $\therefore$ (pr. 47, B. 1.),

⸻^{2} + ⸻^{2} = $2 \cdot$ ⸺ $\cdot$ ⸻ + ⸻^{2},

$\therefore$ ⸻^{2} ⊐ ⸻^{2} + ⸻^{2} by $2 \cdot$ ⸺ $\cdot$ ⸻.

Q. E. D.

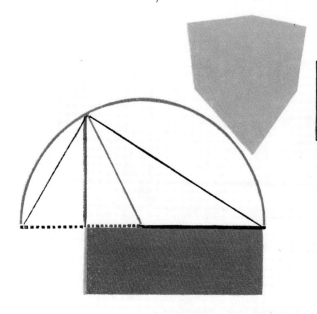

 O *draw a right line of which the square shall be equal to a given rectilinear figure.*

To draw ———— *such that,*

$$\text{————}^2 = \;$$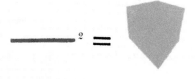

Make ▬▬▬ = ⬠   (pr. 45, B. 1.),

produce ·····——— until ▪▪▪▪▪▪ = ——— ;
take ▪▪·▪▪▪▪ = ———   (pr. 10, B. 1.),

Defcribe ⌒———— (poft. 3.),
and produce ——— to meet it : draw ————·

$$\text{———}^2 \text{ or } \text{———}^2 = \text{▪▪▪▪·····——} + \text{·····}^2$$
(pr. 5, B. 2.),

but $\text{———}^2 = \text{———}^2 + \text{·····}^2$ (pr. 47, B. 1.);

∴ $\text{———}^2 + \text{·····}^2 = \text{▪▪▪▪·····——} + \text{·····}^2$,

∴ $\text{———}^2 = \text{▪▪▪▪·····——}$, and

∴ $\text{———}^2 = $ ▬▬▬ = ⬠

Q. E. D.

BOOK III.

DEFINITIONS.

I.

EQUAL circles are thofe whofe diameters are equal.

II.

A right line is said to touch a circle when it meets the circle, and being produced does not cut it.

III.

Circles are faid to touch one another which meet but do not cut one another.

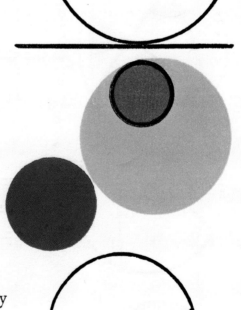

IV.

Right lines are faid to be equally diftant from the centre of a circle when the perpendiculars drawn to them from the centre are equal.

V.

And the ſtraight line on which the greater perpendicular falls is ſaid to be farther from the centre.

VI.

A ſegment of a circle is the figure contained by a ſtraight line and the part of the circumference it cuts off.

VII.

An angle in a ſegment is the angle contained by two ſtraight lines drawn from any point in the circumference of the ſegment to the extremities of the ſtraight line which is the baſe of the ſegment.

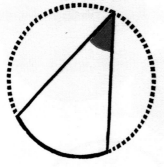

VIII.

An angle is ſaid to ſtand on the part of the circumference, or the arch, intercepted between the right lines that contain the angle.

IX.

A ſector of a circle is the figure contained by two radii and the arch between them.

X.

Similar ſegments of circles are thoſe which contain equal angles.

Circles which have the ſame centre are called *concentric circles*.

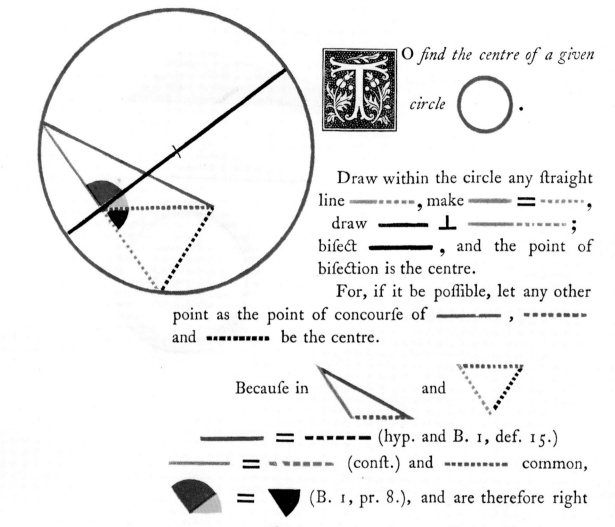

T O *find the centre of a given circle* ⬭ .

Draw within the circle any ftraight line ▬ ▪ ▪ ▪ , make ▬▬ = ▪ ▪ ▪ , draw ▬ ⊥ ▬▬▬ ; bifect ▬▬ , and the point of bifection is the centre.

For, if it be poffible, let any other point as the point of concourfe of ▬▬ , ▪ ▪ ▪ ▪ and ▪ ▪ ▪ ▪ ▪ be the centre.

Becaufe in ◺ and ◸

▬▬ = ▪ ▪ ▪ (hyp. and B. 1, def. 15.)

▬▬ = ▪ ▪ ▪ (conft.) and ▪ ▪ ▪ ▪ common,

◣ = ▼ (B. 1, pr. 8.), and are therefore right angles ; but ▼ = ◹ (conft.) ▼ = ▼ (ax.11.) which is abfurd ; therefore the affumed point is not the centre of the circle ; and in the fame manner it can be proved that no other point which is not on ▬▬ is the centre, therefore the centre is in ▬▬ , and therefore the point where ▬▬ is bifected is the centre.

Q. E. D.

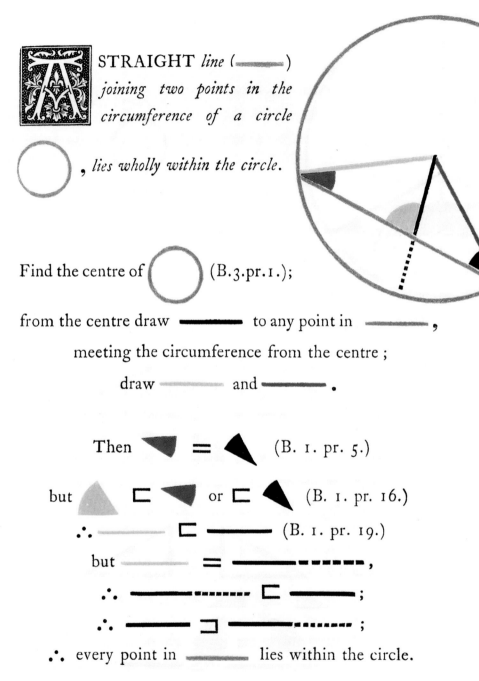

STRAIGHT *line* (———)
joining two points in the
circumference of a circle

, *lies wholly within the circle.*

Find the centre of ◯ (B.3.pr.1.);

from the centre draw ━━━━ to any point in ———— ,

meeting the circumference from the centre ;

draw ———— and ━━━━ .

Then ◤ = ◀ (B. 1. pr. 5.)

but ◭ ⊏ ◤ or ⊏ ◀ (B. 1. pr. 16.)

∴ ———— ⊏ ━━━ (B. 1. pr. 19.)

but ———— = ━━ ┅┅┅ ,

∴ ━━┅┅┅ ⊏ ━━━ ;

∴ ━━ ⊐ ━━┅┅┅ ;

∴ every point in ———— lies within the circle.

Q. E. D.

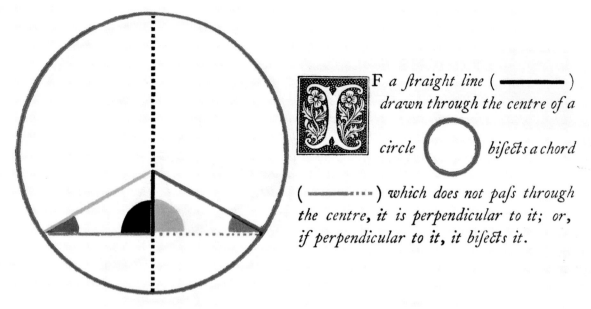

IF *a straight line* (————) *drawn through the centre of a circle* ◯ *bifects a chord* (——— ••••) *which does not pafs through the centre, it is perpendicular to it; or, if perpendicular to it, it bifects it.*

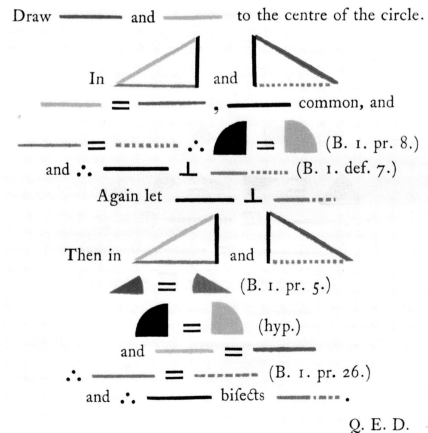

Draw ———— and ———— to the centre of the circle.

In ◿ and ◺ ———— = ———— , ———— common, and

———— = ••••••• ∴ ◼ = ◣ (B. 1. pr. 8.)

and ∴ ———— ⊥ ———— (B. 1. def. 7.)

Again let ———— ⊥ ————

Then in ◿ and ◺ ◣ = ◣ (B. 1. pr. 5.)

◼ = ◣ (hyp.)

and ———— = ———— ∴ ———— = ••••••• (B. 1. pr. 26.)

and ∴ ———— bifects ———— •••• .

Q. E. D.

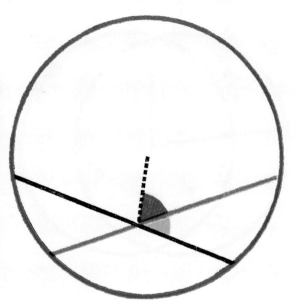

F *in a circle two straight lines cut one another, which do not both pass through the centre, they do not bisect one another.*

If one of the lines pass through the centre, it is evident that it cannot be bisected by the other, which does not pass through the centre.

But if neither of the lines ——— or ———

pass through the centre, draw ━━━━━━━

from the centre to their intersection.

If ——— be bisected, ━━━━━━ ⊥ to it (B. 3. pr. 3.)

∴ ◗ = ◗ and if ——— be

bisected, ━━━━━━ ⊥ ——— (B. 3. pr. 3.)

∴ ◗ = ◗

and ∴ ◗ = ◗ ; a part

equal to the whole, which is absurd :

∴ ——— and ———

do not bisect one another.

Q. E. D.

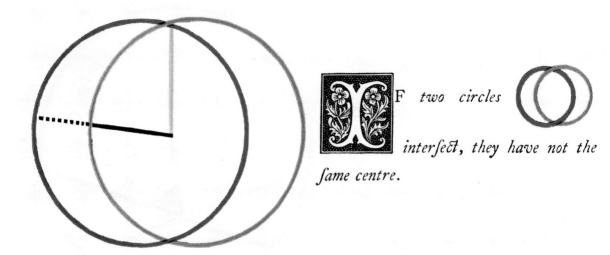

F *two circles*

interſeĉt, they have not the ſame centre.

Suppoſe it poſſible that two interſecting circles have a common centre; from ſuch ſuppoſed centre draw ——————— to the interſecting point, and ——————·········· meeting the circumferences of the circles.

Then ——————— = ——————— (B. 1. def. 15.)

and ——————— = ——————·········· (B. 1. def. 15.)

∴ ——————— = ——————······· ; a part

equal to the whole, which is abſurd:

∴ circles ſuppoſed to interſect in any point cannot

have the ſame centre.

Q. E. D.

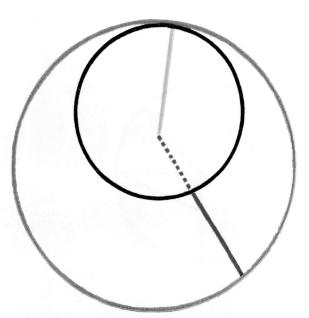

F *two circles*  *touch*

one another internally, they
have not the same centre.

For, if it be poffible, let both circles have the fame
centre; from fuch a fuppofed centre draw ▬ ▬ ▬ ▬ ▬▬▬▬▬
cutting both circles, and ▬▬▬▬▬▬ to the point of contact.

Then ▬▬▬▬▬▬ = ▬ ▬ ▬ ▬ ▬ (B. 1. def. 15.)

and ▬▬▬▬▬▬ = ▬▬▬▬▬▬ (B. 1. def. 15.)

∴ ▬ ▬ ▬ ▬ ▬ = ▬▬▬▬▬▬; a part

equal to the whole, which is abfurd;
therefore the affumed point is not the centre of both circles; and in the fame manner it can be demonftrated that
no other point is.

Q. E. D.

FIGURE I.

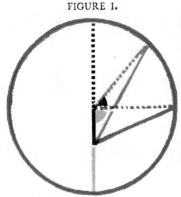

 F *from any point within a circle*

which is not the centre, lines {

are drawn to the circumference; the greateſt of thoſe lines is that (━━━━ ▪▪▪▪ *) which paſſes through the centre, and the leaſt is the remaining part (* ━━━━ *) of the diameter.*

Of the others, that (━━━━ *) which is nearer to the line paſſing through the centre, is greater than that (* ━━━━ *) which is more remote.*

FIGURE II.

Fig. 2. The two lines (━━━ ▪▪▪▪ *and* ━━━━ *) which make equal angles with that paſſing through the centre, on oppoſite ſides of it, are equal to each other; and there cannot be drawn a third line equal to them, from the ſame point to the circumference.*

FIGURE I.

To the centre of the circle draw ━ ━ ━ ━ and ▪▪▪ ▪▪▪ ▪;

then ▪▪▪▪▪▪▪▪ = ━━ ▪▪▪▪ (B. 1. def. 15.)

▪▪▪▪━━ = ━━ + ▪▪▪▪ ⊏ ━━ (B. 1. pr. 20.)

in like manner ▪▪▪▪▪━ may be ſhewn to be greater than ━━━, or any other line drawn from the ſame point to the circumference. Again, by (B. 1. pr. 20.)

━━ + ━━ ⊏ ▪▪▪▪▪ = ━━ + ━━,

take ━━ from both; ∴ ━━━ ⊏ ━━━ (ax.),

and in like manner it may be ſhewn that ━━━━ is leſs

than any other line drawn from the fame point to the cir-

cumference. Again, in 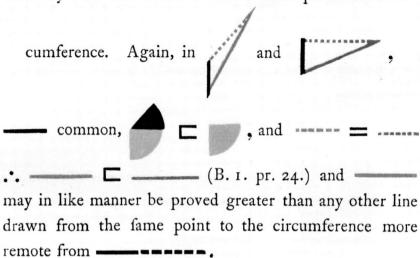 and ,

—— common, ⊏ , and ---- = ·······

∴ ——— ⊏ ——— (B. 1. pr. 24.) and ———
may in like manner be proved greater than any other line
drawn from the fame point to the circumference more
remote from ——————.

FIGURE II.

If 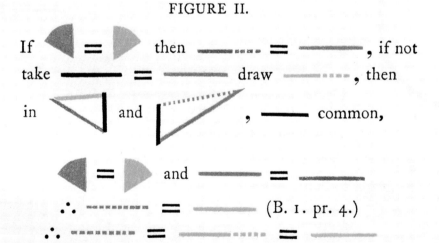 = then ——— = ———, if not

take —— = ——— draw ———, then

in and , —— common,

= and ——— = ———

∴ ——— = ——— (B. 1. pr. 4.)

∴ ——— = ——— = ———

a part equal to the whole, which is abfurd :

∴ ——— = ———; and no other line is equal to
——— drawn from the fame point to the circumference ; for if it were nearer to the one paffing through the
centre it would be greater, and if it were more remote it
would be lefs.

Q. E. D.

The original text of this propofition is here divided into three parts.

I.

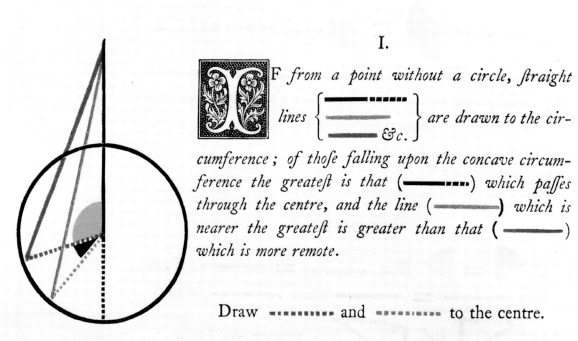

IF *from a point without a circle, ſtraight lines* { ═══ } *are drawn to the cir-cumference; of thoſe falling upon the concave circumference the greateſt is that* (══───) *which paſſes through the centre, and the line* (═════) *which is nearer the greateſt is greater than that* (─────) *which is more remote.*

Draw ·········· and ·········· to the centre.

Then, ──···· which paſſes through the centre, is greateſt; for ſince ········· = ········· , if ───── be added to both, ──···· = ───── + ··········· ; but ⊏ ───── (B. 1. pr. 20.) ∴ ──···· is greater than any other line drawn from the ſame point to the concave circumference.

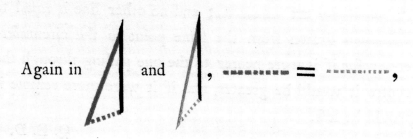

Again in ◿ and ◿ , ·········· = ·········· ,

and ————— common, but 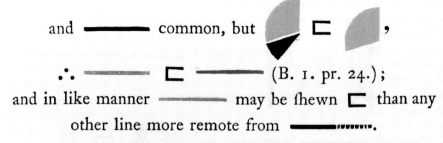 ,

∴ ————— ⊏ ————— (B. 1. pr. 24.);
and in like manner ————— may be ſhewn ⊏ than any
other line more remote from ——— ·········.

II.

*Of thoſe lines falling on the convex circumference the
leaſt is that (·········-) which being produced would
paſs through the centre, and the line which is nearer to
the leaſt is leſs than that which is more remote.*

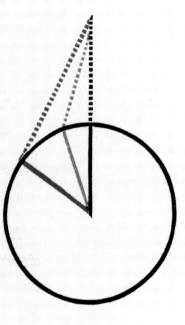

For, ſince ———— + ········ ⊏ ————— (B. 1. pr. 20.)

and ————— = ————— ,

∴ ········ ⊏ ·········· (ax. 5.)

And again, ſince ———— + ········ ⊏

————— + ········ (B. 1. pr. 21.),

and ———— = ————— ,

∴ ········ ⊐ ········ . And ſo of others.

III.

*Alſo the lines making equal angles with that which
paſſes through the centre are equal, whether falling on
the concave or convex circumference ; and no third line
can be drawn equal to them from the ſame point to the
circumference.*

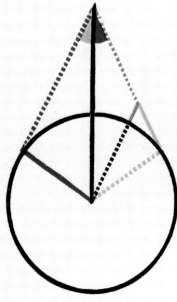

For if ········ ⊏ ········ , but making ◣ = ◢ ;

make ········ = ········ , and draw ········ .

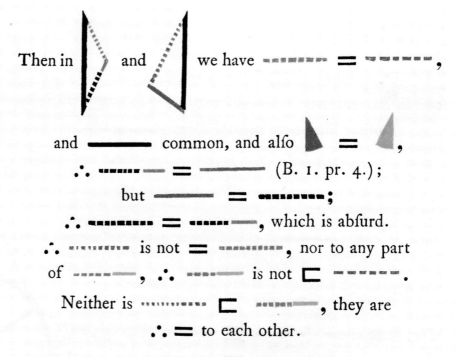

Then in ⟋ and ⟍ we have ▬▬▬ ▬ ▬▬▬,

and ▬▬▬ common, and alfo ◤ = ◣,

∴ ▬▬▬ ▬ ▬▬▬ (B. 1. pr. 4.);

but ▬▬▬ ▬ ▬▬▬;

∴ ▬▬▬ ▬ ▬▬▬, which is abfurd.

∴ ▬▬▬ is not ▬ ▬▬▬, nor to any part

of ▬▬▬, ∴ ▬▬▬ is not ⊏ ▬▬▬.

Neither is ▬▬▬ ⊏ ▬▬▬, they are

∴ ▬ to each other.

And any other line drawn from the fame point to the circumference muft lie at the fame fide with one of thefe lines, and be more or lefs remote than it from the line paff-ing through the centre, and cannot therefore be equal to it.

Q. E. D.

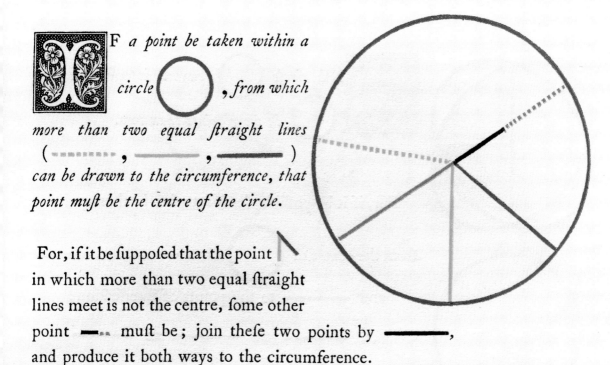

TF *a point be taken within a* *circle* ⭕ , *from which* more *than two equal ſtraight lines* (▬▬▬ , ▬▬▬ , ▬▬▬) *can be drawn to the circumference, that point muſt be the centre of the circle.*

For, if it be ſuppoſed that the point ⋀ in which more than two equal ſtraight lines meet is not the centre, ſome other point ▬ muſt be; join theſe two points by ▬▬▬, and produce it both ways to the circumference.

Then ſince more than two equal ſtraight lines are drawn from a point which is not the centre, to the circumference, two of them at leaſt muſt lie at the ſame ſide of the diameter ▬▬▬▬▬; and ſince from a point ⋀, which is not the centre, ſtraight lines are drawn to the circumference; the greateſt is ▬▬▬, which paſſes through the centre: and ▬▬▬ which is nearer to ▬▬▬, ⊏ ▬▬ which is more remote (B. 3. pr. 8.); but ▬▬▬ = ▬▬▬ (hyp.) which is abſurd.

The ſame may be demonſtrated of any other point, different from ⋀, which muſt be the centre of the circle.

Q. E. D.

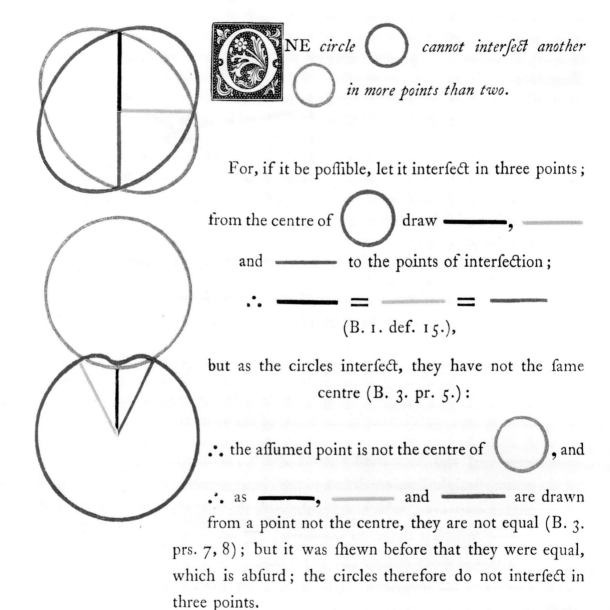

NE *circle* *cannot interfect another in more points than two.*

For, if it be poffible, let it interfect in three points;

from the centre of draw ━━━, ▬▬▬

and ━━━ to the points of interfection;

∴ ━━━ = ▬▬▬ = ━━━

(B. 1. def. 15.),

but as the circles interfect, they have not the fame centre (B. 3. pr. 5.):

∴ the affumed point is not the centre of , and

∴ as ━━━, ▬▬▬ and ━━━ are drawn from a point not the centre, they are not equal (B. 3. prs. 7, 8); but it was fhewn before that they were equal, which is abfurd; the circles therefore do not interfect in three points.

Q. E. D.

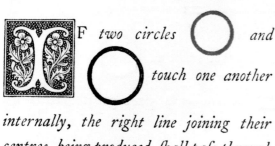F *two circles* ◯ *and* ◯ *touch one another*

internally, the right line joining their centres, being produced, shall pass through a point of contact.

For, if it be possible, let ▬▬▬ join their centres, and produce it both ways; from a point of contact draw

▬▬▬ to the centre of ◯ , and from the same point

of contact draw •••••••• to the centre of ◯.

Because in ▲ ;  (B. 1. pr. 20.),

and ▬▬ ▬▬ as they are radii of

◯ ,

but ▬ **+** ▬▬ **⊏** ▬▬▬▬▬ ; take

away ▬▬ which is common,

and ▬▬ **⊏** ▬▬▬ ;

but ▬▬ **=** ▬▬ ,

becaufe they are radii of 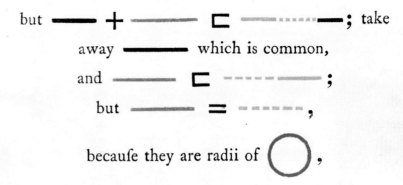 ,

and ∴ ▬▬▬ **⊏** ▬▬ a part greater than the whole, which is abfurd.

The centres are not therefore fo placed, that a line joining them can pafs through any point but a point of contact.

Q. E. D.

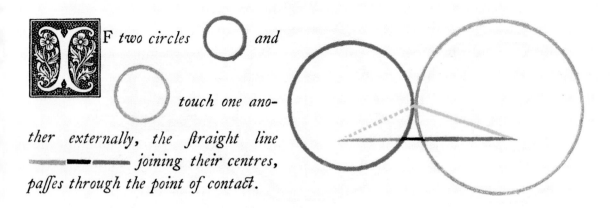

F *two circles* ⭕ *and* ⭕ *touch one ano-ther externally, the straight line* ▬▬▬ *joining their centres, passes through the point of contact.*

If it be possible, let ▬▬▬ join the centres, and not pass through a point of contact; then from a point of contact draw ▬▬▬ and ▬▬▬ to the centres.

Because ▬▬▬ + ▬▬▬ ⊏ ▬▬▬ (B. 1. pr. 20.),

and ▬▬▬ = ▬▬▬ (B. 1. def. 15.),

and ▬▬▬ = ▬▬▬ (B. 1. def. 15.),

∴ ▬▬▬ + ▬▬▬ ⊏ ▬▬▬, a part greater than the whole, which is abfurd.

The centres are not therefore fo placed, that the line joining them can pafs through any point but the point of contact.

Q. E. D.

N

FIGURE I.   FIGURE II.

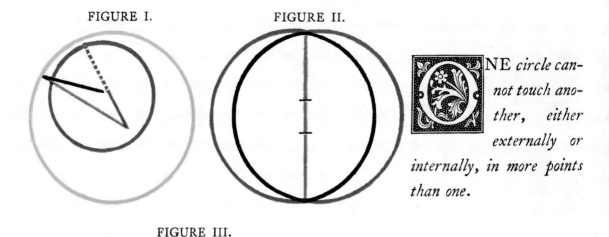

ONE *circle cannot touch another, either externally or internally, in more points than one.*

FIGURE III.

Fig. 1. For, if it be poffible, let

and ◯ touch one

another internally in two points;

draw ———— joining their cen-

tres, and produce it until it pafs

through one of the points of contact (B. 3. pr. 11.);

draw ———— and ————,

But ------ = ———— (B. 1. def. 15.),

∴ if ———— be added to both,

——— = ———— + ————;

but ———— = ———— (B. 1. def. 15.),

and ∴ ———— + ———— = ————; but

———— + ———— ⊏ ———— (B. 1. pr. 20.),

which is abfurd.

Fig. 2. But if the points of contact be the extremities of the right line joining the centres, this ftraight line muft be bifected in two different points for the two centres; becaufe it is the diameter of both circles, which is abfurd.

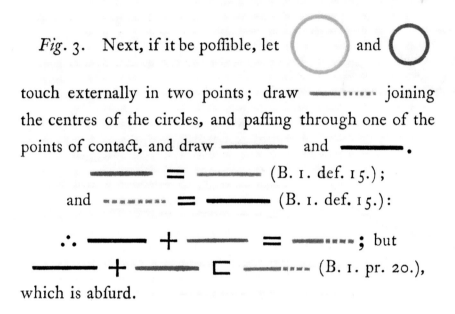

Fig. 3. Next, if it be poffible, let ◯ and ⬤

touch externally in two points; draw ▬▬▬····· joining the centres of the circles, and paffing through one of the points of contact, and draw ▬▬▬ and ▬▬▬.

▬▬▬ = ▬▬▬ (B. 1. def. 15.);

and ·····≈ = ▬▬▬ (B. 1. def. 15.):

∴ ▬▬▬ + ▬▬▬ = ▬▬▬·····; but

▬▬▬ + ▬▬▬ ⊏ ▬▬▬····· (B. 1. pr. 20.),

which is abfurd.

There is therefore no cafe in which two circles can touch one another in two points.

Q. E. D.

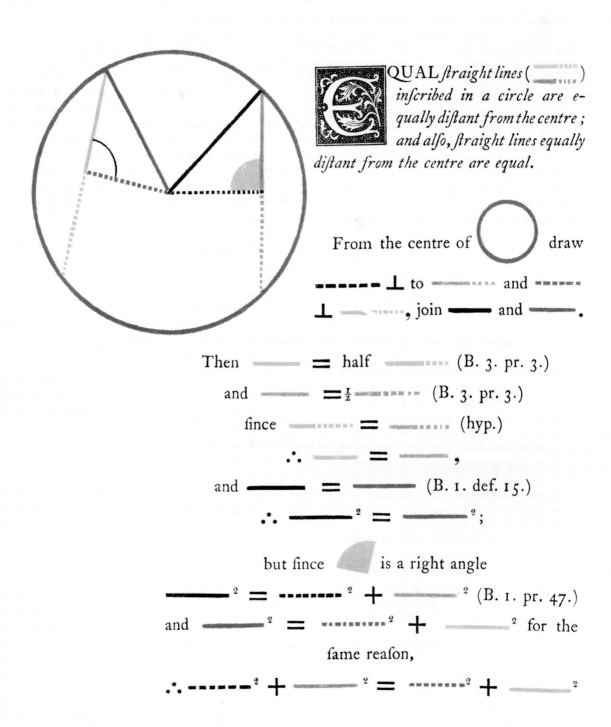

EQUAL *ſtraight lines* (▬▬▬) *inſcribed in a circle are equally diſtant from the centre; and alſo, ſtraight lines equally diſtant from the centre are equal.*

From the centre of ◯ draw

▬ ⊥ to ▬ and ▬

⊥ ▬, join ▬ and ▬.

Then ▬ = half ▬ (B. 3. pr. 3.)

and ▬ = $\frac{1}{2}$ ▬ (B. 3. pr. 3.)

ſince ▬ = ▬ (hyp.)

∴ ▬ = ▬,

and ▬ = ▬ (B. 1. def. 15.)

∴ ▬^{2} = ▬^{2};

but ſince ◢ is a right angle

▬^{2} = ▬^{2} + ▬^{2} (B. 1. pr. 47.)

and ▬^{2} = ▬^{2} + ▬^{2} for the same reaſon,

∴ ▬^{2} + ▬^{2} = ▬^{2} + ▬^{2}

∴ ⸺² = ⸺²,

∴ ⸺ = ⸺.

Alſo, if the lines ⸺ and ⸺ be equally diſtant from the centre; that is to ſay, if the perpendiculars ⸺ and ⸺ be given equal, then ⸺ = ⸺.

For, as in the preceding caſe,

⸺² + ⸺² = ⸺² + ⸺²;

but ⸺² = ⸺²:

∴ ⸺² = ⸺², and the doubles of theſe ⸺ and ⸺ are alſo equal.

Q. E. D.

FIGURE I.

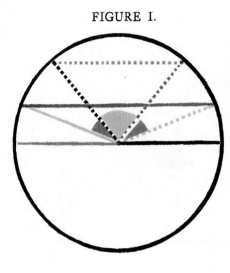

 HE *diameter is the greateſt ſtraight line in a circle : and, of all others, that which is neareſt to the centre is greater than the more remote.*

FIGURE I.

The diameter ⚊⚊ is ⊏ any line ⚊ .

For draw ⚊⚊ and ⚊⚊ .

Then ⚊⚊ = ⚊⚊

and ⚊⚊ = ⚊⚊ ,

∴ ⚊ + ⚊⚊ = ⚊ ⚊

but ⚊ + ⚊⚊ ⊏ ⚊ (B. 1. pr. 20.)

∴ ⚊ ⚊ ⊏ ⚊ .

Again, the line which is nearer the centre is greater than the one more remote.

Firſt, let the given lines be ⚊⚊ and ⚊⚊ , which are at the ſame ſide of the centre and do not interſect ;

draw $\left\{ \begin{array}{c} \end{array} \right.$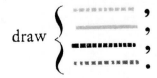

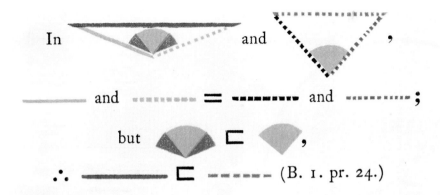

In _____ and _____ ,

and _____ and •••••••••• = ▬▬▬▬ and •••••••••• ;

but ◤◥ ⊏ ◢ ,

∴ ▬▬▬▬▬▬ ⊏ – – – – – – (B. 1. pr. 24.)

FIGURE II.

Let the given lines be ▬▬▬ and _____ which either are at different fides of the centre, or interfect ; from the centre draw •••••–•–•– and •–•–•– ⊥ _____ and _____ , make •••••••• = •–•–•– , and draw ▬▬▬ ⊥ •–•–•– .

FIGURE II.

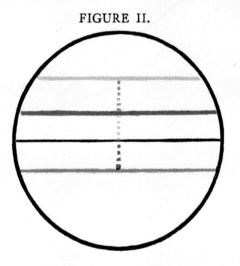

Since _____ and ▬▬▬▬ are equally diftant from the centre, ▬▬▬ = ▬▬▬ (B. 3. pr. 14.);

but ▬▬▬ ⊏ _____ (Pt. 1. B. 3. pr. 15.),

∴ ▬▬▬ ⊏ _____ .

Q. E. D.

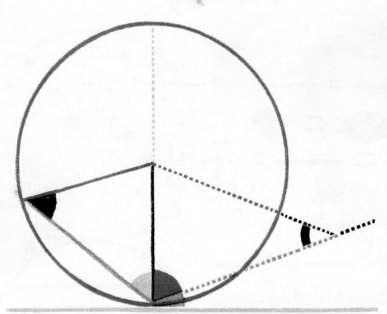

HE *ſtraight line drawn from the extremity of the diame-ter* ━━━ *of a circle perpendicular to it falls without the circle.*

And if any ſtraight line ━━━━ *be drawn from a point within that perpendi-*cular *to the point of contaƈt, it cuts the circle.*

PART I

If it be poſſible, let ━━━━, which meets the circle again, be ⊥ ━━━, and draw ━━━━.

Then, becauſe ━━━ = ━━━,

◀ = ◀ (B. 1. pr. 5.),

and ∴ each of these angles is acute. (B. 1. pr. 17.)

but ◀ = ◠ (hyp.), which is abſurd, therefore

━━━ drawn ⊥ ━━━ does not meet

the circle again.

PART II.

Let ———— be ⊥ ———— and let ━ ━ ━ be

drawn from a point ⟋ between ———— and the

circle, which, if it be poſſible, does not cut the circle.

Becauſe ◣ = ◗ ,

∴ ◣ is an acute angle ; ſuppoſe

━━━━━ ⊥ ━ ━ ━, drawn from the centre of the

circle, it muſt fall at the ſide of ◣ the acute angle.

∴ ▷ which is ſuppoſed to be a right angle, is ⊏ ◣ ,

∴ ———— ⊏ ━ ━ ━ ;

but ━ ━ = ———— ,

and ∴ ━ ━ ⊏ ━ ━ ━, a part greater than

the whole, which is abſurd. Therefore the point does

not fall outſide the circle, and therefore the ſtraight line

━ ━ cuts the circle.

Q. E. D.

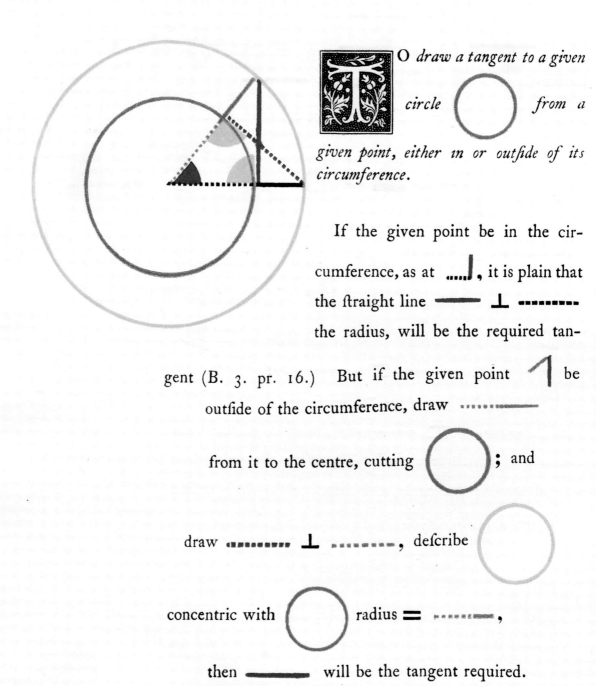

T O *draw a tangent to a given circle* ◯ *from a given point, either in or outside of its circumference.*

If the given point be in the circumference, as at .....⌐, it is plain that the ſtraight line ━━ ⊥ ┄┄┄┄ the radius, will be the required tangent (B. 3. pr. 16.) But if the given point ⌐ be outſide of the circumference, draw ┄┄┄━ from it to the centre, cutting ◯ ; and draw ┅┅ ⊥ ┄┄┄, deſcribe ◯ concentric with ◯ radius ═ ┄┄┄, then ━━ will be the tangent required.

For in 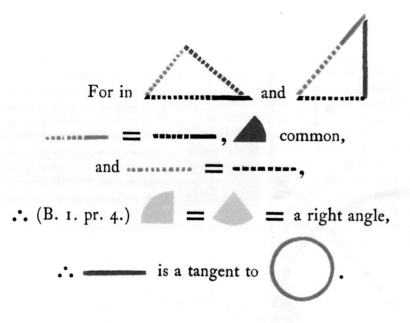 and

══ ════, ◣ common,

and ┈┈┈ ══ ┄┄┄,

∴ (B. 1. pr. 4.) ◣ ══ ◣ ══ a right angle,

∴ ━━━ is a tangent to ◯ .

Q. E. D.

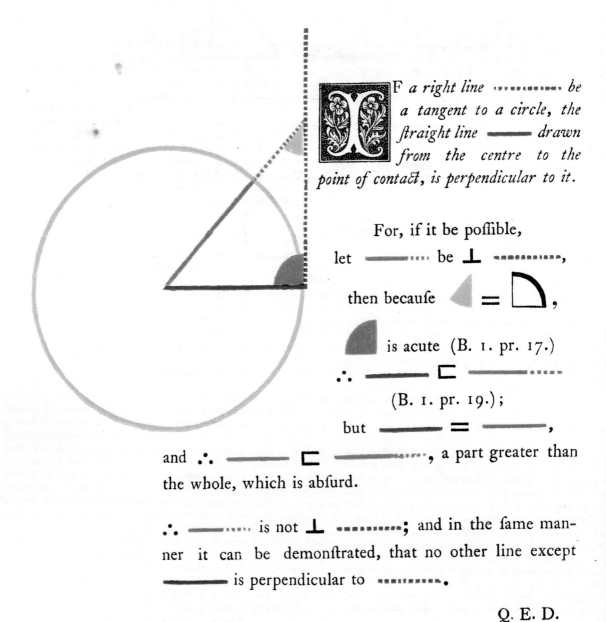

IF *a right line* .... *be a tangent to a circle, the ſtraight line* ——— *drawn from the centre to the point of contaċt, is perpendicular to it.*

For, if it be poſſible,

let ——— .... be ⊥ ....,

then becauſe ◣ = ◗ ,

◗ is acute (B. 1. pr. 17.)

∴ ——— ⊏ ——— ......

(B. 1. pr. 19.);

but ——— = ——— ,

and ∴ ——— ⊏ ———......, a part greater than the whole, which is abſurd.

∴ ——— .... is not ⊥ ....; and in the ſame manner it can be demonſtrated, that no other line except ——— is perpendicular to ....

Q. E. D.

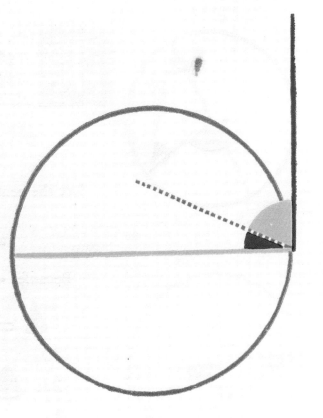

F *a straight line* —— *be a tangent to a circle, the straight line* ——, *drawn perpendicular to it* from *point of the contact, paſſes through the centre of the circle.*

For, if it be poſſible, let the centre be without ——, and draw ·········· from the ſuppoſed centre to the point of contact.

Becauſe ·········· ⊥ ——
(B. 3. pr. 18.)

∴ ◢ = ◗ , a right angle;

but ◢ = ◗ (hyp.), and ∴ ◗ = ◢ ,
a part equal to the whole, which is abſurd.

Therefore the aſſumed point is not the centre; and in the ſame manner it can be demonſtrated, that no other point without —— is the centre.

Q. E. D.

FIGURE I

 HE *angle at the centre of a circle, is double the angle at the circumference, when they have the fame part of the circumference for their bafe.*

FIGURE I.

Let the centre of the circle be on ▬▬▬ ▪▪▪▪

a fide of ◣ .

Becaufe ▬▬ = ▬▬ ,

◣ = ◤ (B. 1. pr. 5.).

But ◗ = ◣ + ◤ ,

or ◗ = twice ◣ (B. 1. pr. 32).

FIGURE II.

FIGURE II.

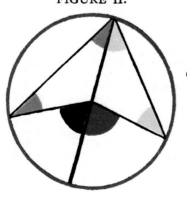

Let the centre be within ◣ , the angle at the

circumference; draw ▬▬▬ from the angular

point through the centre of the circle;

then ◀ = ▶ , and ◣ = ◤ ,

becaufe of the equality of the fides (B. 1. pr. 5).

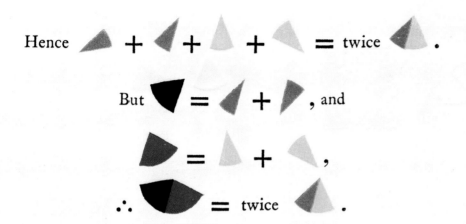

Hence 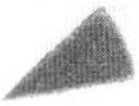 +  +  +  = twice 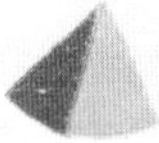.

But 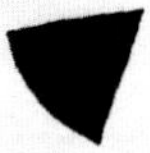 =  + , and

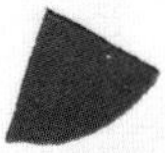 = 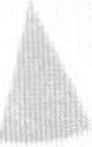 + ,

∴ 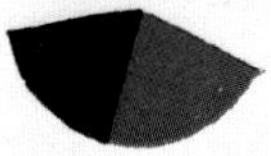 = twice 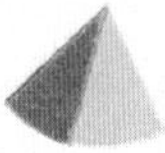.

FIGURE III.

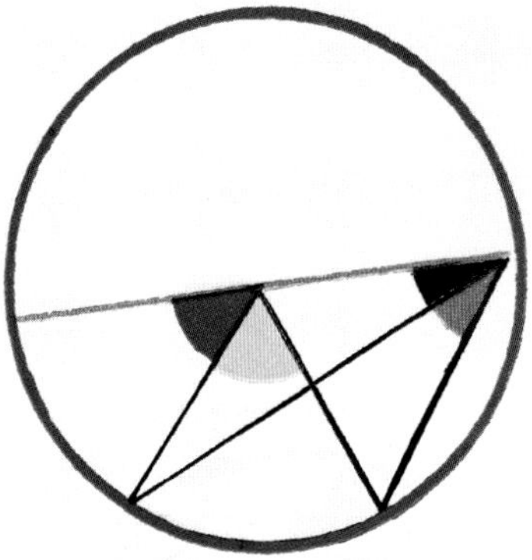

FIGURE III.

Let the centre be without  and draw , the diameter.

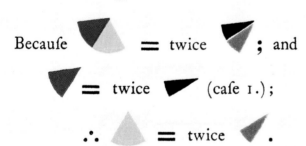

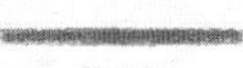

Becauſe 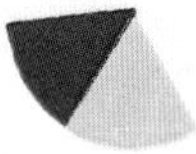 = twice 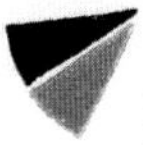; and

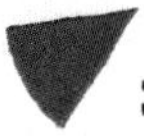 = twice  (caſe 1.);

∴  = twice 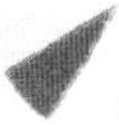.

Q. E. D.

FIGURE I.

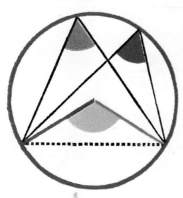

THE *angles* (,) *in the same segment of a circle are equal.*

FIGURE I.

Let the ſegment be greater than a ſemicircle, and draw ———— and ———— to the centre.

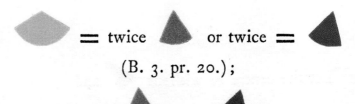

= twice or twice =

(B. 3. pr. 20.);

∴ = .

FIGURE II.

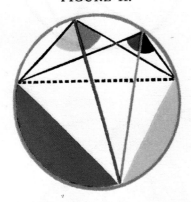

FIGURE II.

Let the ſegment be a ſemicircle, or leſs than a ſemicircle, draw ———— the diameter, alſo draw ———— .

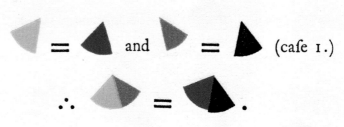

= and = (caſe 1.)

∴ = .

Q. E. D.

HE *opposite angles*

and , and

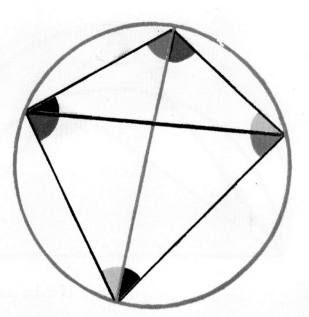

of any quadrilateral figure infcribed in a circle, are together equal to
two right angles.

Draw ———— and ————

the diagonals; and becaufe angles in

the fame fegment are equal 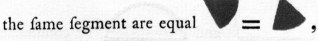 ,

and 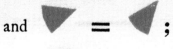 ;

add to both.

∴  =

two right angles (B. 1. pr. 32.). In like manner it may
be fhown that,

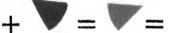 .

Q. E. D.

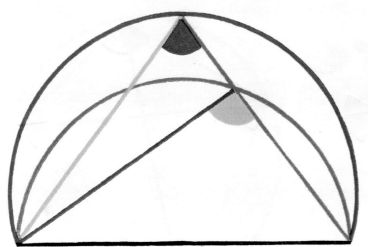

PON *the same*
straight line,
and upon the
same side of it,
two similar segments of cir-
cles cannot be constructed
which do not coincide.

For if it be possible, let two similar segments

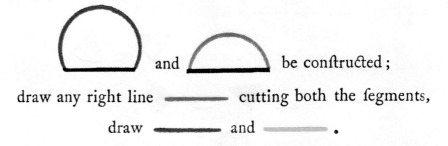

and   be constructed;

draw any right line ——————— cutting both the segments,

draw ——————— and ———————— .

Because the segments are similar,

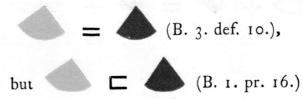

= ▲   (B. 3. def. 10.),

but   ⊏ ▲   (B. 1. pr. 16.)

which is absurd : therefore no point in either of

the segments falls without the other, and

therefore the segments coincide.

Q. E. D.

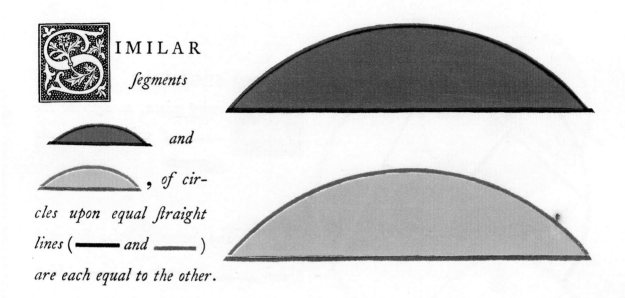

SIMILAR *ſegments* *and* , *of cir-*
cles upon equal ſtraight
lines (——— *and* ———)
are each equal to the other.

For, if be ſo applied to ,
that ——— may fall on ———, the extremities of
——— may be on the extremities ——— and
 at the ſame ſide as ;

becauſe ——— = ———,
——— muſt wholly coincide with ——— ;
and the ſimilar ſegments being then upon the ſame
ſtraight line and at the ſame ſide of it, muſt
alſo coincide (B. 3. pr. 23.), and
are therefore equal.

Q. E. D.

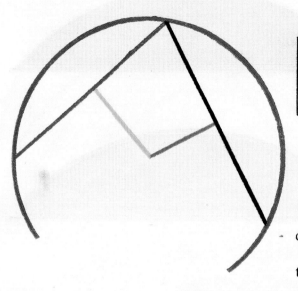

 SEGMENT *of a circle being given, to deſcribe the circle of which it is the ſegment.*

From any point in the ſegment draw ———— and ———— biſect them, and from the points of biſection

draw ———— ⊥ ————

and ———— ⊥ ————

where they meet is the centre of the circle.

Becauſe ———— terminated in the circle is biſected perpendicularly by ————, it paſſes through the centre (B. 3. pr. 1.), likewiſe ———— paſſes through the centre, therefore the centre is in the interſection of theſe perpendiculars.

Q. E. D.

N *equal circles* 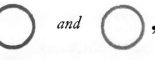 *and* , *the arcs* , *on which* *ftand equal angles, whether at the centre or circum- ference, are equal.*

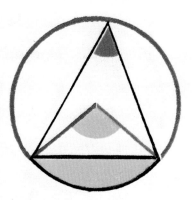

First, let 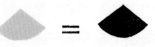 = at the centre,

draw —— and ------- .

Then fince ○ = ○ ,

△ and △ have

—— = —— = ------ = ------ ,

and = ,

∴ —— = ------- (B. 1. pr. 4.).

But ▲ = ▲ (B. 3. pr. 20.);

∴ ◠ and ◠ are fimilar (B. 3. def. 10.);

they are alfo equal (B. 3. pr. 24.)

If therefore the equal fegments be taken from the equal circles, the remaining fegments will be equal;

hence ⬤ = ⬤ (ax. 3.);

and ∴ ⌣ = ⌣.

But if the given equal angles be at the circumference, it is evident that the angles at the centre, being double of thofe at the circumference, are alfo equal, and therefore the arcs on which they ftand are equal.

Q. E. D.

N *equal circles,* 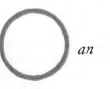 *an*

the angles *and* (dark triangle) *which* ſ*tand upon equal*

arches are equal, whether they be at the centres or at

the circumferences.

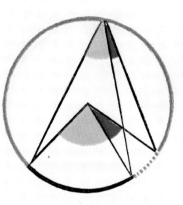

For if it be poſſible, let one of them

(dark triangle) be greater than the other (light triangle)

and make

(light triangle) = (dark triangle)

∴ ⌣ = ⌣ (B. 3. pr. 26.)

but ⌣ = ⌣ (hyp.)

∴ ⌣ = ⌣ a part equal

to the whole, which is abſurd; ∴ neither angle

is greater than the other, and

∴ they are equal.

Q. E. D.

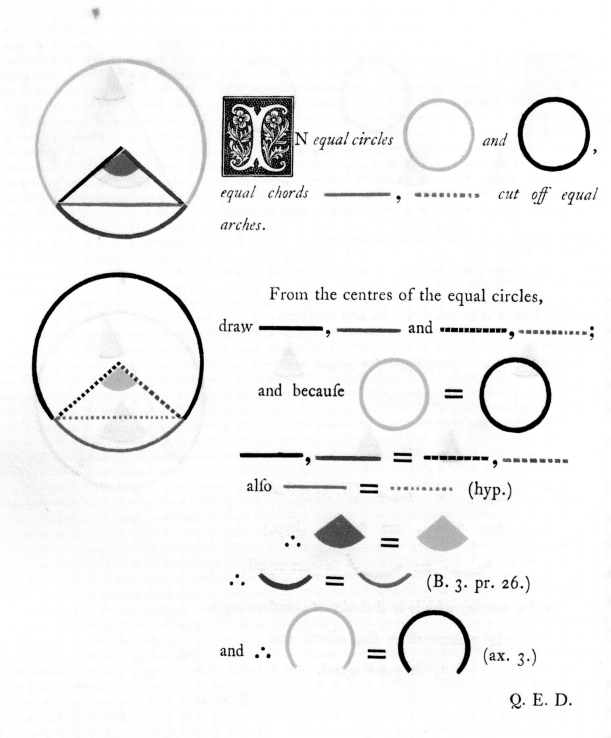

IN *equal circles* 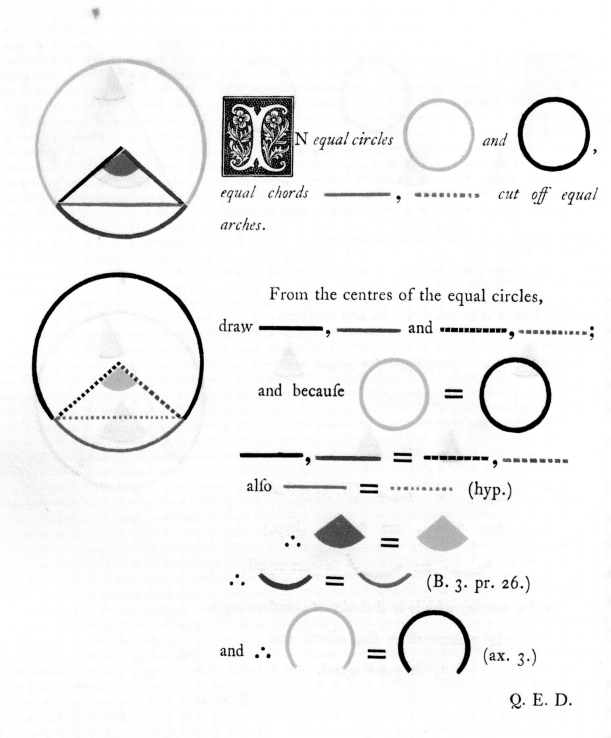 *and* , *equal chords* ——————, ·········· *cut off equal arches.*

From the centres of the equal circles, draw ——————, —————— and ▬▬▬▬, ··········;

and becauſe =

——————, —————— = ▬▬▬▬, ··········

alſo —————— = ·········· (hyp.)

∴ =

∴ ‿ = ‿ (B. 3. pr. 26.)

and ∴ = (ax. 3.)

Q. E. D.

N *equal circles* 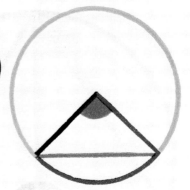 *and*

the chords ———— *and* ·········· *which fub-*

tend equal arcs are equal.

If the equal arcs be femicircles the propofition is

evident. But if not,

let ————, ————, and ▪▪▪▪▪▪▪▪▪, ««««««««

be drawn to the centres ;

becaufe ⌣ = ⌣ (hyp.)

and ◢ = ◣ (B. 3. pr. 27.);

but ———— and ———— = ▪▪▪▪▪▪▪▪▪ and ««««««««

∴ ———— = ·········· (B. 1. pr. 4.);

but thefe are the chords fubtending

the equal arcs.

Q. E. D.

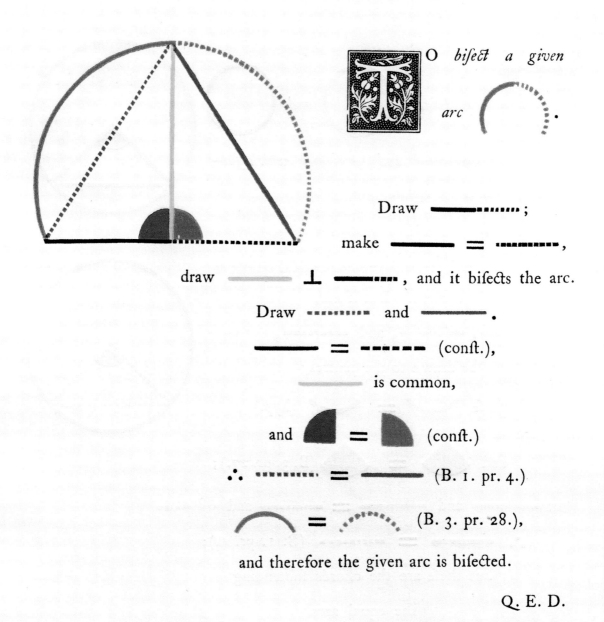

O *bifect a given arc* .

Draw ▬▬▬▬·········· ;

make ▬▬▬▬ = ·············· ,

draw ▬▬▬▬ ⊥ ▬▬▬ , and it bifects the arc.

Draw ·········· and ▬▬▬▬ .

▬▬▬▬ = ▬ ▬ ▬ ▬ (conft.),

▬▬▬▬ is common,

and ◖ = ◗ (conft.)

∴ ·········· = ▬▬▬▬ (B. 1. pr. 4.)

◠ = ⌒ (B. 3. pr. 28.),

and therefore the given arc is bifected.

Q. E. D.

N a circle the angle in a *femicircle is a right angle, the angle in a fegment greater than a femicircle is acute, and the angle in a fegment lefs than a femicircle is obtufe.*

FIGURE I.

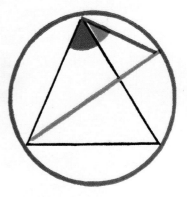

FIGURE I.

The angle in a femicircle is a right angle.

Draw ▬▬▬ and ▬▬▬

△ = △ and △ = ▶ (B. 1. pr. 5.)

△ + △ = ◢ = the half of two

right angles ═ a right angle. (B. 1. pr. 32.)

FIGURE II.

The angle ◭ in a segment greater than a femi-circle is acute.

Draw ▬▬▬ the diameter, and ·▬▬▬

∴ ◢ ═ a right angle

∴ ◭ is acute.

FIGURE II.

FIGURE III.

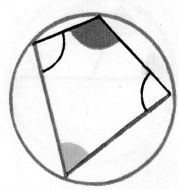

FIGURE III.

The angle 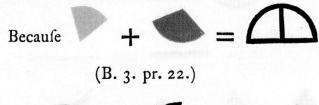 in a segment less than semi-circle is obtuse.

Take in the opposite circumference any point, to which draw ———— and ————.

Because

(B. 3. pr. 22.)

but  (part 2.),

∴ is obtuse.

Q. E. D.

F *a right line* —— *be a tangent to a circle, and from the point of contact a right line* ——

be drawn cutting the circle, the angle

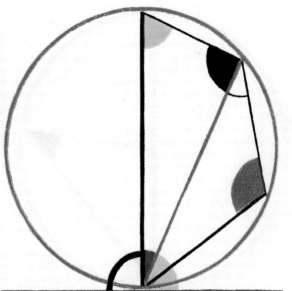

made by this line with the tangent

is equal to the angle ▷ *in the alter- ate fegment of the circle.*

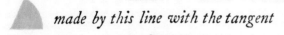

If the chord fhould pafs through the centre, it is evi- dent the angles are equal, for each of them is a right angle. (B. 3. prs. 16, 31.)

But if not, draw —— ⊥ —— from the point of contact, it muft pafs through the centre of the circle, (B. 3. pr. 19.)

∴ ◣ = ◿ (B. 3. pr. 31.)

▷ + ◢ = ◿ = ◤ (B. 1. pr. 32.)

∴ ◿ = ◿ (ax.).

Again ◖ = ⬒ = ▷ + ◆ (B. 3. pr. 22.)

∴ ◿ = ◆ , (ax.), which is the angle in the alternate fegment.

Q. E. D.

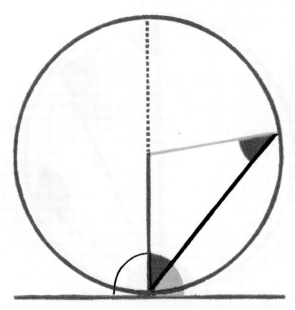

 N *a given straight line* ———— *to describe a segment of a circle that shall contain an angle equal to a given angle*

If the given angle be a right angle, bifect the given line, and defcribe a femicircle on it, this will evidently contain a right angle. (B. 3. pr. 31.)

If the given angle be acute or obtufe, make with the given line, at its extremity,

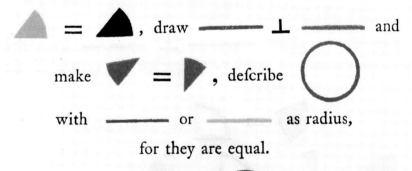

with ———— or ———— as radius, for they are equal.

———— is a tangent to 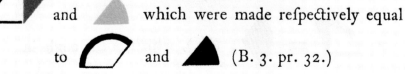 (B. 3. pr. 16.)

∴ ———— divides the circle into two fegments capable of containing angles equal to

and   which were made refpectively equal

to   and   (B. 3. pr. 32.)

Q. E. D.

O *cut off from a given cir-*

cle a *segment*

which fhall contain an angle equal to a

given angle .

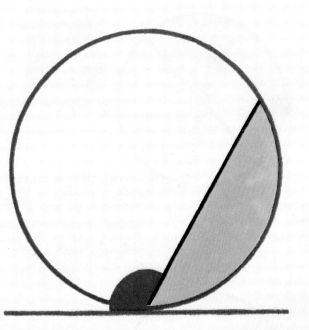

Draw ———— (B. 3. pr. 17.),

a tangent to the circle at any point ;

at the point of contact make

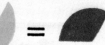 = the given angle ;

and contains an angle = the given angle.

Becaufe ———— is a tangent,

and ———— cuts it, the

angle in = (B. 3. pr. 32.),

but = (conft.)

Q. E. D.

FIGURE I.

 F *two chords* { } *in a circle intersect each other, the rectangle contained by the segments of the one is equal to the rectangle contained by the segments of the other.*

FIGURE I.

If the given right lines pass through the centre, they are bisected in the point of intersection, hence the rectangles under their segments are the squares of their halves, and are therefore equal.

FIGURE II.

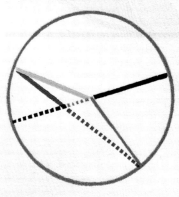

FIGURE II.

Let ▬▬▬ pass through the centre, and ▬▬▬ not; draw ▬▬▬ and ▬▬▬.

Then ▬▬ × ▬▬ = ▬▬² − ▬▬² (B. 2. pr. 6.),

or ▬▬ × ▬▬ = ▬▬² − ▬▬²,

∴ ▬▬ × ▬▬ = ▬▬ × ▬▬ (B. 2. pr. 5.).

FIGURE III.

FIGURE III.

Let neither of the given lines pass through the centre, draw through their intersection a diameter ▬▬▬,

and ▬▬ × ▬▬ = ▬▬ × ▬▬ (Part. 2.),

also ▬▬ × ▬▬ = ▬▬ × ▬▬ (Part. 2.);

∴ ▬▬ × ▬▬ = ▬▬ × ▬▬.

Q. E. D.

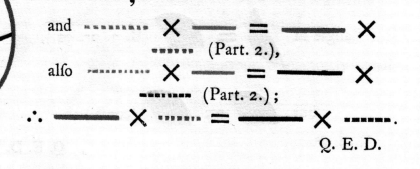

IF *from a point without a circle two straight lines be drawn to it, one of which* ────── *is a tangent to the circle, and the other* ─── *cuts it ; the rectangle under the whole cutting line* ─── *and the external segment* ─── *is equal to the square of the tangent* ─── .

FIGURE I.

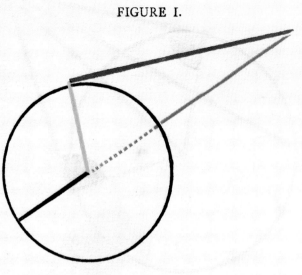

FIGURE I.

Let ─── pass through the centre;

draw ─── from the centre to the point of contact;

─── ^{2} = ───^{2} minus ───^{2} (B. 1. pr. 47),

or ───^{2} = ───^{2} minus ───^{2},

∴ ───^{2} = ─── × ─── (B. 2. pr. 6).

FIGURE II.

FIGURE II.

If ─── do not pass through the centre, draw ─── and ───.

Then ─── × ─── = ───^{2} minus ───^{2} (B. 2. pr. 6), that is,

─── × ─── = ───^{2} minus ───^{2},

∴ ─── × ─── = ───^{2} (B. 3. pr. 18).

Q. E. D.

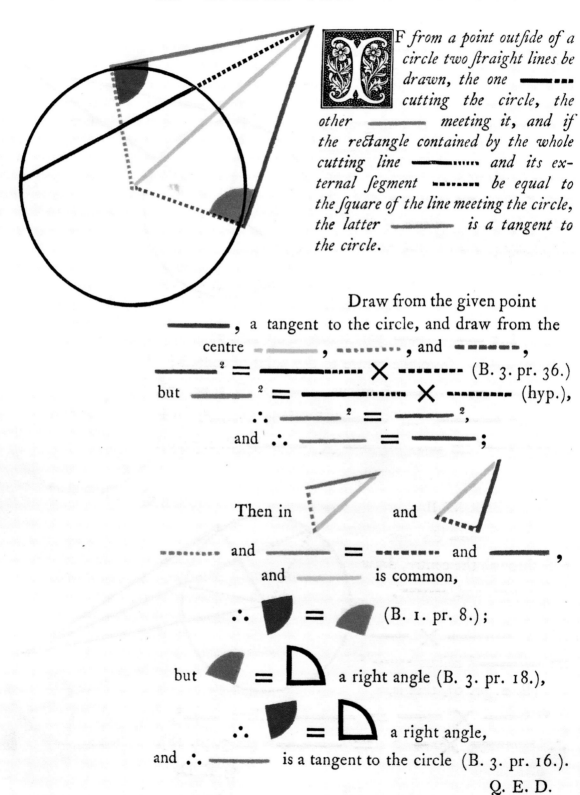

IF *from a point outſide of a circle two ſtraight lines be drawn, the one* ━━ ▬▬ *cutting the circle, the other* ━━━ *meeting it, and if the rectangle contained by the whole cutting line* ━━ ······ *and its external ſegment* ▬▬▬▬ *be equal to the ſquare of the line meeting the circle, the latter* ━━━ *is a tangent to the circle.*

Draw from the given point ━━━━, a tangent to the circle, and draw from the centre ━━━ , ·········· , and ▬▬▬▬ ,

━━━━² = ━━ ······ ✕ ▬▬▬▬ (B. 3. pr. 36.)

but ━━━² = ▬▬ ···· ✕ ▬▬▬▬ (hyp.),

∴ ━━━² = ━━━²,

and ∴ ━━━ = ━━━ ;

Then in ◿ and ◺

·········· and ━━━ = ▬▬▬▬ and ━━━ ,

and ━━━ is common,

∴ ◗ = ◖ (B. 1. pr. 8.);

but ◗ = ◖ a right angle (B. 3. pr. 18.),

∴ ◗ = ◖ a right angle,

and ∴ ━━━ is a tangent to the circle (B. 3. pr. 16.).

Q. E. D.

BOOK IV.

DEFINITIONS.

I.

 RECTILINEAR figure is said to be *inscribed in* another, when all the angular points of the inscribed figure are on the sides of the figure in which it is said to be inscribed.

II.

A FIGURE is said to be *described about* another figure, when all the sides of the circumscribed figure pass through the angular points of the other figure.

III.

A RECTILINEAR figure is said to be *inscribed in* a circle, when the vertex of each angle of the figure is in the circumference of the circle.

IV.

A RECTILINEAR figure is said to be *circumscribed about* a circle, when each of its sides is a tangent to the circle.

V.

A CIRCLE is faid to be *infcribed in* a rectilinear figure, when each fide of the figure is a tangent to the circle.

VI.

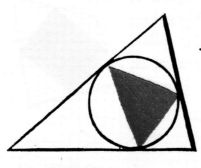

A CIRCLE is faid to be *circum-fcribed about* a rectilinear figure, when the circumference paffes through the vertex of each angle of the figure.

 is circumfcribed.

VII.

A STRAIGHT line is faid to be *infcribed in* a circle, when its extremities are in the circumference.

The Fourth Book of the Elements is devoted to the folution of problems, chiefly relating to the infcription and circumfcrip-tion of regular polygons and circles.

A regular polygon is one whofe angles and fides are equal.

I N *a given circle*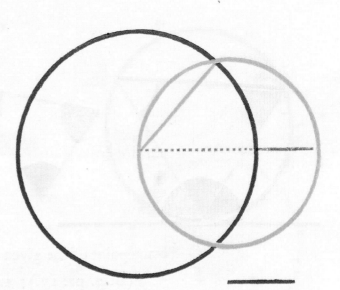

to place a straight line,

equal to a given straight line (———),

not greater than the diameter of the

circle.

Draw ·······——, the diameter of ◯ ;

and if ·······—— ＝ ————— , then

the problem is solved.

But if ·······—— be not equal to ————— ,

·······—— ⊏ ———— (hyp.);

make ·······—— ＝ ———— (B. 1. pr. 3.) with

— — — — — as radius,

defcribe ◯ , cutting ◯ , and

draw ———— , which is the line required.

For ———— ＝ ·········· ＝ ————

(B. 1. def. 15. conft.)

Q. E. D.

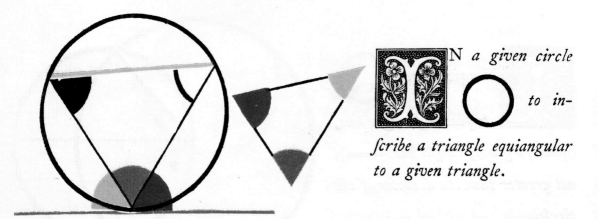

N *a given circle* *to in-* ſcribe a triangle equiangular to a given triangle.

To any point of the given circle draw ———, a tangent (B. 3. pr. 17.); and at the point of contact

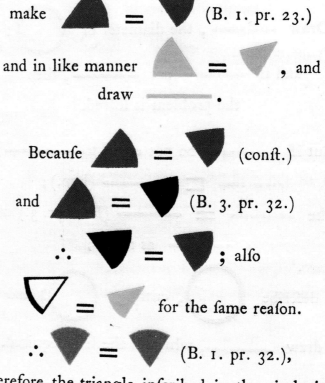

make ◢ = ◣ (B. 1. pr. 23.)

and in like manner ◢ = ◣ , and draw ——— .

Becauſe ◢ = ◣ (conſt.)

and ◢ = ◣ (B. 3. pr. 32.)

∴ ◣ = ◣ ; alſo

▽ = ◣ for the ſame reaſon.

∴ ◣ = ◣ (B. 1. pr. 32.),

and therefore the triangle inſcribed in the circle is equi-angular to the given one.

Q. E. D.

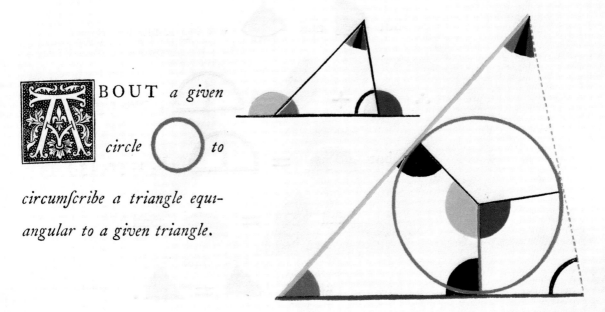

A BOUT *a given circle* ⃝ *to circumſcribe a triangle equi-angular to a given triangle.*

Produce any ſide ⸻, of the given triangle both ways; from the centre of the given circle draw ⸺, any radius.

Make 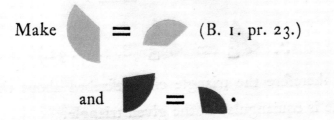 (B. 1. pr. 23.)

and 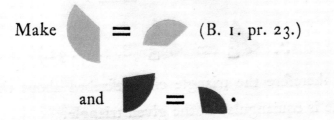 .

At the extremities of the three radii, draw ⸺, ⸺ and ┅┅┅, tangents to the given circle. (B. 3. pr. 17.)

The four angles of 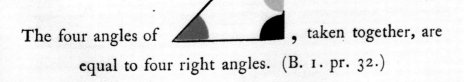 , taken together, are equal to four right angles. (B. 1. pr. 32.)

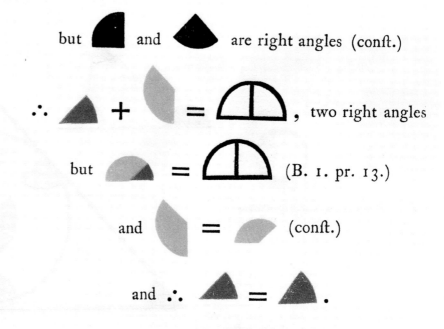

but  and  are right angles (conſt.)

∴  +  = , two right angles

but  =  (B. 1. pr. 13.)

and  =  (conſt.)

and ∴  = .

In the ſame manner it can be demonſtrated that

 = ;

∴  =  (B, 1. pr. 32.)

and therefore the triangle circumſcribed about the given circle is equiangular to the given triangle.

Q. E. D.

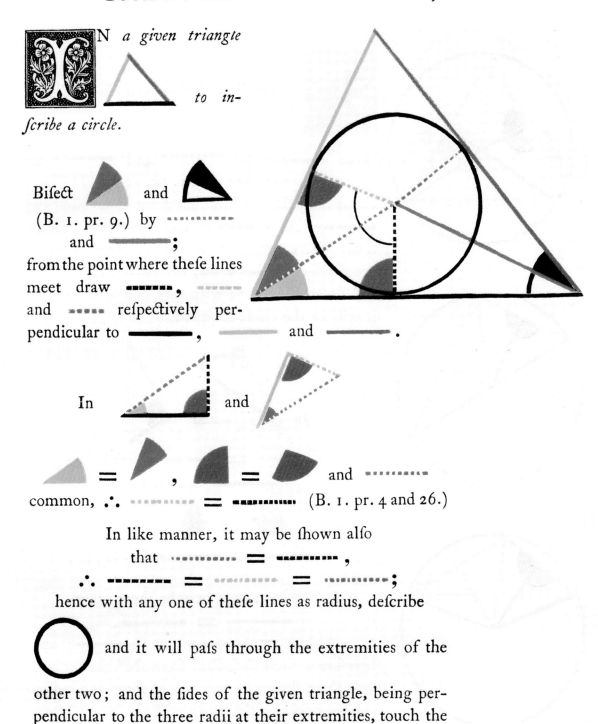

N *a given triangle* *to in-*
ſcribe a circle.

Biſect 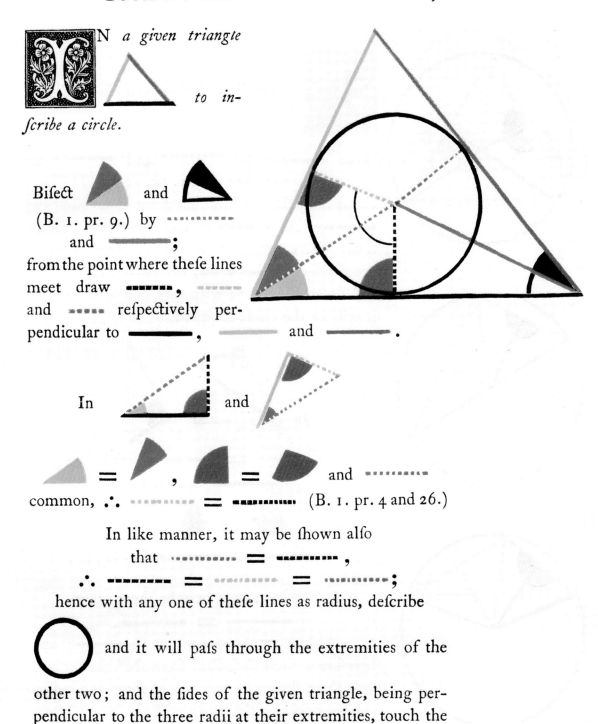 and
(B. 1. pr. 9.) by ···········
and ——————;
from the point where theſe lines
meet draw ■■■■■■, ━ ━ ━ ━,
and ▪▪▪▪▪ reſpectively perpendicular to ——————,
——————— and ——————.

In and

 = , = and ···········
common, ∴ ▪▪▪▪▪▪▪▪▪ = ■■■■■■■ (B. 1. pr. 4 and 26.)

In like manner, it may be ſhown alſo
that ··········· ═ ■■■■■■■,
∴ ━ ━ ━ ━ ━ ═ ▪▪▪▪▪▪▪▪ ═ ···········;
hence with any one of theſe lines as radius, deſcribe

and it will paſs through the extremities of the
other two; and the ſides of the given triangle, being perpendicular to the three radii at their extremities, touch the
circle (B. 3. pr. 16.), which is therefore inſcribed in the
given circle.

s   Q. E. D.

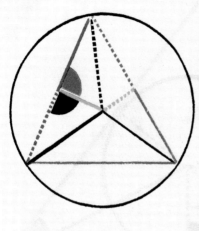

 O *defcribe a circle about a given triangle.*

Make ——— = ·········· and ——— = ········· (B. 1. pr. 10.)

From the points of bifection draw ——— and ········· ⊥ ——— and ——— refpec- tively (B. 1. pr. 11.), and from their point of concourfe draw ———, ············ and ——— and defcribe a circle with any one of them, and it will be the circle required.

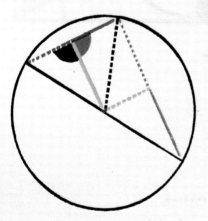

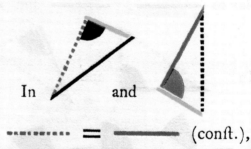

In and

········· = ——— (conft.),

common,

◗ = ◗ (conft.),

∴ ——— = ············ (B. 1. pr. 4.).

In like manner it may be fhown that

——— = ············.

∴ ············ = ——— = ———; and

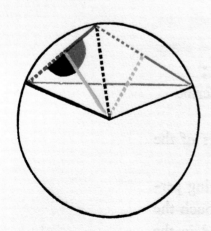

therefore a circle defcribed from the concourfe of thefe three lines with any one of them as a radius will circumfcribe the given triangle.

Q. E. D.

N *a given circle* 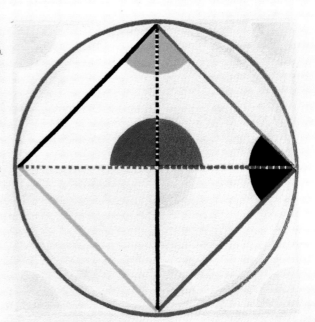 *to*

inſcribe a ſquare.

Draw the two diameters of the circle ⊥ to each other, and draw ——— , ——— , ——— and ———

 is a ſquare.

For, ſince and are, each of them, in

a ſemicircle, they are right angles (B. 3. pr. 31),

∴ ——— ‖ ——— (B. 1. pr. 28):

and in like manner ——— ‖ ——— .

And becauſe ◗ = ◖ (conſt.), and

·········· = ▬▬▬ = ·········· (B. 1. def. 15).

∴ ——— = ——— (B. 1. pr. 4);

and ſince the adjacent ſides and angles of the parallelo-

gram are equal, they are all equal (B. 1. pr. 34);

and ∴ , inſcribed in the given circle, is a

ſquare. Q. E. D.

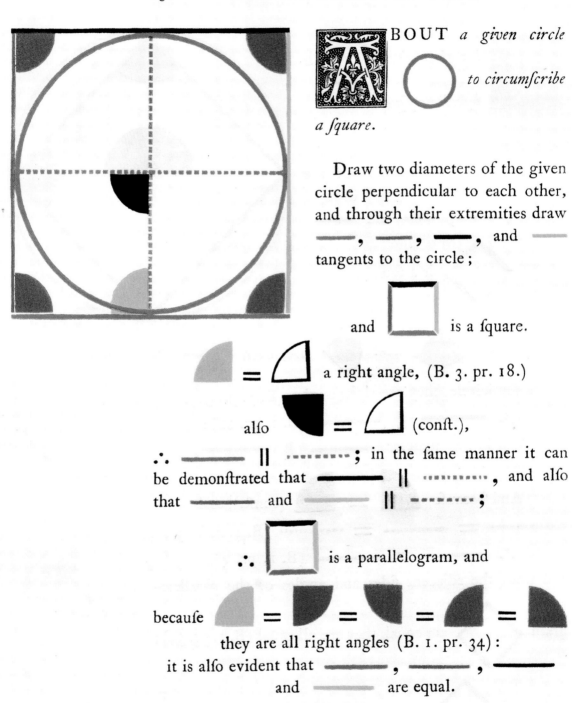

BOUT *a given circle* *to circumſcribe* *a ſquare.*

Draw two diameters of the given circle perpendicular to each other, and through their extremities draw ▬▬ , ▬▬ , ▬▬ , and ▬▬ tangents to the circle;

and ▢ is a ſquare.

◢ = ◿ a right angle, (B. 3. pr. 18.)

alſo ◣ = ◿ (conſt.),

∴ ▬▬ ‖ ┈┈┈ ; in the ſame manner it can be demonſtrated that ▬▬ ‖ ┈┈┈ , and alſo that ▬▬ and ▬▬ ‖ ┈┈┈ ;

∴ ▢ is a parallelogram, and

becauſe ◺ = ◢ = ◣ = ◥ = ◤

they are all right angles (B. 1. pr. 34):

it is alſo evident that ▬▬ , ▬▬ , ▬▬ and ▬▬ are equal.

∴ ▢ is a ſquare.

Q. E. D.

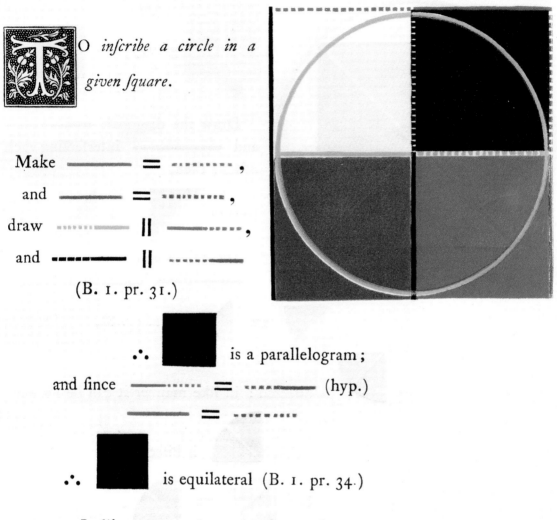

T O *infcribe a circle in a given fquare.*

Make ——— = ·········· ,

and ——— = ·•·•·•·•·•· ,

draw ·········· ‖ ——·—·—· ,

and ——·——·—— ‖ ·—·—·—·—· ,

(B. 1. pr. 31.)

∴ ■ is a parallelogram ;

and fince ———······· = ·—·—·—·— (hyp.)

—————— = ·—·—·—·—

∴ ■ is equilateral (B. 1. pr. 34.)

In like manner, it can be fhown that

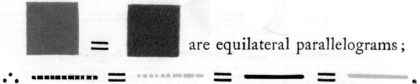 are equilateral parallelograms ;

∴ ——·——·— = ·—·—·—·— = ——————— = ———————— ,

and therefore if a circle be defcribed from the concourfe of thefe lines with any one of them as radius, it will be infcribed in the given fquare. (B. 3. pr. 16.)

Q. E. D.

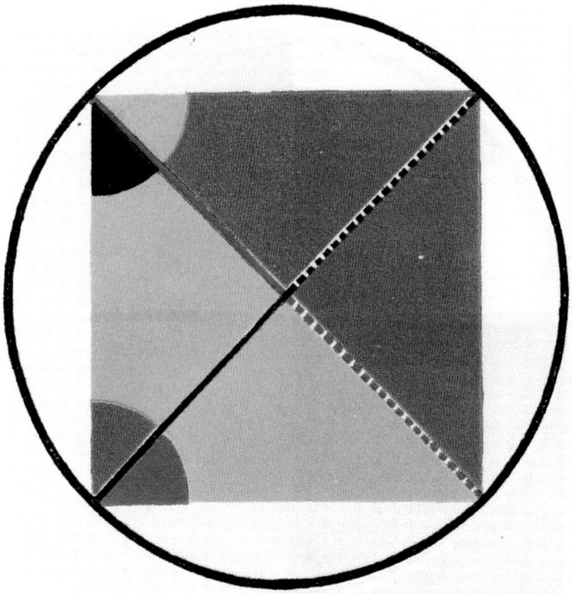

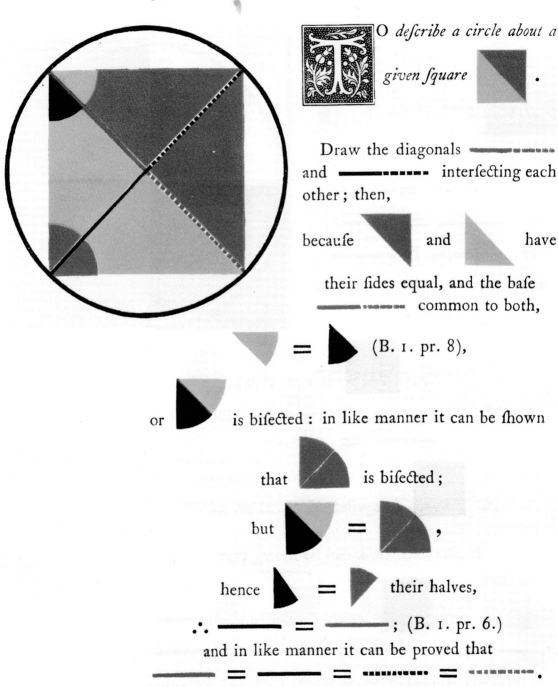

T*O describe a circle about a given ſquare*  .

Draw the diagonals —— and —— interſecting each other; then,

becauſe  and  have their ſides equal, and the baſe —— common to both,

 =  (B. 1. pr. 8),

or  is biſected: in like manner it can be ſhown

that  is biſected;

but  =  ,

hence  =  their halves,

∴ —— = ——; (B. 1. pr. 6.)

and in like manner it can be proved that

—— = —— = —— = ——.

If from the confluence of theſe lines with any one of them as radius, a circle be deſcribed, it will circumſcribe the given ſquare.

Q. E. D.

O *conftruct an ifofceles triangle, in which each of the angles at the bafe fhail be double of the vertical angle.*

Take any ftraight line ━━━━ •••••• and divide it fo that

━━━ •••• ✕ ••••• ═ ━━━━ ²

(B. 2. pr. 11.)

With ━━━━ ••••• as radius, defcribe ◯ and place

in it from the extremity of the radius, ━━ ═ ━━ ,

(B. 4. pr. 1); draw ━━━ .

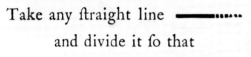 Then ◿ is the required triangle.

For, draw ━━━ and defcribe

◯ about ◺ (B. 4. pr. 5.)

Since ━━ •••••• ✕ ━━ •••••• ═ ━━ ² ═ ━━ ²,

∴ ━━ is a tangent to ◯ (B. 3. pr. 37.)

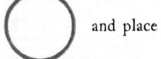 ∴ ◭ ═ △ (B. 3. pr. 32),

add ◀ to each,

∴ ▲ + ◀ = △ + ◀ ;

but ◀ + ◣ or ◤ = ◤ (B. 1. pr. 5) :

ſince ▬▬ = ▬▬⋯ (B. 1. pr. 5.)

conſequently ◤ = △ + ◀ = ◤

(B. 1. pr. 32.)

∴ ▬▬ = ▬▬ (B. 1. pr. 6.)

∴ ▬▬▬ = ▬▬▬ = ▬▬▬ (conſt.)

∴ △ = ◀ (B. 1. pr. 5.)

∴ ◤ = ◤ = ◤ = △ +

◀ = twice △ ; and conſequently each angle at the baſe is double of the vertical angle.

Q. E. D.

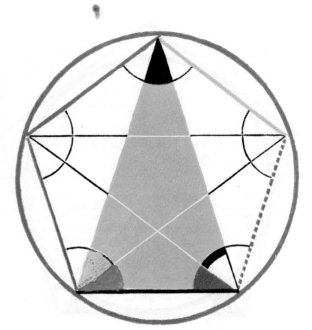

N *a given circle*

*to infcribe an equilateral and equi-
angular pentagon.*

Conftruct an ifofceles triangle, in
which each of the angles at the bafe
fhall be double of the angle at the
vertex, and infcribe in the given

circle a triangle equiangular to it ; (B. 4. pr. 2.)

Bifect and and (B. 1. pr. 9.)

draw ——— , ——— , ——— and ------- .

Becaufe each of the angles

 , , , and are equal,

the arcs upon which they ftand are equal, (B. 3. pr. 26.)
and ∴ ——— , ——— , ——— , ——— and
------- which fubtend thefe arcs are equal (B. 3. pr. 29.)
and ∴ the pentagon is equilateral, it is alfo equiangular,
as each of its angles ftand upon equal arcs. (B. 3. pr. 27).

Q. E. D.

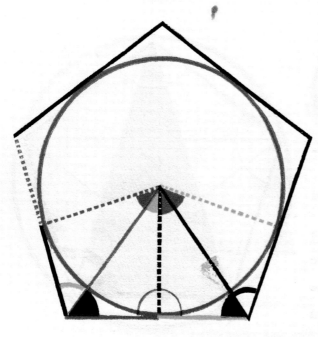

 O *defcribe an equilateral and equiangular pentagon about a given circle* .

Draw five tangents through the vertices of the angles of any regular pentagon infcribed in the given circle (B. 3. pr. 17).

Thefe five tangents will form the required pentagon.

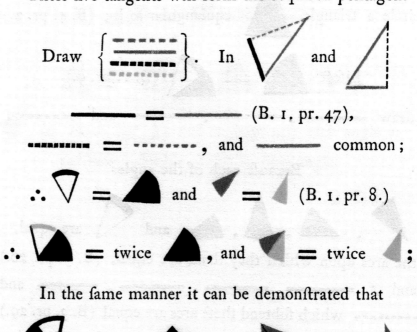

Draw ⎰⎱. In ◺ and ◹

▬ = ▬ (B. 1. pr. 47),

▬▬ = ······, and ▬ common;

∴ ◹ = ◣ and ◥ = ◥ (B. 1. pr. 8.)

∴ ◣ = twice ◣, and ◥ = twice ◥;

In the fame manner it can be demonftrated that

◣ = twice ◣, and ◥ = twice ◥;

but ◥ = ◥ (B. 3. pr. 27),

∴ their halves ◢ = ◣, alſo ◪ = ◩, and

▬▬▬ common;

∴ ▲ = ▲ and ▬▬▬ = ▬▬▬,

∴ ▬▬▬ = twice ▬▬ ;

In the ſame manner it can be demonſtrated

that ▬▬▬ = twice ▬▬,

but ▬▬ = ▬▬

∴ ▬▬▬ = ▬▬▬ ;

In the ſame manner it can be demonſtrated that the other ſides are equal, and therefore the pentagon is equilateral, it is alſo equiangular, for

◣ = twice ▲ and ◤ = twice ▲,

and therefore ▲ = ▲,

∴ ◣ = ◤ ; in the ſame manner it can be demonſtrated that the other angles of the deſcribed pentagon are equal.

Q. E. D

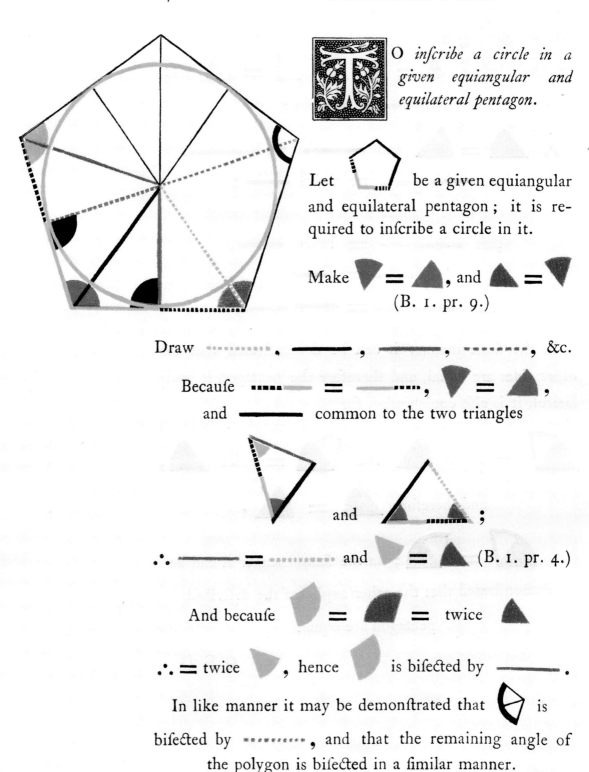

T O inscribe a circle in a given equiangular and equilateral pentagon.

Let ⬠ be a given equiangular and equilateral pentagon; it is required to inscribe a circle in it.

Make ◣ = ◢, and ◢ = ◣, (B. 1. pr. 9.)

Draw ⋯⋯⋯, ▬▬▬, ▬▬▬, ▭▭▭, &c.

Because ▬▬ = ▬▬, ◣ = ◢,

and ▬▬▬ common to the two triangles

and ;

∴ ▬▬ = ⋯⋯⋯ and ◣ = ◢ (B. 1. pr. 4.)

And because ◗ = ◗ = twice ◢

∴ ⬭ = twice ◗, hence ◗ is bisected by ▬▬▬.

In like manner it may be demonstrated that ⬙ is bisected by ⋯⋯⋯, and that the remaining angle of the polygon is bisected in a similar manner.

Draw ———— , ----- , &c. perpendicular to the
fides of the pentagon.

Then in the two triangles 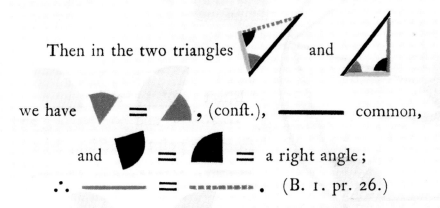 and

we have ▼ = ▲ , (conft.), ———— common,

and ◗ = ◖ = a right angle ;

∴ ———— = ----- . (B. 1. pr. 26.)

In the fame way it may be fhown that the five perpendiculars on the fides of the pentagon are equal to one
another.

Defcribe ◯ with any one of the perpendicu-
lars as radius, and it will be the infcribed circle required.
For if it does not touch the fides of the pentagon, but cut
them, then a line drawn from the extremity at right angles
to the diameter of a circle will fall within the circle, which
has been fhown to be abfurd. (B. 3. pr. 16.)

Q. E. D.

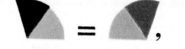

T O *defcribe a circle about a given equilateral and equi-angular pentagon.*

Bifect ◢ and ◣

by ·········· and ··········· , and

from the point of fection, draw

———— , ········ , and ▬▬▬ .

◢ = ◣ ,

△ = △ , ∴ ······ = ······· (B. 1. pr. 6);

and fince in ◺ and ◹ ,

———— = ———— , and ·········· common,

alfo ▼ = ▲ ;

∴ ▬▬▬ = ·········· (B. 1. pr. 4).

In like manner it may be proved that

········ = ———— = ▬▬▬ , and

therefore ········ = ▬▬▬ = ·········· =

·········· = ———— :

Therefore if a circle be defcribed from the point where
thefe five lines meet, with any one of them
as a radius, it will circumfcribe
the given pentagon.

Q. E. D.

O *inscribe an equilateral and equiangular hexagon in a given circle*

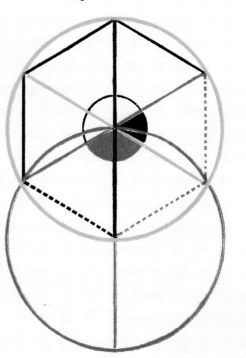

From any point in the circumference of the given circle describe ⬭ passing through its centre, and draw the diameters ▬▬▬ , ▬▬▬ and ▬▬▬ ; draw ▬▬▬ , ┄┄┄ , ┄┄┄ , &c. and the required hexagon is inscribed in the given circle.

Since ▬▬▬ passes through the centres of the circles, ◁ and ▷ are equilateral triangles, hence ◖ = ◗ = one-third of two right angles ; (B. 1. pr. 32) but ◓ = ◒ (B. 1. pr. 13);

∴ ◀ = ▶ = ◣ = one-third of ◒ (B. 1. pr. 32), and the angles vertically opposite to these are all equal to one another (B. 1. pr. 15), and stand on equal arches (B. 3. pr. 26), which are subtended by equal chords (B. 3. pr. 29); and since each of the angles of the hexagon is double of the angle of an equilateral triangle, it is also equiangular. Q. E. D.

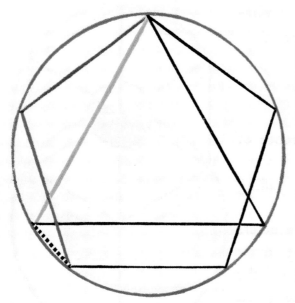

 O *infcribe an equilateral and equiangular quindecagon in a given circle.*

Let ———— and ———— be the fides of an equilateral pentagon infcribed in the given circle, and ———— the fide of an inscribed equilateral triangle.

$$\left.\text{The arc fubtended by} \atop \text{———— and ————}\right\} = \tfrac{2}{5} = \tfrac{6}{15} \left\{\text{of the whole} \atop \text{circumference.}\right.$$

$$\left.\text{The arc fubtended by} \atop \text{————}\right\} = \tfrac{1}{3} = \tfrac{5}{15} \left\{\text{of the whole} \atop \text{circumference}\right.$$

$$\text{Their difference} = \tfrac{1}{15}$$

∴ the arc fubtended by ·········· $= \tfrac{1}{15}$ difference of the whole circumference.

Hence if ftraight lines equal to ·········· be placed in the circle (B. 4. pr. 1), an equilateral and equiangular quindecagon will be thus infcribed in the circle.

Q. E. D.

BOOK V.

DEFINITIONS.

I.

 LESS magnitude is faid to be an aliquot part or fubmultiple of a greater magnitude, when the lefs meafures the greater; that is, when the lefs is contained a certain number of times exactly in the greater.

II.

A GREATER magnitude is faid to be a multiple of a lefs, when the greater is meafured by the lefs; that is, when the greater contains the lefs a certain number of times exactly.

III.

RATIO is the relation which one quantity bears to another of the fame kind, with refpect to magnitude.

IV.

MAGNITUDES are faid to have a ratio to one another, when they are of the fame kind; and the one which is not the greater can be multiplied fo as to exceed the other.

The other definitions will be given throughout the book where their aid is firft required.

AXIOMS.

I.

QUIMULTIPLES or equiſubmultiples of the ſame, or of equal magnitudes, are equal.

If A = B, then
twice A = twice B, that is,
2 A = 2 B;
3 A = 3 B;
4 A = 4 B;
&c. &c.
and ½ of A = ½ of B;
⅓ of A = ⅓ of B;
&c. &c.

II.

A MULTIPLE of a greater magnitude is greater than the ſame multiple of a leſs.

Let A ⊏ B, then
2 A ⊏ 2 B;
3 A ⊏ 3 B;
4 A ⊏ 4 B;
&c. &c.

III.

THAT magnitude, of which a multiple is greater than the ſame multiple of another, is greater than the other.

Let 2 A ⊏ 2 B, then
A ⊏ B;
or, let 3 A ⊏ 3 B, then
A ⊏ B;
or, let *m* A ⊏ *m* B, then
A ⊏ B.

F *any number of magnitudes be equimultiples of as many others, each of each: what multiple soever any one of the firſt is of its part, the ſame multiple ſhall of the firſt magnitudes taken together be of all the others taken together.*

Let ⌂⌂⌂⌂⌂ be the ſame multiple of ⌂,

that ♥♥♥♥♥ is of ♥.

that ◇◇◇◇◇ is of ◇.

Then is evident that

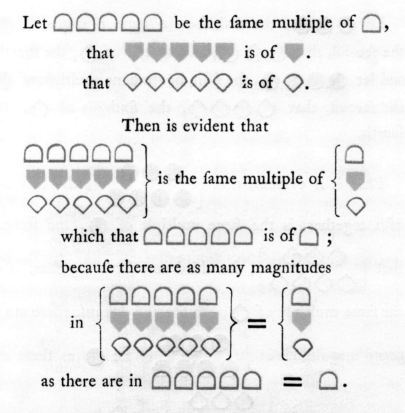

which that ⌂⌂⌂⌂⌂ is of ⌂ ;

becauſe there are as many magnitudes

as there are in ⌂⌂⌂⌂⌂ = ⌂.

The ſame demonſtration holds in any number of magnitudes, which has here been applied to three.

∴ If any number of magnitudes, &c.

F *the firſt magnitude be the ſame multiple of the ſecond that the third is of the fourth, and the fifth the ſame multiple of the ſecond that the ſixth is of the fourth, then ſhall the firſt, together with the fifth, be the ſame multiple of the ſecond that the third, together with the ſixth, is of the fourth.*

Let ⬤⬤⬤, the firſt, be the ſame multiple of ⬤, the ſecond, that ◇◇◇, the third, is of ◇, the fourth; and let ⬤⬤⬤⬤, the fifth, be the ſame multiple of ⬤, the ſecond, that ◇◇◇◇, the ſixth, is of ◇, the fourth.

Then it is evident, that $\left\{ \begin{matrix} ●●● \\ ⬤⬤⬤⬤ \end{matrix} \right\}$, the firſt and fifth together, is the ſame multiple of ⬤, the ſecond, that $\left\{ \begin{matrix} ◇◇◇ \\ ◇◇◇◇ \end{matrix} \right\}$, the third and ſixth together, is of the ſame multiple of ◇, the fourth; becauſe there are as many magnitudes in $\left\{ \begin{matrix} ●●● \\ ⬤⬤⬤⬤ \end{matrix} \right\} = ●$ as there are in $\left\{ \begin{matrix} ◇◇◇ \\ ◇◇◇◇ \end{matrix} \right\} = ◇$.

∴ If the firſt magnitude, &c.

F *the firſt of four magnitudes be the ſame multiple of the ſecond that the third is of the fourth, and if any equimultiples whatever of the firſt and third be taken, thoſe ſhall be equimultiples; one of the ſecond, and the other of the fourth.*

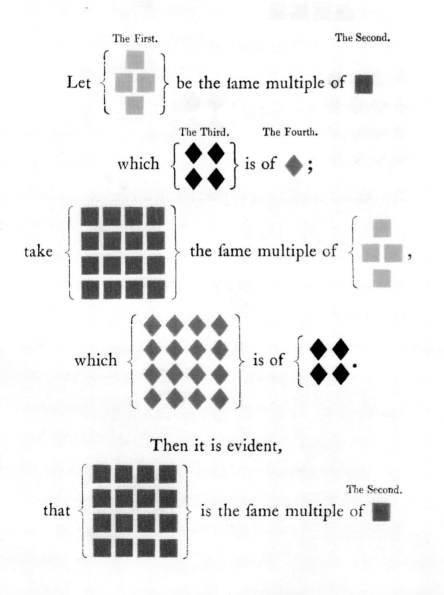

which 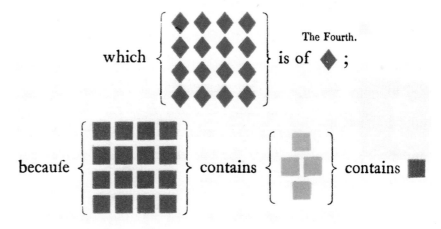 is of ◆ ;

The Fourth.

becaufe  contains ⬜⬜⬜⬜ contains ⬛

as many times as

◆◆◆◆ contains ◆◆◆◆ contains ◆ .

The fame reafoning is applicable in all cafes.

∴ If the firft four, &c.

DEFINITION V.

FOUR magnitudes, ⬤ , ▪ , ◆ , ▼ , are faid to be proportionals when every equimultiple of the firft and third be
taken, and every equimultiple of the fecond and fourth, as,

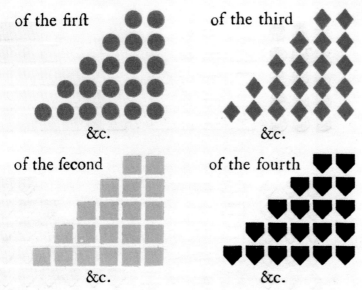

Then taking every pair of equimultiples of the firft and
third, and every pair of equimultiples of the fecond and
fourth,

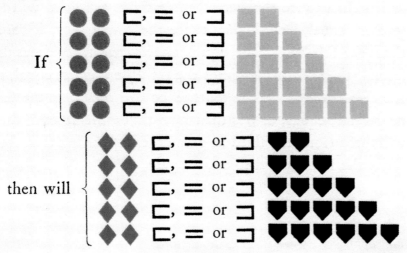

That is, if twice the firſt be greater, equal, or leſs than twice the ſecond, twice the third will be greater, equal, or leſs than twice the fourth; or, if twice the firſt be greater, equal, or leſs than three times the ſecond, twice the third will be greater, equal, or leſs than three times the fourth, and ſo on, as above expreſſed.

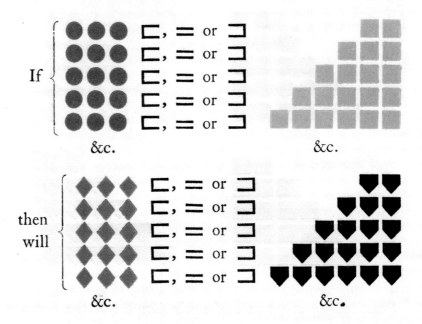

In other terms, if three times the firſt be greater, equal, or leſs than twice the ſecond, three times the third will be greater, equal, or leſs than twice the fourth; or, if three times the firſt be greater, equal, or leſs than three times the ſecond, then will three times the third be greater, equal, or leſs than three times the fourth; or if three times the firſt be greater, equal, or leſs than four times the ſecond, then will three times the third be greater, equal, or leſs than four times the fourth, and ſo on. Again,

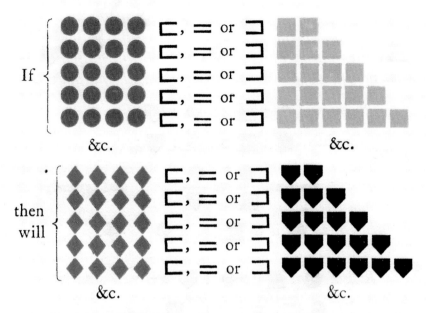

And so on, with any other equimultiples of the four magnitudes, taken in the fame manner.

Euclid expreffes this definition as follows :—

The firft of four magnitudes is faid to have the fame ratio to the fecond, which the third has to the fourth, when any equimultiples whatfoever of the firft and third being taken, and any equimultiples whatfoever of the fecond and fourth; if the multiple of the firft be lefs than that of the fecond, the multiple of the third is alfo lefs than that of the fourth; or, if the multiple of the firft be equal to that of the fecond, the multiple of the third is alfo equal to that of the fourth; or, ir the multiple of the firft be greater than that of the fecond, the multiple of the third is alfo greater than that of the fourth.

In future we fhall exprefs this definition generally, thus :

Then we infer that ●, the firſt, has the ſame ratio to ▨, the ſecond, which ◆, the third, has to ▼ the fourth : expreſſed in the ſucceeding demonſtrations thus :

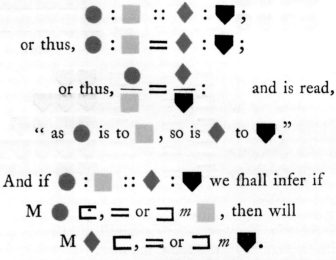

$$ ● : ▨ :: ◆ : ▼ ; $$

or thus, $ ● : ▨ = ◆ : ▼ ; $

or thus, $ \dfrac{●}{▨} = \dfrac{◆}{▼} : $ and is read,

" as ● is to ▨ , so is ◆ to ▼."

And if ● : ▨ :: ◆ : ▼ we ſhall infer if

M ● ⊏, ═ or ⊐ *m* ▨ , then will

M ◆ ⊏, ═ or ⊐ *m* ▼.

That is, if the firſt be to the ſecond, as the third is to the fourth ; then if M times the firſt be greater than, equal to, or leſs than *m* times the ſecond, then ſhall M times the third be greater than, equal to, or leſs than *m* times the fourth, in which M and *m* are not to be conſidered particular multiples, but every pair of multiples whatever ; nor are ſuch marks as ●, ▼, ▨ , &c. to be conſidered any more than repreſentatives of geometrical magnitudes.

The ſtudent ſhould thoroughly underſtand this definition before proceeding further.

F *the firſt of four magnitudes have the ſame ratio to the ſecond, which the third has to the fourth, then any equimultiples whatever of the firſt and third ſhall have the ſame ratio to any equimultiples of the ſecond and fourth; viz., the equimultiple of the firſt ſhall have the ſame ratio to that of the ſecond, which the equimultiple of the third has to that of the fourth.*

Let ● : ■ :: ◆ : ▼, then 3 ● : 2 ■ :: 3 ◆ : 2 ▼, every equimultiple of 3 ● and 3 ◆ are equimultiples of ● and ◆, and every equimultiple of 2 ■ and 2 ▼, are equimultiples of ■ and ▼ (B. 5, pr. 3.)

That is, M times 3 ● and M times 3 ◆ are equimultiples of ● and ◆, and *m* times 2 ■ and *m* 2 ▼ are equimultiples of 2 ■ and 2 ▼; but ● : ■ :: ◆ : ▼ (hyp); ∴ if M 3 ● ⊏, =, or ⊐ *m* 2 ■, then M 3 ◆ ⊏, =, or ⊐ *m* 2 ▼ (def. 5.) and therefore 3 ● : 2 ■ :: 3 ◆ : 2 ▼ (def. 5.)

The ſame reaſoning holds good if any other equimultiple of the firſt and third be taken, any other equimultiple of the ſecond and fourth.

∴ If the firſt four magnitudes, &c.

F *one magnitude be the same multiple of another,*
which a magnitude taken from the first is of a mag-
nitude taken from the other, the remainder shall be
the same multiple of the remainder, that the whole
is of the whole.

$$\text{Let } \bigcirc\!\!\bigcirc\!\!\bigcirc\!\!\bigcup = M' \, \blacktriangle \; \blacksquare$$

$$\text{and } \bigcup = M' \; \blacksquare,$$

$$\therefore \; \bigcirc\!\!\bigcirc\!\!\bigcirc\!\!\bigcup \text{ minus } \bigcup = M' \, \blacktriangle \; \blacksquare \text{ minus } M' \; \blacksquare,$$

$$\therefore \; \bigcirc\!\!\bigcirc\!\!\bigcirc = M' \, (\blacktriangle \; \blacksquare \text{ minus } \blacksquare),$$

$$\text{and } \therefore \; \bigcirc\!\!\bigcirc\!\!\bigcirc = M' \, \blacktriangle.$$

∴ If one magnitude, &c.

F *two magnitudes be equimultiples of two others,
and if equimultiples of thefe be taken from the firft
two, the remainders are either equal to thefe others,
or equimultiples of them.*

Let $= M' \blacksquare$; and ⊍⊍ $= M' \blacktriangle$;

then minus $m' \blacksquare =$

$M' \blacksquare$ minus $m' \blacksquare = (M'$ minus $m') \blacksquare$,

and ⊍⊍ minus $m' \blacktriangle = M' \blacktriangle$ minus $m' \blacktriangle =$

$(M'$ minus $m') \blacktriangle$.

Hence, $(M'$ minus $m') \blacksquare$ and $(M'$ minus $m') \blacktriangle$ are equimultiples of $\blacksquare$ and $\blacktriangle$, and equal to $\blacksquare$ and $\blacktriangle$,
when M' minus $m' = 1$.

$\therefore$ If two magnitudes be equimultiples, &c.

F *the firſt of the four magnitudes has the ſame ratio to the ſecond which the third has to the fourth, then if the firſt be greater than the ſecond, the third is alſo greater than the fourth ; and if equal, equal ; if leſs, leſs.*

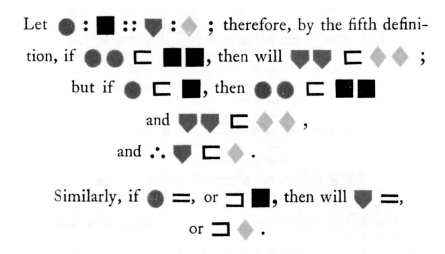

Let ● : ■ :: ▼ : ◆ ; therefore, by the fifth definition, if ●● ⊏ ■■, then will ▼▼ ⊏ ◆◆ ;
but if ● ⊏ ■, then ●● ⊏ ■■
and ▼▼ ⊏ ◆◆ ,
and ∴ ▼ ⊏ ◆ .

Similarly, if ● =, or ⊐ ■, then will ▼ =,
or ⊐ ◆ .

∴ If the firſt of four, &c.

DEFINITION XIV.

GEOMETRICIANS make uſe of the technical term " Invertendo," by inverſion, when there are four proportionals,
and it is inferred, that the ſecond is to the firſt as the fourth
to the third.

Let A : B :: C : D, then, by " invertendo" it is inferred
B : A :: D : C.

F *four magnitudes are proportionals, they are pro-portionals alſo when taken inverſely.*

Let ▼ : ◡ :: ■ : ◆ ,

then, inverſely, ◡ : ▼ :: ◆ : ■ .

If M ▼ ⊐ *m* ◡, then M ■ ⊐ *m* ◆
by the fifth definition.

Let M ▼ ⊐ *m* ◡, that is, *m* ◡ ⊏ M ▼,

∴ M ■ ⊐ *m* ◆, or, *m* ◆ ⊏ M ■;

∴ if *m* ◡ ⊏ M ▼, then will *m* ◆ ⊏ M ■.

In the ſame manner it may be ſhown,

that if *m* ◡ = or ⊐ M ▼,

then will *m* ◆ =, or ⊐ M ■;

and therefore, by the fifth definition, we infer

that ◡ : ▼ : ◆ : ■.

∴ If four magnitudes, &c.

F *the firſt be the ſame multiple of the ſecond, or the ſame part of it, that the third is of the fourth; the firſt is to the ſecond, as the third is to the fourth.*

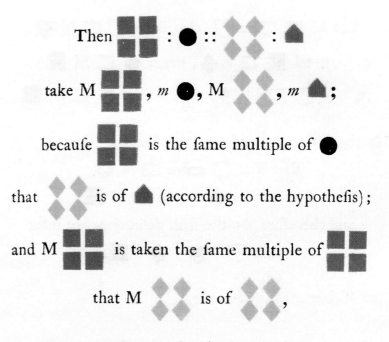

Therefore, if M ▨ be of ⬤ a greater multiple than

m ⬤ is, then M ◈ is a greater multiple of ▲ than

m ▲ is ; that is, if M ▨ be greater than *m* ⬤, then

M ◈ will be greater than *m* ▲ ; in the ſame manner

it can be ſhewn, if M ▨ be equal *m* ⬤, then

M ◈ will be equal *m* ▲.

And, generally, if M ▨ ⊏, = or ⊐ *m* ⬤

then M ◈ will be ⊏, = or ⊐ *m* ▲ ;

∴ by the fifth definition,

▨ : ⬤ :: ◈ : ▲.

Next, let ⬤ be the ſame part of ▨

that ▲ is of ◈.

In this caſe alſo ⬤ : ▨ :: ▲ : ◈.

For, becauſe

⬤ is the ſame part of ▨ that ▲ is of ◈,

Y

therefore 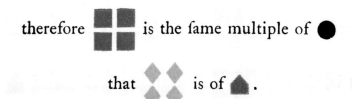 is the fame multiple of ●

that 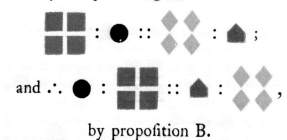 is of ▲.

Therefore, by the preceding cafe,

▦ : ● :: ◈ : ▲ ;

and ∴ ● : ▦ :: ▲ : ◈ ,

by propofition B.

∴ If the firft be the fame multiple, &c.

F *the firft be to the fecond as the third to the fourth,
and if the firft be a multiple, or a part of the
fecond; the third is the fame multiple, or the fame
part of the fourth.*

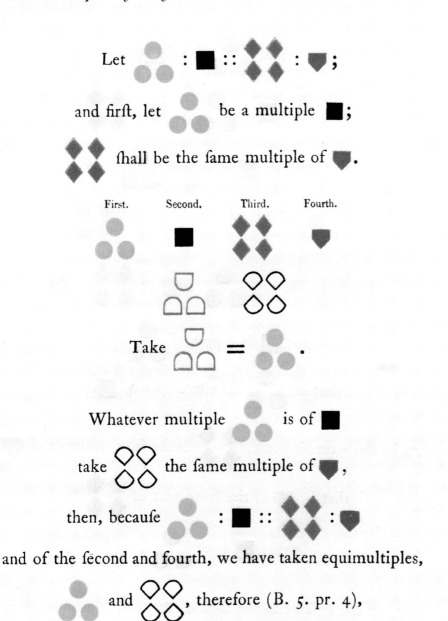

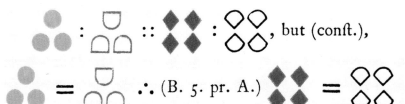

, but (conſt.),

∴ (B. 5. pr. A.)

and ⬡ is the ſame multiple of ⬟

that ⬡ is of ■.

Next, let ■ : ⬡ :: ⬟ : ◆◆ ,

and alſo ■ a part of ⬡ ;

then ⬟ ſhall be the ſame part of ◆◆ .

Inverſely (B. 5.), ⬡ : ■ :: ◆◆ : ⬟ ,

but ■ is a part of ⬡ ;

that is, ⬡ is a multiple of ■ ;

∴ by the preceding caſe, ◆◆ is the ſame multiple of ⬟

that is, ⬟ is the ſame part of ◆◆

that ■ is of ⬡ .

∴ If the firſt be to the ſecond, &c.

QUAL *magnitudes have the same ratio to the same magnitude, and the same has the same ratio to equal magnitudes.*

Let ● = ◆ and ▪ any other magnitude;
then ● : ▪ = ◆ : ▪ and ▪ : ● = ▪ : ◆.

Becaufe ● = ◆,

∴ M ● = M ◆ ;

∴ if M ● ⊏, = or ⊐ *m* ▪, then

M ◆ ⊏, = or ⊐ *m* ▪,

and ∴ ● : ▪ = ◆ : ▪ (B. 5. def. 5).

From the foregoing reafoning it is evident that,

if *m* ▪ ⊏, = or ⊐ M ●, then

m ▪ ⊏, = or ⊐ M ◆

∴ ▪ : ● = ▪ : ◆ (B. 5. def. 5).

∴ Equal magnitudes, &c.

DEFINITION VII.

W HEN of the equimultiples of four magnitudes (taken as in the fifth definition), the multiple of the firſt is greater than that of the ſecond, but the multiple of the third is not greater than the multiple of the fourth; then the firſt is ſaid to have to the ſecond a greater ratio than the third magnitude has to the fourth: and, on the contrary, the third is ſaid to have to the fourth a leſs ratio than the firſt has to the ſecond.

If, among the equimultiples of four magnitudes, compared as in the fifth definition, we ſhould find

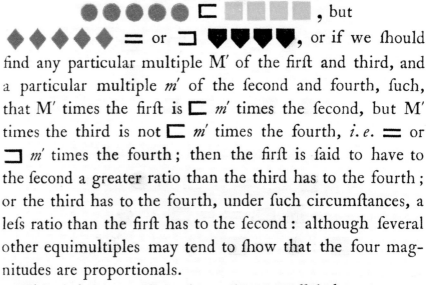

, but

, or if we ſhould find any particular multiple M′ of the firſt and third, and a particular multiple *m′* of the ſecond and fourth, ſuch, that M′ times the firſt is ⊏ *m′* times the ſecond, but M′ times the third is not ⊏ *m′* times the fourth, *i. e.* = or ⊐ *m′* times the fourth; then the firſt is ſaid to have to the ſecond a greater ratio than the third has to the fourth; or the third has to the fourth, under ſuch circumſtances, a leſs ratio than the firſt has to the ſecond: although ſeveral other equimultiples may tend to ſhow that the four magnitudes are proportionals.

This definition will in future be expreſſed thus:—

If M′ ⬥ ⊏ *m′* ⋃, but M′ ▪ = or ⊐ *m′* ◆,

then ⬥ : ⋃ ⊏ ▪ : ◆.

In the above general expreſſion, M′ and *m′* are to be confidered particular multiples, not like the multiples M and *m* introduced in the fifth definition, which are in that definition confidered to be every pair of multiples that can be taken. It muft alfo be here obferved, that ▼, ⊍, ■, and the like fymbols are to be confidered merely the reprefentatives of geometrical magnitudes.

In a partial arithmetical way, this may be fet forth as follows :

Let us take the four numbers, 8, 7, 10, and 9.

Firſt.	Second.	Third.	Fourth.
8	7	10	9
16	14	20	18
24	21	30	27
32	28	40	36
40	35	50	45
48	42	60	54
56	49	70	63
64	56	80	72
72	63	90	81
80	70	100	90
88	77	110	99
96	84	120	108
104	91	130	117
112	98	140	126
&c.	&c.	&c	&c.

Among the above multiples we find 16 ⊏ 14 and 20 ⊏ 18; that is, twice the firſt is greater than twice the fecond, and twice the third is greater than twice the fourth; and 16 ⊐ 21 and 20 ⊐ 27; that is, twice the firſt is lefs than three times the fecond, and twice the third is lefs than three times the fourth; and among the fame multiples we can find 72 ⊏ 56 and 90 ⊏ 72 : that is, 9 times the firſt is greater than 8 times the fecond, and 9 times the third is greater than 8 times the fourth. Many other equimultiples might be selected, which would tend to ſhow that the numbers 8, 7, 10, 9, were proportionals, but they are not, for we can find a multiple of the firſt ⊏ a multiple of the ſecond, but the ſame multiple of the third that has been taken of the firſt not ⊏ the ſame multiple of the fourth which has been taken of the ſecond; for inſtance, 9 times the firſt is ⊏ 10 times the ſecond, but 9 times the third is not ⊏ 10 times the fourth, that is, 72 ⊏ 70, but 90 not ⊏ 90, or 8 times the firſt we find ⊏ 9 times the ſecond, but 8 times the third is not greater than 9 times the fourth, that is, 64 ⊏ 63, but 80 is not ⊏ 81. When any ſuch multiples as theſe can be found, the firſt (8) is ſaid to have to the ſecond (7) a greater ratio than the third (10) has to the fourth (9), and on the contrary the third (10) is ſaid to have to the fourth (9) a leſs ratio than the firſt (8) has to the ſecond (7).

O F *unequal magnitudes the greater has a greater ratio to the same than the less has : and the same magnitude has a greater ratio to the less than it has to the greater.*

Let ■ and ■ be two unequal magnitudes, and ● any other.

We shall first prove that ■ which is the greater of the two unequal magnitudes, has a greater ratio to ● than ■, the less, has to ● ;

that is, ■ : ● ⊏ ■ : ● ;

take M′ ■, m′ ●, M′ ■, and m′ ● ;

such, that M′ ▲ and M′ ■ shall be each ⊏ ● ;

also take m′ ● the least multiple of ●,

which will make m′ ● ⊏ M′ ■ = M′ ■ ;

∴ M′ ■ is not ⊏ m′ ●,

but M′ ■ is ⊏ m′ ●, for,

as m′ ● is the first multiple which first becomes ⊏ M′■,

than (m′ minus 1) ● or m′ ● minus ● is not ⊏ M′ ■,

and ● is not ⊏ M′ ▲,

∴ m′ ● minus ● + ● must be ⊐ M′ ■ + M′ ▲ ;

that is, m′ ● must be ⊐ M′ ■ ;

∴ M′ ■ is ⊏ m′ ● ; but it has been shown above that

z

M′ ▨ is not ⊏ m′ ●, therefore, by the seventh definition, ▨ has to ● a greater ratio than ▨ : ●.

Next we shall prove that ● has a greater ratio to ▨, the less, than it has to ▨, the greater;

or, ● : ▨ ⊏ ● : ▨.

Take m′ ●, M′ ▨, m′ ●, and M′ ▨, the same as in the first case, such, that M′ ▲ and M′ ▨ will be each ⊏ ●, and m′ ● the least multiple of ●, which first becomes greater than M′ ▨ = M′ ▨.

∴ m′ ● minus ● is not ⊏ M′ ▨, and ● is not ⊏ M′ ▲; consequently m′ ● minus ● + ● is ⊐ M′ ▨ + M′ ▲;

∴ m′ ● is ⊐ M′ ▨, and ∴ by the seventh definition, ● has to ▨ a greater ratio than ● has to ▨.

∴ Of unequal magnitudes, &c.

The contrivance employed in this proposition for finding among the multiples taken, as in the fifth definition, a multiple of the first greater than the multiple of the second, but the same multiple of the third which has been taken of the first, not greater than the same multiple of the fourth which has been taken of the second, may be illustrated numerically as follows :—

The number 9 has a greater ratio to 7 than 8 has to 7 : that is, 9 : 7 ⊏ 8 : 7 ; or, 8 + 1 : 7 ⊏ 8 : 7.

The multiple of 1, which firft becomes greater than 7, is 8 times, therefore we may multiply the firft and third by 8, 9, 10, or any other greater number; in this cafe, let us multiply the firft and third by 8, and we have $64 + 8$ and 64: again, the firft multiple of 7 which becomes greater than 64 is 10 times; then, by multiplying the fecond and fourth by 10, we fhall have 70 and 70 ; then, arranging thefe multiples, we have—

8 times the first.	10 times the second.	8 times the third.	10 times the fourth.
$64 + 8$	70	64	70

Confequently $64 + 8$, or 72, is greater than 70 , but 64 is not greater than 70 , ∴ by the feventh definition, 9 has a greater ratio to 7 than 8 has to 7 .

The above is merely illuftrative of the foregoing demonftration, for this property could be fhown of thefe or other numbers very readily in the following manner; becaufe, if an antecedent contains its confequent a greater number of times than another antecedent contains its confequent, or when a fraction is formed of an antecedent for the numerator, and its confequent for the denominator be greater than another fraction which is formed of another antecedent for the numerator and its confequent for the denominator, the ratio of the firft antecedent to its confequent is greater than the ratio of the laft antecedent to its confequent.

Thus, the number 9 has a greater ratio to 7, than 8 has to 7, for $\frac{9}{7}$ is greater than $\frac{8}{7}$.

Again, 17 : 19 is a greater ratio than 13 : 15, becaufe $\frac{17}{19} = \frac{17 \times 15}{19 \times 15} = \frac{255}{285}$, and $\frac{13}{15} = \frac{13 \times 19}{15 \times 19} = \frac{247}{285}$, hence it is evident that $\frac{255}{285}$ is greater than $\frac{247}{285}$, ∴ $\frac{17}{19}$ is greater than

$\frac{13}{15}$, and, according to what has been above fhown, 17 has to 19 a greater ratio than 13 has to 15.

So that the general terms upon which a greater, equal, or lefs ratio exifts are as follows :—

If $\frac{A}{B}$ be greater than $\frac{C}{D}$, A is faid to have to B a greater ratio than C has to D ; if $\frac{A}{B}$ be equal to $\frac{C}{D}$, then A has to B the fame ratio which C has to D ; and if $\frac{A}{B}$ be lefs than $\frac{C}{D}$, A is faid to have to B a lefs ratio than C has to D.

The ftudent fhould underftand all up to this propofition perfectly before proceeding further, in order fully to comprehend the following propofitions of this book. We therefore ftrongly recommend the learner to commence again, and read up to this flowly, and carefully reafon at each ftep, as he proceeds, particularly guarding againft the mifchievous fyftem of depending wholly on the memory. By following thefe inftructions, he will find that the parts which ufually prefent confiderable difficulties will prefent no difficulties whatever, in profecuting the ftudy of this important book.

AGNITUDES *which have the fame ratio to the fame magnitude are equal to one another; and thofe to which the fame magnitude has the fame ratio are equal to one another.*

Let ◆ : ▦ :: ● : ▦, then ◆ = ●.

For, if not, let ◆ ⊏ ●, then will

◆ : ▦ ⊏ ● : ▦ (B. 5. pr. 8),

which is abfurd according to the hypothefis.

∴ ◆ is not ⊏ ●.

In the fame manner it may be fhown, that

● is not ⊏ ◆,

∴ ◆ = ●.

Again, let ▦ : ◆ :: ▦ : ●, then will ◆ = ●.

For (invert.) ◆ : ▦ :: ● : ▦,

therefore, by the firft cafe, ◆ = ●.

∴ Magnitudes which have the fame ratio, &c.

This may be fhown otherwife, as follows :—

Let $A : B = A : C$, then $B = C$, for, as the fraction $\frac{A}{B}$ = the fraction $\frac{A}{C}$, and the numerator of one equal to the numerator of the other, therefore the denominator of thefe fractions are equal, that is $B = C$.

Again, if $B : A = C : A$, $B = C$. For, as $\frac{B}{A} = \frac{C}{A}$, B muft $= C$.

T**HAT** *magnitude which has a greater ratio than another has unto the fame magnitude, is the greater of the two : and that magnitude to which the fame has a greater ratio than it has unto another magnitude, is the lefs of the two.*

Let ▼ : ■ ⊏ ● : ■, then ▼ ⊏ ●.

For if not, let ▼ = or ⊐ ● ;

then, ▼ : ■ = ● : ■ (B. 5. pr. 7) or

▼ : ■ ⊐ ● : ■ (B. 5. pr. 8) and (invert.),

which is abfurd according to the hypothefis.

∴ ▼ is not = or ⊐ ●, and

∴ ▼ muft be ⊏ ●.

Again, let ■ : ● ⊏ ■ : ▼,

then, ● ⊐ ▼.

For if not, ● muft be ⊏ or = ▼,

then ■ : ● ⊐ ■ : ▼ (B. 5. pr. 8) and (invert.);

or ■ : ● = ■ : ▼ (B. 5. pr. 7), which is abfurd (hyp.);

∴ ● is not ⊏ or = ▼,

and ∴ ● muft be ⊐ ▼.

∴ That magnitude which has, &c.

ATIOS *that are the same to the same ratio, are the same to each other.*

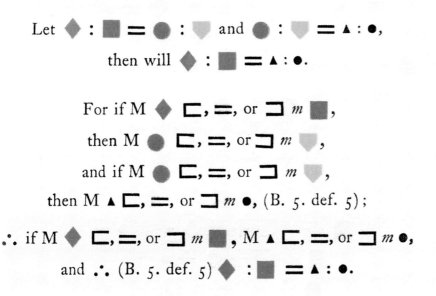

Let ◆ : ■ = ● : ▼ and ● : ▼ = ▲ : ●,

then will ◆ : ■ = ▲ : ●.

For if M ◆ ⊏, =, or ⊐ *m* ■,

then M ● ⊏, =, or ⊐ *m* ▼,

and if M ● ⊏, =, or ⊐ *m* ▼,

then M ▲ ⊏, =, or ⊐ *m* ●, (B. 5. def. 5);

∴ if M ◆ ⊏, =, or ⊐ *m* ■, M ▲ ⊏, =, or ⊐ *m* ●,

and ∴ (B. 5. def. 5) ◆ : ■ = ▲ : ●.

∴ Ratios that are the same, &c.

F *any number of magnitudes be proportionals, as one of the antecedents is to its consequent, so shall all the antecedents taken together be to all the consequents.*

Let ■ : ● = ∪ : ◇ = ◆ : ▽ = • : ▾ = ▲ : ◉ ;

then will ■ : ● =

■ + ∪ + ◆ + • + ▲ : ● + ◇ + ▽ + ▾ + ◉.

For if M ■ ⊏ *m* ●, then M ∪ ⊏ *m* ◇,

and M ◆ ⊏ *m* ▽ M • ⊏ *m* ▾,

also M ▲ ⊏ *m* ◉. (B. 5. def. 5.)

Therefore, if M ■ ⊏ *m* ●, then will

M ■ + M ∪ + M ◆ + M • + M ▲,

or M (■ + ∪ + ◆ + • + ▲) be greater

than *m* ● + *m* ◇ + *m* ▽ + *m* ▾ + *m* ◉,

or *m* (● + ◇ + ▽ + ▾ + ◉).

In the same way it may be shown, if M times one of the antecedents be equal to or less than *m* times one of the consequents, M times all the antecedents taken together, will be equal to or less than *m* times all the consequents taken together. Therefore, by the fifth definition, as one of the antecedents is to its consequent, so are all the antecedents taken together to all the consequents taken together.

∴ If any number of magnitudes, &c.

IF *the firſt has to the ſecond the ſame ratio which the third has to the fourth, but the third to the fourth a greater ratio than the fifth has to the ſixth; the firſt ſhall alſo have to the ſecond a greater ratio than the fifth to the ſixth.*

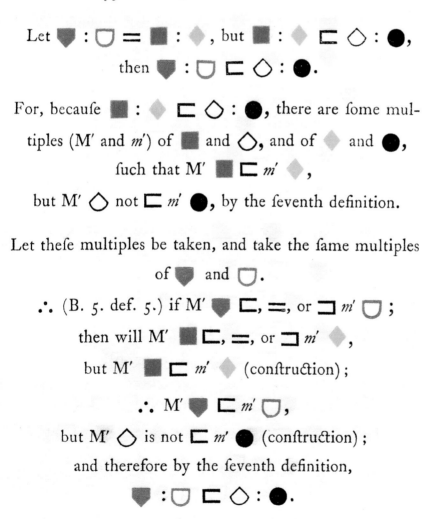

Let ▼ : ◡ = ■ : ◆, but ■ : ◆ ⊏ ◇ : ●,

then ▼ : ◡ ⊏ ◇ : ●.

For, becauſe ■ : ◆ ⊏ ◇ : ●, there are ſome multiples (M′ and *m′*) of ■ and ◇, and of ◆ and ●,
ſuch that M′ ■ ⊏ *m′* ◆,
but M′ ◇ not ⊏ *m′* ●, by the ſeventh definition.

Let theſe multiples be taken, and take the ſame multiples
of ▼ and ◡.

∴ (B. 5. def. 5.) if M′ ▼ ⊏, =, or ⊐ *m′* ◡ ;
then will M′ ■ ⊏, =, or ⊐ *m′* ◆,
but M′ ■ ⊏ *m′* ◆ (conſtruction) ;

∴ M′ ▼ ⊏ *m′* ◡,

but M′ ◇ is not ⊏ *m′* ● (conſtruction) ;
and therefore by the ſeventh definition,

▼ : ◡ ⊏ ◇ : ●.

∴ If the firſt has to the ſecond, &c.

F *the firſt has the ſame ratio to the ſecond which the third has to the fourth ; then, if the firſt be greater than the third, the ſecond ſhall be greater than the fourth ; and if equal, equal ; and if leſs, leſs.*

Let ⬇ : ∪ :: ◻ : ◆, and firſt ſuppoſe

⬇ ⊏ ◻, then will ∪ ⊏ ◆.

For ⬇ : ∪ ⊏ ◻ : ∪ (B. 5. pr. 8), and by the

hypotheſis, ⬇ : ∪ = ◻ : ◆ ;

∴ ◻ : ◆ ⊏ ◻ : ∪ (B. 5. pr. 13),

∴ ◆ ⊐ ∪ (B. 5. pr. 10.), or ∪ ⊏ ◆.

Secondly, let ⬇ = ◻, then will ∪ = ◆.

For ⬇ : ∪ = ◻ : ∪ (B. 5. pr. 7),

and ⬇ : ∪ = ◻ : ◆ (hyp.);

∴ ◻ : ∪ = ◻ : ◆ (B. 5. pr. 11),

and ∴ ∪ = ◆ (B. 5, pr. 9).

Thirdly, if ⬇ ⊐ ◻, then will ∪ ⊐ ◆ ;

becauſe ◻ ⊏ ⬇ and ◻ : ◆ = ⬇ : ∪ ;

∴ ◆ ⊏ ∪, by the firſt caſe,

that is, ∪ ⊐ ◆.

∴ If the firſt has the ſame ratio, &c.

AGNITUDES *have the same ratio to one another which their equimultiples have.*

Let ● and ▢ be two magnitudes;

then, ● : ▢ :: M′ ● : M′ ▢.

For ● : ▢ = ● : ▢

= ● : ▢

= ● : ▢

∴ ● : ▢ :: 4 ● : 4 ▢. (B. 5. pr. 12).

And as the same reasoning is generally applicable, we have

● : ▢ :: M′ ● : M′ ▢.

∴ Magnitudes have the same ratio, &c.

DEFINITION XIII.

THE technical term permutando, or alternando, by permutation or alternately, is ufed when there are four proportionals, and it is inferred that the firft has the fame ratio to the third which the fecond has to the fourth; or that the firft is to the third as the fecond is to the fourth: as is fhown in the following propofition :—

Let ● : ◆ :: ▼ : ■,

by " permutando" or " alternando" it is

inferred ● : ▼ :: ◆ : ■.

It may be neceffary here to remark that the magnitudes ●, ◆, ▼, ■, muft be homogeneous, that is, of the fame nature or fimilitude of kind; we muft therefore, in fuch cafes, compare lines with lines, furfaces with furfaces, folids with folids, &c. Hence the ftudent will readily perceive that a line and a furface, a furface and a folid, or other heterogenous magnitudes, can never ftand in the relation of antecedent and confequent.

F *four magnitudes of the same kind be proportionals, they are also proportionals when taken alternately.*

Let ▼ : ◡ :: ▢ : ◆, then ▼ : ▢ :: ◡ : ◆.

For M ▼ : M ◡ :: ▼ : ◡ (B. 5. pr. 15),

and M ▼ : M ◡ :: ▢ : ◆ (hyp.) and (B. 5. pr. 11);

also *m* ▢ : *m* ◆ :: ▢ : ◆ (B. 5. pr. 15);

∴ M ▼ : M ◡ :: *m* ▢ : *m* ◆ (B. 5. pr. 14),

and ∴ if M ▼ ⊏, =, or ⊐ *m* ▢,

then will M ◡ ⊏, =, or ⊐ *m* ◆ (B. 5. pr. 14);

therefore, by the fifth definition,

▼ : ▢ :: ◡ : ◆.

∴ If four magnitudes of the same kind, &c.

DEFINITION XVI.

DIVIDENDO, by divifion, when there are four proportionals, and it is inferred, that the excefs of the firft above the fecond is to the fecond, as the excefs of the third above the fourth, is to the fourth.

Let A : B :: C : D ;

by " dividendo " it is inferred

A minus B : B :: C minus D : D.

According to the above, A is fuppofed to be greater than B, and C greater than D ; if this be not the cafe, but to have B greater than A, and D greater than C, B and D can be made to ftand as antecedents, and A and C as confequents, by " invertion "

B : A :: D : C ;

then, by "dividendo," we infer

B minus A : A :: D minus C : C .

F *magnitudes, taken jointly, be proportionals, they shall also be proportionals when taken separately: that is, if two magnitudes together have to one of them the same ratio which two others have to one of these, the remaining one of the first two shall have to the other the same ratio which the remaining one of the last two has to the other of these.*

Let ▽ + ◡ : ◡ :: ▪ + ◆ : ◆,

then will ▽ : ◡ :: ▪ : ◆.

Take M ▽ ⊏ *m* ◡ to each add M ◡,

then we have M ▽ + M ◡ ⊏ *m* ◡ + M ◡,

or M (▽ + ◡) ⊏ (*m* + M) ◡ :

but because ▽ + ◡ : ◡ :: ▪ + ◆ : ◆ (hyp.),

and M (▽ + ◡) ⊏ (*m* + M) ◡ ;

∴ M (▪ + ◆) ⊏ (*m* + M) ◆ (B. 5. def. 5) ;

∴ M ▪ + M ◆ ⊏ *m* ◆ + M ◆ ;

∴ M ▪ ⊏ *m* ◆, by taking M ◆ from both sides :

that is, when M ▽ ⊏ *m* ◡, then M ▪ ⊏ *m* ◆.

In the same manner it may be proved, that if

M ▽ = or ⊐ *m* ◡, then will M ▪ = or ⊐ *m* ◆ ;

and ∴ ▽ : ◡ :: ▪ : ◆ (B. 5. def. 5).

∴ If magnitudes taken jointly, &c.

DEFINITION XV.

THE term componendo, by compofition, is ufed when there are four proportionals; and it is inferred that the firft together with the fecond is to the fecond as the third together with the fourth is to the fourth.

$$\text{Let } A : B :: C : D \ ;$$

then, by the term "componendo," it is inferred that

$$A + B : B :: C + D : D.$$

By "invertion" B and D may become the firft and third, A and C the fecond and fourth, as

$$B : A :: D : C,$$

then, by "componendo," we infer that

$$B + A : A :: D + C : C.$$

I F *magnitudes, taken separately, be proportionals, they shall also be proportionals when taken jointly: that is, if the first be to the second as the third is to the fourth, the first and second together shall be to the second as the third and fourth together is to the fourth.*

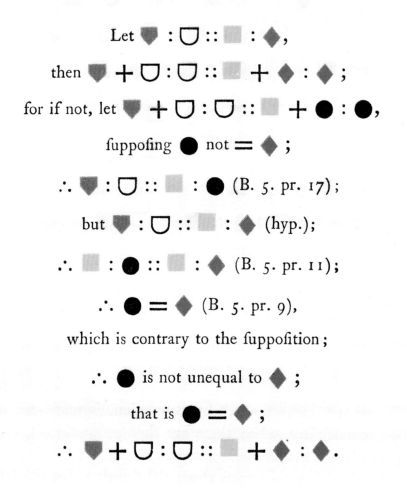

Let ▼ : ∪ :: ■ : ◆,

then ▼ + ∪ : ∪ :: ■ + ◆ : ◆ ;

for if not, let ▼ + ∪ : ∪ :: ■ + ● : ● ,

supposing ● not = ◆ ;

∴ ▼ : ∪ :: ■ : ● (B. 5. pr. 17) ;

but ▼ : ∪ :: ■ : ◆ (hyp.) ;

∴ ■ : ● :: ■ : ◆ (B. 5. pr. 11) ;

∴ ● = ◆ (B. 5. pr. 9),

which is contrary to the supposition ;

∴ ● is not unequal to ◆ ;

that is ● = ◆ ;

∴ ▼ + ∪ : ∪ :: ■ + ◆ : ◆.

∴ If magnitudes, taken separately, &c.

F *a whole magnitude be to a whole, as a magnitude taken from the firſt, is to a magnitude taken from the other; the remainder ſhall be to the remainder, as the whole to the whole.*

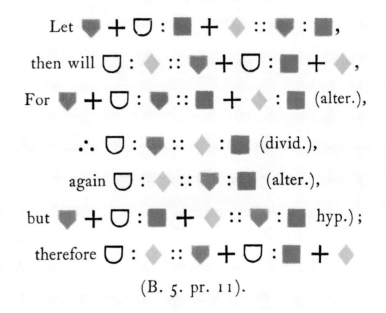

(B. 5. pr. 11).

∴ If a whole magnitude be to a whole, &c.

DEFINITION XVII.

THE term "convertendo," by converſion, is made uſe of by geometricians, when there are four proportionals, and it is inferred, that the firſt is to its exceſs above the ſecond, as the third is to its exceſs above the fourth. See the following propoſition :—

F *four magnitudes be proportionals, they are alſo proportionals by converſion: that is, the firſt is to its exceſs above the ſecond, as the third to its exceſs above the fourth.*

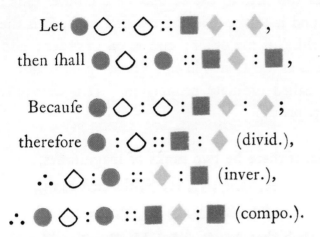

∴ If four magnitudes, &c.

DEFINITION XVIII.

" Ex æquali" (ſc. diſtantiâ), or ex æquo, from equality of diſtance: when there is any number of magnitudes more than two, and as many others, ſuch that they are proportionals when taken two and two of each rank, and it is inferred that the firſt is to the laſt of the firſt rank of magnitudes, as the firſt is to the laſt of the others: " of this there are the two following kinds, which ariſe from the different order in which the magnitudes are taken, two and two."

DEFINITION XIX.

" Ex æquali," from equality. This term is ufed fimply by itfelf, when the firft magnitude is to the fecond of the firft rank, as the firft to the fecond of the other rank ; and as the fecond is to the third of the firft rank, fo is the fecond to the third of the other ; and fo on in order : and the inference is as mentioned in the preceding definition ; whence this is called ordinate proportion.   It is demonftrated in Book 5. pr. 22.

Thus, if there be two ranks of magnitudes,

A, B, C, D, E, F, the firft rank,

and L, M, N, O, P, Q, the fecond,

fuch that A : B :: L : M, B : C :: M : N,

C : D :: N : O, D : E :: O : P, E : F :: P : Q ;

we infer by the term " ex æquali " that

A : F :: L : Q.

DEFINITION XX.

" Ex æquali in proportione perturbatâ feu inordinatâ," from equality in perturbate, or diforderly proportion. This term is ufed when the firft magnitude is to the fecond of the firft rank as the laft but one is to the laft of the fecond rank ; and as the fecond is to the third of the firft rank, fo is the laft but two to the laft but one of the fecond rank ; and as the third is to the fourth of the firft rank, fo is the third from the laft to the laft but two of the fecond rank ; and fo on in a crofs order : and the inference is in the 18th definition. It is demonftrated in B. 5. pr. 23.

Thus, if there be two ranks of magnitudes,

A , B , C , D , E , F , the firft rank,

and L , M , N , O , P , Q , the fecond,

fuch that A : B :: P : Q, B : C :: O : P,

C : D :: N : O, D : E :: M : N, E : F :: L : M ;

the term " ex æquali in proportione perturbatâ feu inordi-

natâ" infers that

A : F :: L : Q.

F *there be three magnitudes, and other three, which, taken two and two, have the same ratio ; then, if the first be greater than the third, the fourth shall be greater than the sixth ; and if equal, equal ; and if less, less.*

Let ▼, ◡, ▨, be the first three magnitudes,

and ◆, ◇, ●, be the other three,

such that ▼ : ◡ :: ◆ : ◇, and ◡ : ▨ :: ◇ : ●.

Then, if ▼ ⊏, =, or ⊐ ▨, then will ◆ ⊏, =,

or ⊐ ●.

From the hypothesis, by alternando, we have

▼ : ◆ :: ◡ : ◇,

and ◡ : ◇ :: ▨ : ● ;

∴ ▼ : ◆ :: ▨ : ● (B. 5. pr. 11);

∴ if ▼ ⊏, =, or ⊐ ▨, then will ◆ ⊏, =,

or ⊐ ● (B. 5. pr. 14).

∴ If there be three magnitudes, &c.

F there be three magnitudes, and other three which have the fame ratio, taken two and two, but in a crofs order; then if the firft magnitude be greater than the third, the fourth fhall be greater than the fixth; and if equal, equal; and if lefs, lefs.

Let ▽, ▲, ■, be the firft three magnitudes,

and ◆, ◇, ●, the other three,

fuch that ▽ : ▲ :: ◇ : ●, and ▲ : ■ :: ◆ : ◇.

Then, if ▽ ⊏, =, or ⊐ ■, then

will ◆ ⊏, =, ⊐ ●.

Firft, let ▽ be ⊏ ■ :

then, becaufe ▲ is any other magnitude,

▽ : ▲ ⊏ ■ : ▲ (B. 5. pr. 8);

but ◇ : ● :: ▽ : ▲ (hyp.);

∴ ◇ : ● ⊏ ■ : ▲ (B. 5. pr. 13);

and becaufe ▲ : ■ :: ◆ : ◇ (hyp.);

∴ ■ : ▲ :: ◇ : ◆ (inv.),

and it was fhown that ◇ : ● ⊏ ■ : ▲,

∴ ◇ : ● ⊏ ◇ : ◆ (B. 5. pr. 13);

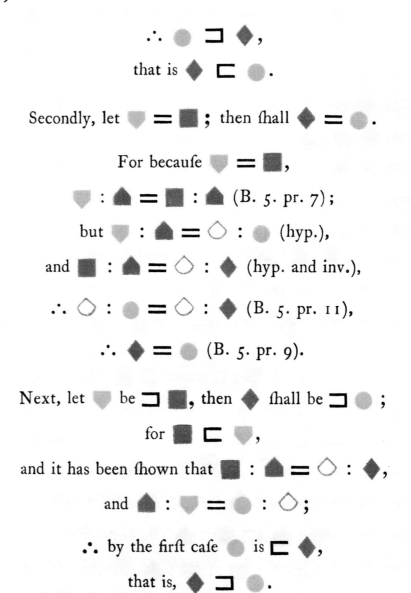

∴ ● ⊐ ◆,

that is ◆ ⊏ ●.

Secondly, let ▽ = ■ ; then ſhall ◆ = ●.

For becauſe ▽ = ■,

▽ : ▲ = ■ : ▲ (B. 5. pr. 7) ;

but ▽ : ▲ = ◇ : ● (hyp.),

and ■ : ▲ = ◇ : ◆ (hyp. and inv.),

∴ ◇ : ● = ◇ : ◆ (B. 5. pr. 11),

∴ ◆ = ● (B. 5. pr. 9).

Next, let ▽ be ⊐ ■, then ◆ ſhall be ⊐ ● ;

for ■ ⊏ ▽,

and it has been ſhown that ■ : ▲ = ◇ : ◆,

and ▲ : ▽ = ● : ◇ ;

∴ by the firſt caſe ● is ⊏ ◆,

that is, ◆ ⊐ ●.

∴ If there be three, &c.

F *there be any number of magnitudes, and as many others, which, taken two and two in order, have the fame ratio; the firft fhall have to the laft of the firft magnitudes the fame ratio which the firft of the others has to the laft of the fame.*

N.B.—*This is ufually cited by the words " ex æquali," or " ex æquo."*

Firft, let there be magnitudes ▼, ◆, ▪,

and as many others ◆, ◇, ●,

fuch that

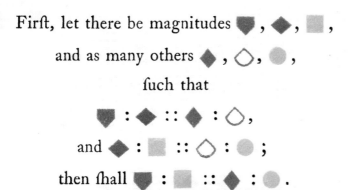

then fhall ▼ : ▪ :: ◆ : ●.

Let thefe magnitudes, as well as any equimultiples whatever of the antecedents and confequents of the ratios, ftand as follows :—

▼, ◆, ▪, ◆, ◇, ●,

and

M ▼, *m* ◆, N ▪, M ◆, *m* ◇, N ●,

becaufe ▼ : ◆ :: ◆ : ◇ ;

∴ M ▼ : *m* ◆ :: M ◆ : *m* ◇ (B. 5. p. 4).

For the fame reafon

m ◆ : N ▪ :: *m* ◇ : N ● ;

and becaufe there are three magnitudes,

M ◗, *m* ◆, N ■,

and other three, M ◆, *m* △, N ●,

which, taken two and two, have the fame ratio ;

∴ if M ◗ ⊏, =, or ⊐ N ■

then will M ◆ ⊏, =, or ⊐ N ●, by (B. 5. pr. 20) ;

and ∴ ◗ : ■ :: ◆ : ● (def. 5).

Next, let there be four magnitudes, ◗, ◆, ■, ◆,

and other four, △, ●, ▬, ▲,

which, taken two and two, have the fame ratio,

that is to fay, ◗ : ◆ :: △ : ●,

◆ : ■ :: ● : ▬,

and ■ : ◆ :: ▬ : ▲,

then fhall ◗ : ◆ :: △ : ▲ ;

for, becaufe ◗, ◆, ■, are three magnitudes,

and △, ●, ▬, other three,

which, taken two and two, have the fame ratio ;

therefore, by the foregoing cafe, ◗ : ■ :: △ : ▬,

but ■ : ◆ :: ▬ : ▲ ;

therefore again, by the firft cafe, ◗ : ◆ :: △ : ▲ ;

and fo on, whatever the number of magnitudes be.

∴ If there be any number, &c.

F *there be any number of magnitudes, and as many others, which, taken two and two in a crofs order, have the fame ratio ; the firft fhall have to the laft of the firft magnitudes the fame ratio which the firft of the others has to the laft of the fame.*

N.B.—*This is ufually cited by the words " ex æquali in proportione perturbatâ ;" or " ex æquo perturbato."*

Firft, let there be three magnitudes, , , ,

and other three, , , ,

which, taken two and two in a crofs order,

have the fame ratio ;

that is, : :: : ,

and : :: : ,

then fhall : :: : .

Let thefe magnitudes and their refpective equimultiples be arranged as follows :—

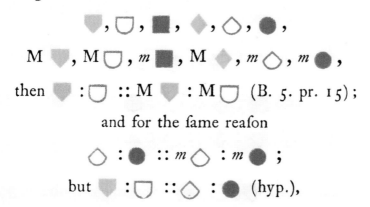

, , , , , ,

M , M , m , M , m , m ,

then : :: M : M (B. 5. pr. 15);

and for the fame reafon

 : :: m : m ;

but : :: : (hyp.),

∴ M ▽ : M ◡ :: ◇ : ● (B. 5. pr. 11);

and becaufe ◡ : ■ :: ◆ : ◇ (hyp.),

∴ M ◡ : *m* ■ :: ◆ : *m* ◇ (B. 5. pr. 4);

then, becaufe there are three magnitudes,

M ▽, M ◡, *m* ■,

and other three, M ◆, *m* ◇, *m* ●,

which, taken two and two in a crofs order, have

the fame ratio;

therefore, if M ▽ ⊏, =, or ⊐ *m* ■,

then will M ◆ ⊏, =, or ⊐ *m* ● (B. 5. pr. 21),

and ∴ ▽ : ■ :: ◆ : ● (B. 5. def. 5).

Next, let there be four magnitudes,

▽, ◡, ■, ◆,

and other four, ◇, ●, ▬, ▲,

which, when taken two and two in a crofs order, have

the fame ratio; namely,

▽ : ◡ :: ▬ : ▲,

◡ : ■ :: ● : ▬,

and ■ : ◆ :: ◇ : ●,

then fhall ▽ : ◆ :: ◇ : ▲.

For, becaufe ▽, ◡, ■ are three magnitudes,

and ● , ■ , ▲ , other three,

which, taken two and two in a crofs order, have the fame ratio,

therefore, by the firſt cafe, ⬟ : ■ :: ● : ▲ ,

but ■ : ◆ :: ◇ : ● ,

therefore again, by the firſt cafe, ⬟ : ◆ :: ◇ : ▲ ;

and ſo on, whatever be the number of ſuch magnitudes.

∴ If there be any number, &c.

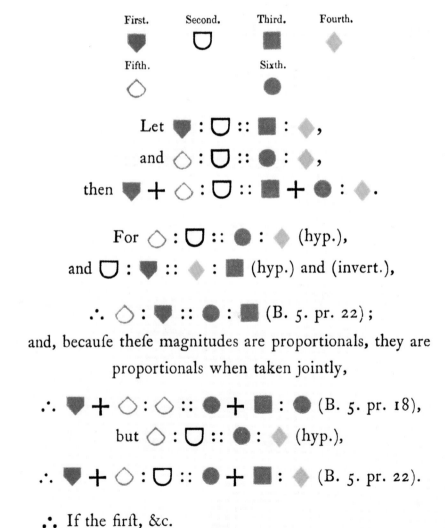

F *the firſt has to the ſecond the ſame ratio which the third has to the fourth, and the fifth to the ſecond the ſame which the ſixth has to the fourth, the firſt and fifth together ſhall have to the ſecond the ſame ratio which the third and ſixth together have to the fourth.*

∴ If the firſt, &c.

F *four magnitudes of the same kind are proportionals, the greatest and least of them together are greater than the other two together.*

Let four magnitudes, ▼ + ∪, ■ + ◆, ∪, and ◆, of the same kind, be proportionals, that is to say,

$$▼ + ∪ : ■ + ◆ :: ∪ : ◆,$$

and let ▼ + ∪ be the greatest of the four, and consequently by pr. A and 14 of Book 5, ◆ is the least;

then will ▼ + ∪ + ◆ be ⊏ ■ + ◆ + ∪;

because ▼ + ∪ : ■ + ◆ :: ∪ : ◆,

∴ ▼ : ■ :: ▼ + ∪ : ■ + ◆ (B. 5. pr. 19),

but ▼ + ∪ ⊏ ■ + ◆ (hyp.),

∴ ▼ ⊏ ■ (B. 5. pr. A);

to each of these add ∪ + ◆,

∴ ▼ + ∪ + ◆ ⊏ ■ + ∪ + ◆.

∴ If four magnitudes, &c.

DEFINITION X.

WHEN three magnitudes are proportionals, the firſt is ſaid to have to the third the duplicate ratio of that which it has to the ſecond.

For example, if A, B, C, be continued proportionals, that is, A : B :: B : C, A is ſaid to have to C the duplicate ratio of A : B ;

$$\text{or } \frac{A}{C} = \text{ the ſquare of } \frac{A}{B}.$$

This property will be more readily ſeen of the quantities $a r^2, a r, a,$ for $a r^2 : a r :: a r : a$;

$$\text{and } \frac{a r^2}{a} = r^2 = \text{ the ſquare of } \frac{a r^2}{a r} = r,$$

$$\text{or of } a, a r, a r^2;$$

$$\text{for } \frac{a}{a r^2} = \frac{1}{r^2} = \text{ the ſquare of } \frac{a}{a r} = \frac{1}{r}.$$

DEFINITION XI.

WHEN four magnitudes are continual proportionals, the firſt is ſaid to have to the fourth the triplicate ratio of that which it has to the ſecond ; and ſo on, quadruplicate, &c. increaſing the denomination ſtill by unity, in any number of proportionals.

For example, let A, B, C, D, be four continued proportionals, that is, A : B :: B : C :: C : D ; A is ſaid to have to D, the triplicate ratio of A to B ;

$$\text{or } \frac{A}{D} = \text{ the cube of } \frac{A}{B}.$$

This definition will be better underſtood, and applied to a greater number of magnitudes than four that are continued proportionals, as follows:—

Let ar^3, ar^2, ar, a, be four magnitudes in continued proportion, that is, $ar^3 : ar^2 :: ar^2 : ar :: ar : a$,

then $\dfrac{ar^3}{a} = r^3 =$ the cube of $\dfrac{ar^3}{ar^2} = r$.

Or, let ar^5, ar^4, ar^3, ar^2, ar, a, be ſix magnitudes in proportion, that is

$$ar^5 : ar^4 :: ar^4 \cdot ar^3 :: ar^3 : ar^2 :: ar^2 : ar :: ar : a,$$

then the ratio $\dfrac{ar^5}{a} = r^5 =$ the fifth power of $\dfrac{ar^5}{ar^4} = r$.

Or, let a, ar, ar^2, ar^3, ar^4, be five magnitudes in continued proportion; then $\dfrac{a}{ar^4} = \dfrac{1}{r^4} =$ the fourth power of $\dfrac{a}{ar} = \dfrac{1}{r}$.

DEFINITION A.

To know a compound ratio:—

When there are any number of magnitudes of the ſame kind, the firſt is ſaid to have to the laſt of them the ratio compounded of the ratio which the firſt has to the ſecond, and of the ratio which the ſecond has to the third, and of the ratio which the third has to the fourth; and ſo on, unto the laſt magnitude.

For example, if A, B, C, D, be four magnitudes of the ſame kind, the firſt A is ſaid to have to the laſt D the ratio compounded of the ratio of A to B, and of the ratio of B to C, and of the ratio of C to D; or, the ratio of

A B C D
E F G H K L
M N

A to D is faid to be compounded of the ratios of A to B, B to C, and C to D.

And if A has to B the fame ratio which E has to F, and B to C the fame ratio that G has to H, and C to D the fame that K has to L; then by this definition, A is said to have to D the ratio compounded of ratios which are the fame with the ratios of E to F, G to H, and K to L. And the fame thing is to be underftood when it is more briefly expreffed by faying, A has to D the ratio compounded of the ratios of E to F, G to H, and K to L.

In like manner, the fame things being fuppofed; if M has to N the fame ratio which A has to D, then for fhort-nefs fake, M is faid to have to N the ratio compounded of the ratios of E to F, G to H, and K to L.

This definition may be better underftood from an arith-metical or algebraical illuftration; for, in fact, a ratio com-pounded of feveral other ratios, is nothing more than a ratio which has for its antecedent the continued product of all the antecedents of the ratios compounded, and for its confequent the continued product of all the confequents of the ratios compounded.

Thus, the ratio compounded of the ratios of

2 : 3, 4 : 7, 6 : 11, 2 : 5,

is the ratio of 2 × 4 × 6 × 2 : 3 × 7 × 11 × 5,

or the ratio of 96 : 1155, or 32 : 385.

And of the magnitudes A, B, C, D, E, F, of the fame kind, A : F is the ratio compounded of the ratios of

A : B, B : C, C : D, D : E, E : F;

for A × B × C × D × E : B × C × D × E × F,

or $\frac{A \times B \times C \times D \times E}{B \times C \times D \times E \times F} = \frac{A}{F}$, or the ratio of A : F.

ATIOS *which are compounded of the same ratios are the same to one another.*

Let A : B :: F : G,
    B : C :: G : H,
    C : D :: H : K,
and D : E :: K : L.

A	B	C	D	E
F	G	H	K	L

Then the ratio which is compounded of the ratios of A : B, B : C, C : D, D : E, or the ratio of A : E, is the same as the ratio compounded of the ratios of F : G, G : H, H : K, K : L, or the ratio of F : L.

$$\text{For } \frac{A}{B} = \frac{F}{G},$$

$$\frac{B}{C} = \frac{G}{H},$$

$$\frac{C}{D} = \frac{H}{K},$$

$$\text{and } \frac{D}{E} = \frac{K}{L};$$

$$\therefore \frac{A \times B \times C \times D}{B \times C \times D \times E} = \frac{F \times G \times H \times K}{G \times H \times K \times L},$$

$$\text{and } \therefore \frac{A}{E} = \frac{F}{L},$$

or the ratio of A : E is the same as the ratio of F : L.

The same may be demonstrated of any number of ratios so circumstanced.

Next, let A : B :: K : L,
    B : C :: H : K,
    C : D :: G : H,
    D : E :: F : G.

Then the ratio which is compounded of the ratios of A : B, B : C, C : D, D : E, or the ratio of A : E, is the fame as the ratio compounded of the ratios of K : L, H : K, G : H, F : G, or the ratio of F : L.

$$\text{For } \frac{A}{B} = \frac{K}{L},$$

$$\frac{B}{C} = \frac{H}{K},$$

$$\frac{C}{D} = \frac{G}{H},$$

$$\text{and } \frac{D}{E} = \frac{F}{G};$$

$$\therefore \frac{A \times B \times C \times D}{B \times C \times D \times E} = \frac{K \times H \times G \times F}{L \times K \times H \times G},$$

$$\text{and } \therefore \frac{A}{E} = \frac{F}{L},$$

or the ratio of A : E is the fame as the ratio of F : L.

∴ Ratios which are compounded, &c.

F *several ratios be the same to several ratios, each to each, the ratio which is compounded of ratios which are the same to the first ratios, each to each, shall be the same to the ratio compounded of ratios which are the same to the other ratios, each to each.*

A B C D E F G H	P Q R S T
a b c d e f g h	V W X Y Z

If A : B :: a : b | and A : B :: P : Q | a : b :: V : W
$\quad$ C : D :: c : d | $\quad$ C : D :: Q : R | c : d :: W : X
$\quad$ E : F :: e : f | $\quad$ E : F :: R : S | e : f :: X : Y
and G : H :: g : h | $\quad$ G : H :: S : T | g : h :: Y : Z

then P : T $=$ V : Z.

For $\dfrac{P}{Q} = \dfrac{A}{B} = \dfrac{a}{b} = \dfrac{V}{W},$

$\dfrac{Q}{R} = \dfrac{C}{D} = \dfrac{c}{d} = \dfrac{W}{X},$

$\dfrac{R}{S} = \dfrac{E}{F} = \dfrac{e}{f} = \dfrac{X}{Y},$

$\dfrac{S}{T} = \dfrac{G}{H} = \dfrac{g}{h} = \dfrac{Y}{Z};$

and $\therefore$ $\dfrac{P \times Q \times R \times S}{Q \times R \times S \times T} = \dfrac{V \times W \times X \times Y}{W \times X \times Y \times Z},$

and $\therefore$ $\dfrac{P}{T} = \dfrac{V}{Z},$

or P : T $=$ V : Z.

$\therefore$ If several ratios, &c.

F *a ratio which is compounded of several ratios be the same to a ratio which is compounded of several other ratios; and if one of the first ratios, or the ratio which is compounded of several of them, be the same to one of the last ratios, or to the ratio which is compounded of several of them; then the remaining ratio of the first, or, if there be more than one, the ratio compounded of the remaining ratios, shall be the same to the remaining ratio of the last, or, if there be more than one, to the ratio compounded of these remaining ratios.*

```
A B C D E F G H
P Q R S T X
```

Let A : B, B : C, C : D, D : E, E : F, F : G, G : H, be the first ratios, and P : Q, Q : R, R : S, S : T, T : X, the other ratios; also, let A : H, which is compounded of the first ratios, be the same as the ratio of P : X, which is the ratio compounded of the other ratios; and, let the ratio of A : E, which is compounded of the ratios of A : B, B : C, C : D, D : E, be the same as the ratio of P : R, which is compounded of the ratios P : Q, Q : R.

Then the ratio which is compounded of the remaining first ratios, that is, the ratio compounded of the ratios E : F, F : G, G : H, that is, the ratio of E : H, shall be the same as the ratio of R : X, which is compounded of the ratios of R : S, S : T, T : X, the remaining other ratios.

Becaufe $\dfrac{A \times B \times C \times D \times E \times F \times G}{B \times C \times D \times E \times F \times G \times H} = \dfrac{P \times Q \times R \times S \times T}{Q \times R \times S \times T \times X}$,

or $\dfrac{A \times B \times C \times D}{B \times C \times D \times E} \times \dfrac{E \times F \times G}{F \times G \times H} = \dfrac{P \times Q}{Q \times R} \times \dfrac{R \times S \times T}{S \times T \times X}$,

and $\dfrac{A \times B \times C \times D}{B \times C \times D \times E} = \dfrac{P \times Q}{Q \times R}$,

$\therefore \dfrac{E \times F \times G}{F \times G \times H} = \dfrac{R \times S \times T}{S \times T \times X}$,

$\therefore \dfrac{E}{H} = \dfrac{R}{X}$,

$\therefore E : H = R : X.$

$\therefore$ If a ratio which, &c.

F *there be any number of ratios, and any number of other ratios, such that the ratio which is compounded of ratios, which are the same to the first ratios, each to each, is the same to the ratio which is compounded of ratios, which are the same, each to each, to the last ratios—and if one of the first ratios, or the ratio which is compounded of ratios, which are the same to several of the first ratios, each to each, be the same to one of the last ratios, or to the ratio which is compounded of ratios, which are the same, each to each, to several of the last ratios—then the remaining ratio of the first ; or, if there be more than one, the ratio which is compounded of ratios, which are the same, each to each, to the remaining ratios of the first, shall be the same to the remaining ratio of the last ; or, if there be more than one, to the ratio which is compounded of ratios, which are the same, each to each, to these remaining ratios.*

$$
\begin{array}{ll}
\quad\quad\text{h }\;\text{k m n s} & \\
\text{AB, CD, EF, GH, KL, MN,} & a\;b\;c\;d\;e\;f\;g \\
\quad\text{OP, QR, ST, VW, XY,} & h\;k\;l\;m\;n\;p \\
\quad\quad\text{a b c d}\quad\text{e}\quad\text{f g} &
\end{array}
$$

Let A : B, C : D, E : F, G : H, K : L, M : N, be the first ratios, and O : P, Q : R, S : T, V : W, X : Y, the other ratios ;

$$
\begin{aligned}
\text{and let } A : B &= a : b, \\
C : D &= b : c, \\
E : F &= c : d, \\
G : H &= d : e, \\
K : L &= e : f, \\
M : N &= f : g.
\end{aligned}
$$

Then, by the definition of a compound ratio, the ratio of $a:g$ is compounded of the ratios of $a:b, b:c, c:d, d:e,$ $e:f, f\cdot g,$ which are the fame as the ratio of A : B, C : D, E : F, G : H, K : L, M : N, each to each.

$$
\begin{aligned}
\text{Alfo, } O :P &= h:k,\\
Q :R &= k:l,\\
S :T &= l:m,\\
V :W &= m:n,\\
X :Y &= n:p.
\end{aligned}
$$

Then will the ratio of $h:p$ be the ratio compounded of the ratios of $h:k, k:l, l:m, m:n, n:p,$ which are the fame as the ratios of O :P, Q :R, S :T, V :W, X :Y, each to each.

$\therefore$ by the hypothefis $a:g = h:p.$

Alfo, let the ratio which is compounded of the ratios of A : B, C : D, two of the firft ratios (or the ratios of $a:c,$ for A : B $= a:b,$ and C : D $= b:c$), be the fame as the ratio of a : d, which is compounded of the ratios of a : b, b : c, c : d, which are the fame as the ratios of O :P, Q : R, S : T, three of the other ratios.

And let the ratios of h : s, which is compounded of the ratios of h : k, k : m, m : n, n : s, which are the fame as the remaining firft ratios, namely, E : F, G : H, K : L, M : N ; alfo, let the ratio of e : g, be that which is compounded of the ratios e : f, f : g, which are the fame, each to each, to the remaining other ratios, namely, V : W, X : Y. Then the ratio of h : s fhall be the fame as the ratio of e : g; or h : s $= e:g.$

For $\dfrac{A \times C \times E \times G \times K \times M}{B \times D \times F \times H \times L \times N} = \dfrac{a \times b \times c \times d \times e \times f}{b \times c \times d \times e \times f \times g},$

and $\dfrac{O\times Q\times S\times V\times X}{P\times R\times T\times W\times Y} = \dfrac{h\times k\times l\times m\times n}{k\times l\times m\times n\times p},$

by the compofition of the ratios;

$\therefore \dfrac{a\times b\times c\times d\times e\times f}{b\times c\times d\times e\times f\times g} = \dfrac{h\times k\times l\times m\times n}{k\times l\times m\times n\times p}$ (hyp.),

or $\dfrac{a\times b}{b\times c}\times\dfrac{c\times d\times e\times f}{d\times e\times f\times g} = \dfrac{h\times k\times l}{k\times l\times m}\times\dfrac{m\times n}{n\times p},$

but $\dfrac{a\times b}{b\times c} = \dfrac{A\times C}{B\times D} = \dfrac{O\times Q\times S}{P\times R\times T} = \dfrac{a\times b\times c}{b\times c\times d} = \dfrac{h\times k\times l}{k\times l\times m};$

$\therefore \dfrac{c\times d\times e\times f}{d\times e\times f\times g} = \dfrac{m\times n}{n\times p}.$

And $\dfrac{c\times d\times e\times f}{d\times e\times f\times g} = \dfrac{h\times k\times m\times n}{k\times m\times n\times s}$ (hyp.),

and $\dfrac{m\times n}{n\times p} = \dfrac{e\times f}{f\times g}$ (hyp.),

$\therefore \dfrac{h\times k\times m\times n}{k\times m\times n\times s} = \dfrac{e\,f}{f\,g},$

$\therefore \dfrac{h}{s} = \dfrac{e}{g},$

$\therefore h : s = e : g.$

$\therefore$ If there be any number, &c.

⁎ Algebraical and Arithmetical expositions of the Fifth Book of Euclid are given in Byrne's Doctrine of Proportion; published by WILLIAMS and Co. London. 1841.

BOOK VI.

DEFINITIONS.

I.

RECTILINEAR figures are faid to be fimilar, when they have their feveral angles equal, each to each, and the fides about the equal angles proportional.

II.

Two fides of one figure are faid to be reciprocally proportional to two fides of another figure when one of the fides of the firft is to the fecond, as the remaining fide of the fecond is to the remaining fide of the firft.

III.

A STRAIGHT line is faid to be cut in extreme and mean ratio, when the whole is to the greater fegment, as the greater fegment is to the lefs.

IV.

THE altitude of any figure is the straight line drawn from its vertex perpendicular to its bafe, or the bafe produced.

RIANGLES *and parallelograms having the same altitude are to one another as their bafes.*

Let the triangles ◣ and ◣ have a common vertex, and their bafes ▬ and ▬ in the fame ftraight line.

Produce ▬▬▬ both ways, take fucceffively on ▬▬ produced lines equal to it; and on ▬▬ produced lines fucceffively equal to it; and draw lines from the common vertex to their extremities.

The triangles ◣ thus formed are all equal to one another, fince their bafes are equal. (B. 1. pr. 38.)

∴ ◣ and its bafe are refpectively equi-

multiples of ◢ and the bafe ▬▬▬.

In like manner  and its bafe are refpec-

tively equimultiples of ▲ and the bafe ▬.

∴ If *m* or 6 times ⊏ = or ⊐ *n* or 5 times

then *m* or 6 times ▬ ⊏ = or ⊐ *n* or 5 times ▬,

m and *n* ftand for every multiple taken as in the fifth definition of the Fifth Book. Although we have only fhown that this property exifts when *m* equal 6, and *n* equal 5, yet it is evident that the property holds good for every multiple value that may be given to *m*, and to *n*.

∴ ▲ : ▲ :: ▬ : ▬ (B. 5. def. 5.)

Parallelograms having the fame altitude are the doubles of the triangles, on their bafes, and are proportional to them (Part 1), and hence their doubles, the parallelograms, are as their bafes. (B. 5. pr. 15.)

Q. E. D.

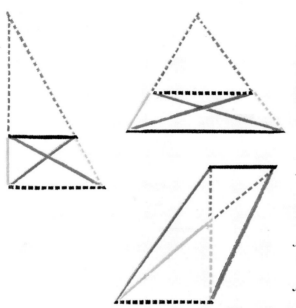

F *a straight line* ━━━ *be drawn parallel to any side* ┅┅┅ *of a triangle, it shall cut the other sides, or those sides produced, into proportional segments.*

And if any straight line ━━━ *divide the sides of a triangle, or those sides produced, into proportional segments, it is parallel to the remaining side* ┅┅┅.

PART I.

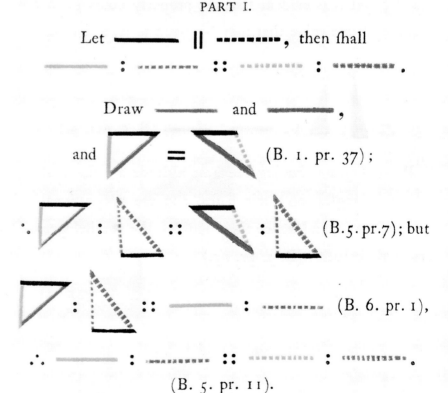

(B. 5. pr. 11).

PART II.

Let ———— : ·········· :: ············ : ··········· ,

then ——— ‖ ·········· .

Let the fame conftruction remain,

becaufe ———— : ·········· :: ▷ : ◺ ⎫
⎬ (B. 6. pr. 1) ;
and ·········· : ·········· :: ◣ : ◺ ⎭

but ———— : ·········· :: ·········· : ··········· (hyp.),

∴ ▷ : ◺ :: ◣ : ◺ (B. 5. pr. 11.)

∴ ▷ = ◣ (B. 5. pr. 9) ;

but they are on the fame bafe ·········· , and at the
fame fide of it, and

∴ ——— ‖ ·········· (B. 1. pr. 39).

Q. E. D.

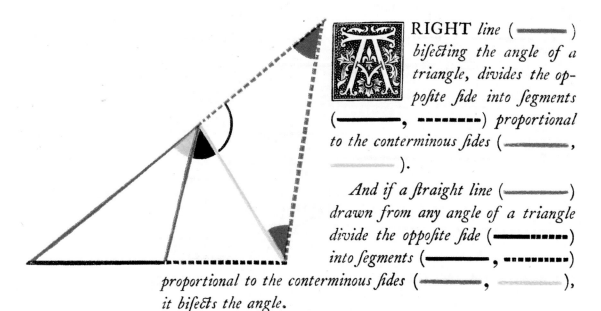

RIGHT *line* (———)
*bisecting the angle of a
triangle, divides the op-
posite side into segments*
(———, ————) *proportional
to the conterminous sides* (———,
————).

And if a straight line (———)
*drawn from any angle of a triangle
divide the opposite side* (———————)
into segments (———————, ————————)
proportional to the conterminous sides (———————, ———————),
it bisects the angle.

PART I.

Draw ———— ‖ ————, to meet ————;

then, ◢ = ◢ (B. 1. pr. 29),

∴ ◣ = ◤ ; but ◣ = ◤, ∴ ◥ = ◢,

∴ ———— = ———— (B. 1. pr. 6);

and because ———— ‖ ————,

———— : ———— ∷ ———— : ————
(B. 6. pr. 2);

but ———— = ————;

∴ ———— : ———— ∷ ———— : ————
(B. 5. pr. 7).

PART II.

Let the fame conftruction remain,

and ▬▬▬ : ▬▬▬ :: ▬▬▬ : ▬▬▬

(B. 6. pr. 2) ;

but ▬▬▬ : ▬▬▬ :: ▬▬▬ : ▬▬▬ (hyp.)

∴ ▬▬▬ : ▬▬▬ :: ▬▬▬ : ▬▬▬

(B. 5. pr. 11).

and ∴ ▬▬▬ = ▬▬▬ (B. 5. pr. 9),

and ∴ ◀ = ▼ (B. 1. pr. 5) ; but fince

▬▬▬ ‖ ▬▬▬ ; ▲ = ▼,

and ◀ = ◀ (B. 1. pr. 29) ;

∴ ◀ = ▼, and ◀ = ▲,

and ∴ ▬▬▬ bifects ◣.

Q. E. D.

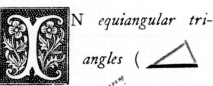 N *equiangular tri-*
angles ( )

and) *the fides*
about the equal angles are pro-
portional, and the fides which are
oppofite to the equal angles are
homologous.

Let the equiangular triangles be fo placed that two fides

━━━ , ┅┅┅ oppofite to equal angles 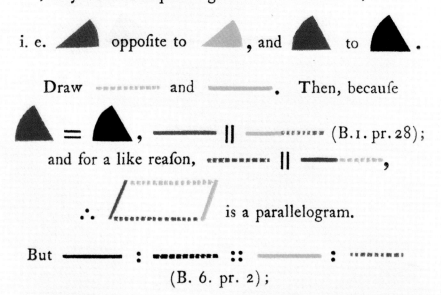 and

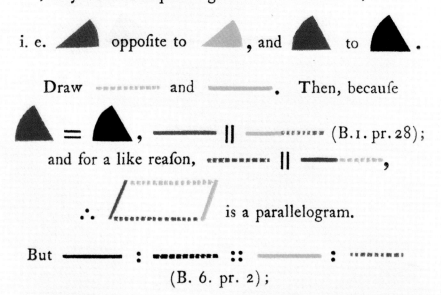 may be conterminous, and in the fame ftraight line;
and that the triangles lying at the fame fide of that ftraight
line, may have the equal angles not conterminous,

i. e. oppofite to , and to .

Draw ┅┅┅ and ━━━. Then, becaufe

 = , ━━━ ‖ ┅┅┅ (B. 1. pr. 28);

and for a like reafon, ┅┅┅ ‖ ━━━,

∴ is a parallelogram.

But ━━━ : ┅┅┅ :: ━━━ : ┅┅┅

(B. 6. pr. 2);

and fince ——— = ——— (B. 1. pr. 34),

——— : ·········· :: ——— : ············ ; and by

alternation, ——— : ——— :: ············ : ············

(B. 5. pr. 16).

In like manner it may be fhown, that

——— : ············ :: ——— : ············ ;

and by alternation, that

——— : ——— :: ············ : ············ ;

but it has been already proved that

——— : ——— :: ············ : ············ ,

and therefore, ex æquali,

——— : ——— :: ············ : ············

(B. 5. pr. 22),

therefore the fides about the equal angles are proportional,
and thofe which are oppofite to the equal angles
are homologous.

Q. E. D.

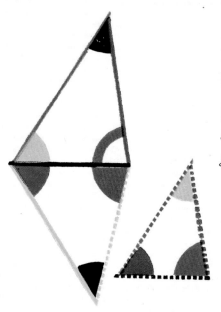

F *two triangles have their fides propor-tional* (▬▬ : ▬▬ :: ▬▬ : ▬▬) *and* (▬▬ : ▬▬ :: ▬▬ : ▬▬) *they are equiangular, and the equal angles are fubtended by the homolo-gous fides.*

From the extremities of ▬▬ , draw ▬▬ and ▬▬ , making

▼ = ◢ ,

◣ = ◢ (B. 1. pr. 23);

and confequently ▼ = ◣ (B. 1. pr. 32),

and fince the triangles are equiangular,

▬▬ : ▬▬ :: ▬▬ : ▬▬

(B. 6. pr. 4);

but ▬▬ : ▬▬ :: ▬▬ : ▬▬ (hyp.);

∴ ▬▬ : ▬▬ :: ▬▬ : ▬▬ ,

and confequently ▬▬ = ▬▬ (B. 5. pr. 9).

In the like manner it may be fhown that

▬▬ = ▬▬ .

Therefore, the two triangles having a common bafe ———, and their fides equal, have alfo equal angles oppofite to equal fides, i. e.

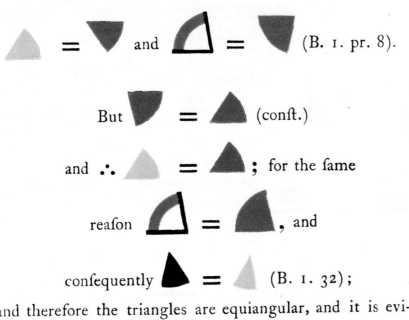

and therefore the triangles are equiangular, and it is evident that the homologous fides fubtend the equal angles.

Q. E. D.

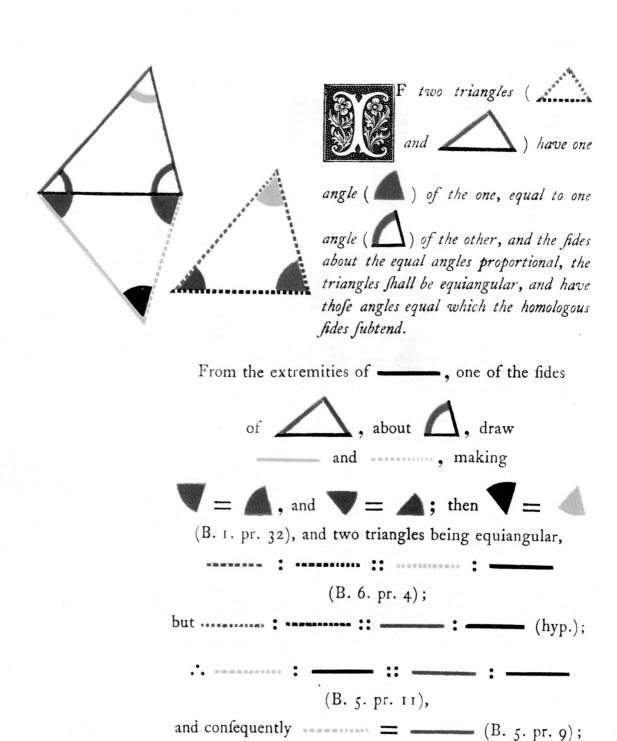

F *two triangles* (*and*) *have one angle* ( ) *of the one, equal to one angle* ( ) *of the other, and the fides about the equal angles proportional, the triangles fhall be equiangular, and have thofe angles equal which the homologous fides fubtend.*

From the extremities of ▬▬▬, one of the fides

of , about , draw

▬▬▬ and ▬▬▬ , making

▼ = ◣ , and ▼ = ◣ ; then ▼ = ◢

(B. 1. pr. 32), and two triangles being equiangular,

▬▬▬ : ▬▬▬ :: ▬▬▬ : ▬▬▬

(B. 6. pr. 4);

but ▬▬▬ : ▬▬▬ :: ▬▬▬ : ▬▬▬ (hyp.);

∴ ▬▬▬ : ▬▬▬ :: ▬▬▬ : ▬▬▬

(B. 5. pr. 11),

and confequently ▬▬▬ = ▬▬▬ (B. 5. pr. 9);

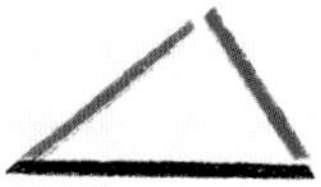

∴ △ = ▽ in every refpect.

(B. 1. pr. 4).

But ▼ = ▲ (conft.),

and ∴ △ = ▲ ; and

fince alfo △ = ◢ ,

△ = ◣ (B. 1. pr. 32) ;

and ∴ △ and △ are equiangular, with their equal angles oppofite to homologous fides.

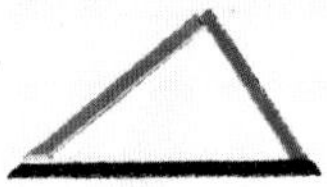

Q. E. D.

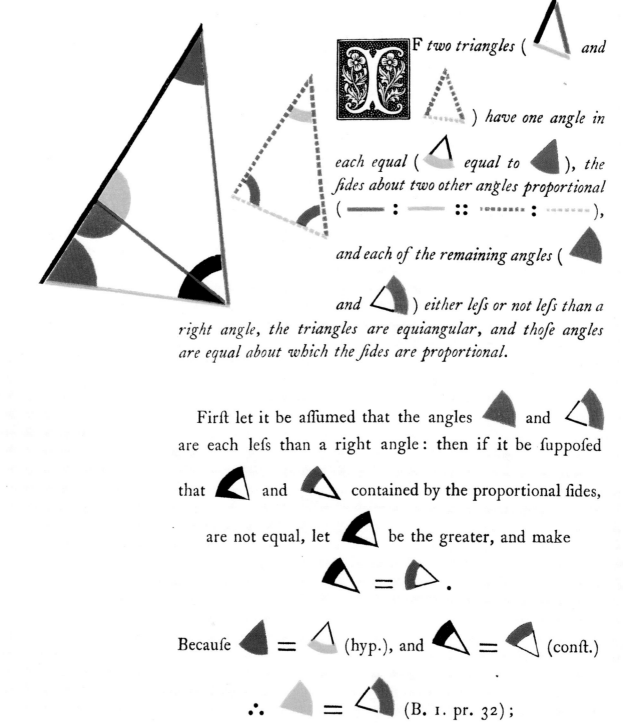

F *two triangles* (and

) *have one angle in*
each equal (equal to), *the*
fides about two other angles proportional
(— : — :: ⋯⋯ : ⋯⋯),

and each of the remaining angles (

and) *either lefs or not lefs than a*
right angle, the triangles are equiangular, and thofe angles
are equal about which the fides are proportional.

First let it be affumed that the angles and
are each lefs than a right angle: then if it be fuppofed

that and contained by the proportional fides,

are not equal, let be the greater, and make

$$ = .$$

Becaufe = (hyp.), and = (conft.)

∴ = (B. 1. pr. 32);

∴ —— : —— :: —— : ——

(B. 6. pr. 4),

but —— : —— :: —— : —— (hyp.)

∴ —— : —— :: —— : —— ;

∴ —— = —— (B. 5. pr. 9),

and ∴ ◢ = ◣ (B. 1. pr. 5).

But ◢ is lefs than a right angle (hyp.)

∴ ◢ is lefs than a right angle ; and ∴ ◣ muſt be greater than a right angle (B. 1. pr. 13), but it has been proved = ◣ and therefore lefs than a right angle, which is abſurd. ∴ ◢ and ◣ are not unequal;

∴ they are equal, and ſince ◢ = ◣ (hyp.)

∴ ◢ = ◣ (B. 1. pr. 32), and therefore the triangles are equiangular.

But if ◢ and ◣ be aſſumed to be each not lefs than a right angle, it may be proved as before, that the triangles are equiangular, and have the ſides about the equal angles proportional. (B. 6. pr. 4).

Q. E. D.

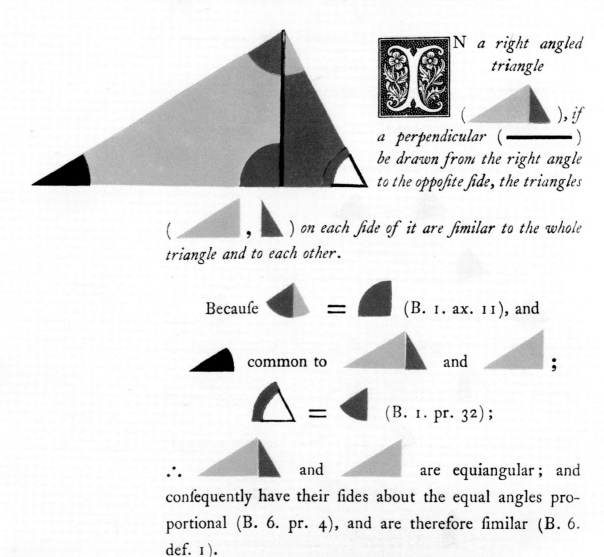

N *a right angled triangle*

( ), *if a perpendicular* (——————) *be drawn from the right angle to the oppofite fide, the triangles*

(,) *on each fide of it are fimilar to the whole triangle and to each other.*

Becaufe = (B. 1. ax. 11), and

common to and ;

= (B. 1. pr. 32);

∴ and are equiangular; and confequently have their fides about the equal angles pro-portional (B. 6. pr. 4), and are therefore fimilar (B. 6. def. 1).

In like manner it may be proved that is fimilar to

; but has been fhewn to be fimilar

to ; ∴ and are fimilar to the whole and to each other.

Q. E. D.

ROM *a given straight line* (━━ ▪ ▪ ▪) *to cut off any required part.*

From either extremity of the given line draw ━━▪▪▪▪ making any angle with ━━ ▪ ▪ ; and produce ━━▪▪▪ till the whole produced line ━━▪▪▪▪ contains ━━ as often as ━━▪▪▪ contains the required part.

Draw ━━, and draw ▪▪▪▪▪ ‖ ━━.

━━ is the required part of ━━ ▪ ▪ ▪.

For since ▪▪▪▪▪ ‖ ━━

━━ : ▪▪▪▪▪ :: ━━ : ▪▪▪▪▪

(B. 6. pr. 2), and by composition (B. 5. pr. 18);

━━ : ━━ :: ━━▪▪▪ : ━━ ;

but ━━▪▪▪ contains ━━ as often as ━━▪▪▪ contains the required part (conft.);

∴ ━━ is the required part.

Q. E. D.

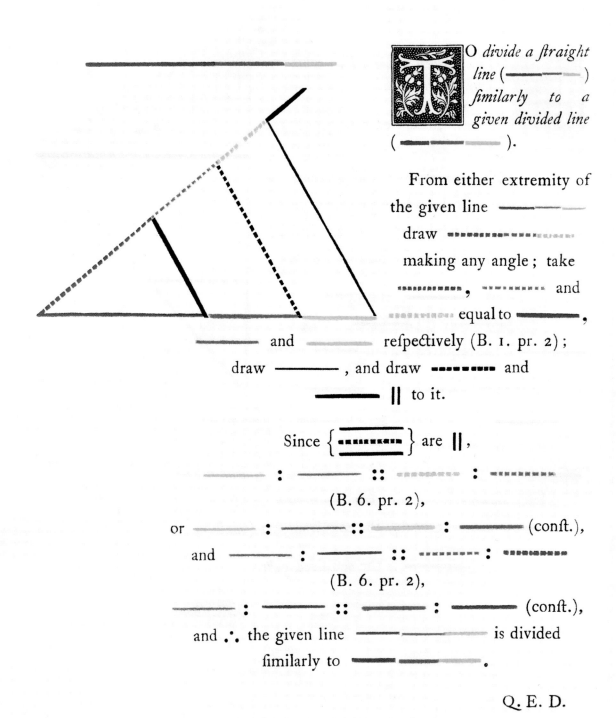

T O *divide a straight line* (━━━━━) *similarly to a given divided line* (━━━━━).

From either extremity of the given line ━━━━━ draw ▬▬▬▬▬▬ making any angle ; take ▬▬▬, ▬▬▬ and ▬▬▬ equal to ━━━, respectively (B. 1. pr. 2); draw ───────, and draw ▰▰▰▰▰ and ━━━━ ‖ to it.

Since { ▰▰▰▰▰ } are ‖,

━━━ : ━━━ :: ━━━ : ━━━

(B. 6. pr. 2),

or ━━━ : ━━━ :: ━━━ : ━━━ (conſt.),

and ━━━ : ━━━ :: ▰▰▰ : ▰▰▰

(B. 6. pr. 2),

━━━ : ━━━ :: ━━━ : ━━━ (conſt.),

and ∴ the given line ━━━━━ is divided ſimilarly to ━━━━━ .

Q. E. D.

T O *find a third proportional to two given straight lines* (———— *and* ————).

At either extremity of the given line ———— draw ━ ━ ━ ━ making an angle; take ┅┅┅┅ = ————, and draw ▬▬▬ ; make ━━━ = ————, and draw ┄┄┄ || ▬▬▬ ; (B. 1. pr. 31.) ———— is the third proportional to ———— and ————.

For fince ▬▬▬ || ━ ━ ━ ,

∴ ———— : ━━━ :: ┅┅┅┅ : ▬▬▬ (B. 6 pr. 2);

but ━━━ = ┅┅┅┅ = ———— (conft.);

∴ ———— : ━━━ :: ———— : ———— .

(B. 5. pr. 7).

Q. E. D.

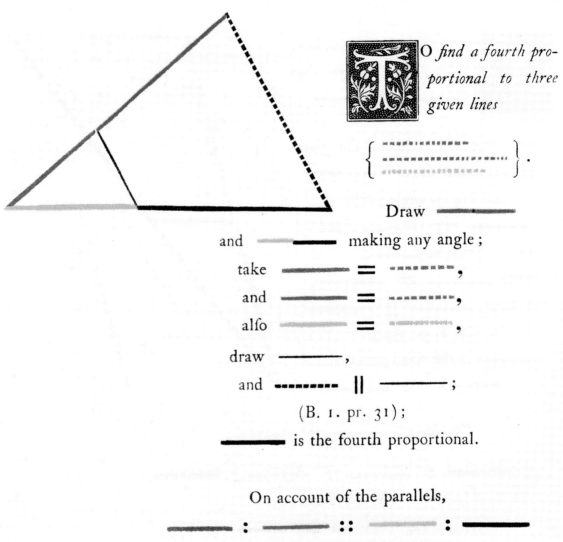

T O *find a fourth proportional to three given lines*

$\left\{ \begin{array}{c} \rule{2cm}{0.4pt} \\ \rule{2cm}{0.4pt} \\ \rule{2cm}{0.4pt} \end{array} \right\}$.

Draw ▬▬▬

and ▬▬▬ making any angle;

take ▬▬▬ = ▬▬▬ ,

and ▬▬▬ = ▬▬▬ ,

alfo ▬▬▬ = ▬▬▬ ,

draw ———— ,

and ▪▪▪▪▪▪ ‖ ———— ;

(B. 1. pr. 31);

▬▬▬ is the fourth proportional.

On account of the parallels,

▬▬▬ : ▬▬▬ :: ▬▬▬ : ▬▬▬

(B. 6. pr. 2);

but $\left\{ \begin{array}{c} \rule{1.5cm}{0.4pt} \\ \rule{1.5cm}{0.4pt} \end{array} \right\}$ = $\left\{ \begin{array}{c} \rule{1.5cm}{0.4pt} \\ \rule{1.5cm}{0.4pt} \end{array} \right\}$ (conft.);

∴ ▬▬▬ : ▬▬▬ :: ▬▬▬ : ▬▬▬ .

(B. 5. pr. 7).

Q. E. D.

O *find a mean propor-
tional between two given
ftraight lines*

{ ⸻ }.

Draw any ftraight line ⸻,

make ⸻ = ⸻,

and ⸻ = ⸻; bifect ⸻:

and from the point of bifection as a centre, and half the

line as a radius, defcribe a femicircle ⌒,

draw ⸻ ⊥ ⸻:

⸻ is the mean proportional required.

Draw ⸻ and ⸻.

Since ◢ is a right angle (B. 3. pr. 31),

and ⸻ is ⊥ from it upon the oppofite fide,

∴ ⸻ is a mean proportional between

⸻ and ⸻ (B. 6. pr. 8),

and ∴ between ⸻ and ⸻ (conft.).

Q. E. D

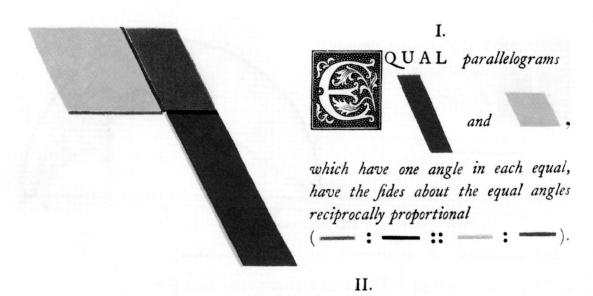

I.

QUAL *parallelograms* and ,

which have one angle in each equal, have the fides about the equal angles reciprocally proportional

(━━━ : ━━━ :: ━━━ : ━━━).

II.

And parallelograms which have one angle in each equal, and the fides about them reciprocally proportional, are equal.

Let ━━━ and ━━━; and ━━━ and ━━━, be fo placed that ━━━ and ━━━ may be continued right lines. It is evident that they may affume this pofition. (B. 1. prs. 13, 14, 15.)

Complete .

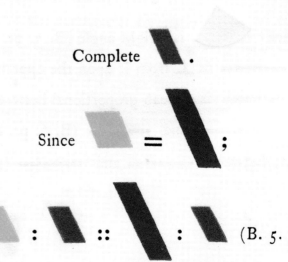

Since = ;

∴ : :: :   (B. 5. pr. 7.)

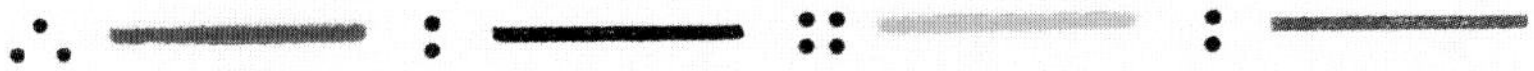

∴ ——— : ——— :: ——— : ———

(B. 6. pr. 1.)

The fame conftruction remaining :

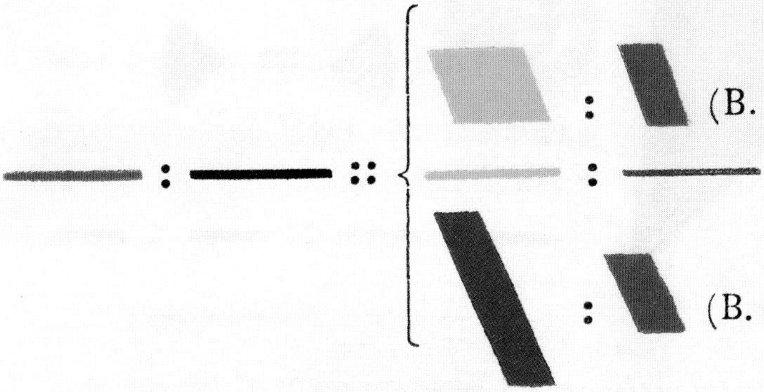

⬛ : ⬛ (B. 6. pr. 1.)

——— : ——— :: { ——— : ——— (hyp.)

⬛ : ⬛ (B. 6. pr. 1.)

∴ ⬛ : ⬛ :: ⬛ : ⬛ (B. 5. pr. 11.)

and ∴ ⬛ = ⬛ (B. 5. pr. 9).

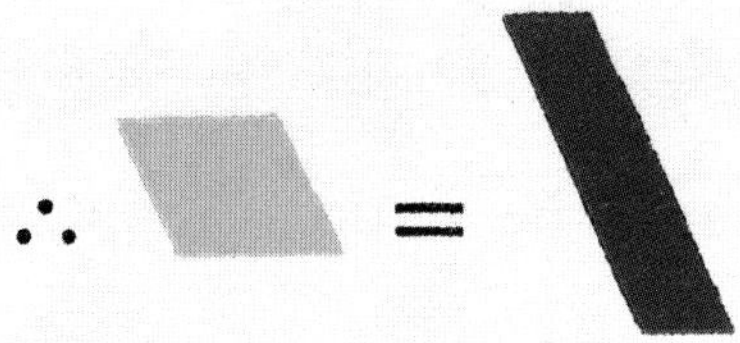

Q. E. D.

I.

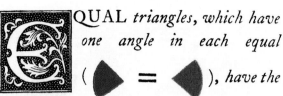QUAL *triangles, which have one angle in each equal* (=), *have the fides about the equal angles reciprocally proportional*

(—— : —— :: —— : ——).

II.

And two triangles which have an angle of the one equal to an angle of the other, and the fides about the equal angles reciprocally proportional, are equal.

I.

Let the triangles be fo placed that the equal angles ◣ and ◢ may be vertically oppofite, that is to fay, fo that —— and —— may be in the fame ftraight line. Whence alfo —— and —— muft be in the fame ftraight line. (B. 1. pr. 14.)

Draw ▪▪▪▪▪▪▪, then

—— : —— :: ◣ : ▼ (B. 6. pr. 1.)

:: ◤ : ▼ (B. 5. pr. 7.)

:: —— : —— (B. 6. pr. 1.)

∴ ▬ : ▬ :: ▬ : ▬

(B. 5. pr. 11.)

II.

Let the fame conftruction remain, and

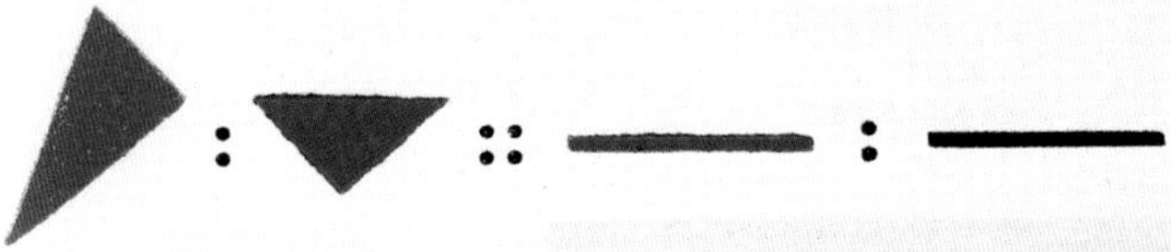

▲ : ▼ :: ▬ : ▬ (B. 6. pr. 1.)

and ▬ : ▬ :: ◀ : ▼

(B. 6. pr. 1.)

But ▬ : ▬ :: ▬ : ▬ , (hyp.)

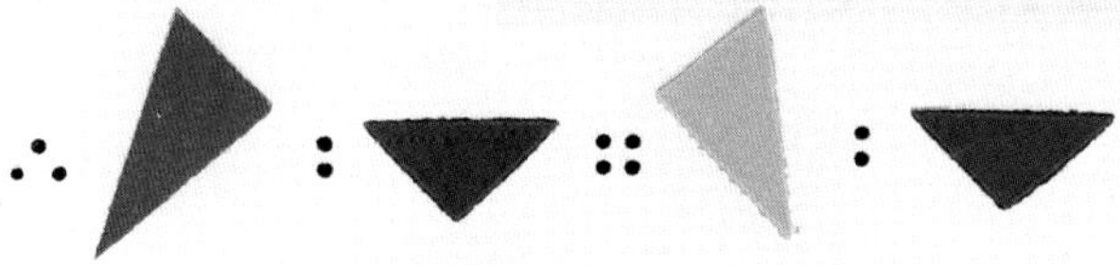

∴ ▲ : ▼ :: ◀ : ▼ (B. 5 pr. 11);

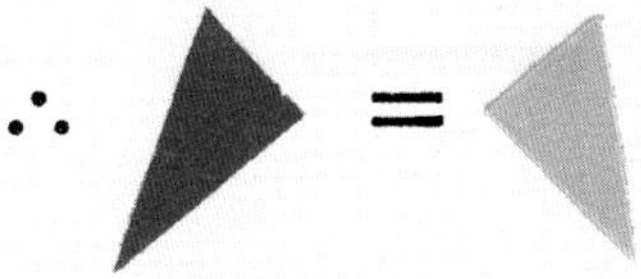

∴ ▲ = ◀ (B. 5. pr. 9.)

Q. E. D.

PART I.

F *four straight lines be proportional*

(—— : —— :: ·—·—· : ·····—·),

the rectangle (—— ✕ ·····—·) *contained*
by the extremes, is equal to the rectangle

(—— ✕ ·····—·) *contained by the means.*

PART II.

And if the rect-
angle contained by
the extremes be equal
to the rectangle con-
tained by the means,
the four straight lines
are proportional.

PART I.

From the extremities of —— and —— draw
—— and —— ⊥ to them and ═ ·····—·
and ·—·—· respectively: complete the parallelograms

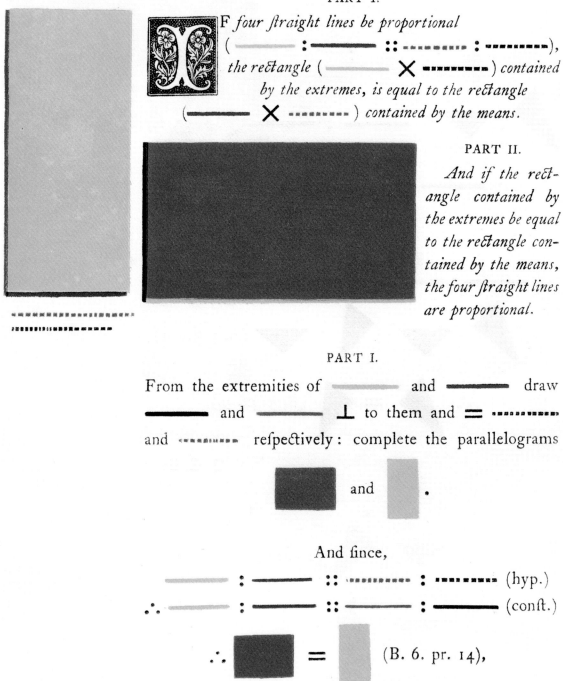

and .

And since,

—— : —— :: ·—·—· : ·····—· (hyp.)

∴ —— : —— :: —— : —— (conft.)

∴ ▢ = ▢ (B. 6. pr. 14),

that is, the rectangle contained by the extremes, equal to
the rectangle contained by the means.

PART II.

Let the fame conſtruction remain; becauſe

━━━━━ = ━━━━━ , ▬▬▬ = ▮

and ━━━━━ = ━━━━━ ,

∴ ━━━━━ : ━━━━━ :: ━━━━━ : ━━━━━

(B. 6. pr. 14).

But ━━━━━ = ━━━━━ ,

and ━━━━━ = ━━━━━ (conſt.)

∴ ━━━━━ : ━━━━━ :: ━━━━━ : ━━━━━

(B. 5. pr. 7).

Q. E. D.

PART I

F *three ſtraight lines be pro-portional* (———— : ———— :: ———— : ————) *the rectangle under the extremes is equal to the ſquare of the mean.*

PART II.

And if the rectangle under the ex-tremes be equal to the ſquare of the mean, the three ſtraight lines are proportional.

PART I.

Aſſume ———— = ————, and

ſince ———— : ———— :: ———— : ————,

then ———— : ———— :: ———— : ————,

∴ ———— × ———— = ———— × ————

(B. 6. pr. 16).

But ———— = ————,

∴ ———— × ———— = ———— × ————,

or = ————^{2}; therefore, if the three ſtraight lines are proportional, the rectangle contained by the extremes is equal to the ſquare of the mean.

PART II.

Aſſume ———— = ————, then

———— × ———— = ———— × ————,

∴ ———— : ———— :: ———— : ————

(B. 6. pr. 16), and

∴ ———— : ———— :: ———— : ————.

Q. E. D.

N a given *ſtraight line* (────) to *conſtruct a rectilinear figure ſimilar to a given one* ( ) and *ſimilarly placed.*

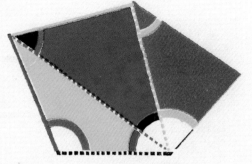

Reſolve the given figure into triangles by drawing the lines ──────── and ──────── .

At the extremities of ──── make

▲ = △ and ◣ = ◗ :

again at the extremities of ──── make ◀ = ◣

and ◀ = ◁ : in like manner make

◣ = ▷ and ▶ = ▶ .

Then ◹ is ſimilar to ◹ .

It is evident from the conſtruction and (B. 1. pr. 32) that the figures are equiangular; and ſince the triangles

◸ and ◸ are equiangular; then by (B. 6. pr. 4),

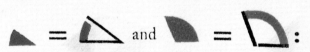

and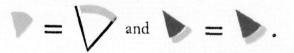

Again, becaufe 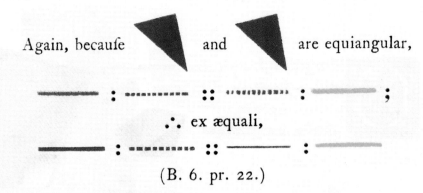 and ⬛ are equiangular,

▬▬▬ : ▬▬▬ :: ▬▬▬ : ▬▬▬ ;

∴ ex æquali,

▬▬▬ : ▬▬▬ :: ▬▬▬ : ▬▬▬

(B. 6. pr. 22.)

In like manner it may be fhown that the remaining fides of the two figures are proportional.

∴ by (B. 6. def. 1.)

 is fimilar to

and fimilarly fituated; and on the given line ▬▬▬ .

Q. E. D.

IMILAR *trian-*

gles (

and) *are to one another in the duplicate ratio of their homologous ſides.*

Let ▲ and ▲ be equal angles, and ▪▪▪▪▪▪▪ ▬▬▬

and ▬▬▬▬▬ homologous ſides of the ſimilar triangles

▲ and ▲ and on ▪▪▪▪▪▪▬▬▬ the greater

of theſe lines take ▪▪▪▪▪ a third proportional, ſo that

▪▪▪▪▪▬▬▬ : ▬▬▬▬ :: ▬▬▬▬ : ▪▪▪▪▪▪▪ ;

draw ▪▪▪▪▪▪▪▪▪ .

▪▪▪▪▬▬▬ : ▬▬▬▬ :: ▬▬▬▬ : ▬▬▬▬

(B. 6. pr. 4) ;

∴ ▪▪▪▪▬▬▬ : ▬▬▬▬ :: ▬▬▬▬ : ▬▬▬▬

(B. 5. pr. 16, alt.),

but ▪▪▪▪▬▬▬ : ▬▬▬▬ :: ▬▬▬▬ : ▪▪▪▪▪▪▪ (conſt.),

∴ ▬▬▬▬ : ▪▪▪▪▪▪▪ :: ▬▬▬▬ : ▬▬▬▬ conſequently 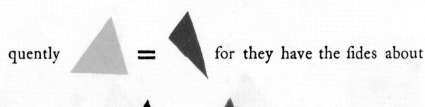 for they have the fides about

the equal angles 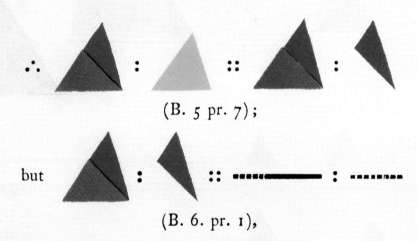 and reciprocally proportional

(B. 6. pr. 15);

(B. 5 pr. 7);

but

(B. 6. pr. 1),

that is to fay, the triangles are to one another in the duplicate ratio of their homologous fides

—— and ⋯⋯—— (B. 5. def. 11).

Q. E. D.

SIMILAR *poly-gons may be divided into the same number of similar triangles, each similar pair of which are proportional to the polygons; and the polygons are to each other in the duplicate ratio of their homologous sides.*

Draw ——— and ▪▪▪▪▪▪▪, and ——— and ----------, resolving the polygons into triangles. Then because the polygons are similar, ◖ = ◗ , and ——— : ▪▪▪▪▪ :: ——— : ---------- ∴ ◺ and ◺ are similar, and ◀ = ◀ (B. 6. pr. 6);

but ◣ = ◣ because they are angles of similar polygons; therefore the remainders ◣ and ◣ are equal; hence ▪▪▪▪▪ : ▪▪▪▪▪ :: ---------- : ▪▪▪▪▪ , on account of the similar triangles, and 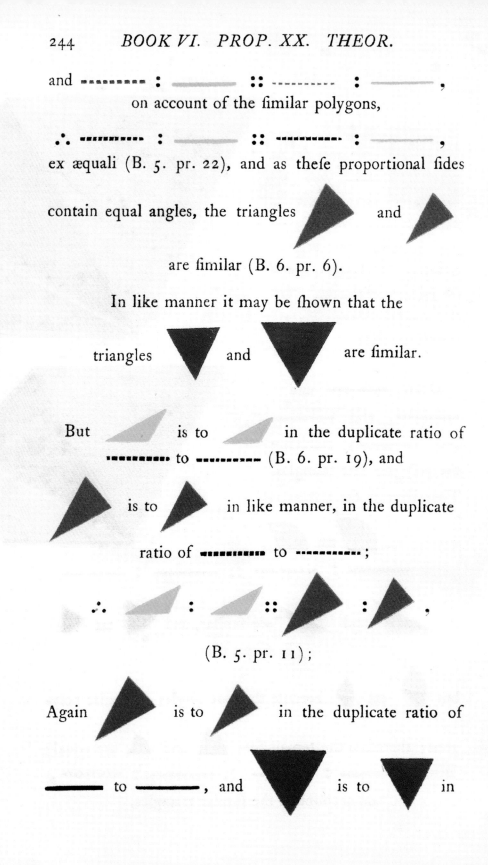 ⁚ ⸺ ⸬ ⋯⋯ ⁚ ⸺ ,

on account of the fimilar polygons,

∴ ⸺ ⁚ ⸺ ⸬ ⋯⋯ ⁚ ⸺ ,

ex æquali (B. 5. pr. 22), and as thefe proportional fides

contain equal angles, the triangles   and

are fimilar (B. 6. pr. 6).

In like manner it may be fhown that the

triangles   and   are fimilar.

But   is to   in the duplicate ratio of

⸺ to ⋯⋯ (B. 6. pr. 19), and

is to   in like manner, in the duplicate

ratio of ⸺ to ⋯⋯ ;

∴   ⁚   ⸬   ⁚   ,

(B. 5. pr. 11);

Again   is to   in the duplicate ratio of

⸺ to ⸺ , and   is to   in

the duplicate ratio of ▬▬▬ to ▬▬▬,

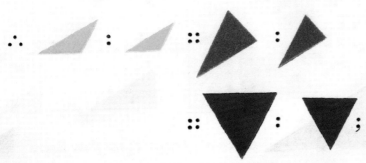

and as one of the antecedents is to one of the confequents, fo is the fum of all the antecedents to the fum of all the confequents; that is to fay, the fimilar triangles have to one another the fame ratio as the polygons (B. 5. pr. 12).

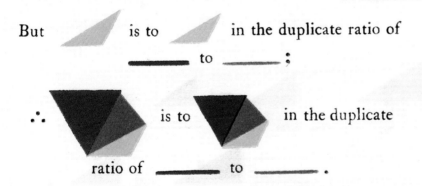

Q. E. D

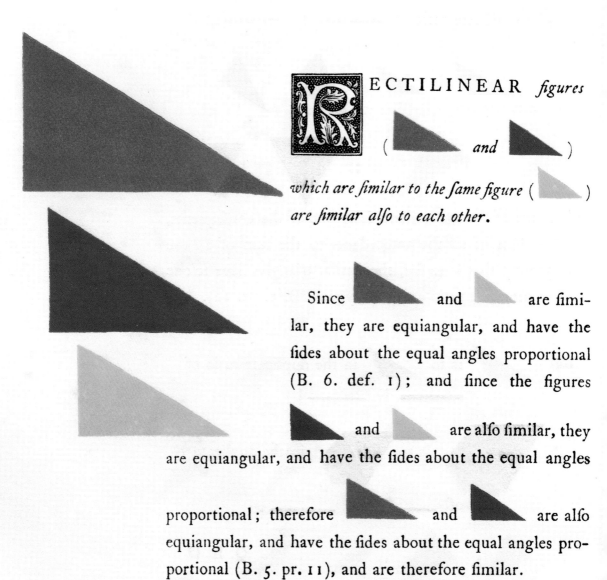

RECTILINEAR *figures* (and) which are *fimilar to the fame figure* ( ) are *fimilar alfo to each other.*

Since and are fimilar, they are equiangular, and have the fides about the equal angles proportional (B. 6. def. 1); and fince the figures and are alfo fimilar, they are equiangular, and have the fides about the equal angles proportional; therefore and are alfo equiangular, and have the fides about the equal angles proportional (B. 5. pr. 11), and are therefore fimilar.

Q. E. D.

PART I.

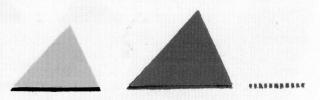

F *four ftraight lines be pro-portional* (——— : ——— :: ——— : ———), *the ſimilar rectilinear figures ſimilarly deſcribed on them are alſo pro-portional.*

PART II.

And if four ſimilar rectilinear figures, ſimilarly deſcribed on four ſtraight lines, be proportional, the ſtraight lines are alſo proportional.

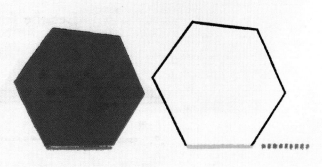

PART I.

Take ---------- a third proportional to ———

and ———, and ---------- a third proportional

to ——— and ——— (B. 6. pr. 11);

ſince ——— : ——— :: ——— : ——— (hyp.),

——— : ---------- :: ——— : ---------- (conſt.)

∴ ex æquali,

——— : ---------- :: ——— : ---------- ;

but △ : △ :: ——— : ———

(B. 6. pr. 20),

and ⬡ : ⬡ :: ——— : ---------- ;

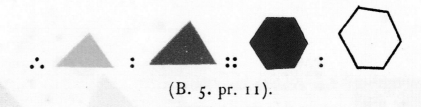

$$\therefore \quad \blacktriangle \quad : \quad \blacktriangle \quad :: \quad \hexagon \quad : \quad \hexagon$$

(B. 5. pr. 11).

PART II.

Let the fame conftruction remain :

$$\blacktriangle \quad : \quad \blacktriangle \quad :: \quad \hexagon \quad : \quad \hexagon \qquad \text{(hyp.)},$$

$$\therefore \quad \rule{2cm}{1mm} \quad : \quad \cdots\cdots :: \quad \rule{2cm}{0.5mm} \quad : \quad ----- \quad \text{(conft.)}$$

$$\text{and} \quad \therefore \quad \rule{2cm}{1mm} \quad : \quad \rule{2cm}{1mm} \quad :: \quad \rule{2cm}{0.5mm} \quad : \quad \rule{2cm}{0.3mm} \quad .$$

(B. 5. pr. 11).

Q. E. D.

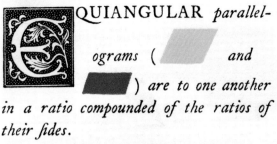QUIANGULAR *parallel-ograms* ( *and*) *are to one another in a ratio compounded of the ratios of their fides.*

Let two of the fides ———— and
— — — — about the equal angles be placed
fo that they may form one ftraight
line.

Since + = ,

and = (hyp.),

 + = ,

and ∴ ———— and ———— form one ftraight line
(B. 1. pr. 14);

complete .

Since : :: ———— : — — —
(B. 6. pr. 1),

and : :: ———— : ———— (B. 6. pr. 1),

 has to a ratio compounded of the ratios of
———— to — — —, and of ———— to — — —.

Q. E. D.

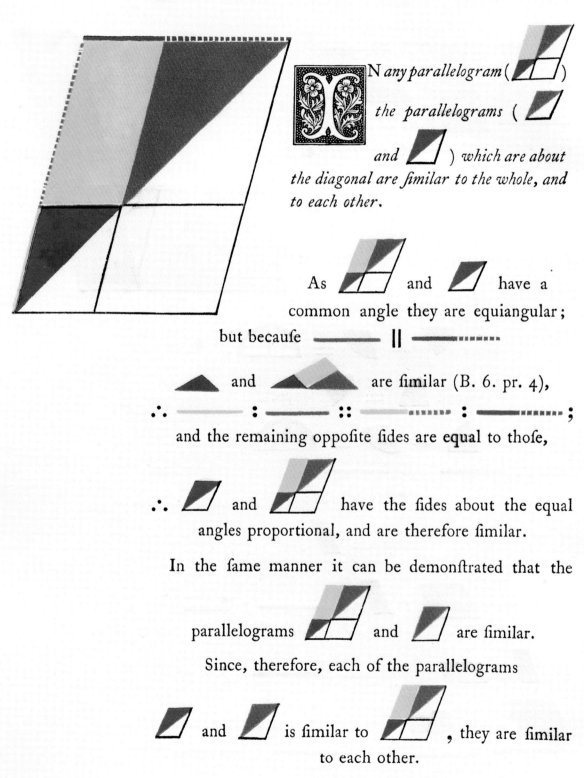

N any parallelogram (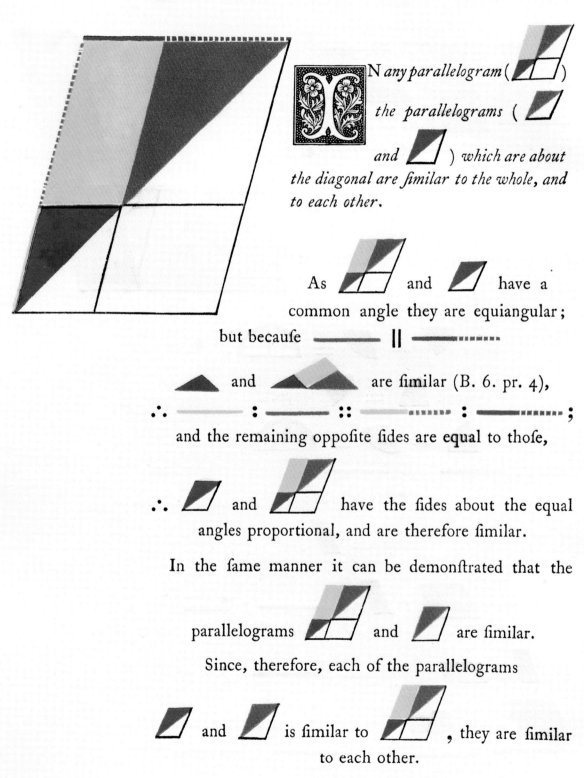)
the parallelograms (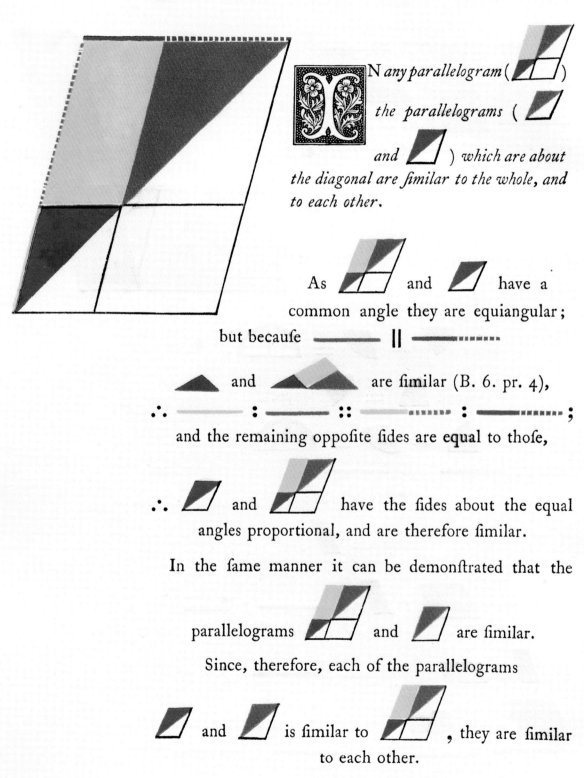
and) which are about
the diagonal are *fimilar* to the *whole, and
to each other.*

As and have a
common angle they are equiangular;
but becaufe ⸺ ‖ ⸺⸺

 and are fimilar (B. 6. pr. 4),

∴ ⸺ : ⸺ :: ⸺ : ⸺ ;

and the remaining oppofite fides are **equal** to thofe,

∴ and have the fides about the equal
angles proportional, and are therefore fimilar.

In the fame manner it can be demonftrated that the

parallelograms and are fimilar.

Since, therefore, each of the parallelograms

 and is fimilar to , they are fimilar
to each other.

Q. E. D.

O *defcribe a rectilinear figure, which fhall be fimilar to a given rectilinear figure (   ), and equal to another (   ).*

Upon _____ defcribe ■ = ▲ ,

and upon _____ defcribe ☐ = ◆ ,

and having ◣ = ◢ (B. 1. pr. 45), and then

_____ and ▬▬▬ will lie in the fame ftraight line (B. 1. prs. 29, 14),

Between _____ and ▬▬▬ find a mean proportional _____ (B. 6. pr. 13), and upon _____

defcribe ▲ , fimilar to ▲ ,

and fimilarly fituated.

Then ▲ = ◆ .

For fince ▲ and ▲ are fimilar, and

_____ : _____ :: _____ : ▬▬▬ (conft.),

▲ : ▲ :: _____ : ▬▬▬

(B. 6. pr. 20);

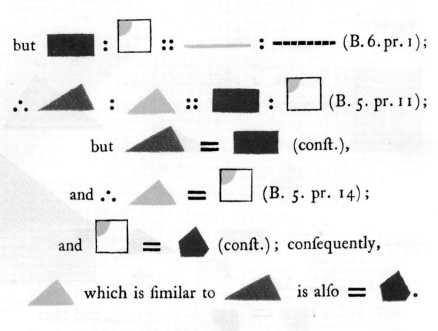

but ▬ : ☐ :: ——— : ------- (B. 6. pr. 1);

∴ ◢ : ◢ :: ▬ : ☐ (B. 5. pr. 11);

but ◢ = ▬ (conſt.),

and ∴ ◢ = ☐ (B. 5. pr. 14);

and ☐ = ⬠ (conſt.); confequently,

◢ which is ſimilar to ◢ is alſo = ⬠ .

Q. E. D.

I F *similar and similarly posited parallelograms*

(⬜ and ⬛)

have a common angle, they are about the same diagonal.

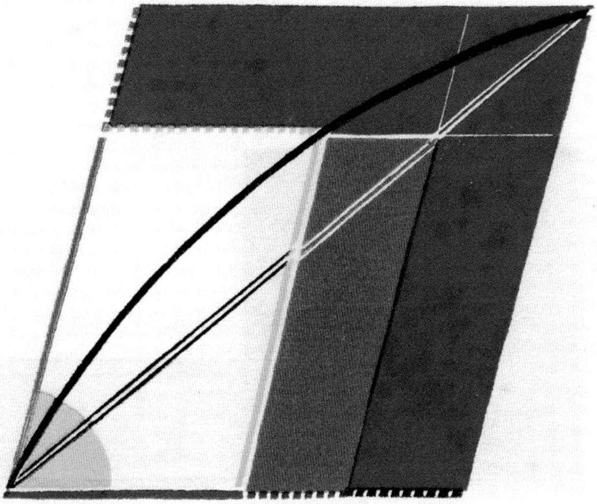

For, if possible, let ⌒

be the diagonal of ⬛ and

draw ── ‖ ── (B. 1. pr. 31).

Since ⬜ and ⬛ are about the same

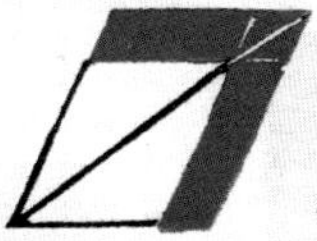

diagonal ⌒, and have ◣ common,

they are similar (B. 6. pr. 24);

∴ ── : ── :: ── : ── ;

but ── : ── :: ── : ── (hyp.),

∴ ── : ── :: ── : ── ,

and ∴ ── = ── (B. 5. pr. 9.),

which is absurd.

∴ ⌒ is not the diagonal of ⬛

in the same manner it can be demonstrated that no other

line is except ══ .

Q. E. D.

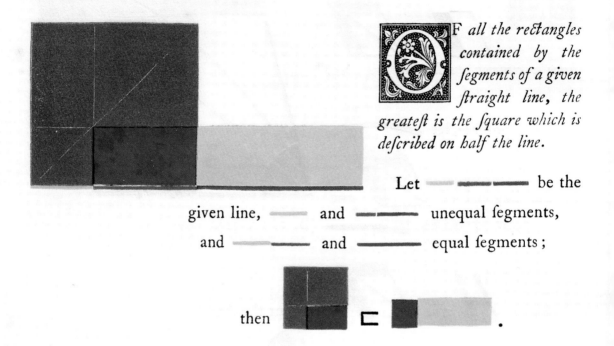

F *all the rectangles contained by the segments of a given straight line, the greatest is the square which is described on half the line.*

Let ━━━ be the given line, ━━━ and ━━━ unequal segments, and ━━━ and ━━━ equal segments;

then ⊏ .

For it has been demonſtrated already (B. 2. pr. 5), that the ſquare of half the line is equal to the rectangle contained by any unequal ſegments together with the ſquare of the part intermediate between the middle point and the point of unequal ſection. The ſquare deſcribed on half the line exceeds therefore the rectangle contained by any unequal ſegments of the line.

Q. E. D.

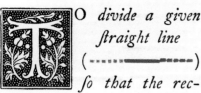 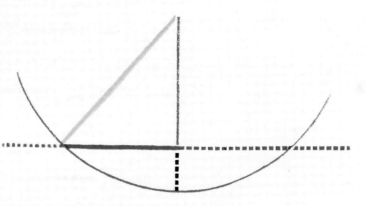

O *divide a given ſtraight line* (———) *ſo that the rectangle contained by its segments may be equal to a given area, not exceeding the ſquare of half the line.*

Let the given area be $=$ ———^{2}.

Biſect ———, or

make ——— $=$ ———;

and if ———^{2} $=$ ———^{2},

the problem is ſolved.

But if ———^{2} $\neq$ ———^{2}, then

muſt ——— $\sqsubset$ ——— (hyp.).

Draw ——— $\perp$ ——— $=$ ———;

make ——— $=$ ——— or ———;

with ——— as radius deſcribe a circle cutting the given line; draw ———.

Then ——— $\times$ ——— $+$ ———^{2} $=$ ———^{2}

(B. 2. pr. 5.) $=$ ———^{2}.

But ———^{2} $=$ ———^{2} $+$ ———^{2}

(B. 1. pr. 47);

$$\therefore \; \rule{1.5cm}{0.4pt} \times \rule{3cm}{0.4pt} + \rule{2.5cm}{0.4pt}^{2}$$

$$= \rule{2cm}{0.4pt}^{2} + \rule{2cm}{0.4pt}^{2},$$

from both, take $\rule{2cm}{0.4pt}^{2}$,

and $\rule{1.5cm}{0.4pt} \times \rule{3.5cm}{0.4pt} = \rule{2.5cm}{0.4pt}^{2}.$

But $\rule{2cm}{0.4pt} = \rule{2.5cm}{0.4pt}$ (conſt.),

and $\therefore \rule{4cm}{0.4pt}$ is ſo divided

that $\rule{1.5cm}{0.4pt} \times \rule{3.5cm}{0.4pt} = \rule{3cm}{0.4pt}^{2}.$

Q. E. D.

O *produce a given ſtraight*
line (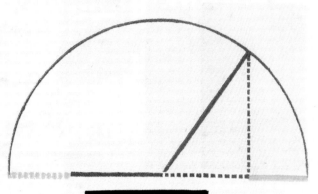), *ſo*
that the rectangle con-
tained by the ſegments
between the extremities of the given
line and the point to which it is pro-
duced, may be equal to a given area,
i. e. equal to the ſquare on ▬▬ .

Make ▬▬ = ▬▬ , and
draw ▬▬ ⊥ ▬▬ = ▬▬ ;
draw ▬▬ ; and
with the radius ▬▬ , deſcribe a circle
meeting ▬▬ produced.

Then ▬▬ ✕ ▬▬ + ▬▬ ^{2} =
▬▬ ^{2} (B. 2. pr. 6.) = ▬▬ ^{2}.

But ▬▬ ^{2} = ▬▬ ^{2} + ▬▬ ^{2} (B. 1. pr. 47.)

∴ ▬▬ ✕ ▬▬ + ▬▬ ^{2} =
▬▬ ^{2} + ▬▬ ^{2},
from both take ▬▬ ^{2},
and ▬▬ ✕ ▬▬ = ▬▬ ^{2};
but ▬▬ = ▬▬ ,
∴ ▬▬ ^{2} = the given area.

Q. E. D.

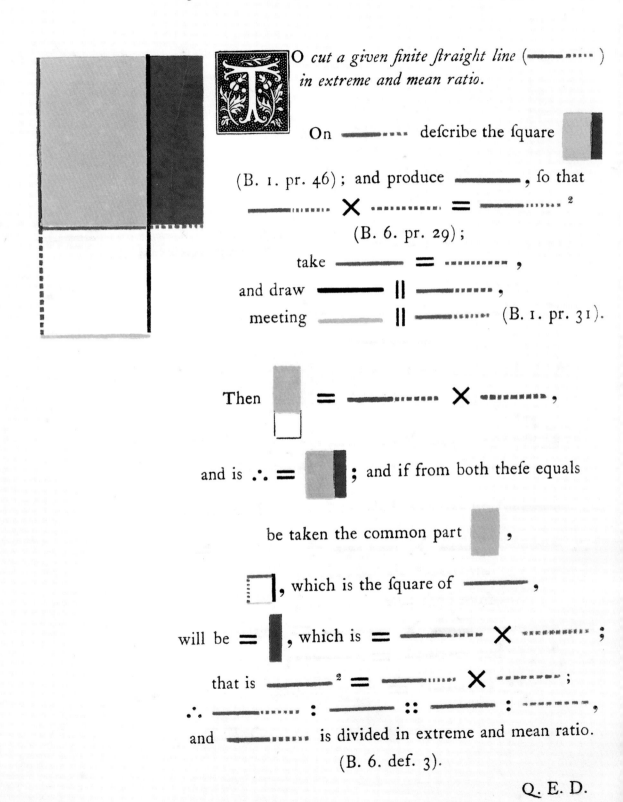

TO *cut a given finite straight line* (━━ ┄┄) *in extreme and mean ratio.*

On ━━ ┄┄ defcribe the fquare (B. 1. pr. 46); and produce ━━━, fo that

$$━━ ┄┄ \times ┄┄┄ = ━━ ┄┄^{2}$$

(B. 6. pr. 29);

take ━━━ = ┄┄┄,

and draw ━━━ ‖ ━━ ┄┄,

meeting ━━━ ‖ ━━ ┄┄ (B. 1. pr. 31).

Then ▯ = ━━ ┄┄ × ┄┄┄,

and is ∴ = ▮ ; and if from both thefe equals

be taken the common part ▯,

▯, which is the fquare of ━━━,

will be = ▮, which is = ━━━ × ┄┄┄ ;

that is ━━━ ^{2} = ━━ ┄┄ × ┄┄┄ ;

∴ ━━ ┄┄ : ━━━ :: ━━━ : ┄┄┄,

and ━━ ┄┄ is divided in extreme and mean ratio.

(B. 6. def. 3).

Q. E. D.

F any *ſimilar reċtilinear figures be ſimilarly deſcribed on the ſides of a right an-*

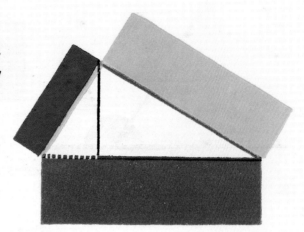

gled triangle (—————), *the figure deſcribed on the ſide* (—————) *ſub-tending the right angle is equal to the ſum of the figures on the other ſides.*

From the right angle draw ———— perpendicular

to ————— ;

then ————— : ————— :: ————— : —————

(B. 6. pr. 8).

∴ � : ▮ :: ————— : —————

(B. 6. pr. 20).

but ▮ : ▪ :: ————— : —————

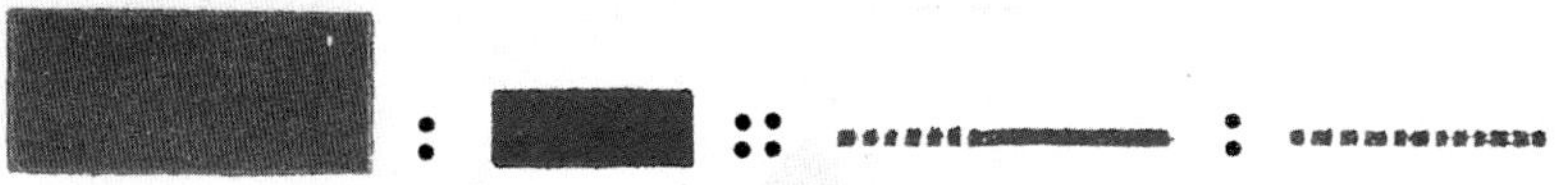

(B. 6. pr. 20).

Hence ————— + ————— : —————

:: ▪ + ▮ : ▮ ;

but ————— + ————— = ————— ;

and ∴ ▪ + ▮ = ▮ .

Q. E. D.

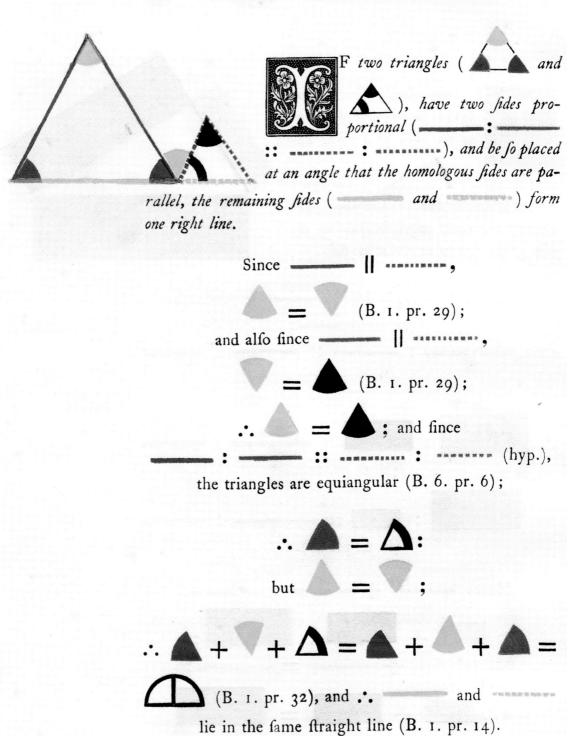

F *two triangles* (*and*

 ), *have two sides pro-*
portional (——— : ———

:: ------- : ··········), *and be so placed*
at an angle that the homologous sides are pa-
rallel, the remaining sides (———— *and* ··········) *form*
one right line.

Since ——— ‖ ··········· ,

= (B. 1. pr. 29) ;

and also since ——— ‖ ··········· ,

= (B. 1. pr. 29) ;

∴ = ; and since

——— : ——— :: ········· : ········· (hyp.),

the triangles are equiangular (B. 6. pr. 6) ;

∴ = :

but = ;

∴ + + = + + =

(B. 1. pr. 32), and ∴ ———— and ··········

lie in the same straight line (B. 1. pr. 14).

Q. E. D.

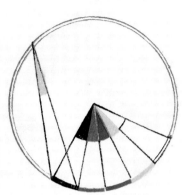

N *equal circles* (◯ , ◯), *angles,* *whether at the centre or circumference, are* *in the fame ratio to one another as the arcs* *on which they ftand* (▲ : ◢ :: ▬ : ▬); *fo alfo are fectors.*

Take in the circumference of ◯ any number of arcs ▬ , ▬ , &c. each ═ ▬ , and alfo in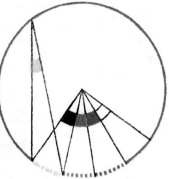

the circumference of ◯ take any number of

arcs ▬ , ▬ , &c. each ═ ▬ , draw the

radii to the extremities of the equal arcs.

Then fince the arcs ▬ , ▬ , ▬ , &c. are all equal,

the angles ▲ , ◣ , ▲ , &c. are alfo equal (B. 3. pr. 27);

∴ ▲ is the fame multiple of ◢ which the arc

▬ is of ▬ ; and in the fame manner ◭

is the fame multiple of ◢ , which the arc ▬

is of the arc ▬ .

Then it is evident (B. 3. pr. 27),

if ▲ (or if *m* times ◢) ⊏, =, ⊐ ⛰

(or *n* times ◢)

then ⌣ (or *m* times ⌒) ⊏, =, ⊐

⌣ (or *n* times ⌒);

∴ ◢ : ◢ :: ⌒ : ⌒ , (B. 5. def. 5), or the angles at the centre are as the arcs on which they ſtand; but the angles at the circumference being halves of the angles at the centre (B. 3. pr. 20) are in the ſame ratio (B. 5. pr. 15), and therefore are as the arcs on which they ſtand.

It is evident, that ſectors in equal circles, and on equal arcs are equal (B. 1. pr. 4; B. 3. prs. 24, 27, and def. 9). Hence, if the ſectors be ſubſtituted for the angles in the above demonſtration, the ſecond part of the propoſition will be eſtabliſhed, that is, in equal circles the ſectors have the ſame ratio to one another as the arcs on which they ſtand.

Q. E. D.

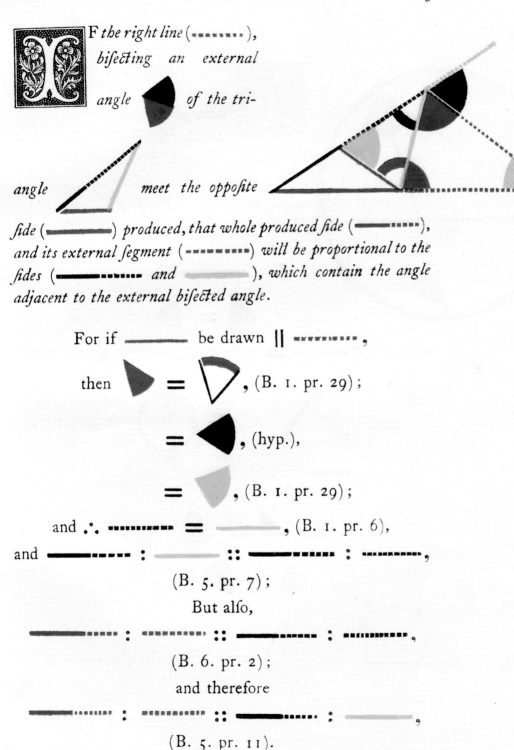

I F *the right line* (----------),
*bisecting an external
angle* of the tri-

angle meet the opposite

side (————) *produced, that whole produced side* (—————),
and its external segment (----------) *will be proportional to the
sides* (——————— *and* ——————), *which contain the angle
adjacent to the external bisected angle.*

For if ———— be drawn ‖ ----------,

then ◗ = ▷ , (B. 1. pr. 29);

= ◖ , (hyp.),

= ◣ , (B. 1. pr. 29);

and ∴ ---------- = ——————, (B. 1. pr. 6),

and ————----- : —————— :: ———————— : ----------,
(B. 5. pr. 7);
But also,
————————----- : ---------- :: ————————— : ----------,
(B. 6. pr. 2);
and therefore
————————---------- : ---------- :: ————————--- : ——————,
(B. 5. pr. 11).

Q. E. D.

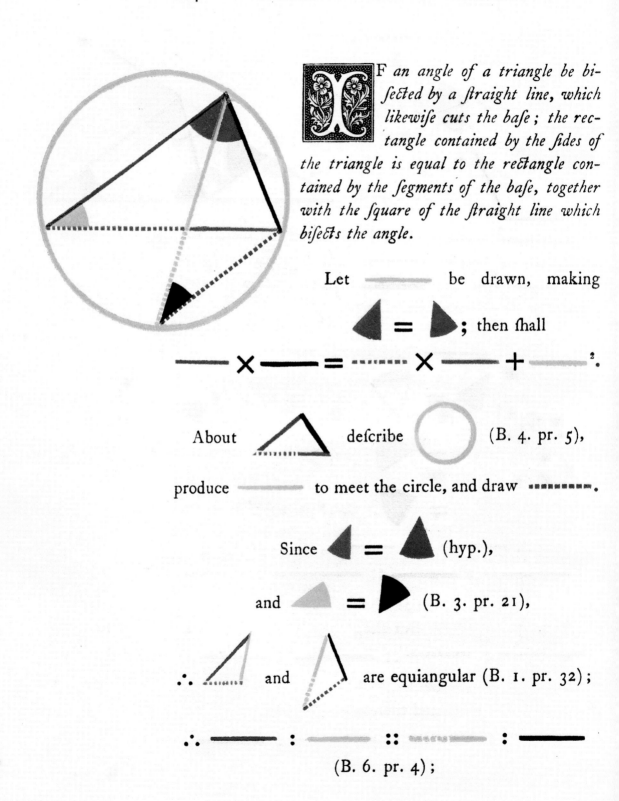

IF *an angle of a triangle be bi-ſected by a ſtraight line, which likewiſe cuts the baſe ; the rec-tangle contained by the ſides of* the triangle is equal to the rectangle con-tained by the ſegments of the baſe, together with the ſquare of the ſtraight line which biſects the angle.

Let ⎯⎯ be drawn, making

◢ = ◣ ; then ſhall

⎯ × ▬ = ┅ × ⎯ + ⎯²·

About ◸ deſcribe ◯ (B. 4. pr. 5),

produce ⎯⎯ to meet the circle, and draw ┅┅┅.

Since ◢ = ◣ (hyp.),

and ◢ = ◣ (B. 3. pr. 21),

∴ ◿ and ◺ are equiangular (B. 1. pr. 32);

∴ ▬ : ⎯ :: ┅ : ▬

(B. 6. pr. 4);

∴ ▬▬ ✕ ▬▬ = ▬▬ ✕ ▬▬

(B. 6. pr. 16.)

= ▬▬ ✕ ▬▬ + ▬▬^{2}

(B. 2. pr. 3);

but ▬▬ ✕ ▬▬ = ▬▬ ✕ ▬▬

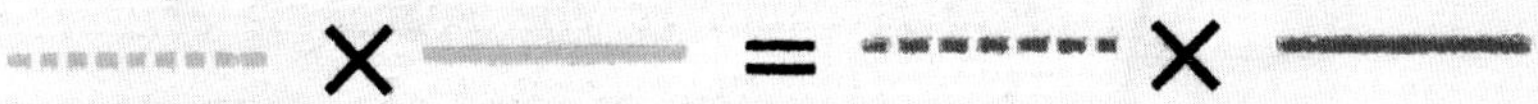

(B. 3. pr. 35);

∴ ▬▬ ✕ ▬▬ = ▬▬ ✕ ▬▬ + ▬▬^{2}.

Q. E. D.

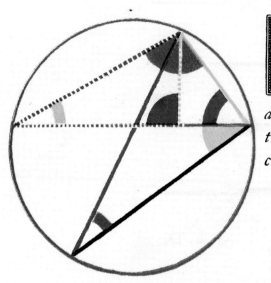

F *from any angle of a triangle a straight line be drawn perpendicular to the base; the rectangle contained by the sides of the triangle is equal to the rectangle contained by the perpendicular and the diameter of the circle described about the triangle.*

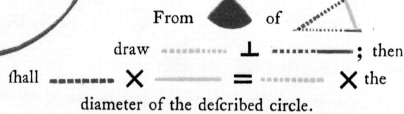

From of

draw ⊥ ; then

shall ✕ = ✕ the

diameter of the described circle.

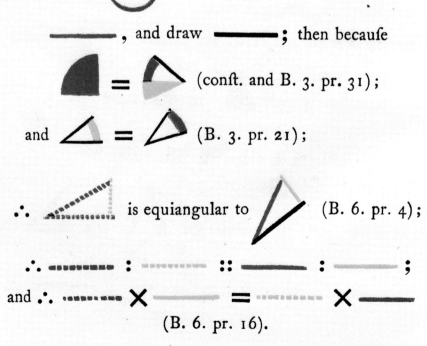

Describe ◯ (B. 4. pr. 5), draw its diameter

———— , and draw ———— ; then because

= (conft. and B. 3. pr. 31);

and △ = △ (B. 3. pr. 21);

∴ is equiangular to (B. 6. pr. 4);

∴ ━━ : ━━ :: ━━ : ━━ ;

and ∴ ━━ ✕ ━━ = ━━ ✕ ━━

(B. 6. pr. 16).

Q. E. D.

HE *rectangle contained by the diagonals of a quadrilateral figure inscribed in a circle, is equal to both the rectangles contained by its opposite sides.*

Let 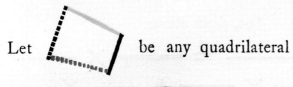 be any quadrilateral

figure inscribed in ◯ ; and draw

.... and ———— ; then

···· ✕ ———— = ········ ✕ ———— + ———— ✕ ········ .

Make ▲ = ▼ (B. 1. pr. 23),

∴ ◢ = ◢ ; and ◢ = ◺ (B. 3. pr. 21);

∴ ———— : ———— :: ———— : ········ (B. 6. pr. 4);

and ∴ ———— ✕ ———— = ———— ✕ ········ (B. 6. pr. 16); again,

because ▲ = ▼ (const.),

and $\bigvee$ $=$ $\bigvee$ (B. 3. pr. 21);

$\therefore$ ▬▬▬ : ▬▬▬ :: ▬▬▬ : ▬▬▬

(B. 6. pr. 4);

and $\therefore$ ▬▬▬ $\times$ ▬▬▬ $=$ ▬▬▬ $\times$ ▬▬▬

(B. 6. pr. 16);

but, from above,

▬▬▬ $\times$ ▬▬▬ $=$ ▬▬▬ $\times$ ▬▬▬;

$\therefore$ ▬▬▬ $\times$ ▬▬▬ $=$ ▬▬▬ $\times$ ▬▬▬ $+$ ▬▬▬ $\times$ ▬▬▬

(B. 2. pr. 1.

Q. E. D.

THE END.

CHISWICK: PRINTED BY C. WHITTINGHAM.